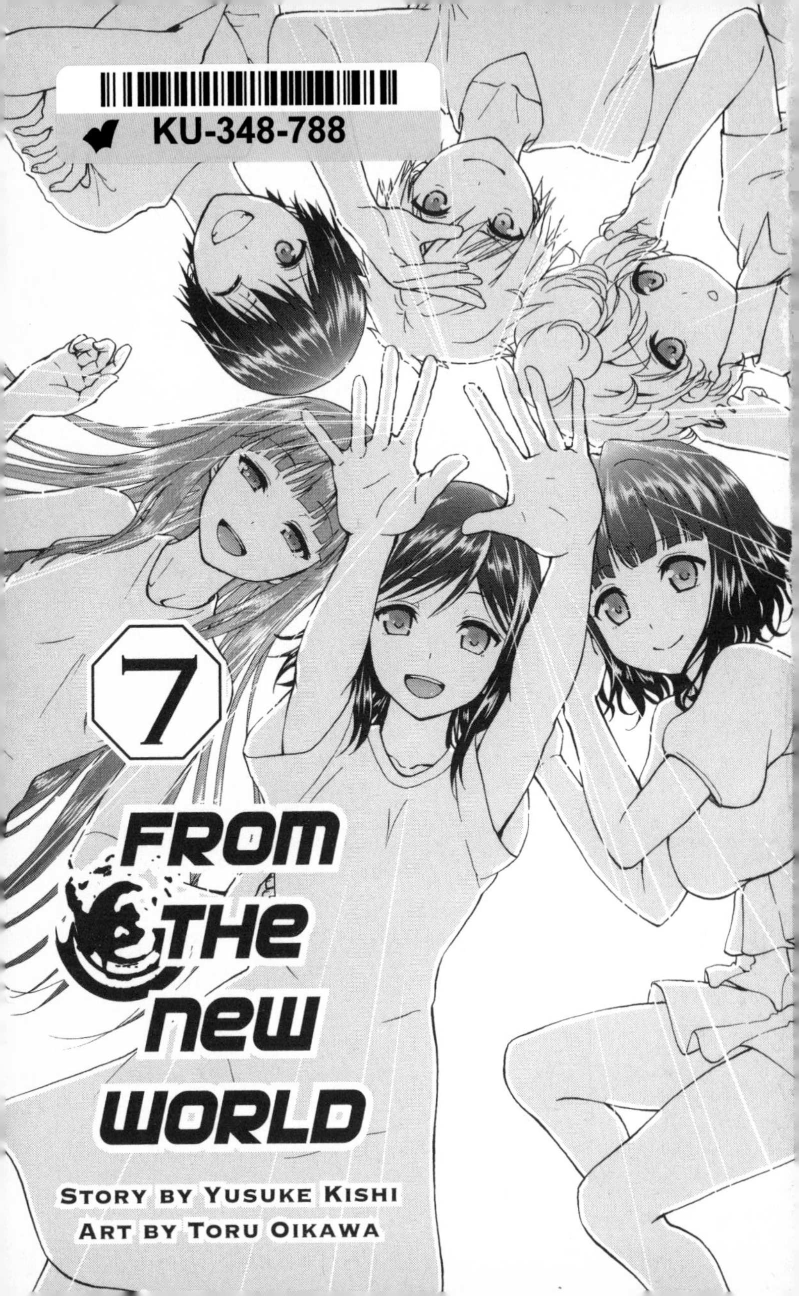
7
FROM THE NEW WORLD
STORY BY YUSUKE KISHI
ART BY TORU OIKAWA

CHARACTERS

FROM THE NEW WORLD

PROFILES

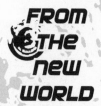

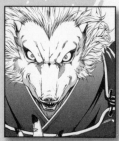

KIROMARU

Former commander-in-chief of the Giant Hornet colony whose forces were wiped out by the Robber Flies.

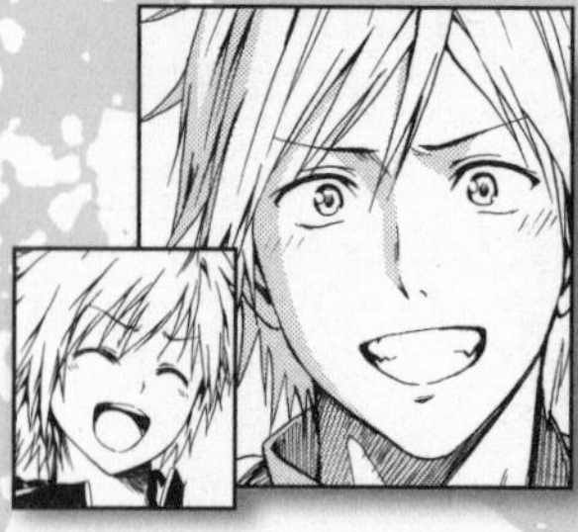

SATORU ASAHINA

A childhood friend of Saki, he was in her grade at Harmony Academy and the Holistic Class. Having done well in school, he now experiments with selective breeding and genetics at the Saddharma Farm.

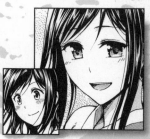

SAKI WATANABE

In addition to an unusually stout mind, she can repair her own DNA. At age 26, others see her as a future leader. She works at the town's health center's non-humans section and observes Morph Rats in the field.

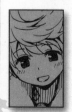

MAMORU ITO

Artistically talented and quiet. Escaped with his beloved Maria in order to protect her.

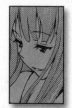

MARIA AKIZUKI

Best friends with Saki. Pretty with a strong will. Targeted for disposal, she skipped town.

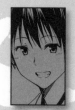

SHUN AONUMA

A prodigy with whom Saki was mutually enamored. As a Karma Demon he left this world.

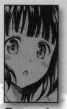

REIKO AMANO

Disposed of via Cats of Impurity because she was unable to control her magick.

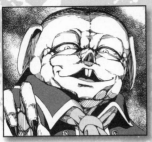

SQUEALER

A savvy Morph Rat. Prolocutor turned Representative of the Robber Flies. Revolts against humans and plans to eradicate them.

THE STORY THUS FAR...

Saki's group lands in Tokyo. But Inui, assigned to the night watch, is killed and suspicion concerning Kiromaru intensifies. Saki, who detects the Fiend's presence amongst their pursuers, decides to venture into the underground, inhabited by dangerous creatures. Suddenly, the Morph Rats' grand fleet appears. Saki's group splits in two, the underground group, who continue to search for the Psycho Buster, and the surface group, who attempt to halt the landing. The surface group is thwarted by the fleet's human shields. Haruka saves the group from this crisis by becoming a Karma Demon. While Haruka sacrifices her life to save Sho, Saki retrieves the Psycho Buster. To forge the future, Saki's group must now face Squealer for the final battle!

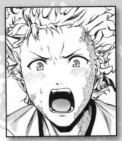

SHO NIIMI

A first year in the Holistic Class. Gave his all to save his beloved Haruka only to witness her final moments.

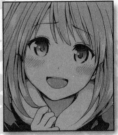

HARUKA SAKAI

Sho's childhood friend. Despite her transformation into a Karma Demon, she saved Sho and her friends from the Morph Rats before dying in battle.

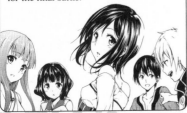

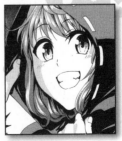

FIEND

A magick user called "Messiah" by the Morph Rats. Revealed to be Maria and Mamoru's child.

CONTENTS

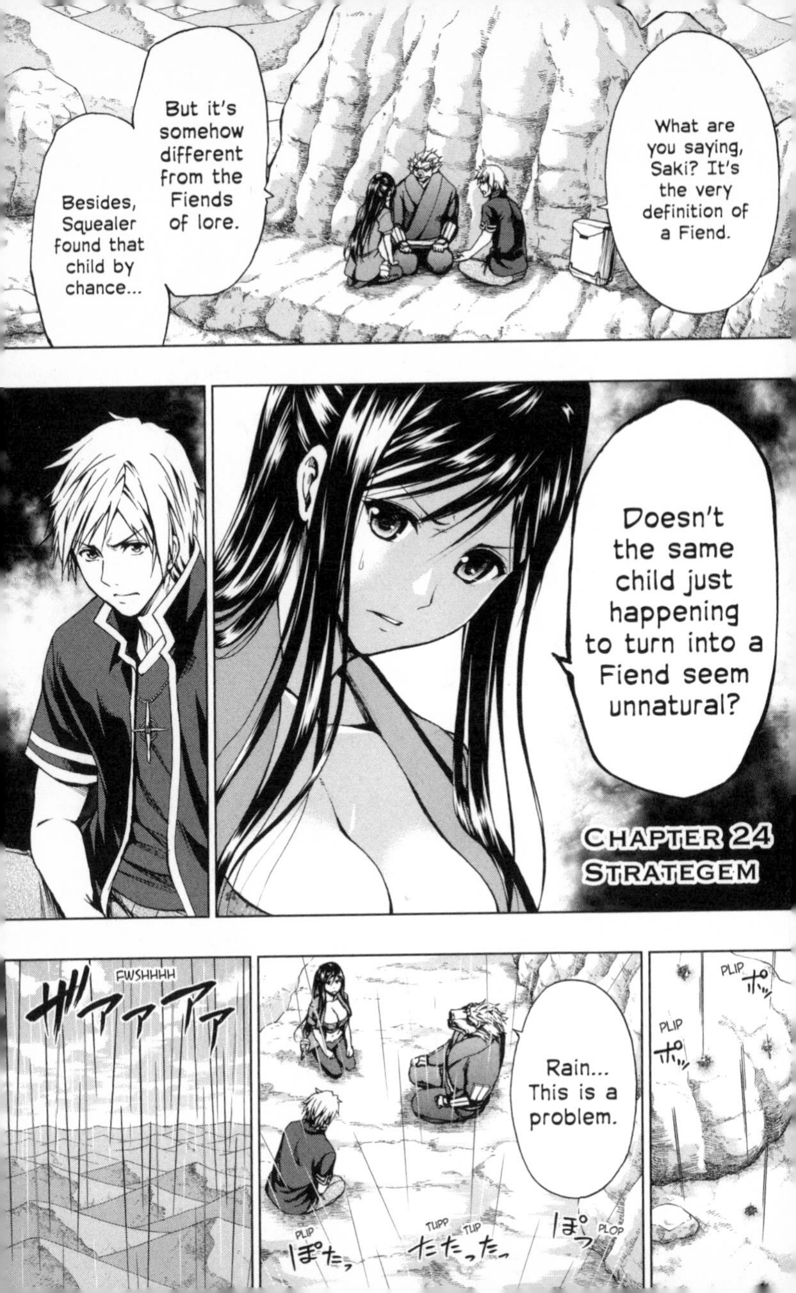
What are you saying, Saki? It's the very definition of a Fiend.
But it's somehow different from the Fiends of lore.
Besides, Squealer found that child by chance...
Doesn't the same child just happening to turn into a Fiend seem unnatural?
CHAPTER 24
STRATEGEM
PLIP ポッ
PLIP ポッ
Rain... This is a problem.
ぽっ PLOP
TUPP TUP たたったっ
PLIP ぽたっ
FWSHHHH ザァァァァ

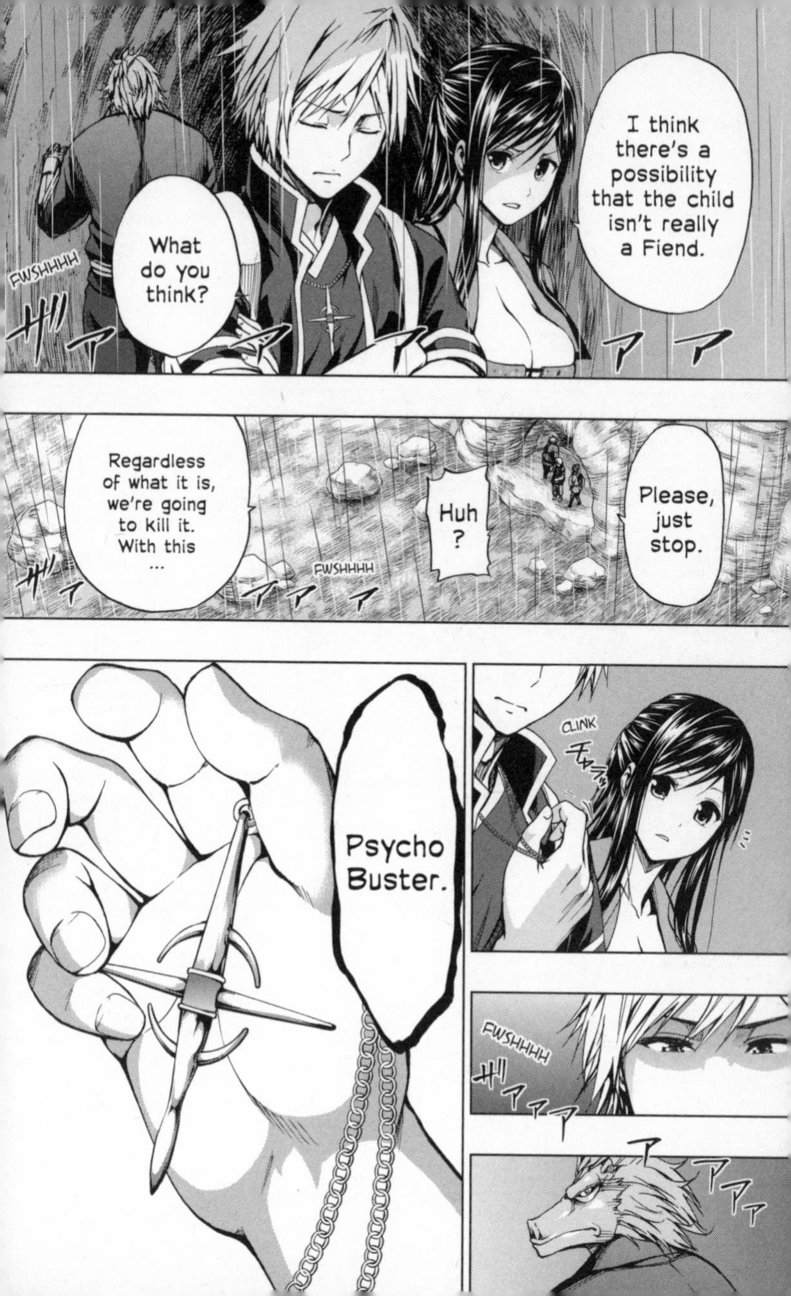
I think there's a possibility that the child isn't really a Fiend.
What do you think?
FWSHHHH
Please, just stop.
Huh?
Regardless of what it is, we're going to kill it. With this ...
FWSHHHH
CLINK
FWSHHHH
Psycho Buster.

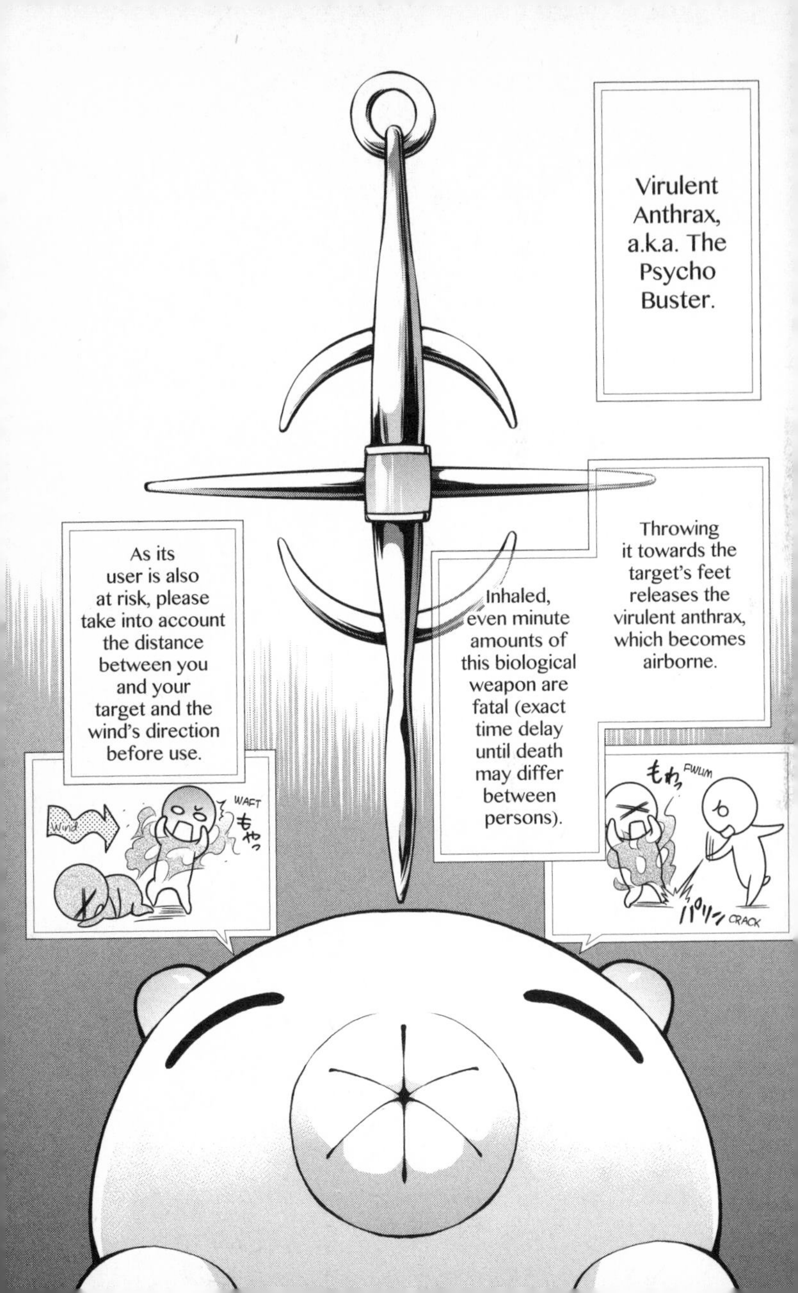
Virulent Anthrax, a.k.a. The Psycho Buster.
Throwing it towards the target's feet releases the virulent anthrax, which becomes airborne.
Inhaled, even minute amounts of this biological weapon are fatal (exact time delay until death may differ between persons).
As its user is also at risk, please take into account the distance between you and your target and the wind's direction before use.
もわっ
FWUM
パリーン
CRACK
Wind
WAFT
もやっ

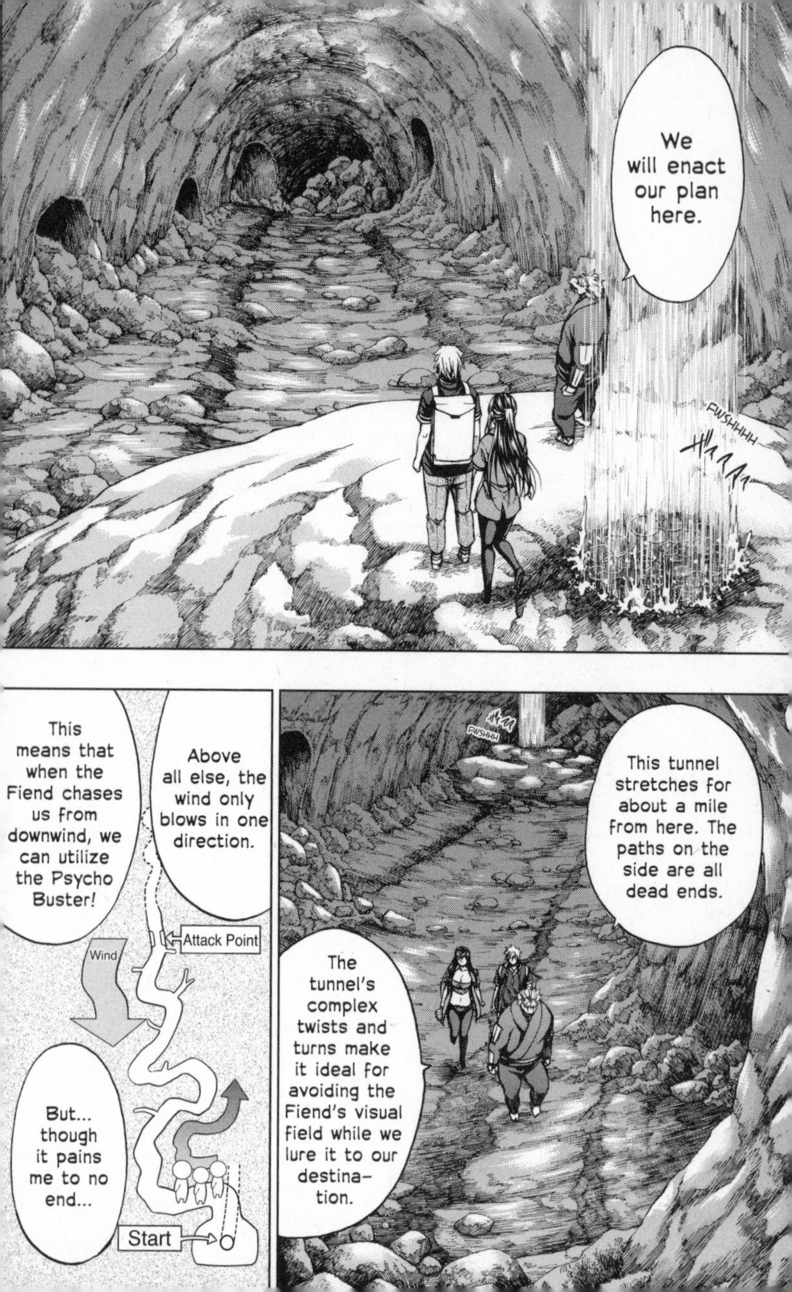
We will enact our plan here.
FWSHHHH
FWSHHH
This tunnel stretches for about a mile from here. The paths on the side are all dead ends.
The tunnel's complex twists and turns make it ideal for avoiding the Fiend's visual field while we lure it to our destination.
Above all else, the wind only blows in one direction.
This means that when the Fiend chases us from downwind, we can utilize the Psycho Buster!
Attack Point
Wind
Start
But... though it pains me to no end...

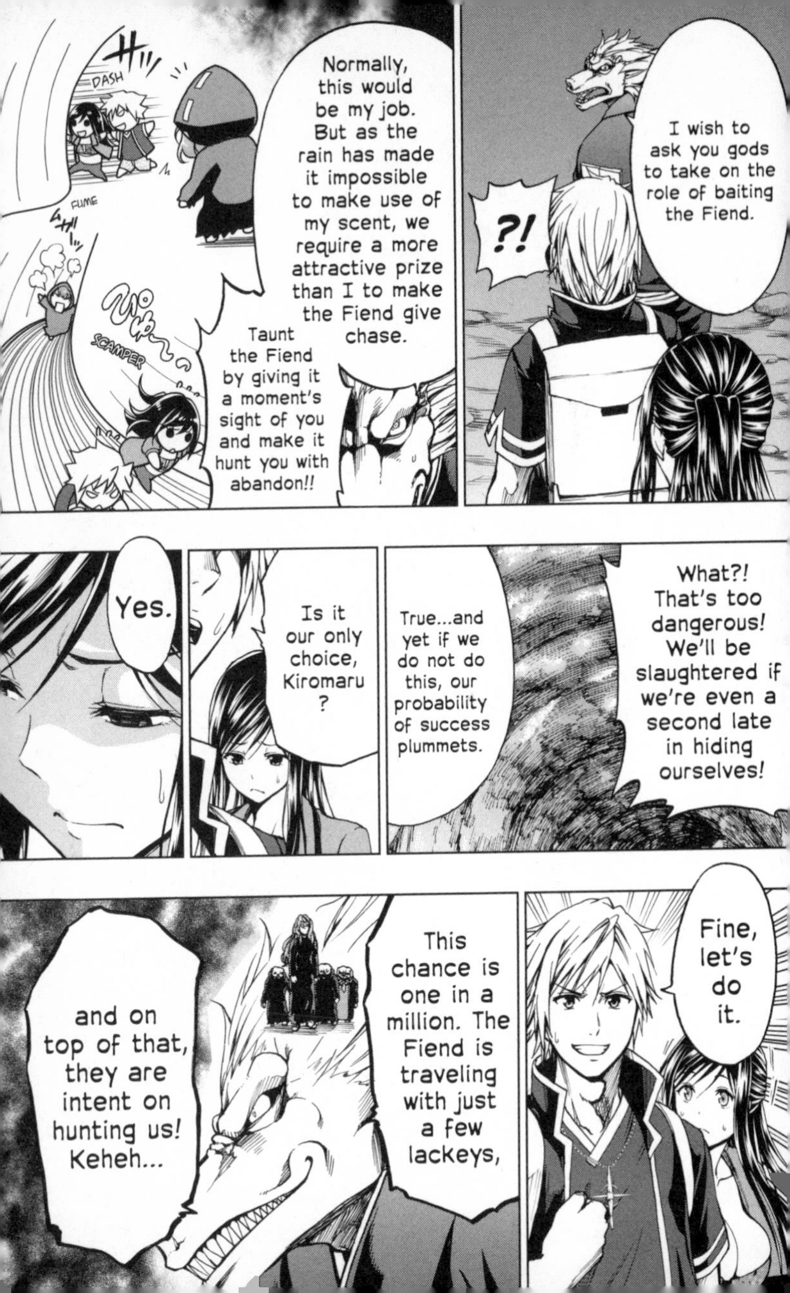
I wish to ask you gods to take on the role of baiting the Fiend.
?!
Normally, this would be my job. But as the rain has made it impossible to make use of my scent, we require a more attractive prize than I to make the Fiend give chase.
Taunt the Fiend by giving it a moment's sight of you and make it hunt you with abandon!!
DASH
FUME
SCAMPER
What?! That's too dangerous! We'll be slaughtered if we're even a second late in hiding ourselves!
True...and yet if we do not do this, our probability of success plummets.
Is it our only choice, Kiromaru ?
Yes.
Fine, let's do it.
This chance is one in a million. The Fiend is traveling with just a few lackeys,
and on top of that, they are intent on hunting us! Keheh...

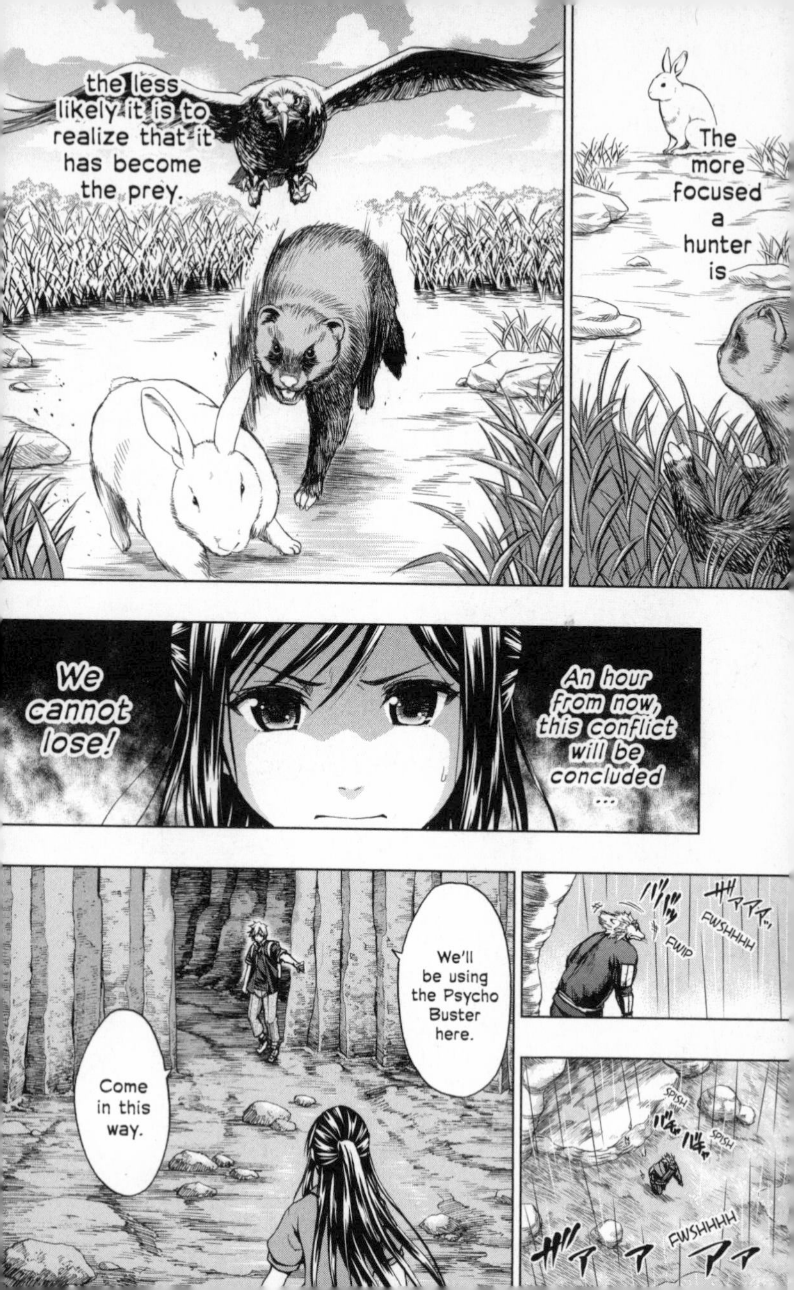
The more focused a hunter is
the less likely it is to realize that it has become the prey.
An hour from now, this conflict will be concluded ...
We cannot lose!
FWIP
FWSHHHH
SPISH
SPISH
FWSHHHH
We'll be using the Psycho Buster here.
Come in this way.

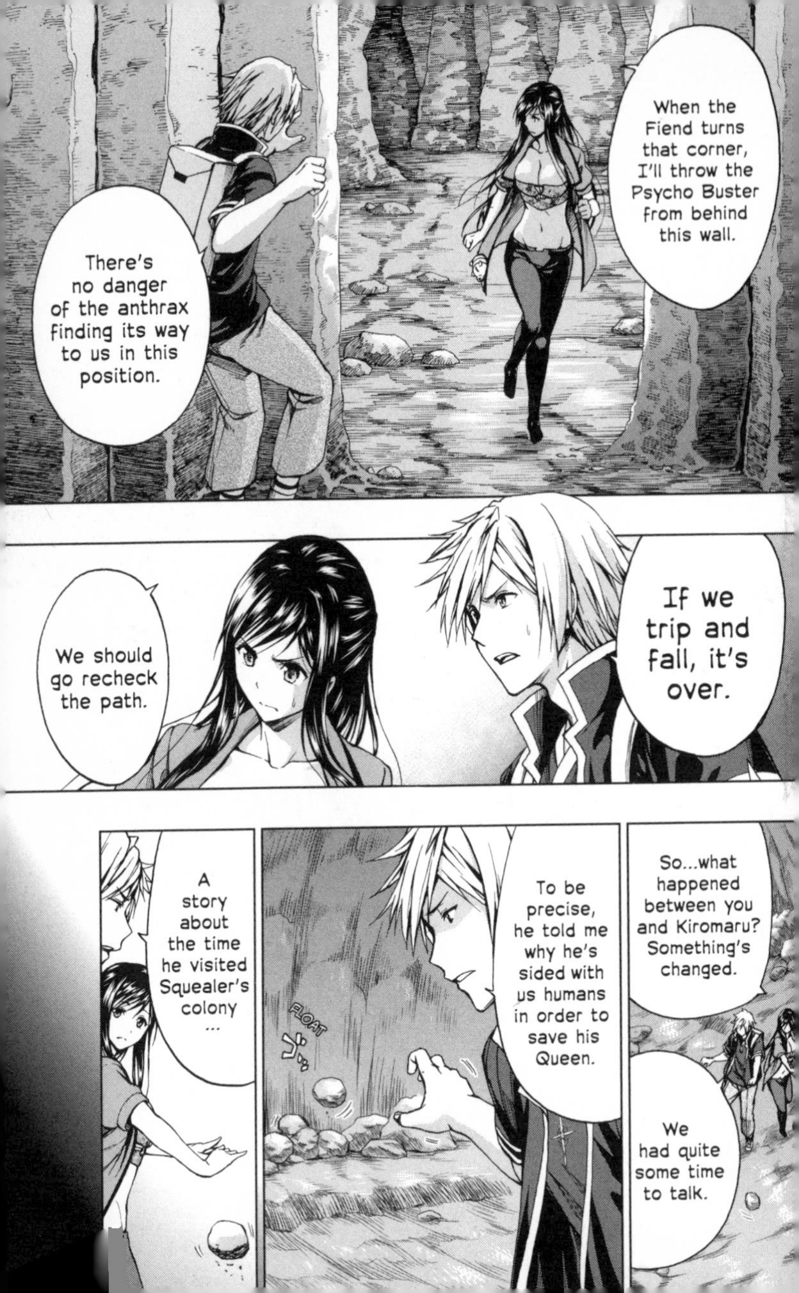
When the Fiend turns that corner, I'll throw the Psycho Buster from behind this wall.
There's no danger of the anthrax finding its way to us in this position.
If we trip and fall, it's over.
We should go recheck the path.
So...what happened between you and Kiromaru? Something's changed.
We had quite some time to talk.
To be precise, he told me why he's sided with us humans in order to save his Queen.
FLOAT
A story about the time he visited Squealer's colony ...

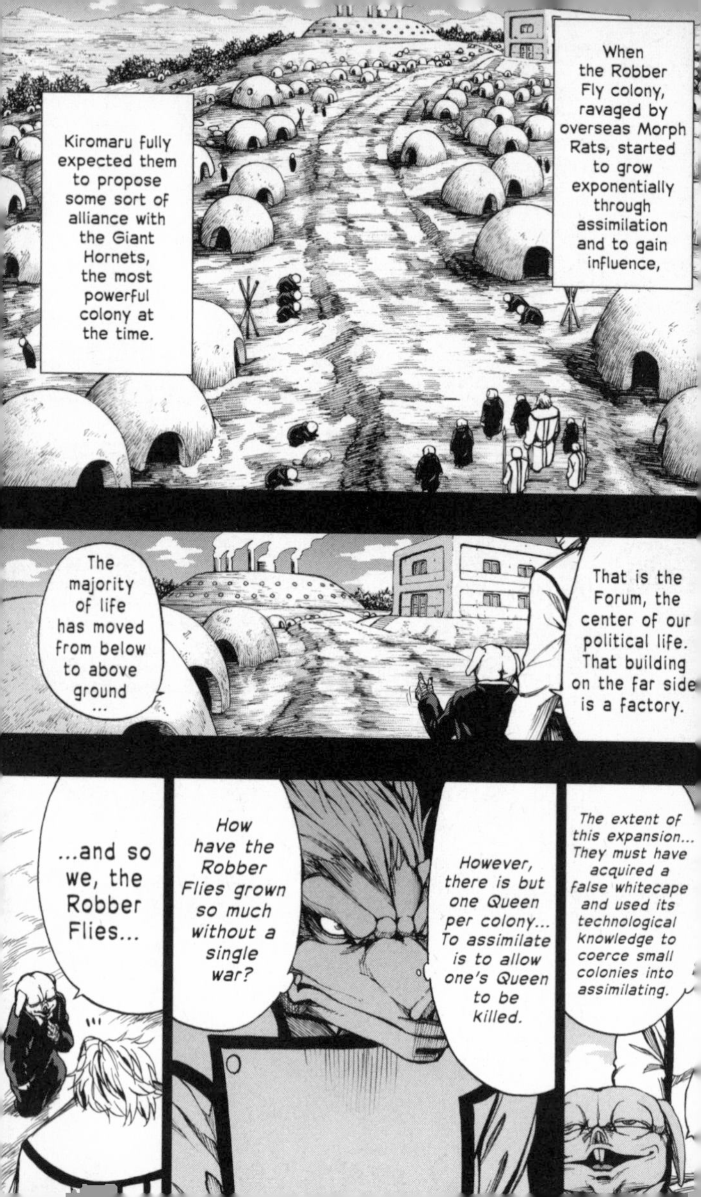
When the Robber Fly colony, ravaged by overseas Morph Rats, started to grow exponentially through assimilation and to gain influence,
Kiromaru fully expected them to propose some sort of alliance with the Giant Hornets, the most powerful colony at the time.
That is the Forum, the center of our political life. That building on the far side is a factory.
The majority of life has moved from below to above ground ...
The extent of this expansion... They must have acquired a false whitecape and used its technological knowledge to coerce small colonies into assimilating.
However, there is but one Queen per colony... To assimilate is to allow one's Queen to be killed.
How have the Robber Flies grown so much without a single war?
...and so we, the Robber Flies...

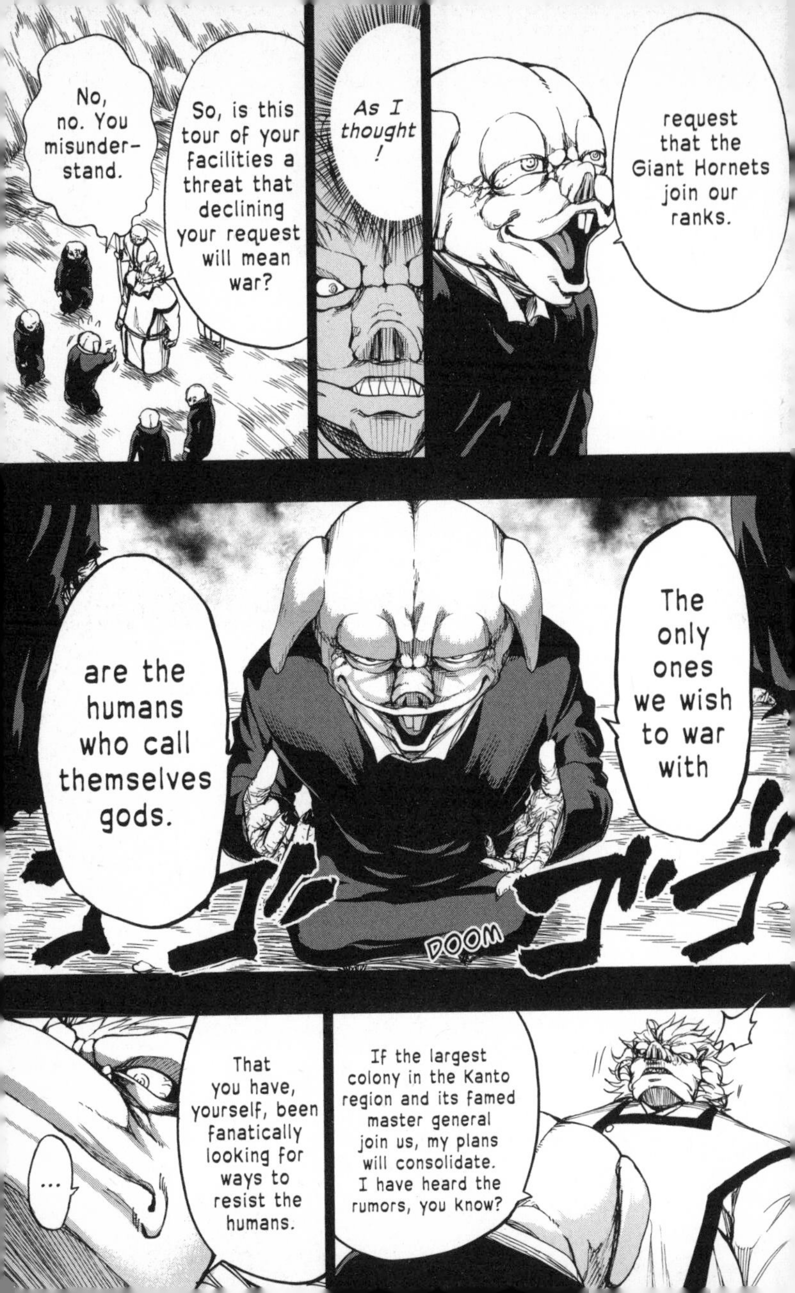
request that the Giant Hornets join our ranks.
As I thought!
So, is this tour of your facilities a threat that declining your request will mean war?
No, no. You misunderstand.
The only ones we wish to war with
are the humans who call themselves gods.
DOOM
If the largest colony in the Kanto region and its famed master general join us, my plans will consolidate. I have heard the rumors, you know?
That you have, yourself, been fanatically looking for ways to resist the humans.
...

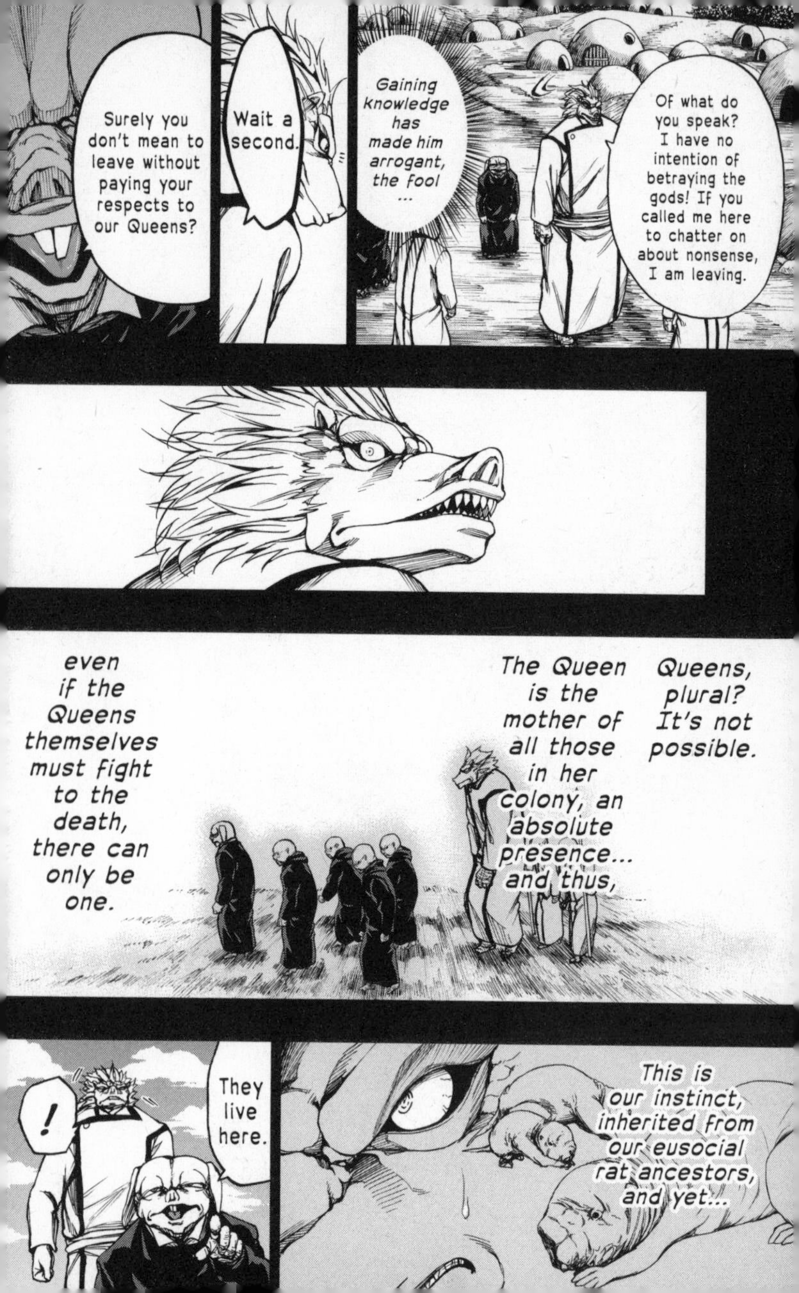
Of what do you speak? I have no intention of betraying the gods! If you called me here to chatter on about nonsense, I am leaving.
Gaining knowledge has made him arrogant, the fool ...
Wait a second.
Surely you don't mean to leave without paying your respects to our Queens?
Queens, plural? It's not possible.
The Queen is the mother of all those in her colony, an absolute presence... and thus,
even if the Queens themselves must fight to the death, there can only be one.
This is our instinct, inherited from our eusocial rat ancestors, and yet...
They live here.
!

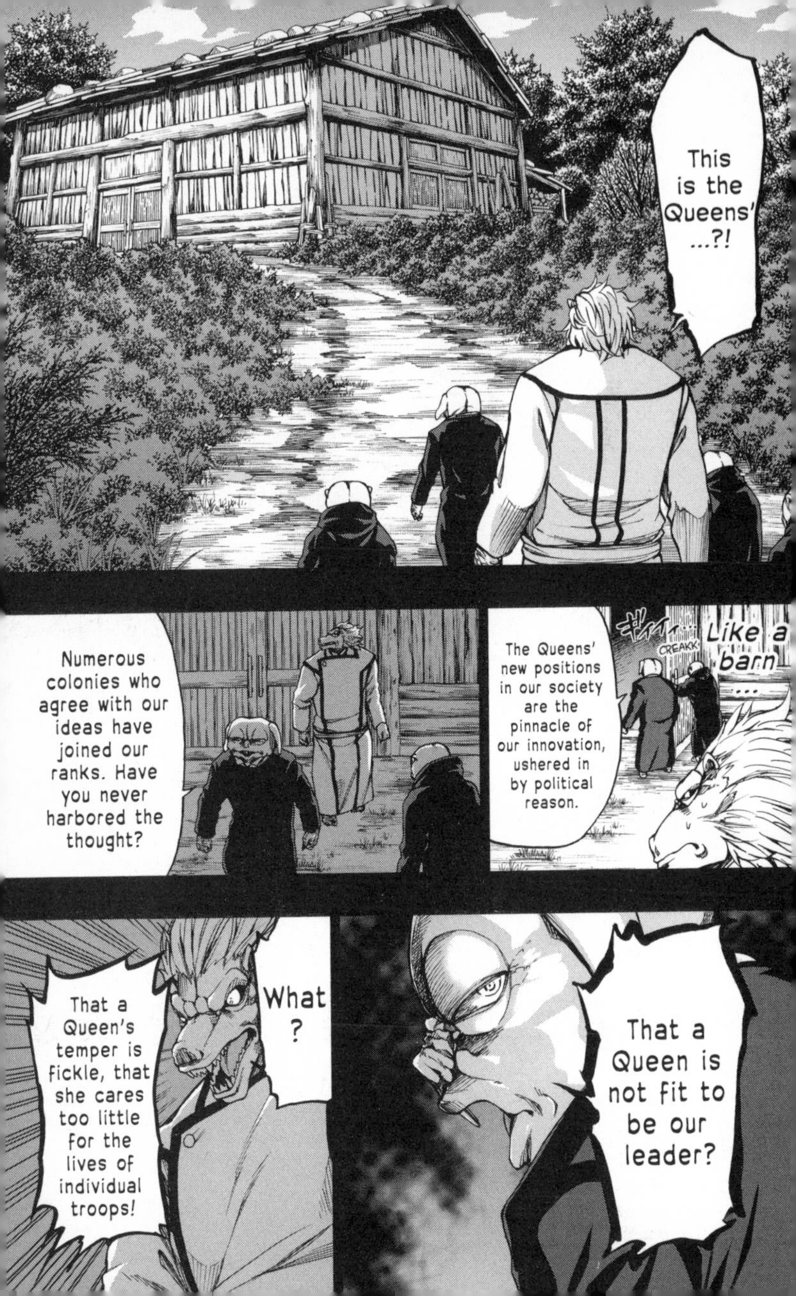
This is the Queens' ...?!
Like a barn ...
CREAKK
The Queens' new positions in our society are the pinnacle of our innovation, ushered in by political reason.
Numerous colonies who agree with our ideas have joined our ranks. Have you never harbored the thought?
That a Queen is not fit to be our leader?
What?
That a Queen's temper is fickle, that she cares too little for the lives of individual troops!

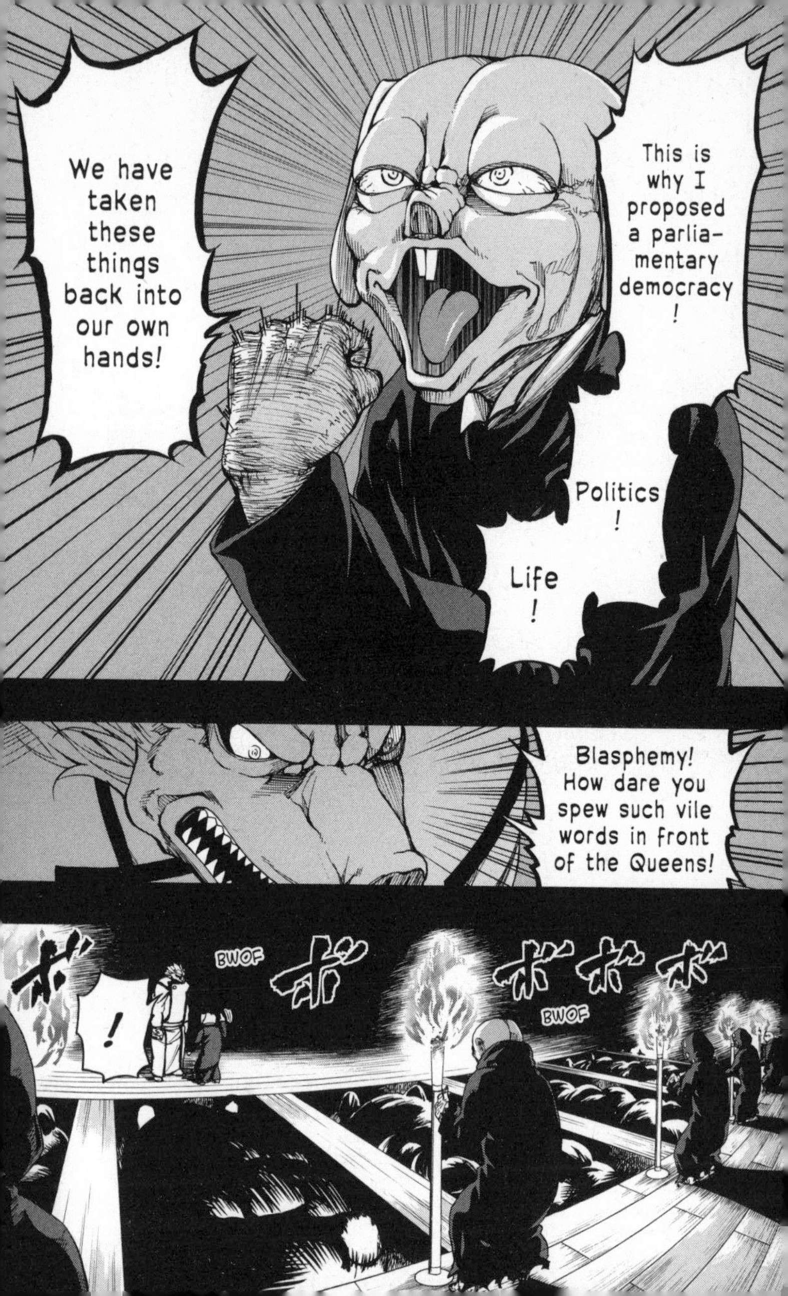
This is why I proposed a parlia-mentary democracy!
Politics!
Life!
We have taken these things back into our own hands!
Blasphemy! How dare you spew such vile words in front of the Queens!
BWOF
BWOF
!

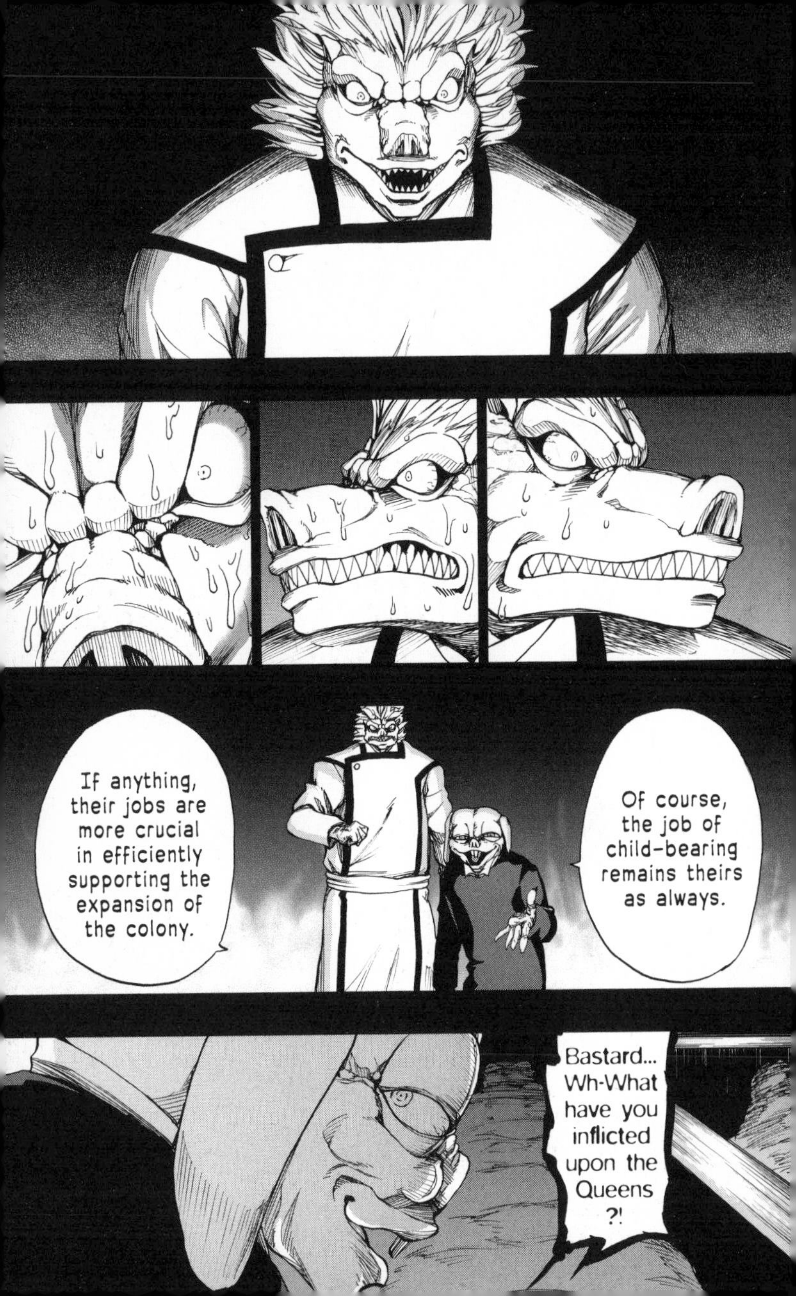
Of course, the job of child-bearing remains theirs as always.
If anything, their jobs are more crucial in efficiently supporting the expansion of the colony.
Bastard... Wh-What have you inflicted upon the Queens?!

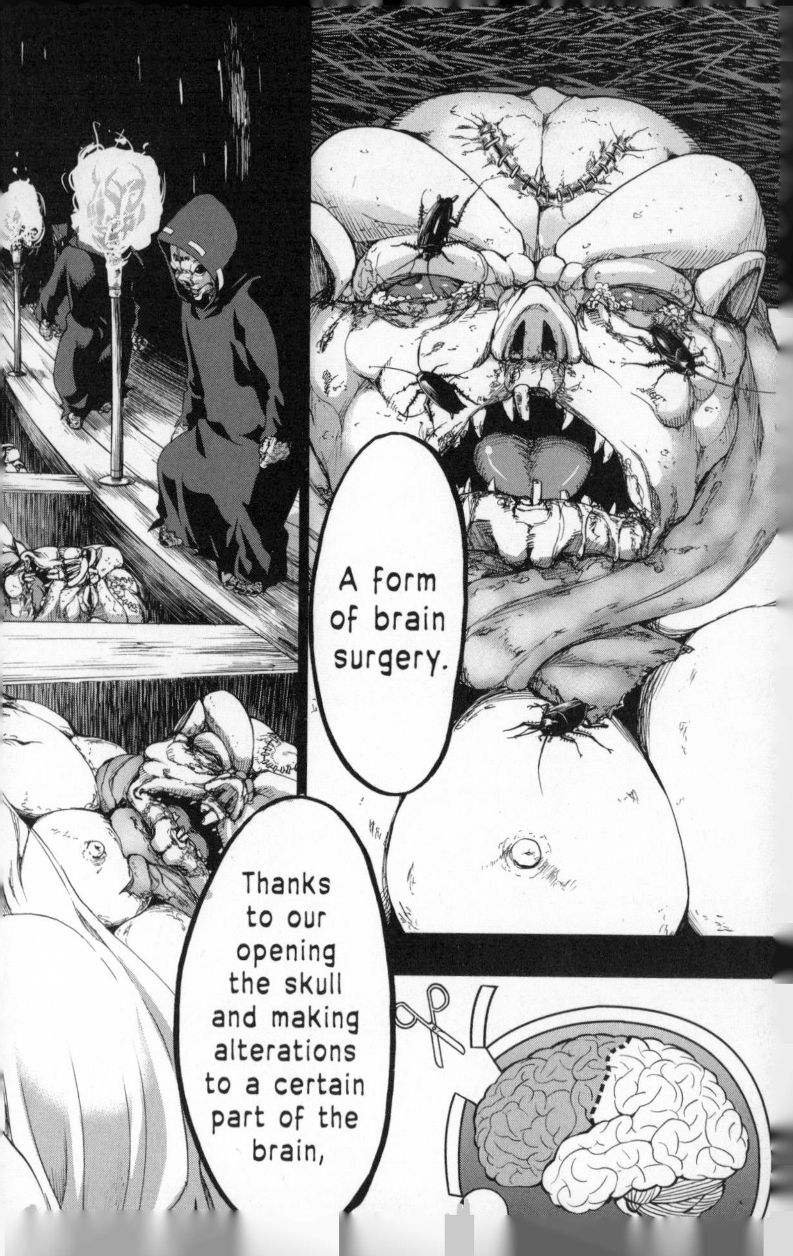
A form of brain surgery.
Thanks to our opening the skull and making alterations to a certain part of the brain,

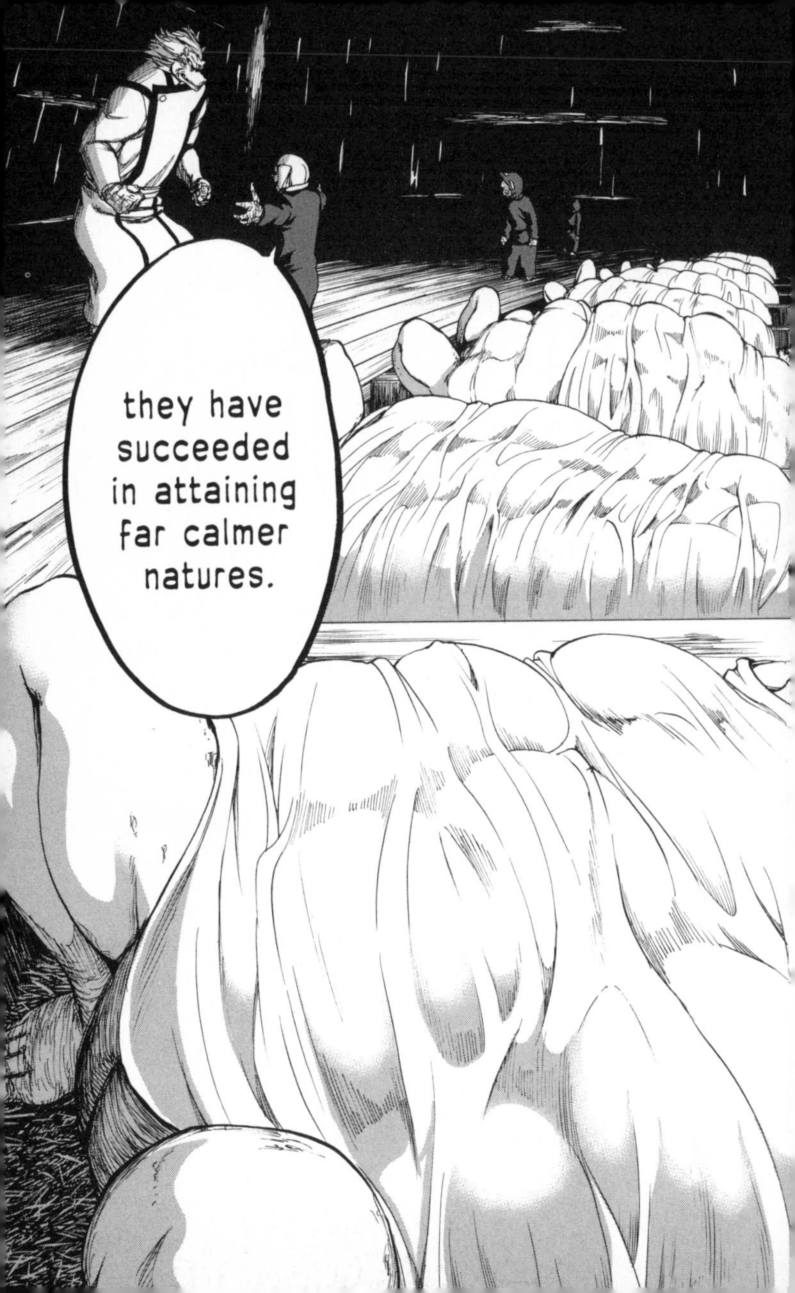
they have succeeded in attaining far calmer natures.

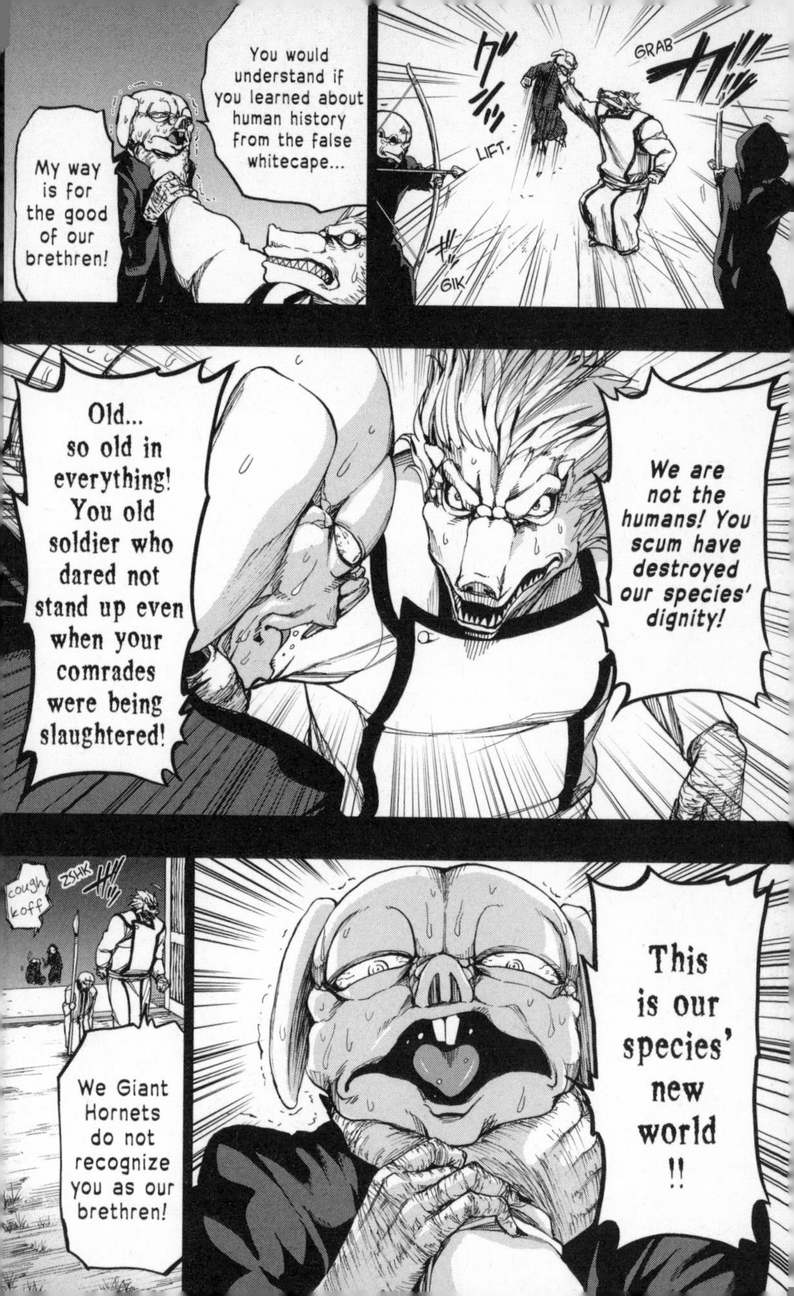
GRAB
LIFT.
GIK
You would understand if you learned about human history from the false whitecape...
My way is for the good of our brethren!
We are not the humans! You scum have destroyed our species' dignity!
Old... so old in everything! You old soldier who dared not stand up even when your comrades were being slaughtered!
This is our species' new world !!
cough koff
ZSHK
We Giant Hornets do not recognize you as our brethren!

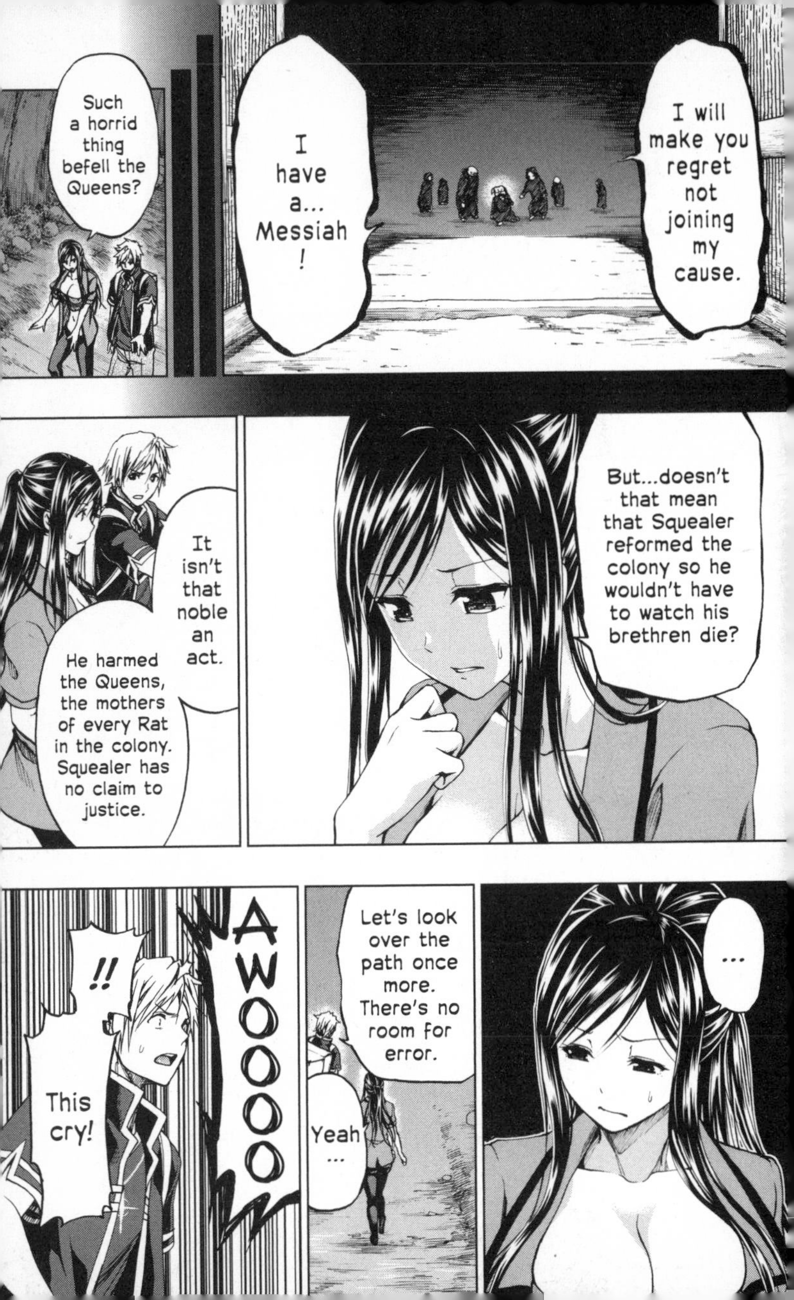
I will make you regret not joining my cause.
I have a... Messiah!
Such a horrid thing befell the Queens?
But...doesn't that mean that Squealer reformed the colony so he wouldn't have to watch his brethren die?
It isn't that noble an act.
He harmed the Queens, the mothers of every Rat in the colony. Squealer has no claim to justice.
...
Let's look over the path once more. There's no room for error.
Yeah...
AWOOOOO
!!
This cry!

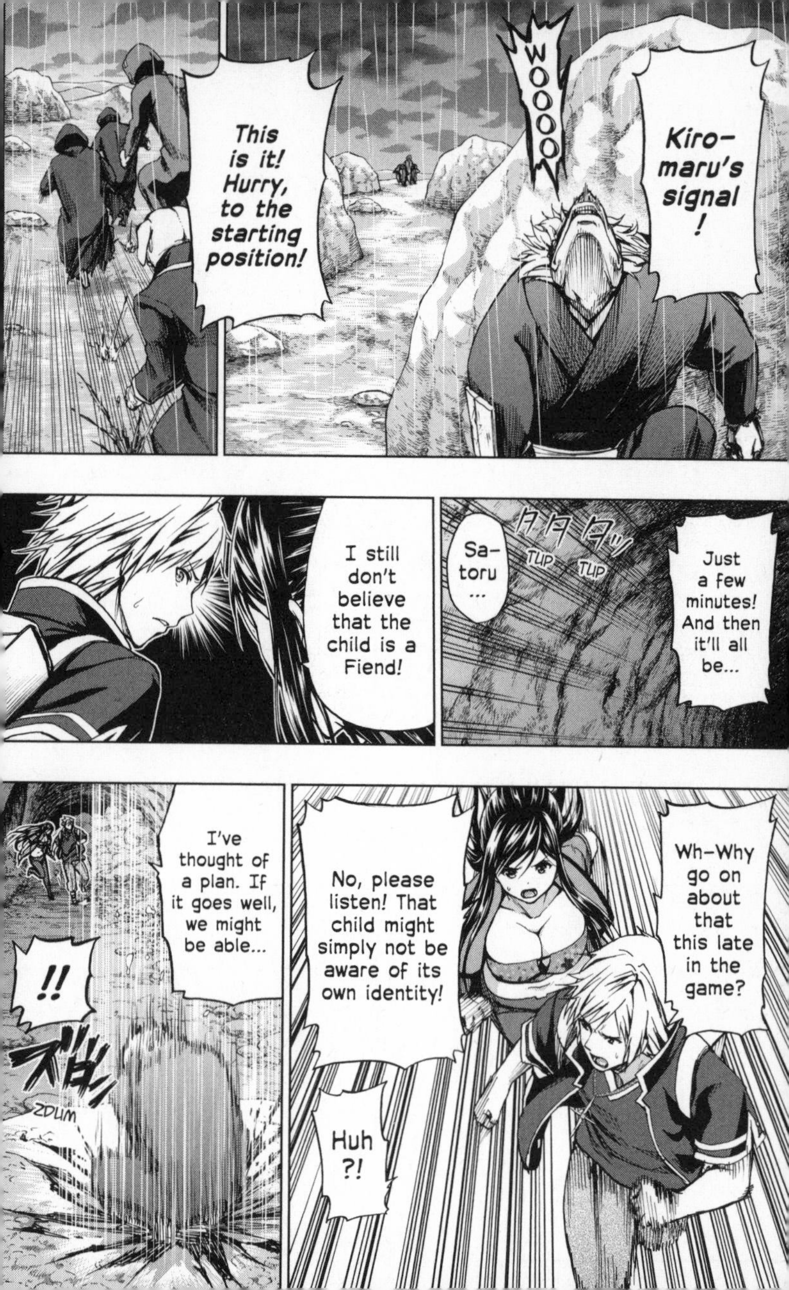
WOOOOO
Kiro-maru's signal!
This is it! Hurry, to the starting position!
Just a few minutes! And then it'll all be...
TUP TUP
Sa-toru...
I still don't believe that the child is a Fiend!
Wh-Why go on about that this late in the game?
No, please listen! That child might simply not be aware of its own identity!
Huh?!
I've thought of a plan. If it goes well, we might be able...
!!
ZDUM

May luck be with you!

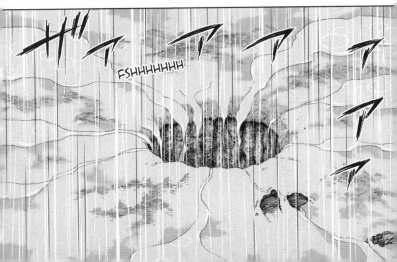

FSHHHHHHH

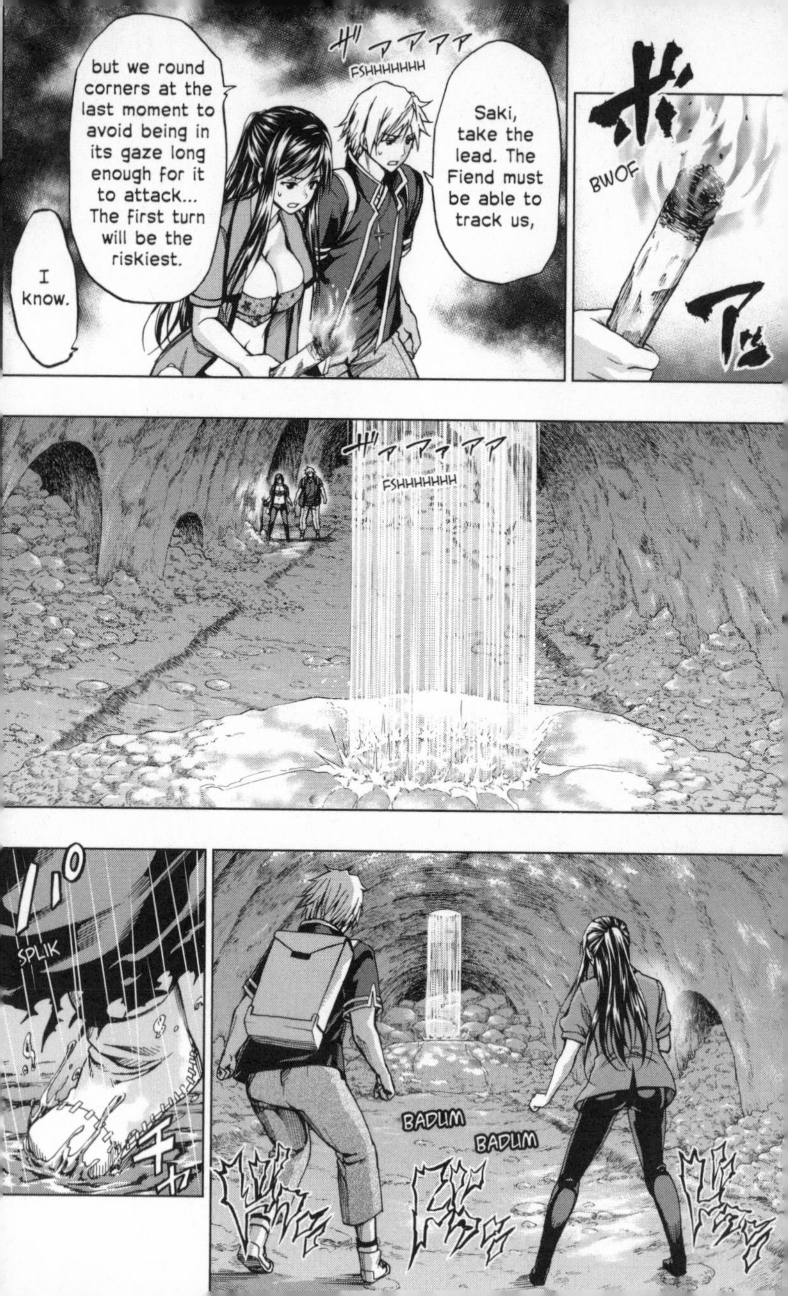
ボ
BWOF
ア
ザァアアア
FSHHHHHHH
Saki, take the lead. The Fiend must be able to track us,
but we round corners at the last moment to avoid being in its gaze long enough for it to attack... The first turn will be the riskiest.
I know.
FSHHHHHHH
BADUM
BADUM
パ
SPLIK
チャ

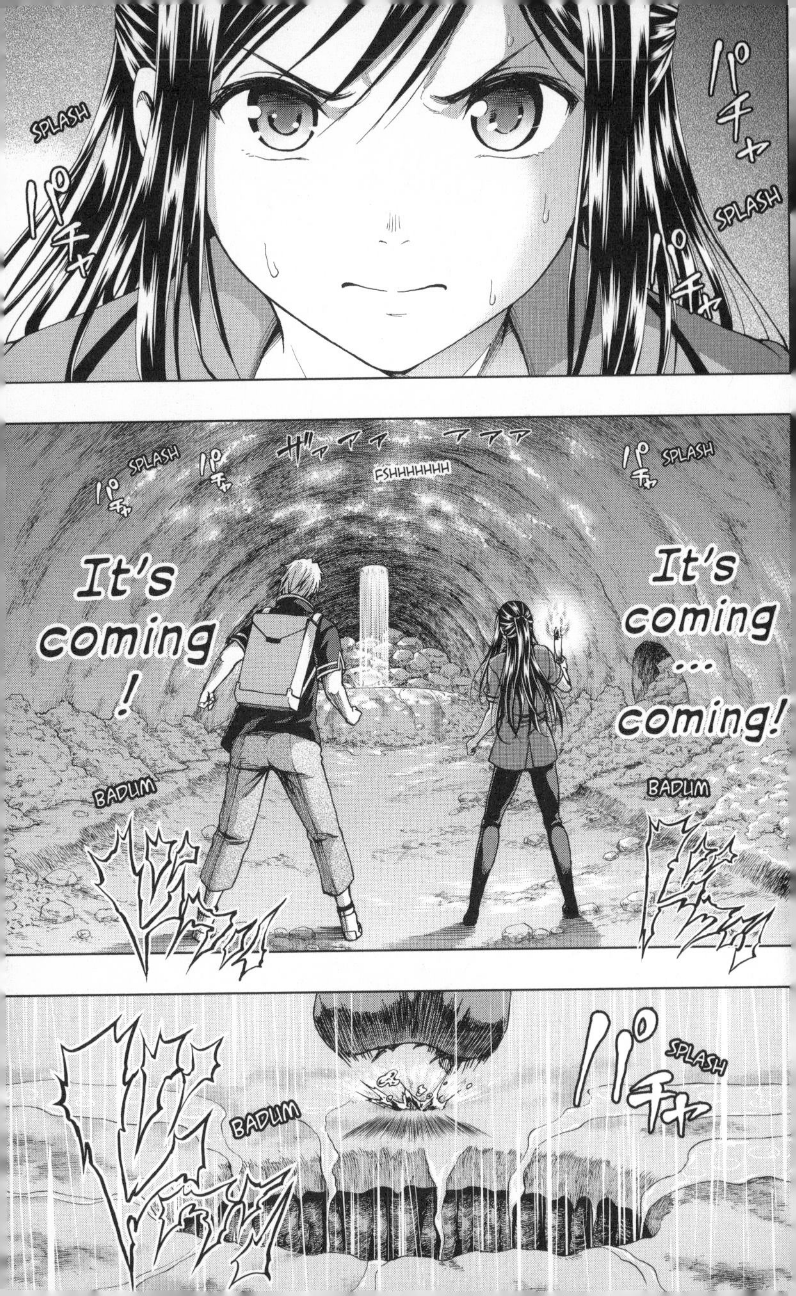

パチャ
SPLASH
パチャ
SPLASH
パチャ
SPLASH
パチャ
SPLASH
It's coming... coming!
BADUM
ザァァァ アァァ
FSHHHHHHH
SPLASH
パチャ
パチャ
It's coming!
BADUM
パチャ
SPLASH
BADUM

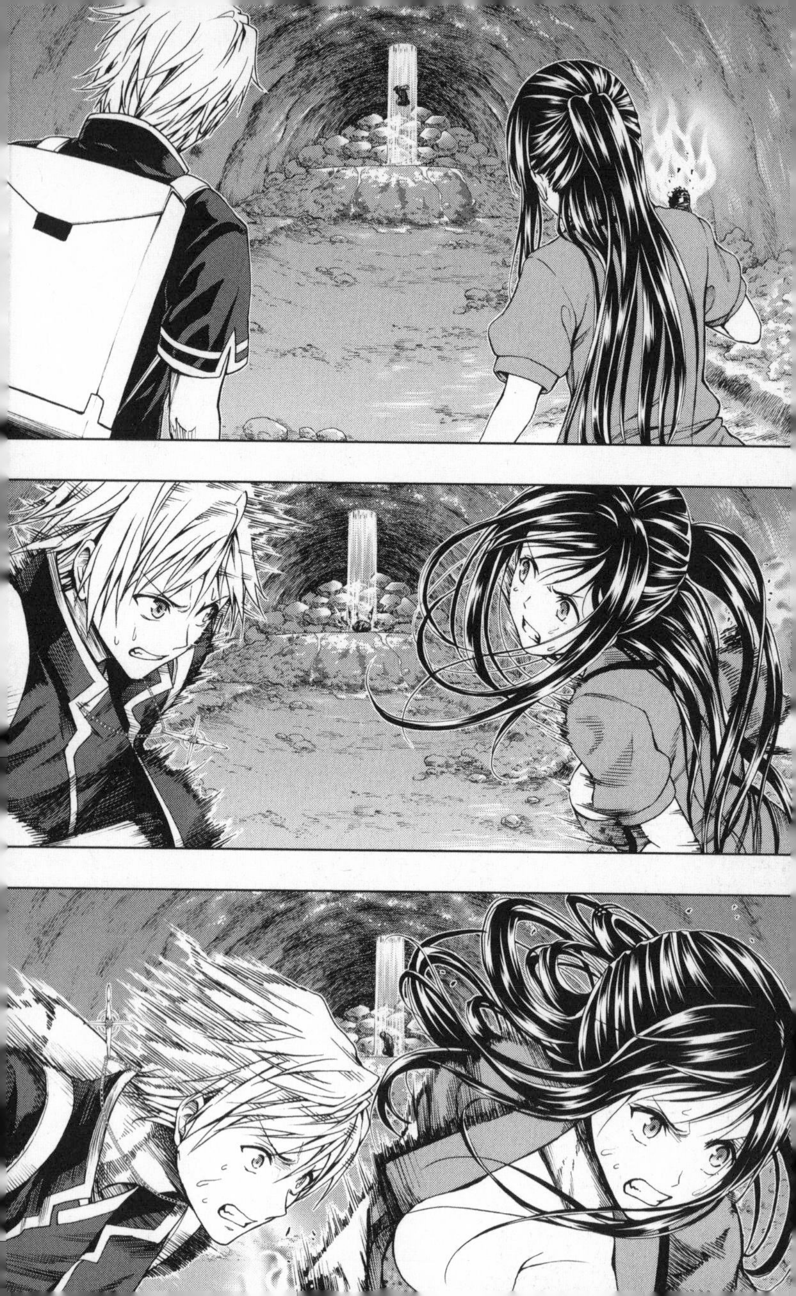

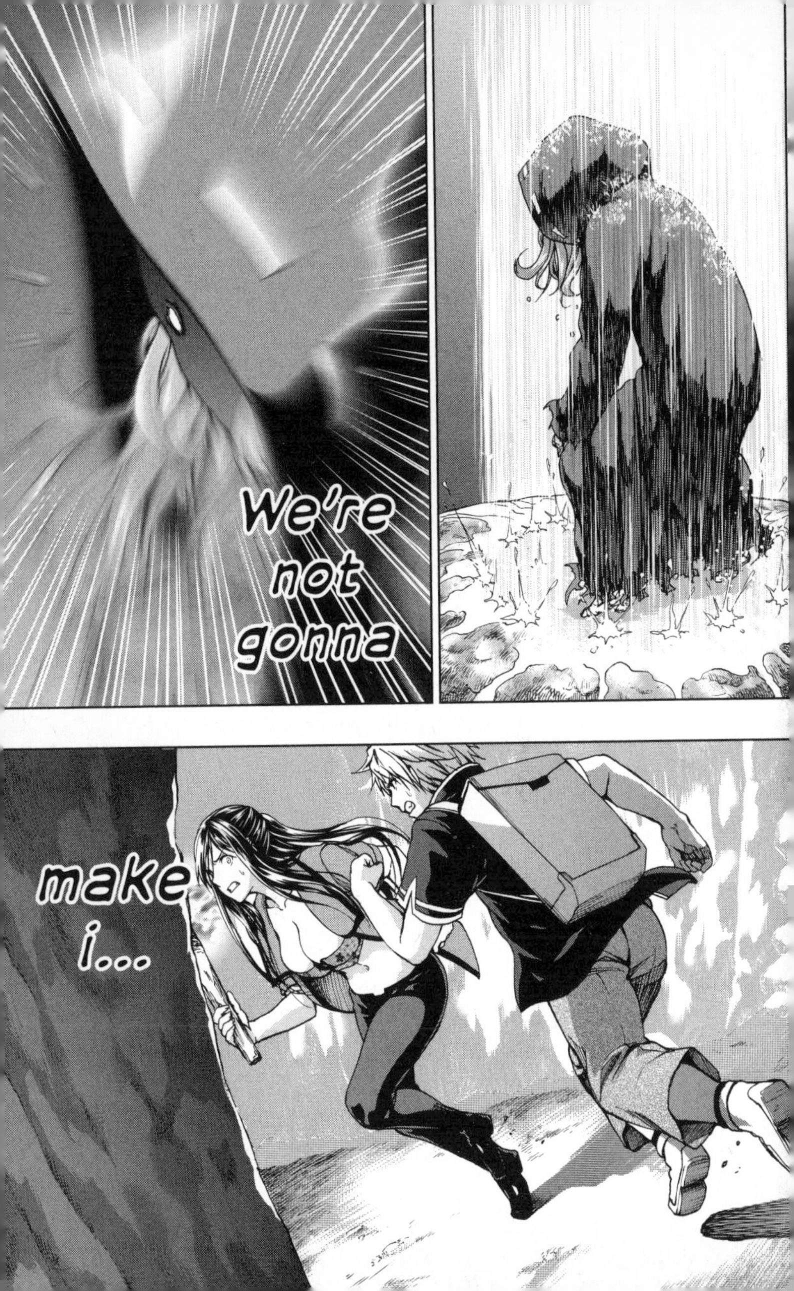
We're not gonna
make i...

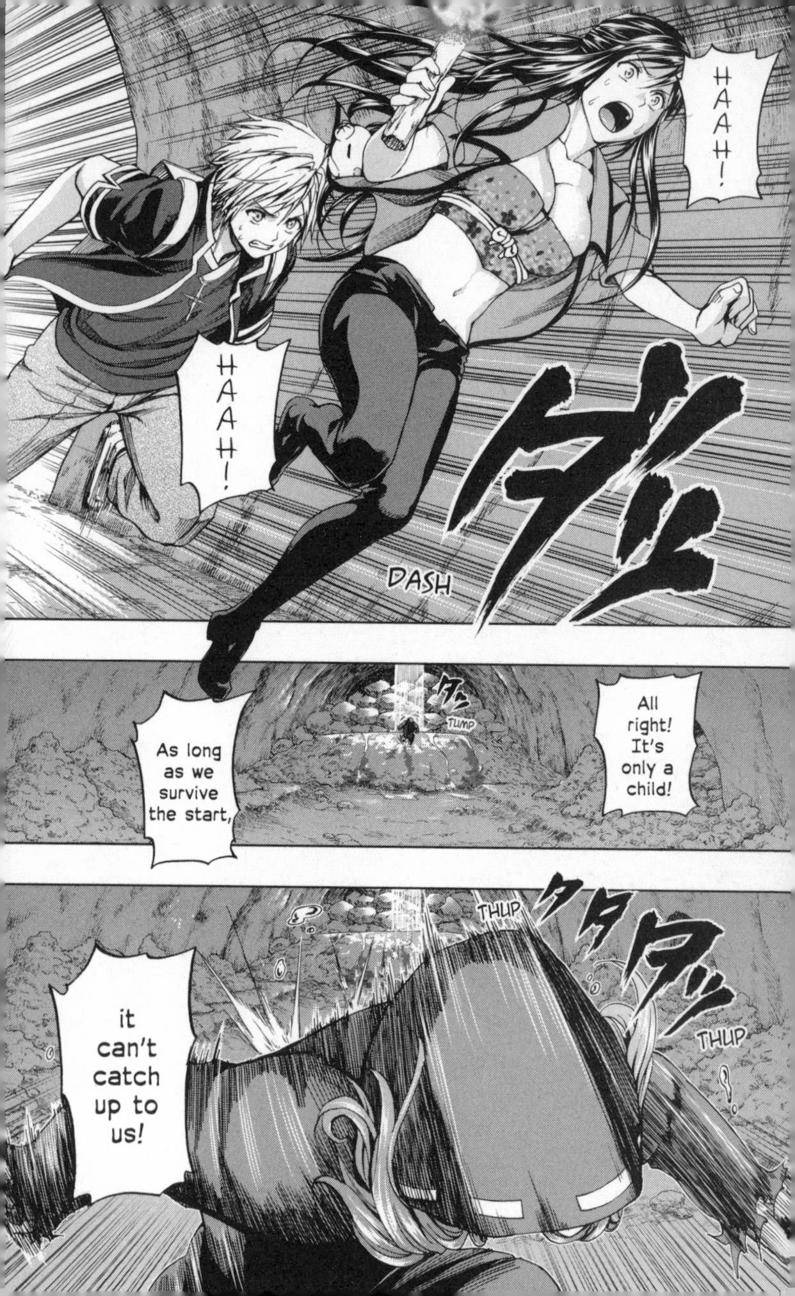
HAAAH!
HAAAH!
DASH
All right! It's only a child!
TUMP
As long as we survive the start,
THUP
THUP
it can't catch up to us!

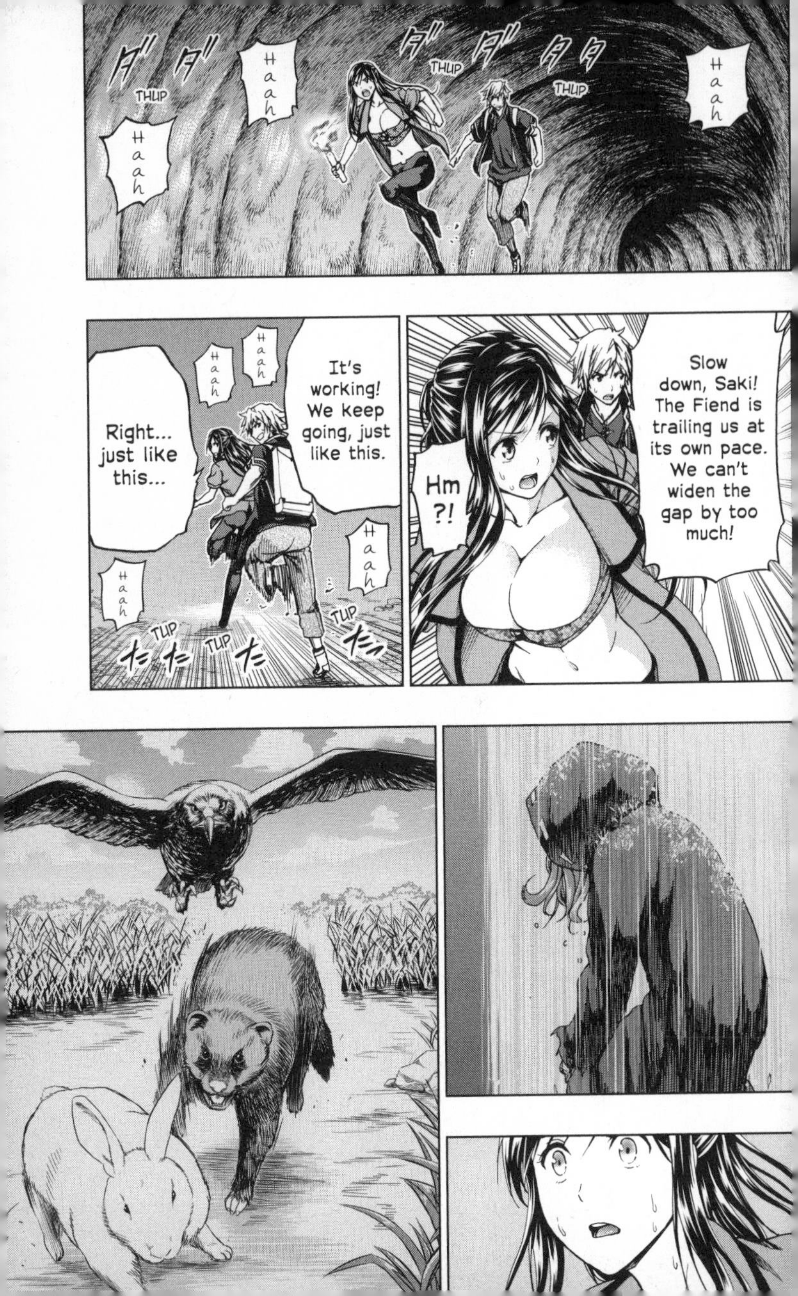
Haah
THUP
THUP
Haah
THUP
Haah
Slow down, Saki! The Fiend is trailing us at its own pace. We can't widen the gap by too much!
Hm?!
It's working! We keep going, just like this.
Haah
Haah
Right... just like this...
Haah
Haah
TUP
TUP
TUP

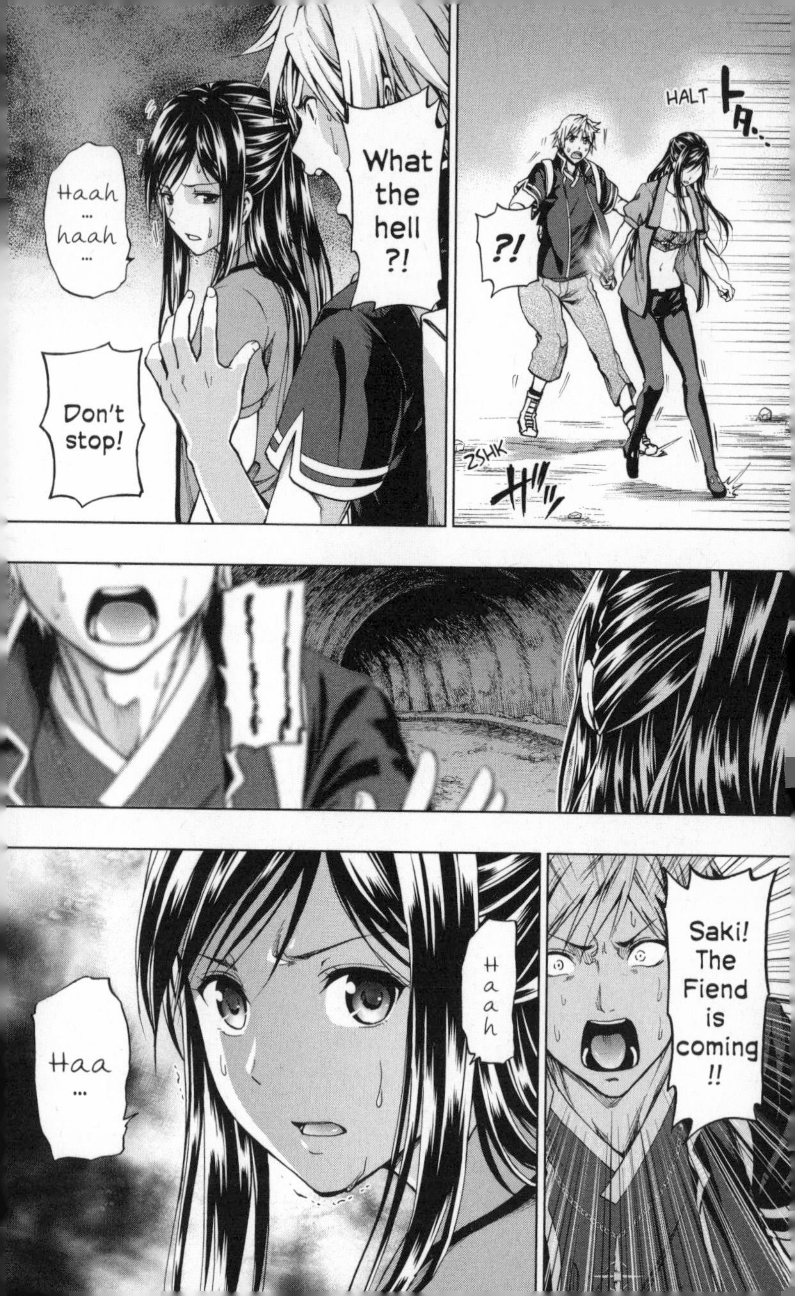
HALT
トタ…
?!
ZSHK
ザッ
What the hell ?!
Haah … haah …
Don't stop!
Saki! The Fiend is coming !!
Haah
Haa …

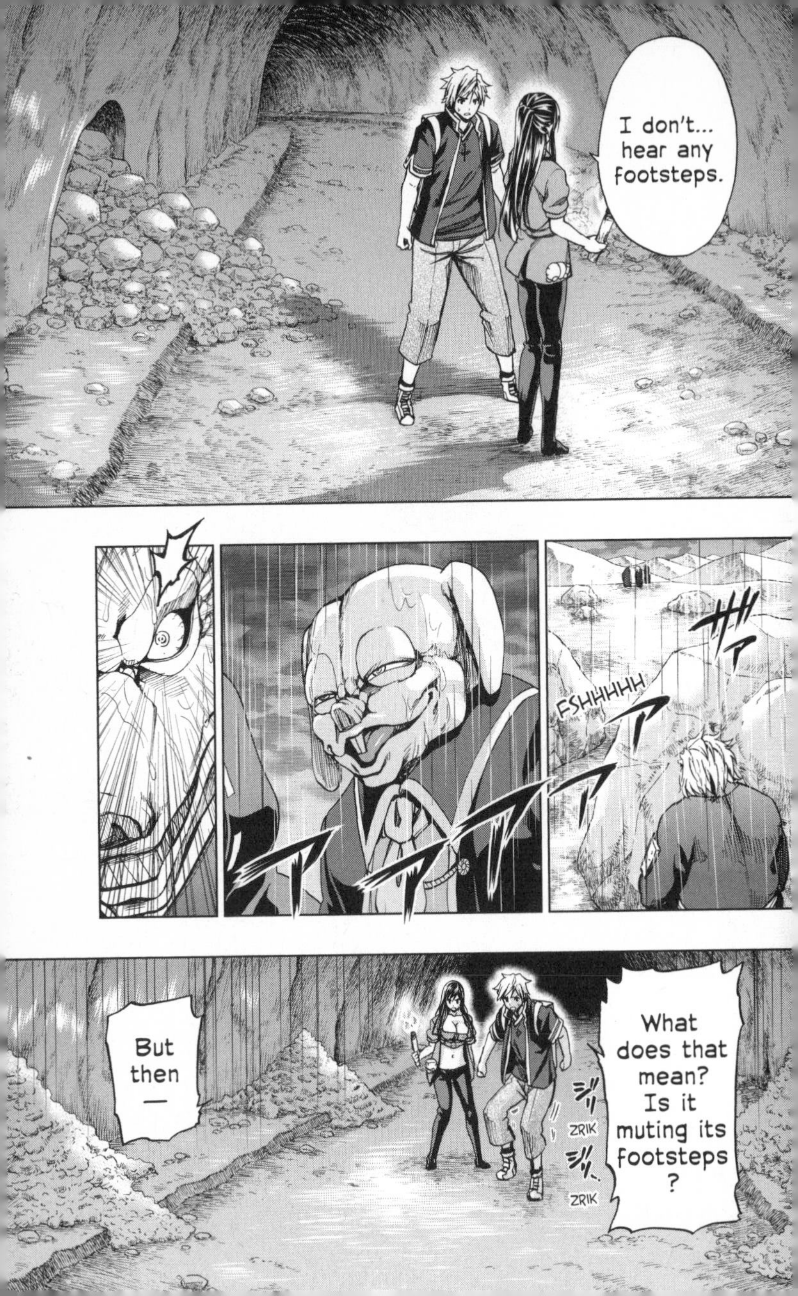
I don't... hear any footsteps.
FSHHHHH
What does that mean? Is it muting its footsteps?
ZRIK
ZRIK
But then —

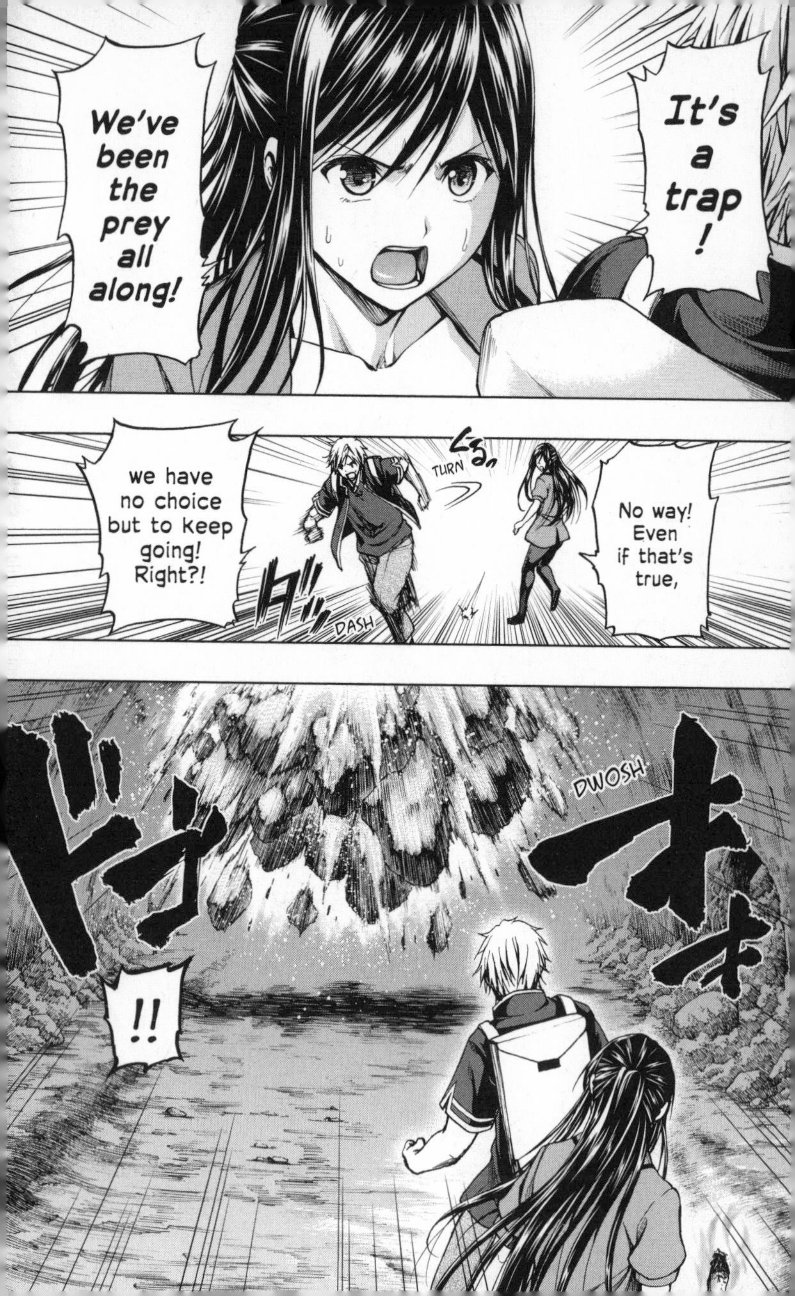
It's a trap!
We've been the prey all along!
No way! Even if that's true,
TURN
we have no choice but to keep going! Right?!
DASH
DWOSH
!!

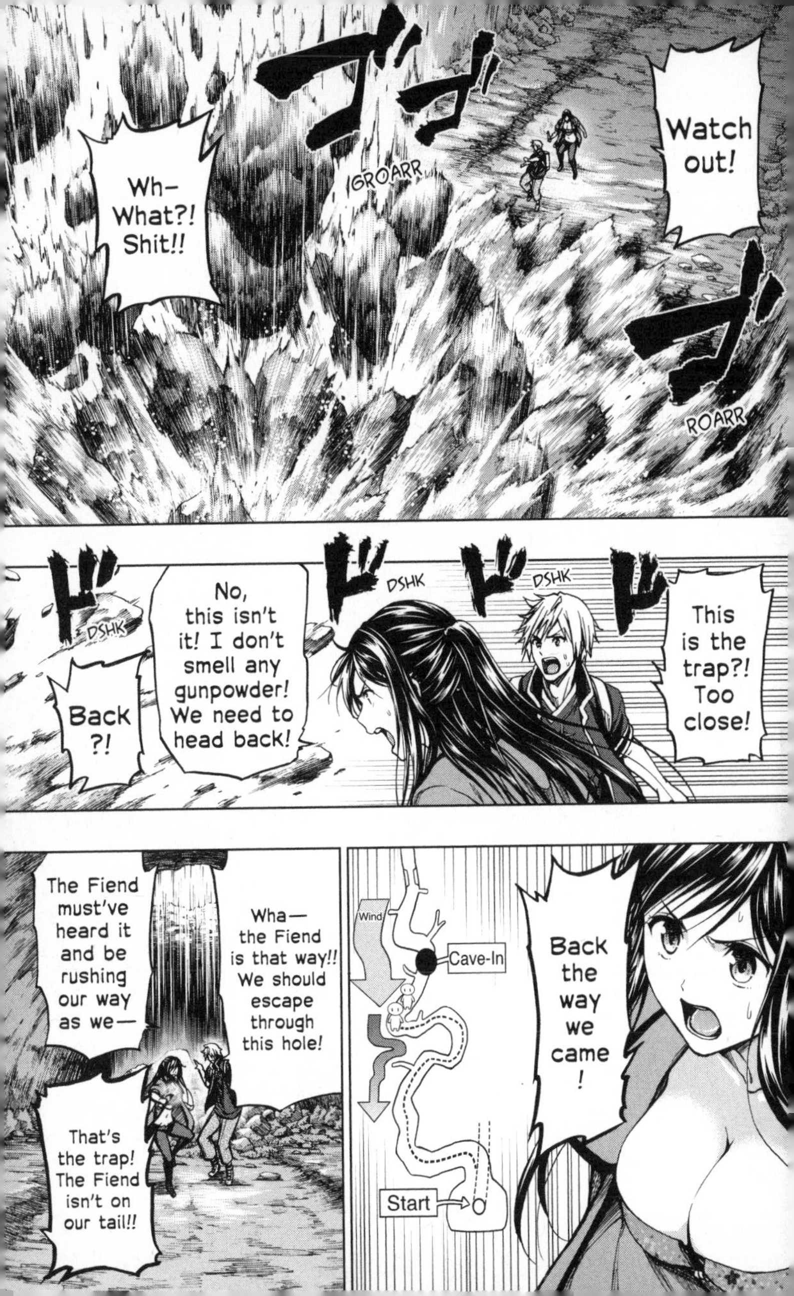
Watch out!
GROARR
ROARR
Wh— What?! Shit!!
This is the trap?! Too close!
DSHK
DSHK
No, this isn't it! I don't smell any gunpowder! We need to head back!
DSHK
Back?!
Back the way we came!
Cave-In
Wind
Start
Wha— the Fiend is that way!! We should escape through this hole!
The Fiend must've heard it and be rushing our way as we—
That's the trap! The Fiend isn't on our tail!!

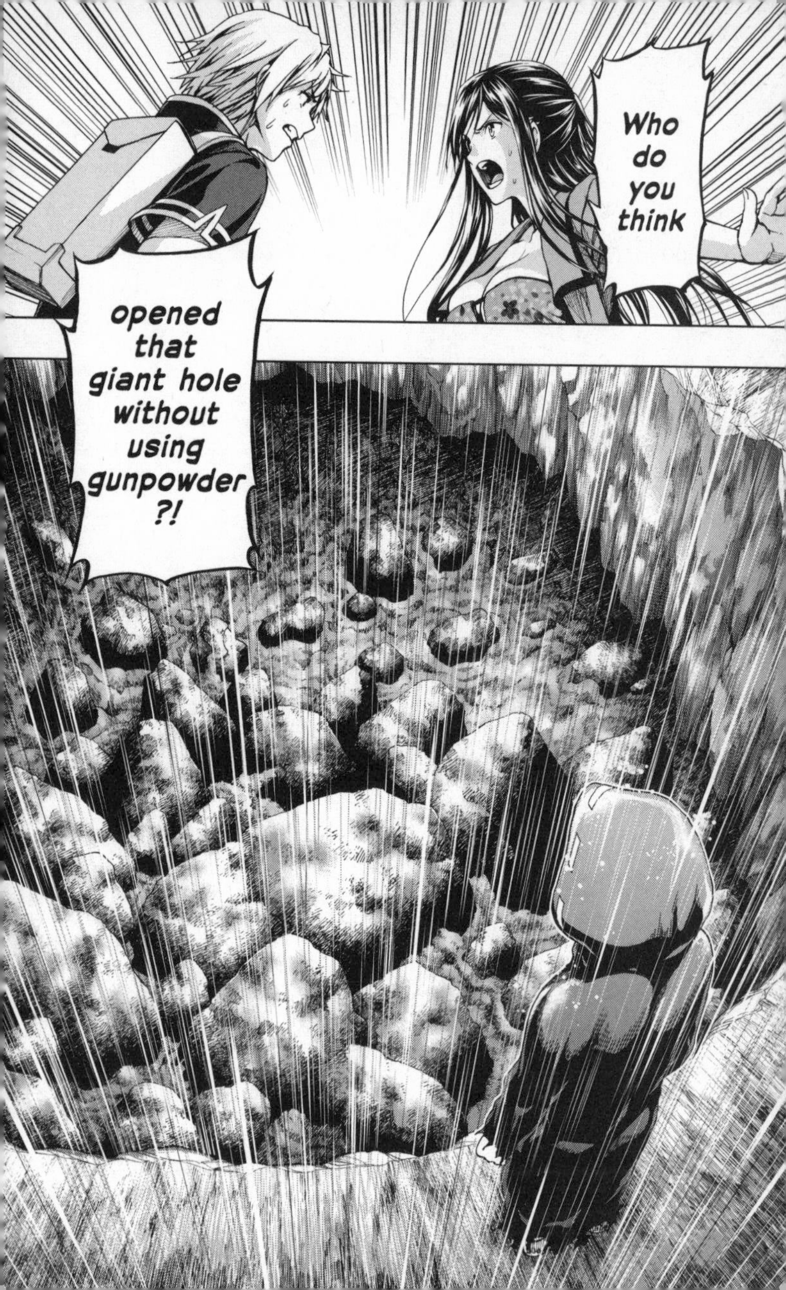
Who do you think
opened that giant hole without using gunpowder ?!

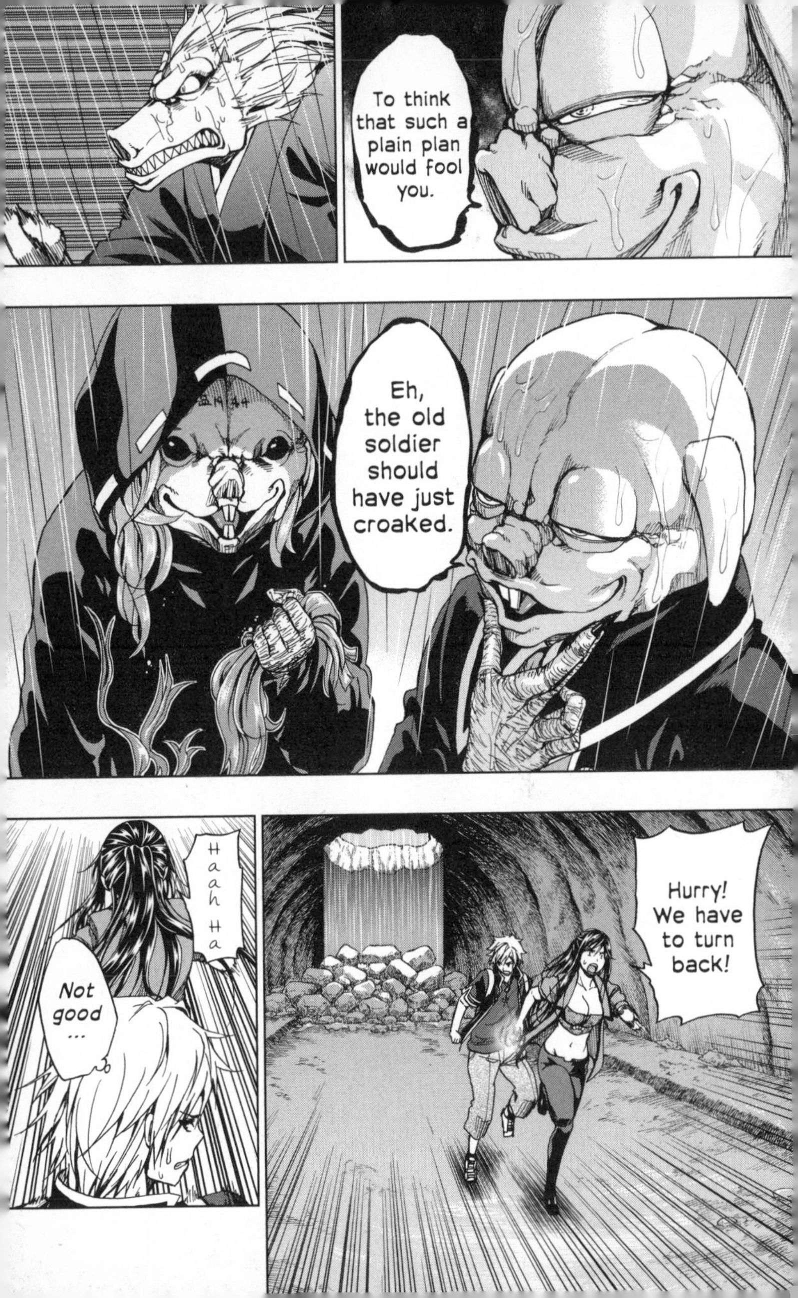
To think that such a plain plan would fool you.
Eh, the old soldier should have just croaked.
Hurry! We have to turn back!
Haah Ha
Not good ...

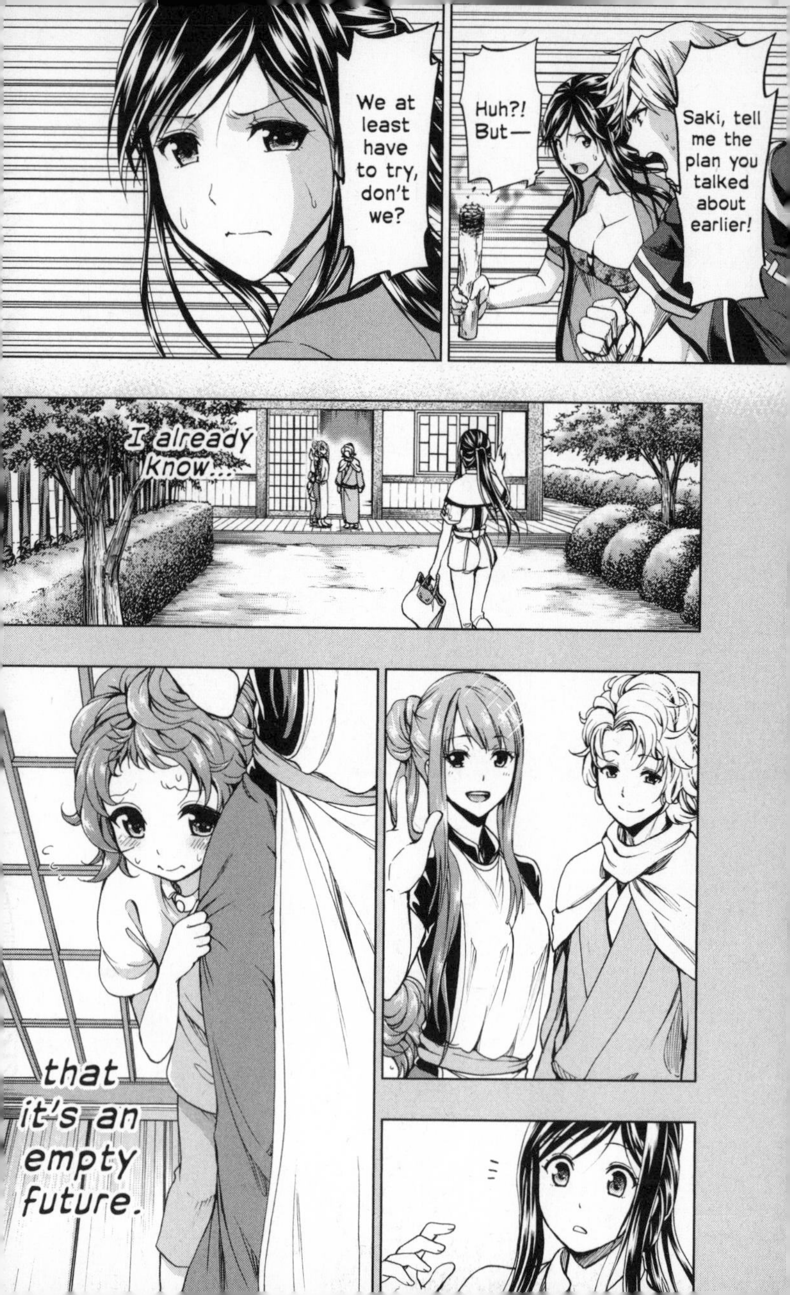
Saki, tell me the plan you talked about earlier!
Huh?! But—
We at least have to try, don't we?
I already know...
that it's an empty future.

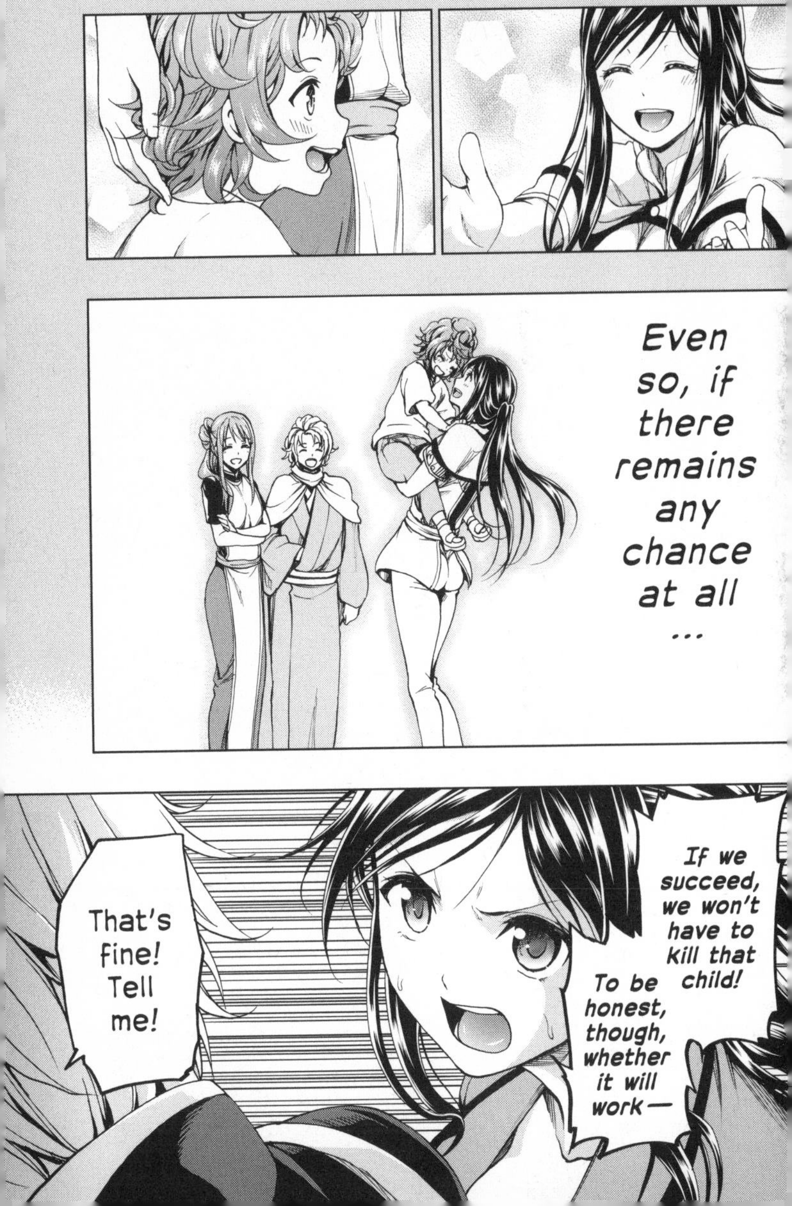
Even so, if there remains any chance at all ...
If we succeed, we won't have to kill that child!
To be honest, though, whether it will work—
That's fine! Tell me!

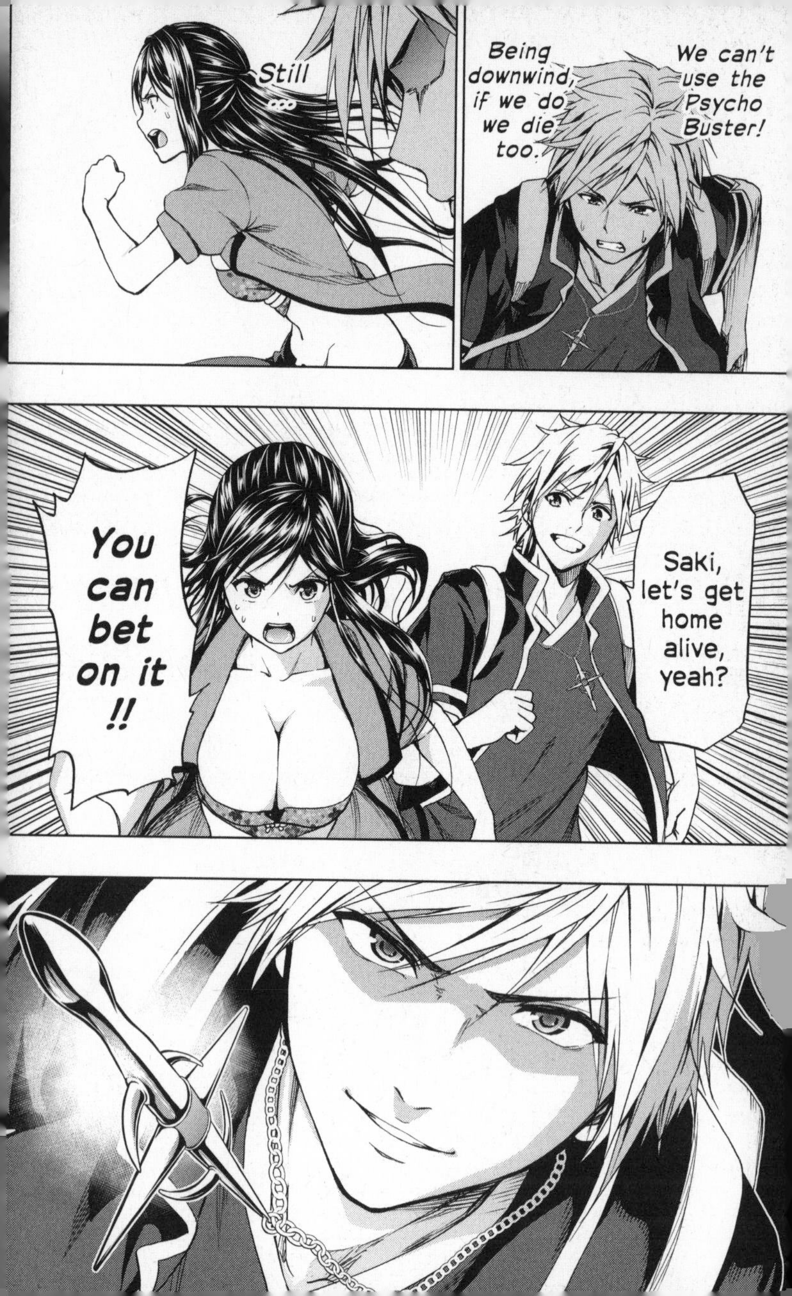
We can't use the Psycho Buster!
Being downwind, if we do we die too.
Still...
Saki, let's get home alive, yeah?
You can bet on it!!

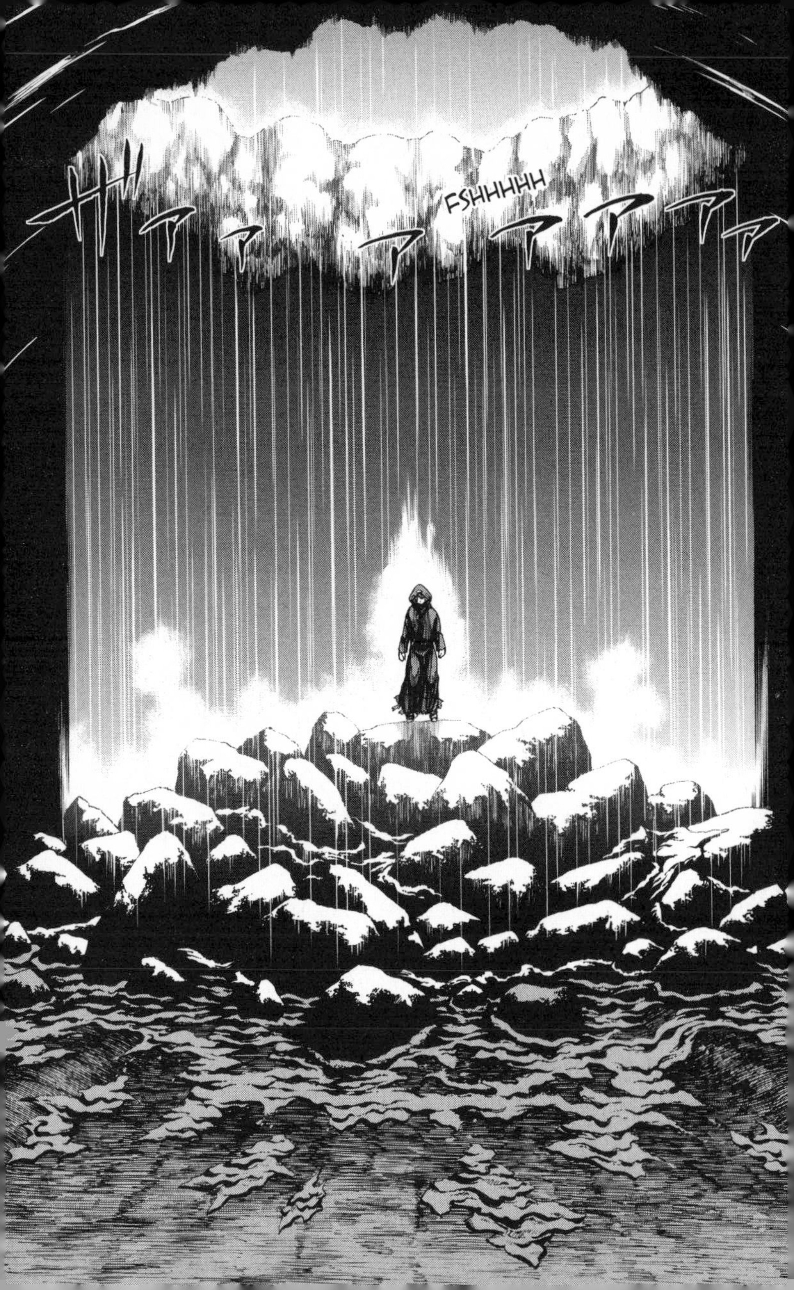
ザァァァァァァァ
FSHHHHH

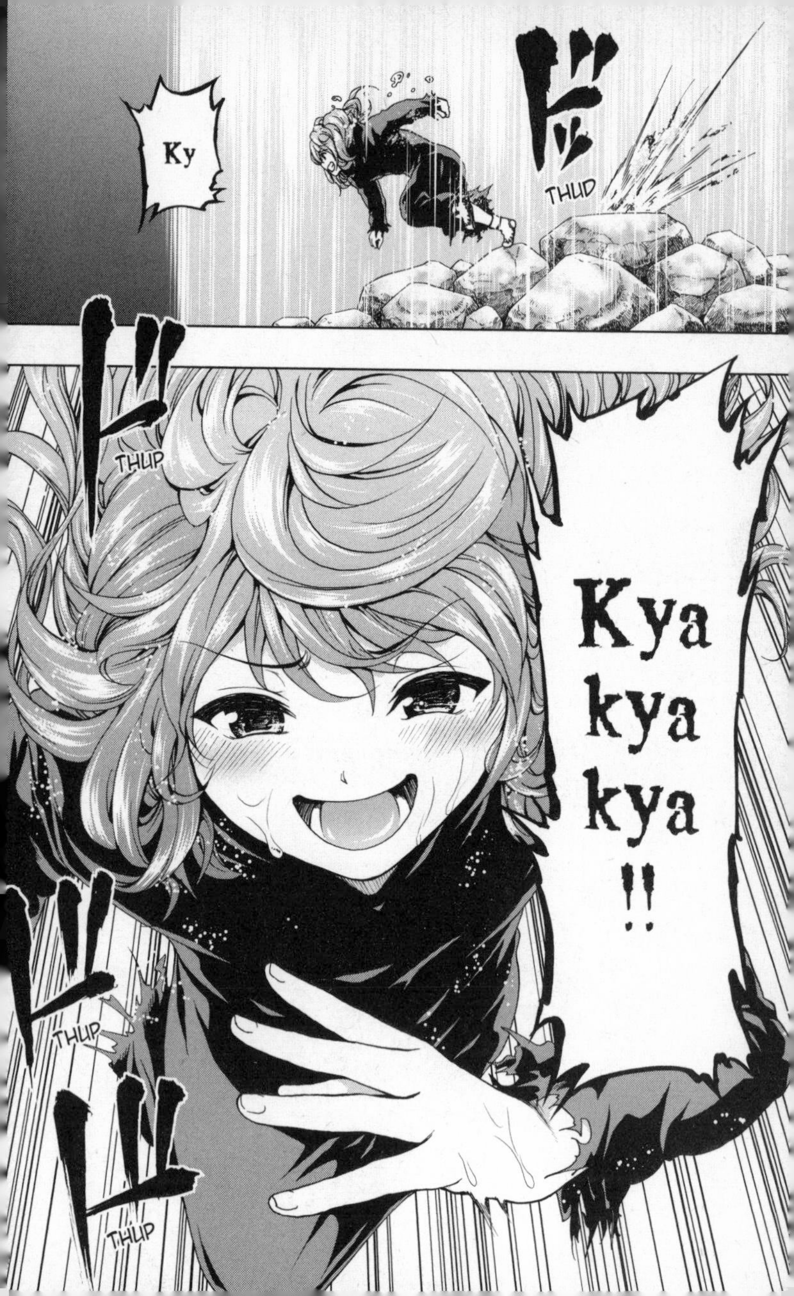
THUD
Ky
Kya kya kya!!
THUP
THUP
THUP

Chapter 25
Trap

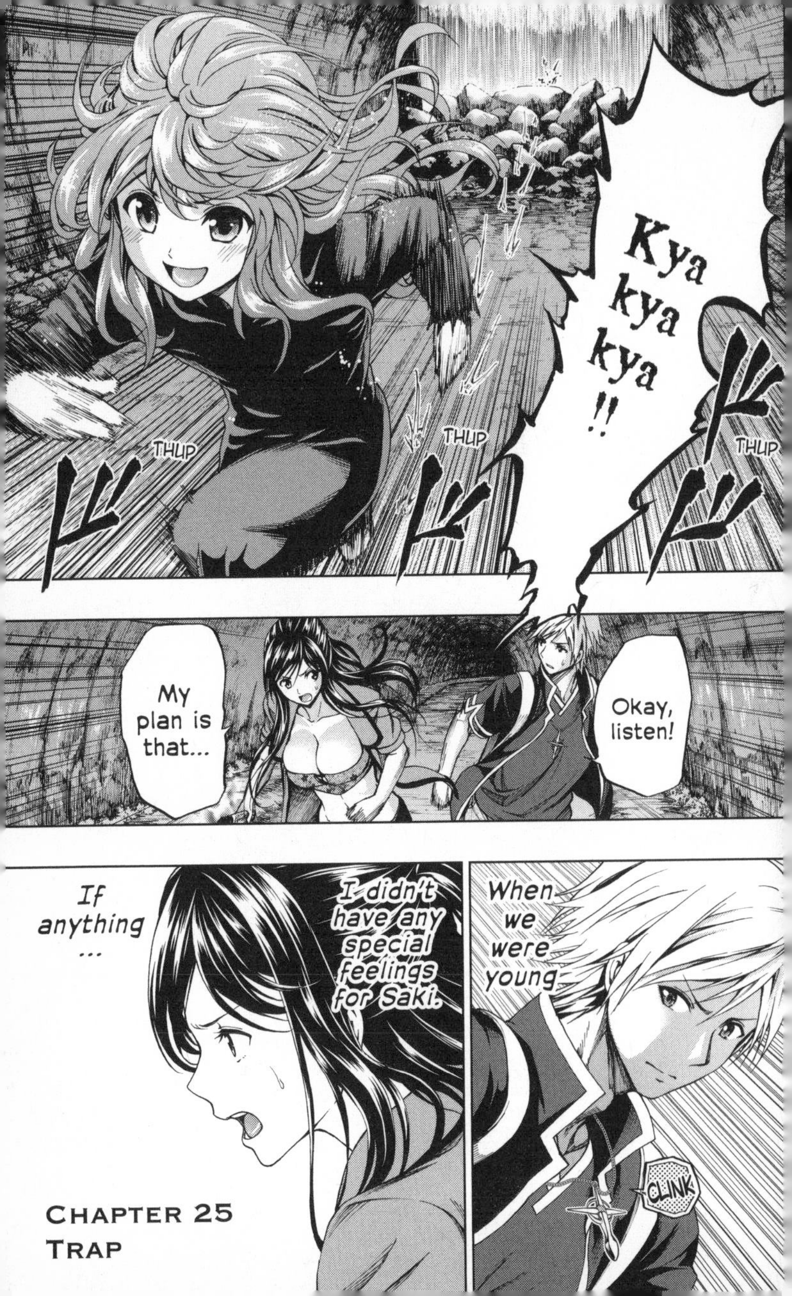

Kya kya kya!!
THUP
THUP
THUP
Okay, listen!
My plan is that...
When we were young
CLINK
I didn't have any special feelings for Saki.
If anything ...

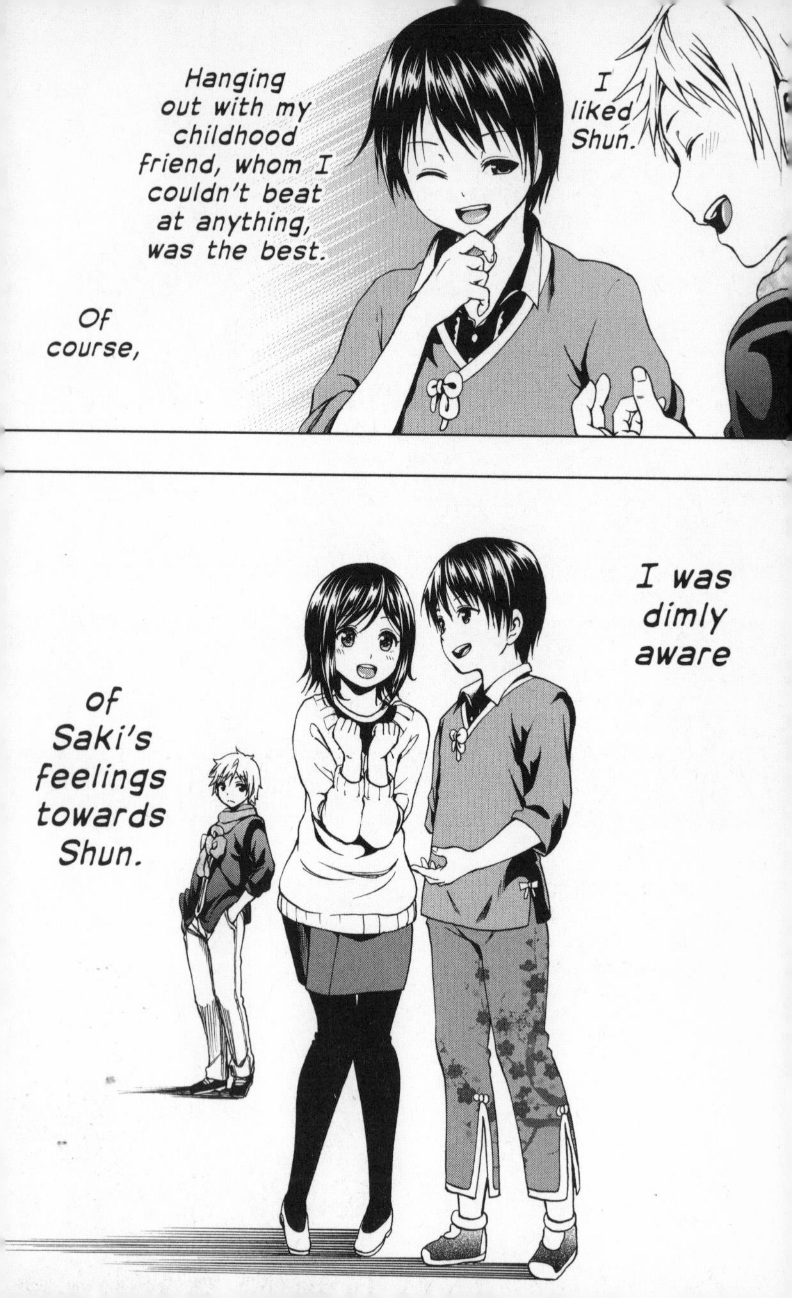
I liked Shun.
Hanging out with my childhood friend, whom I couldn't beat at anything, was the best.
Of course,
I was dimly aware
of Saki's feelings towards Shun.

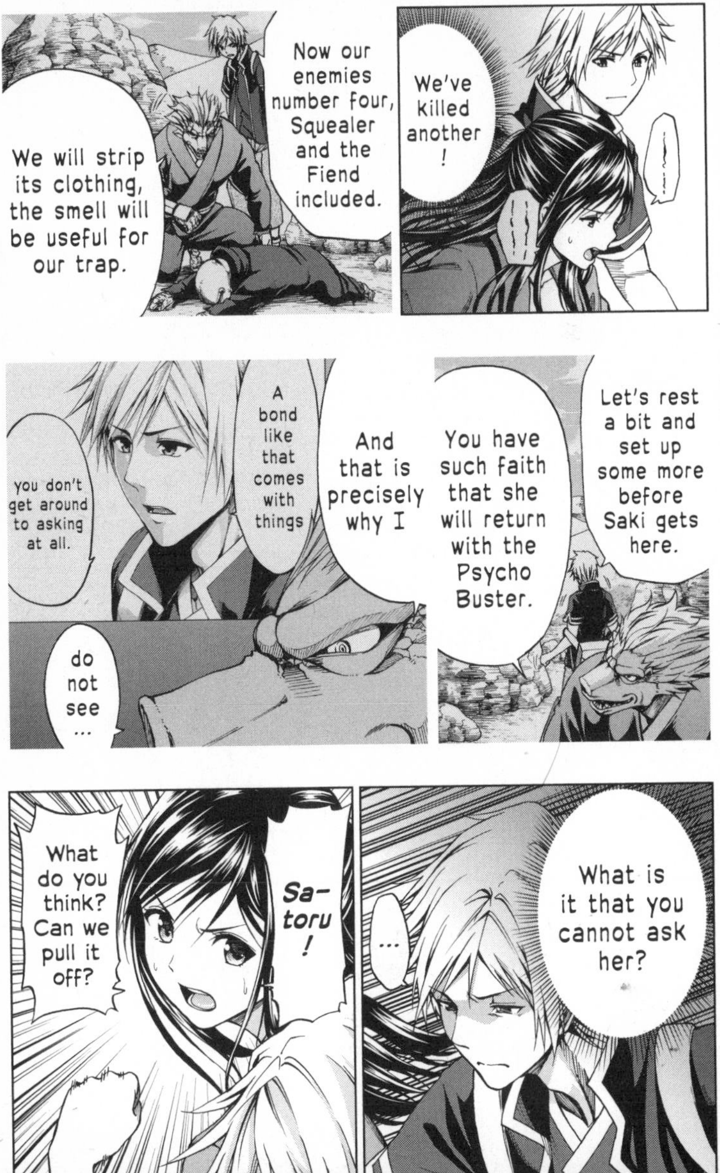
We've killed another!
Now our enemies number four, Squealer and the Fiend included.
We will strip its clothing, the smell will be useful for our trap.
Let's rest a bit and set up some more before Saki gets here.
You have such faith that she will return with the Psycho Buster.
And that is precisely why I
A bond like that comes with things
you don't get around to asking at all.
do not see ...
What is it that you cannot ask her?
...
Sa-toru!
What do you think? Can we pull it off?

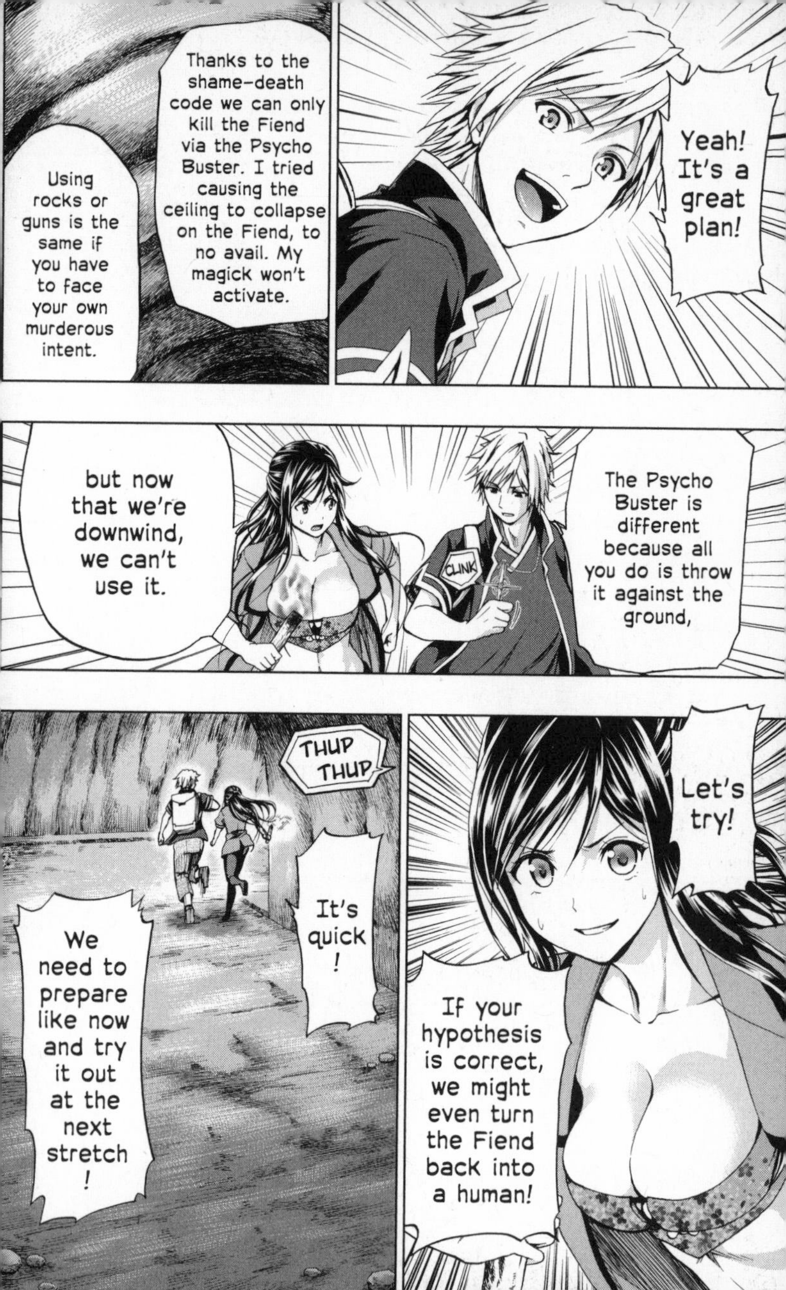
Yeah! It's a great plan!
Thanks to the shame-death code we can only kill the Fiend via the Psycho Buster. I tried causing the ceiling to collapse on the Fiend, to no avail. My magick won't activate.
Using rocks or guns is the same if you have to face your own murderous intent.
The Psycho Buster is different because all you do is throw it against the ground,
CLINK
but now that we're downwind, we can't use it.
Let's try!
If your hypothesis is correct, we might even turn the Fiend back into a human!
THUP THUP
It's quick!
We need to prepare like now and try it out at the next stretch!

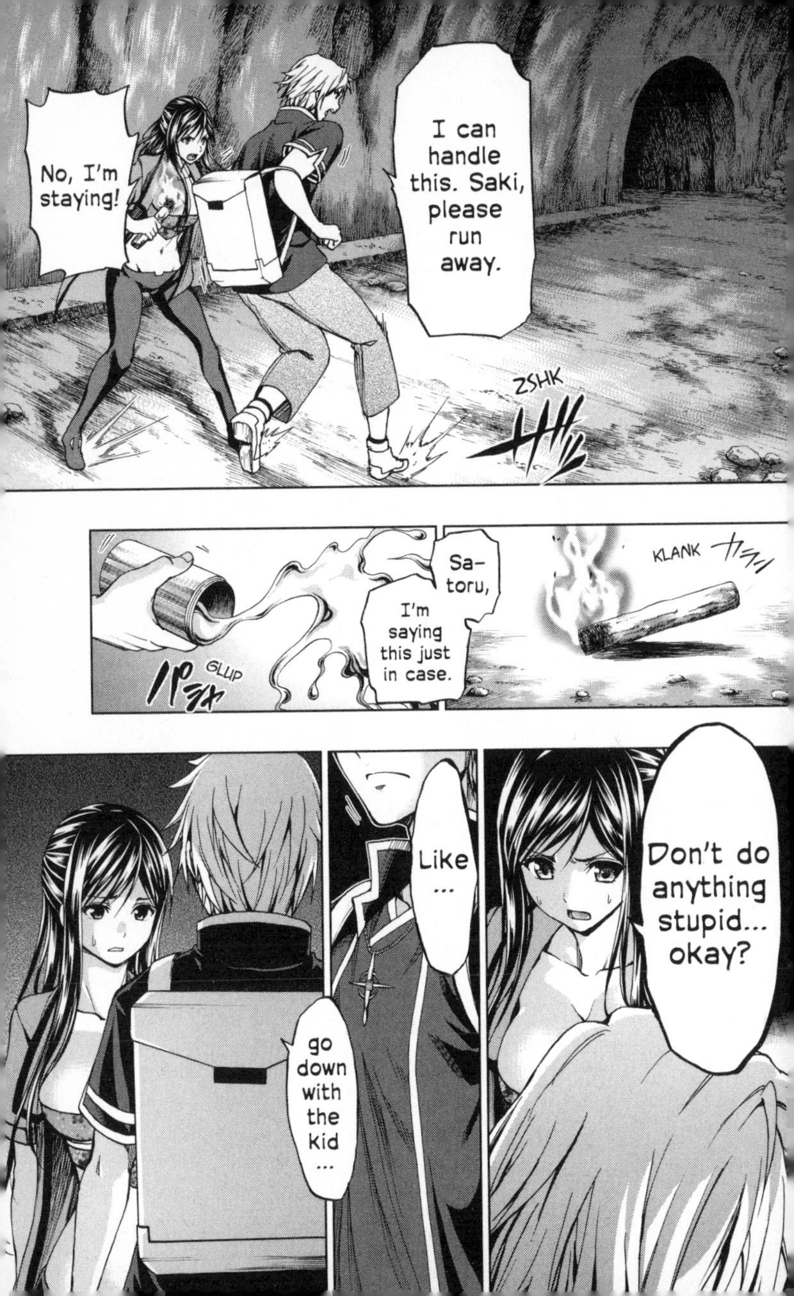
I can handle this. Saki, please run away.
No, I'm staying!
ZSHK
KLANK
Sa-toru,
I'm saying this just in case.
GLUP
Don't do anything stupid... okay?
Like ...
go down with the kid ...

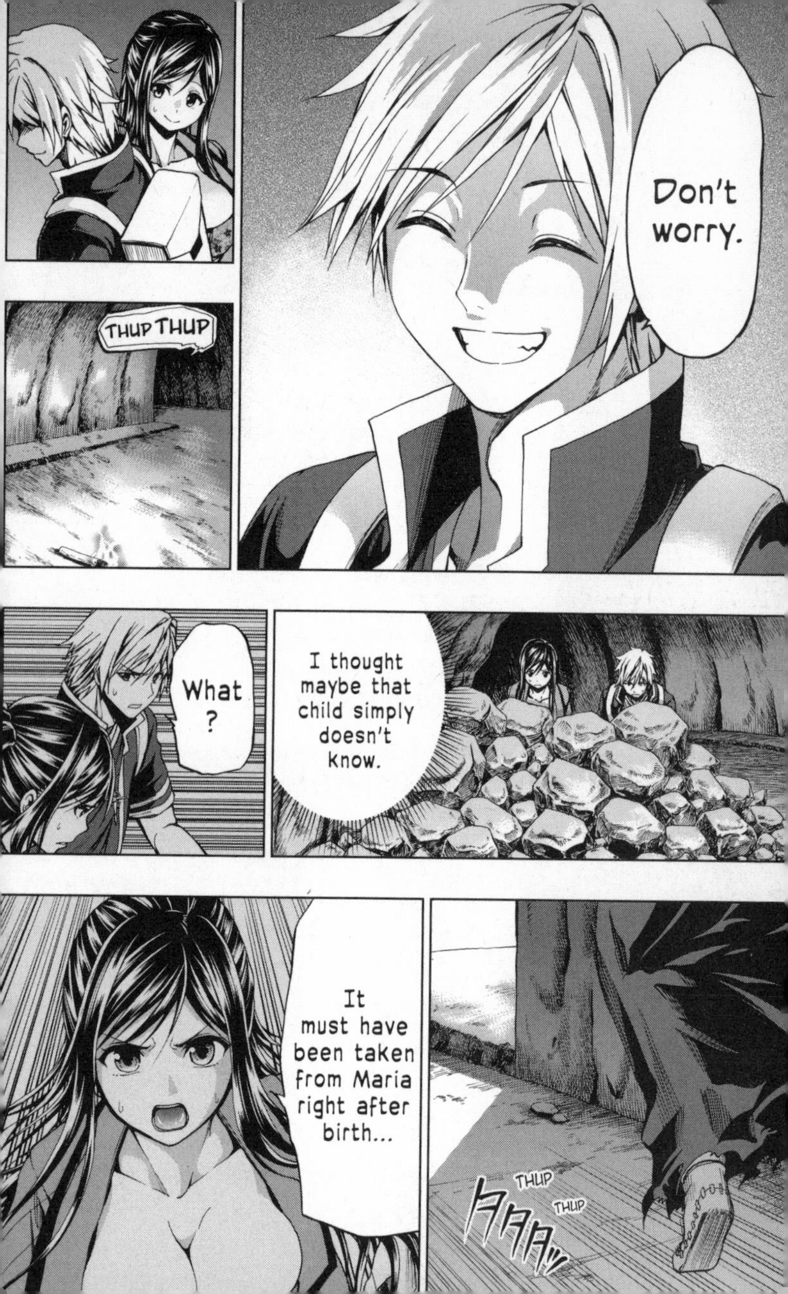
Don't worry.
THUP THUP
I thought maybe that child simply doesn't know.
What?
THUP
THUP
タタタッ
It must have been taken from Maria right after birth...

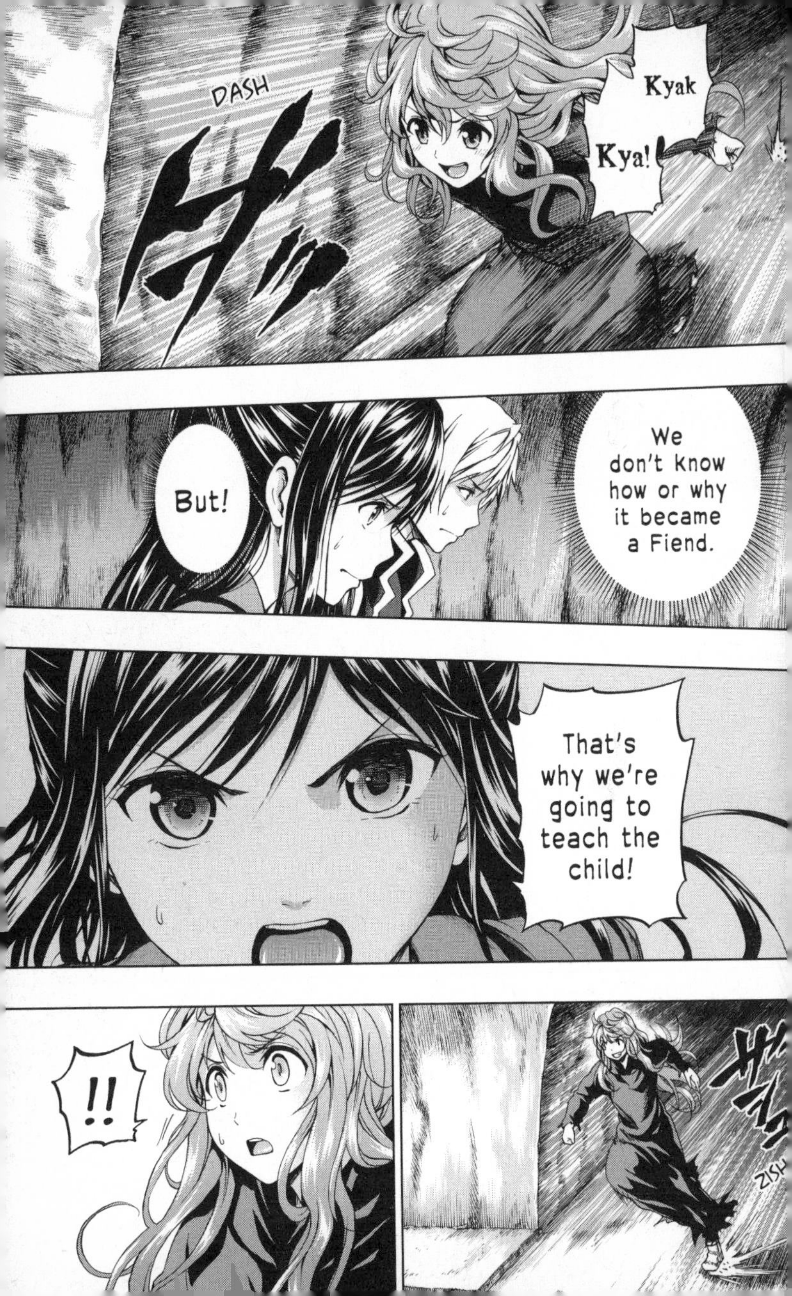
Kyak
Kya!
DASH
We don't know how or why it became a Fiend.
But!
That's why we're going to teach the child!
ZISH
!!

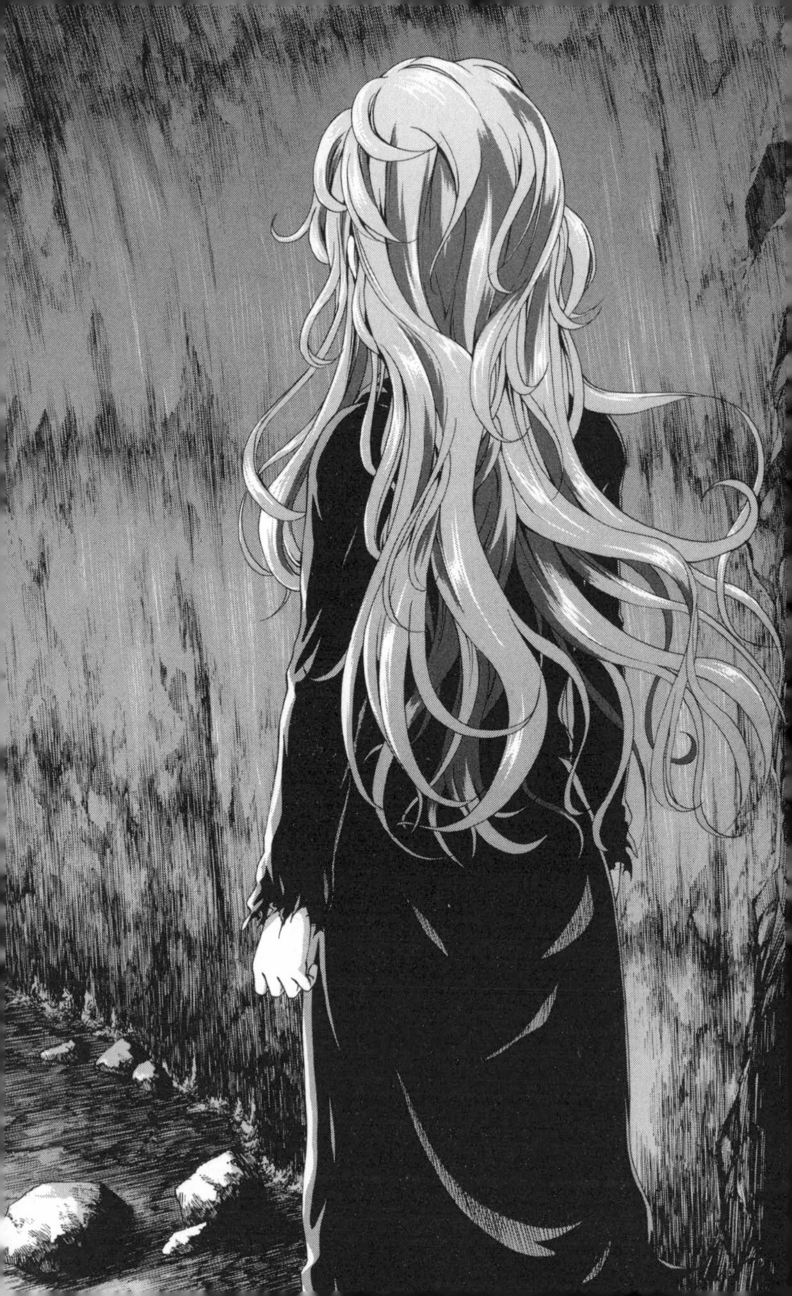

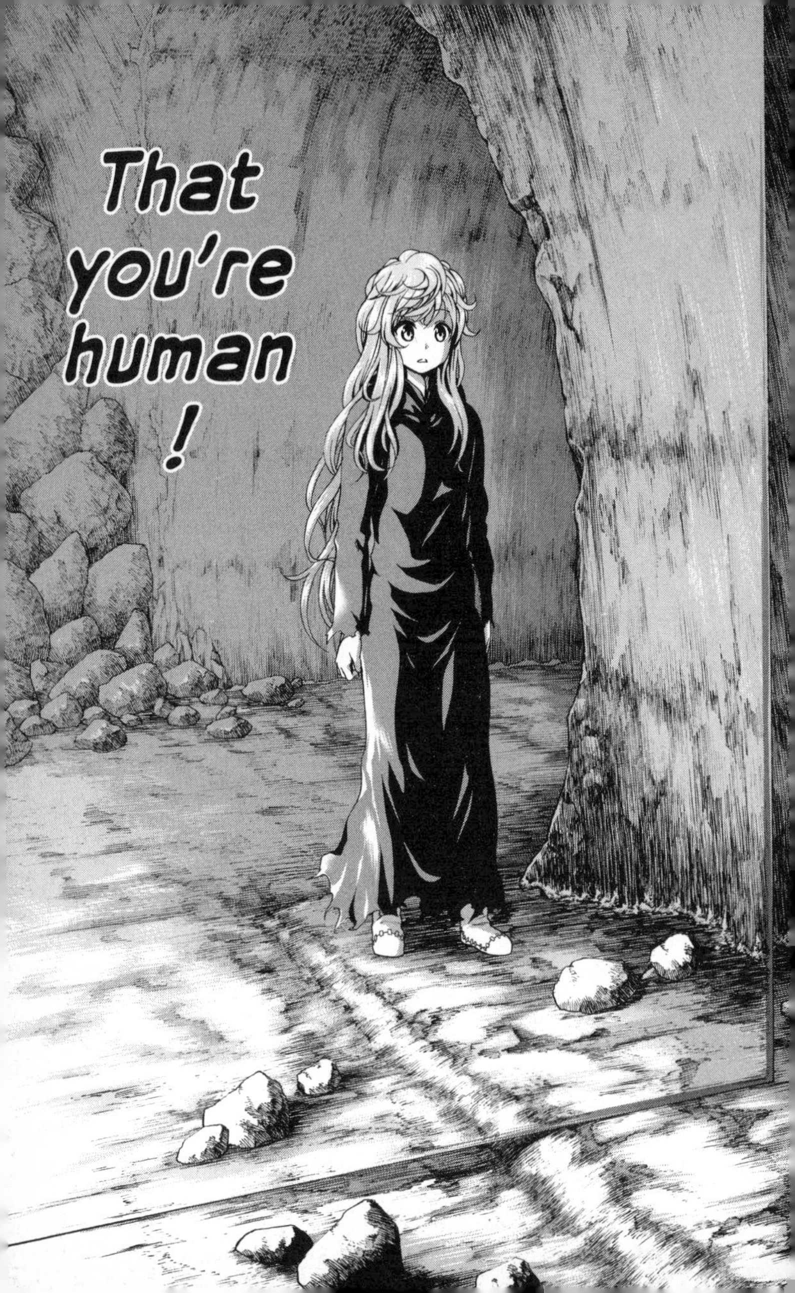
That you're human!

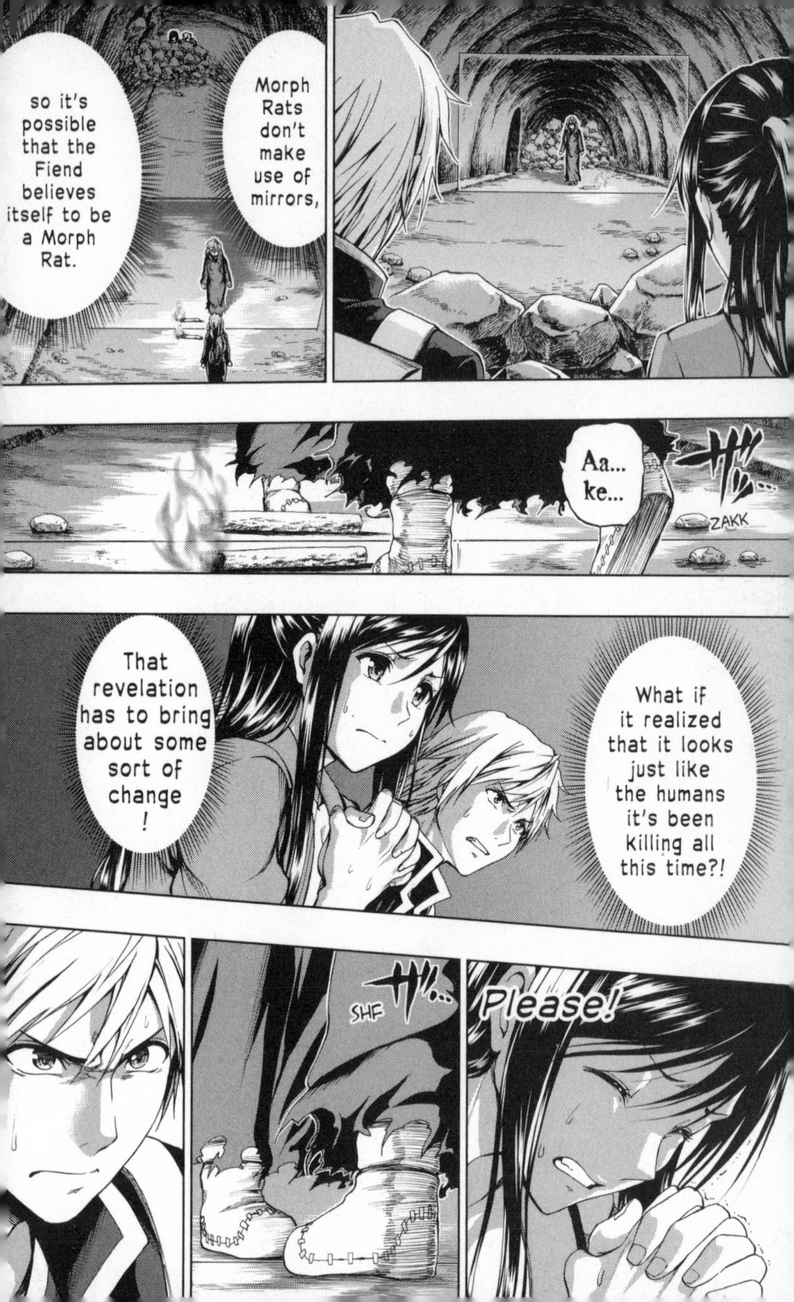
Morph Rats don't make use of mirrors,
so it's possible that the Fiend believes itself to be a Morph Rat.
ZAKK
Aa... ke...
What if it realized that it looks just like the humans it's been killing all this time?!
That revelation has to bring about some sort of change!
Please!
SHF

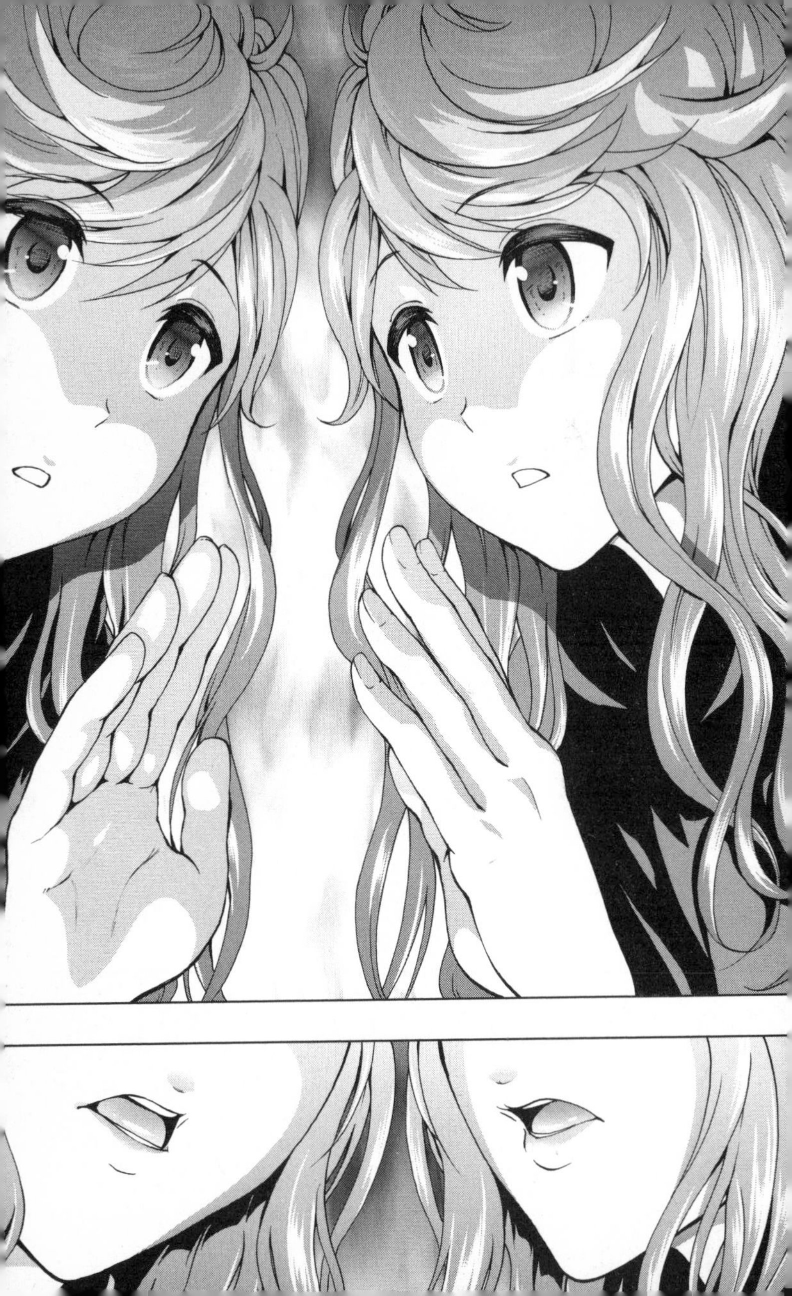

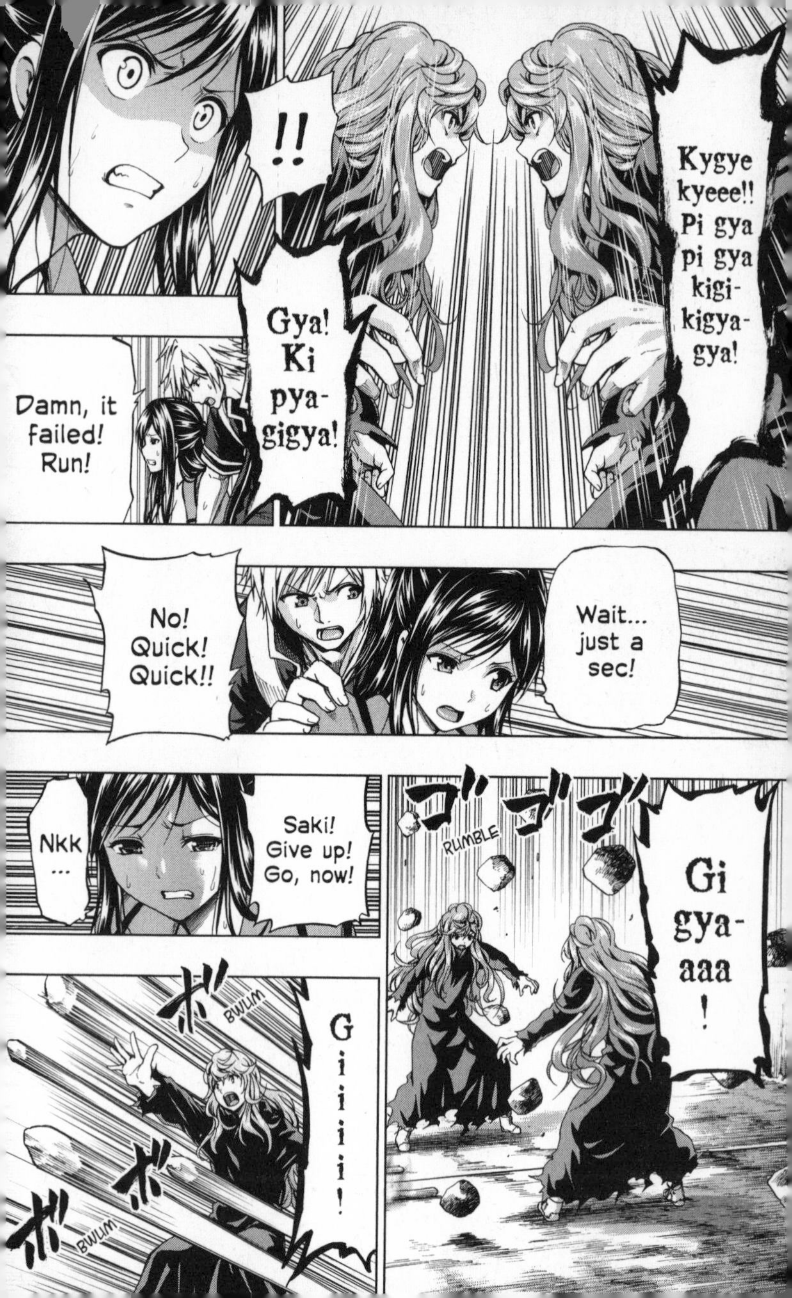
Kygye kyeee!! Pi gya pi gya kigi-kigya-gya!
!!
Gya! Ki pya-gigya!
Damn, it failed! Run!
Wait... just a sec!
No! Quick! Quick!!
ゴゴゴ
RUMBLE
Gi gya-aaa!
Saki! Give up! Go, now!
Nkk...
ボ
BWUM
G i i i i i!
ボ
ボ
BWUM

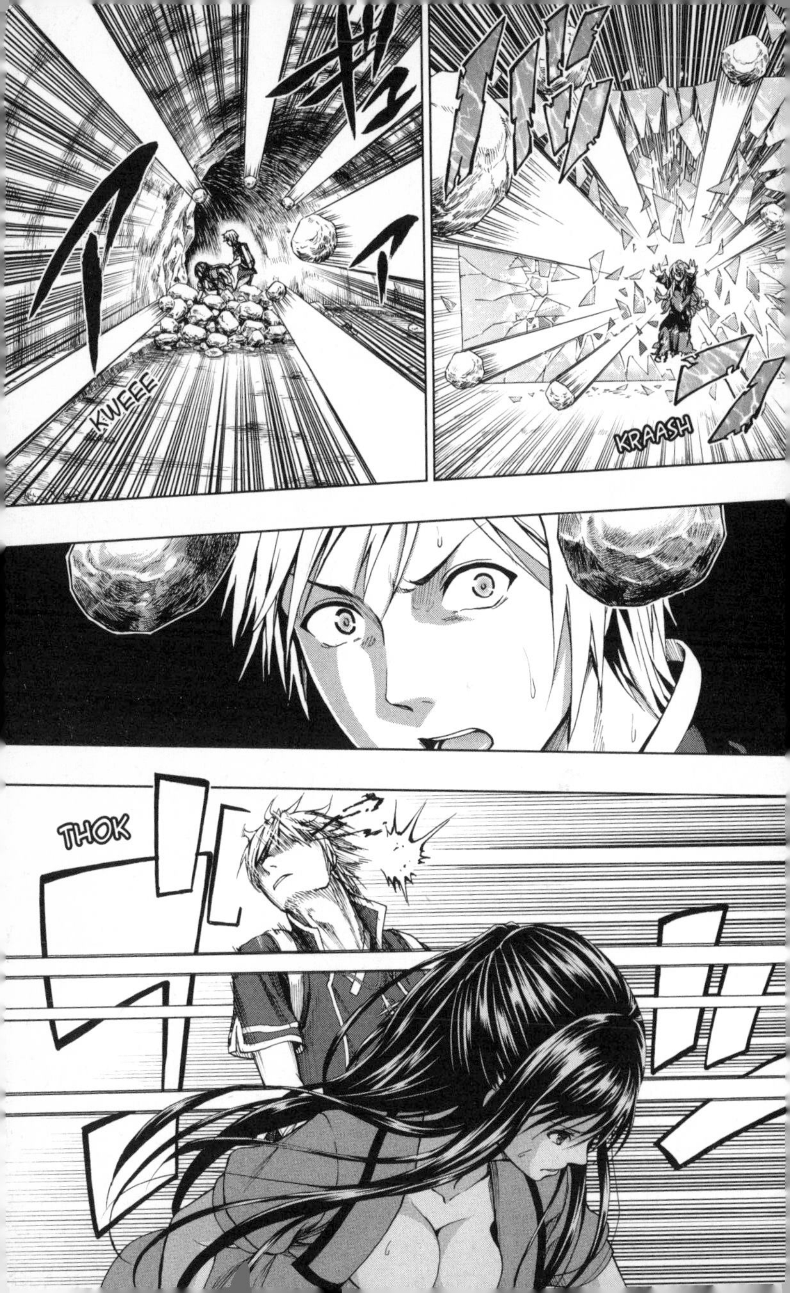
KRAASH
KWEEE
THOK

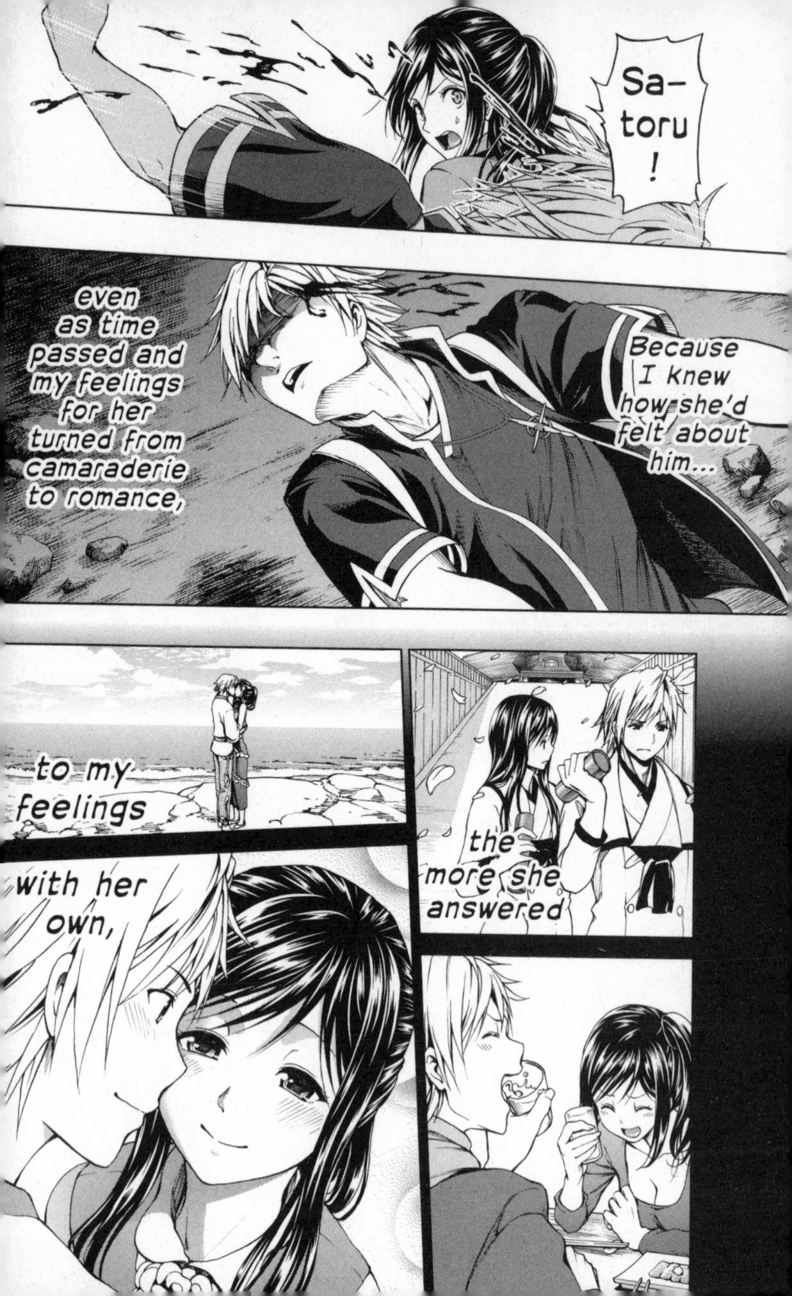
Sa-toru!
Because I knew how she'd felt about him...
even as time passed and my feelings for her turned from camaraderie to romance,
the more she answered
to my feelings
with her own,

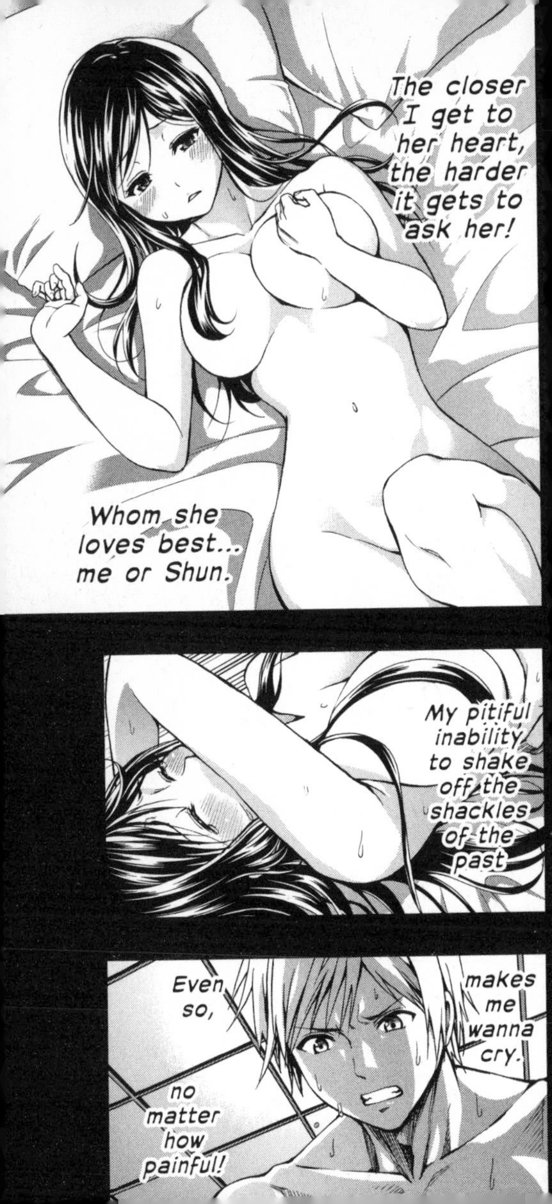
The closer I get to her heart, the harder it gets to ask her!
Whom she loves best... me or Shun.
My pitiful inability to shake off the shackles of the past
makes me wanna cry.
Even so,
no matter how painful!

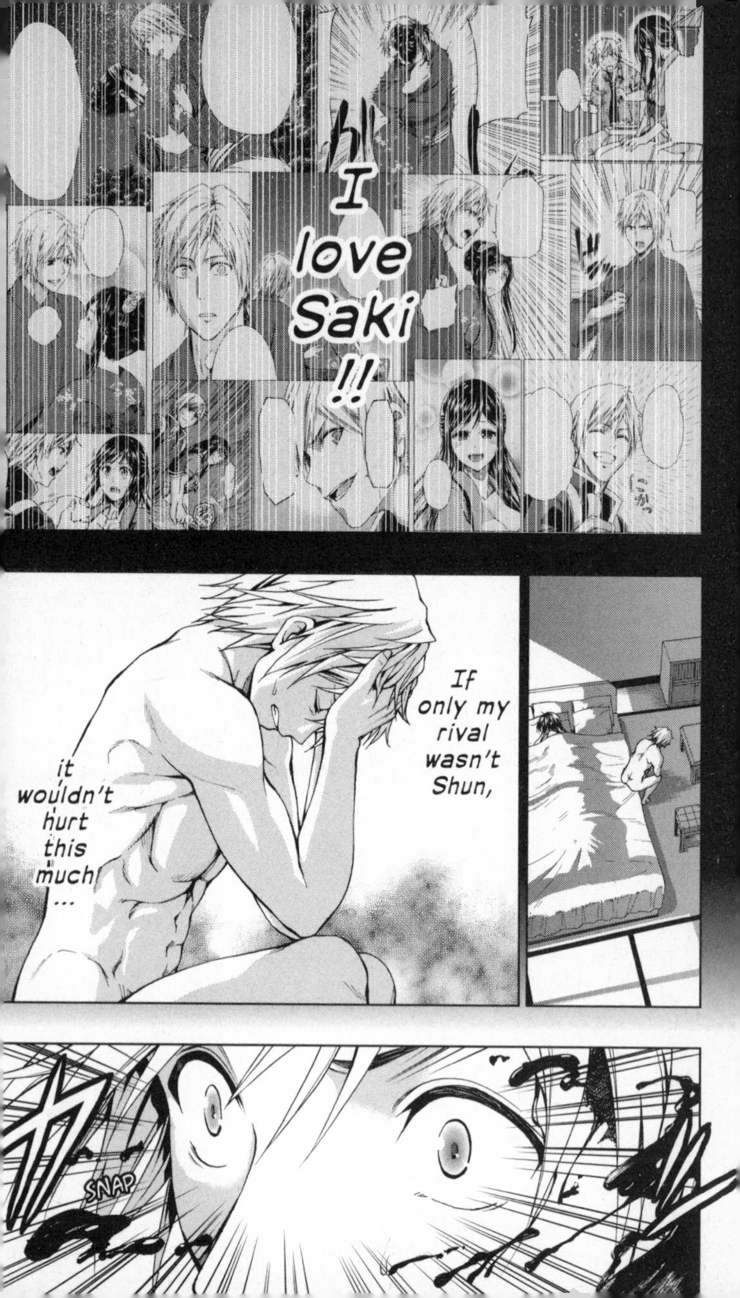
I love Saki !!
If only my rival wasn't Shun,
it wouldn't hurt this much ...
SNAP

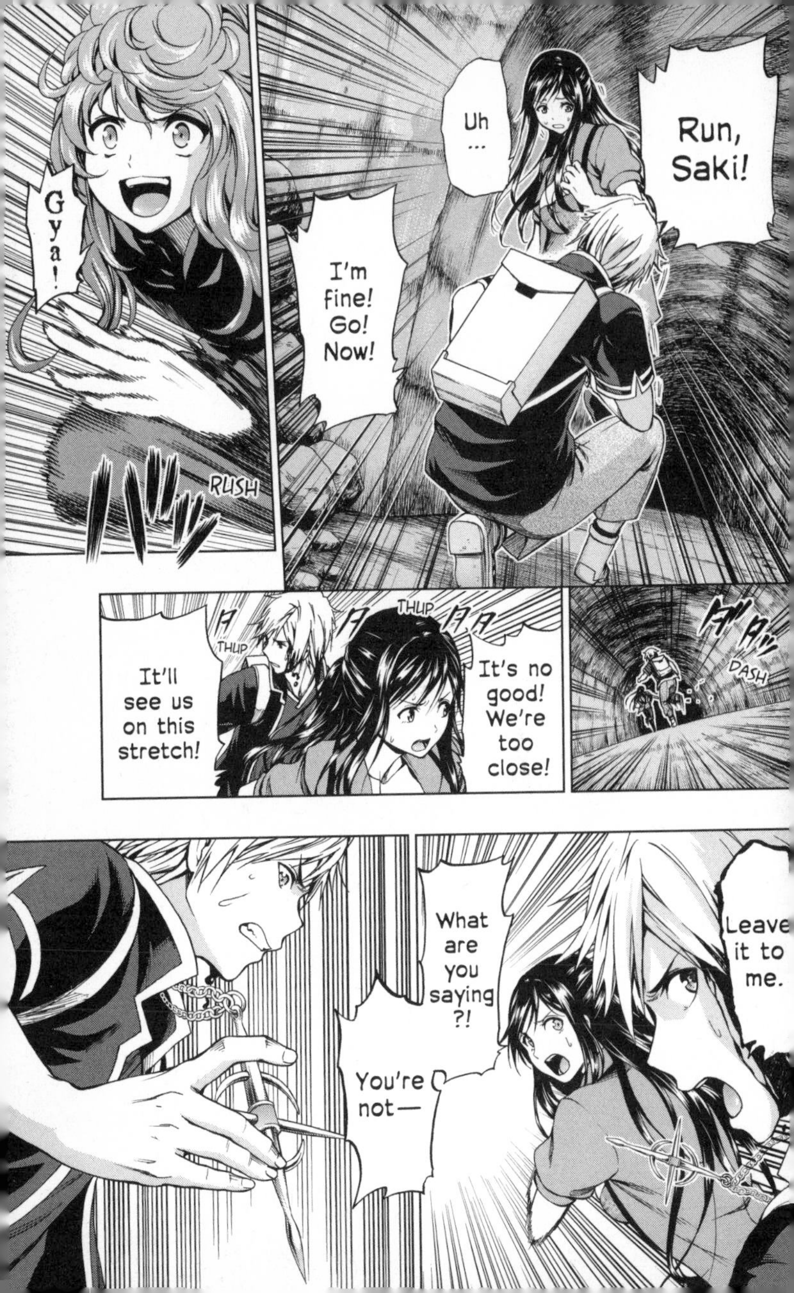
Run, Saki!
Uh ...
I'm fine! Go! Now!
Gya!
RUSH
DASH
THUP
THUP
It's no good! We're too close!
It'll see us on this stretch!
Leave it to me.
What are you saying?!
You're not—

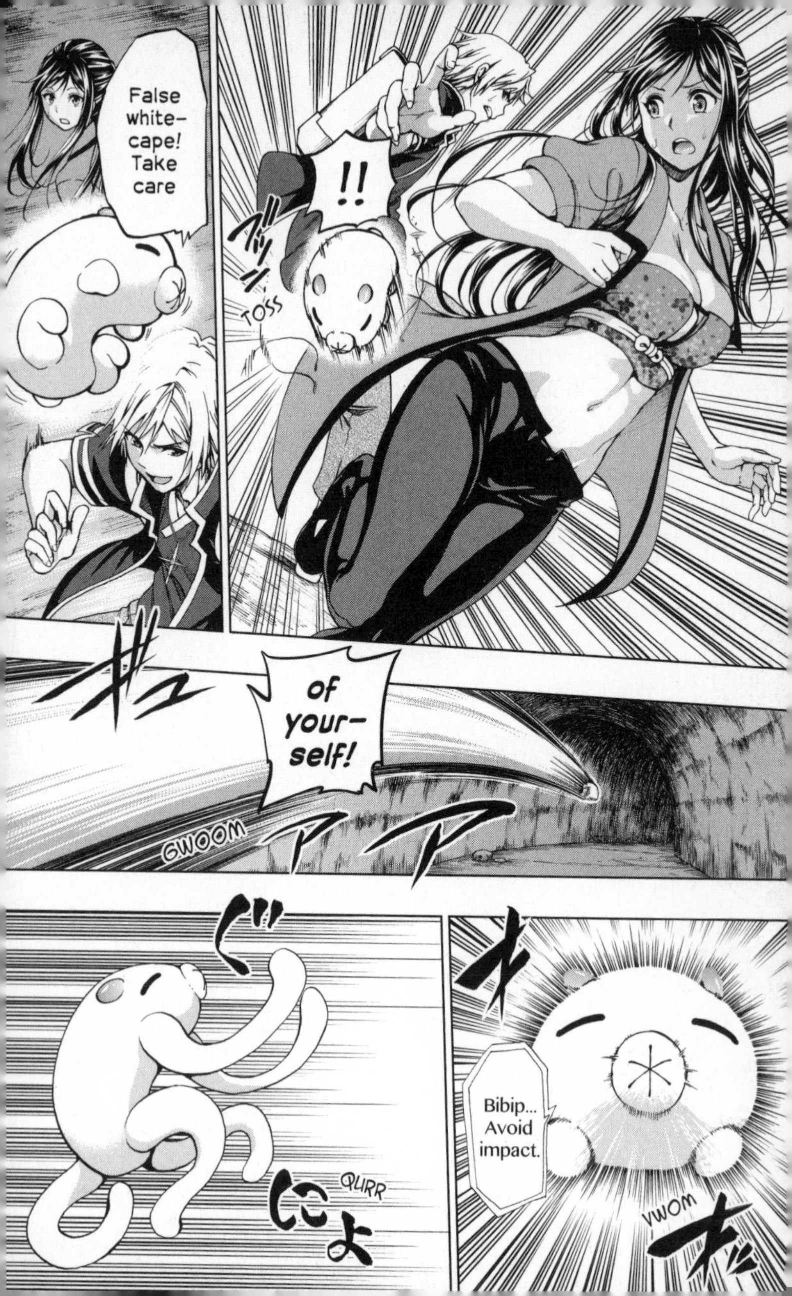
!!
TOSS
False white-cape! Take care
of your-self!
GWOOM
Bibip... Avoid impact.
VWOM
QURR

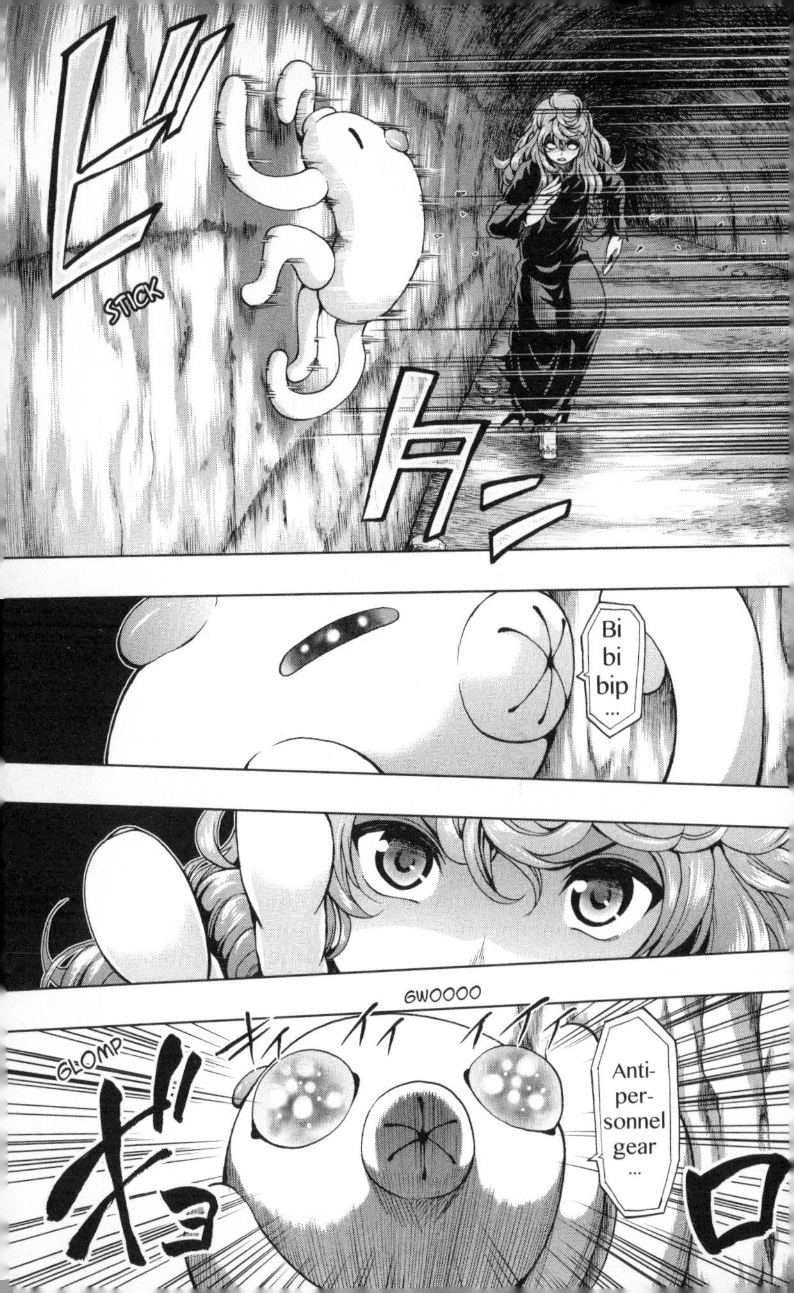
STICK
Bi bi bip ...
GWOOOO
Anti-personnel gear ...
GLOMP

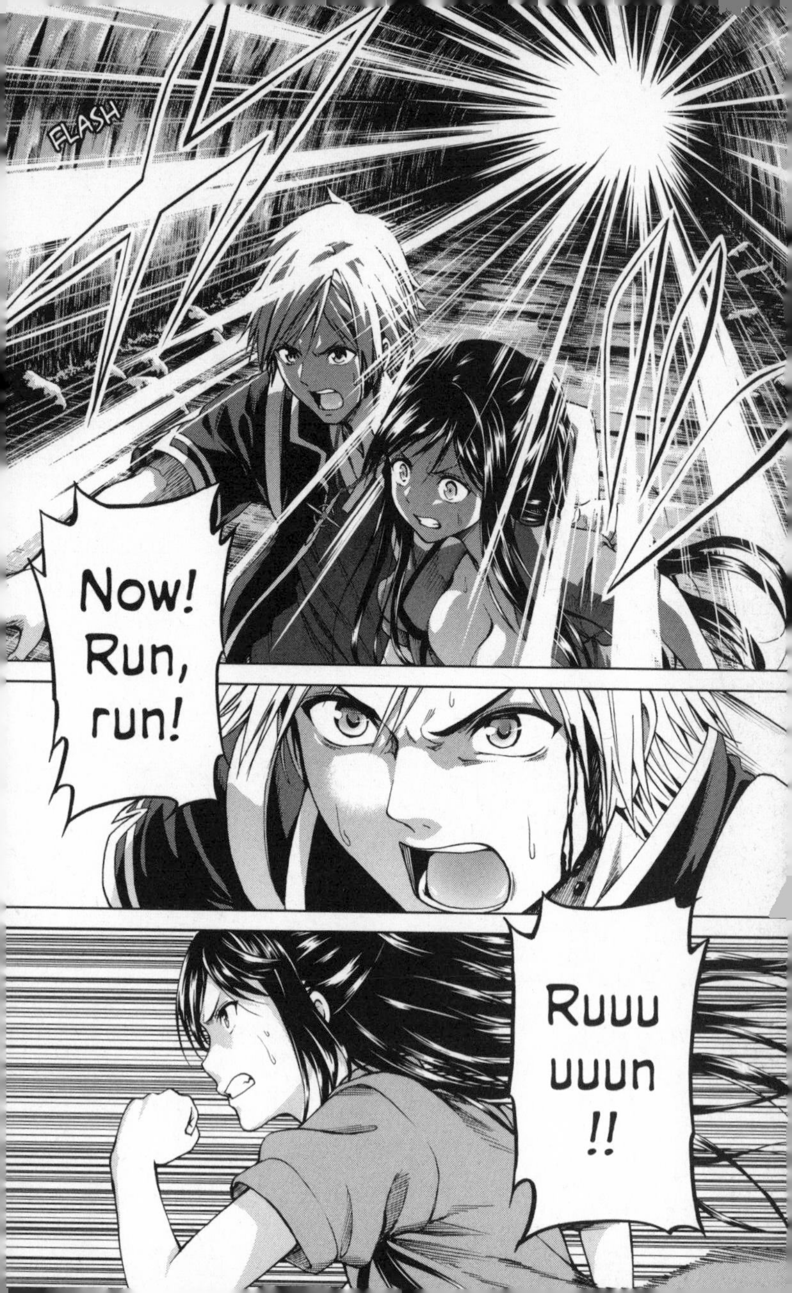
FLASH
Now! Run, run!
Ruuu uuun !!

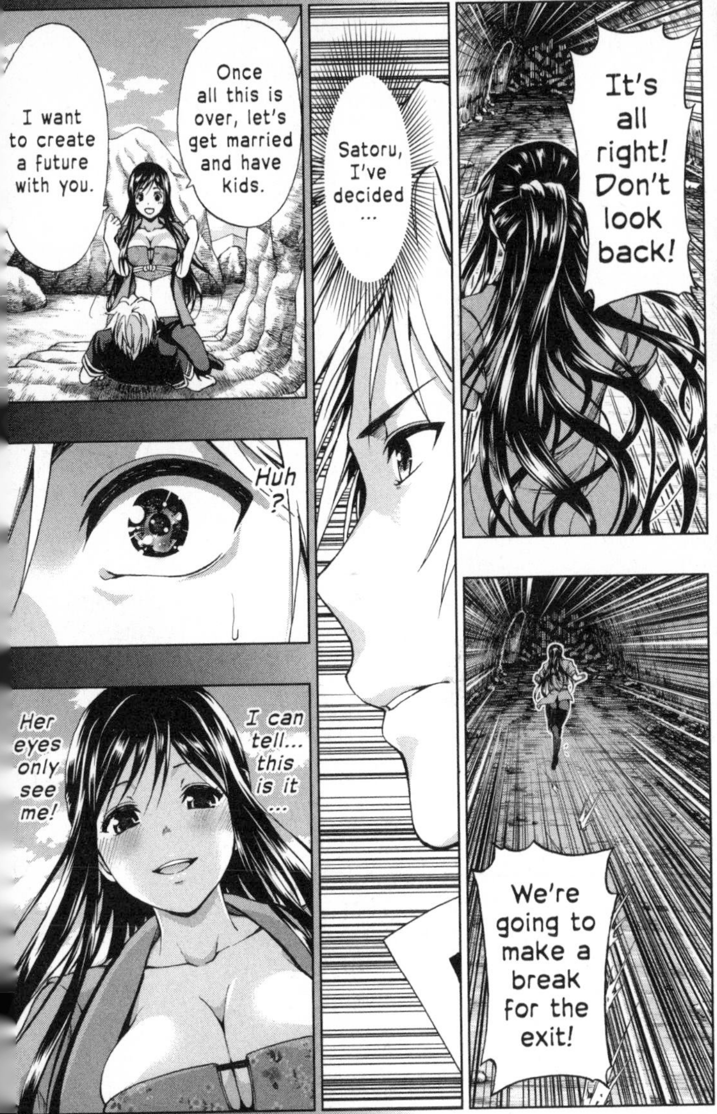
It's all right! Don't look back!
We're going to make a break for the exit!
Satoru, I've decided...
Once all this is over, let's get married and have kids.
I want to create a future with you.
Huh?
I can tell... this is it...
Her eyes only see me!

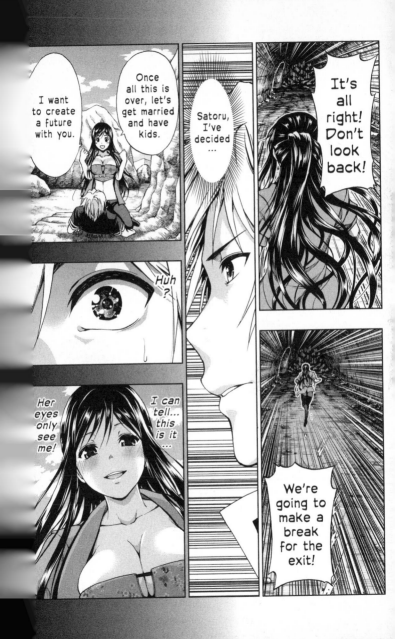

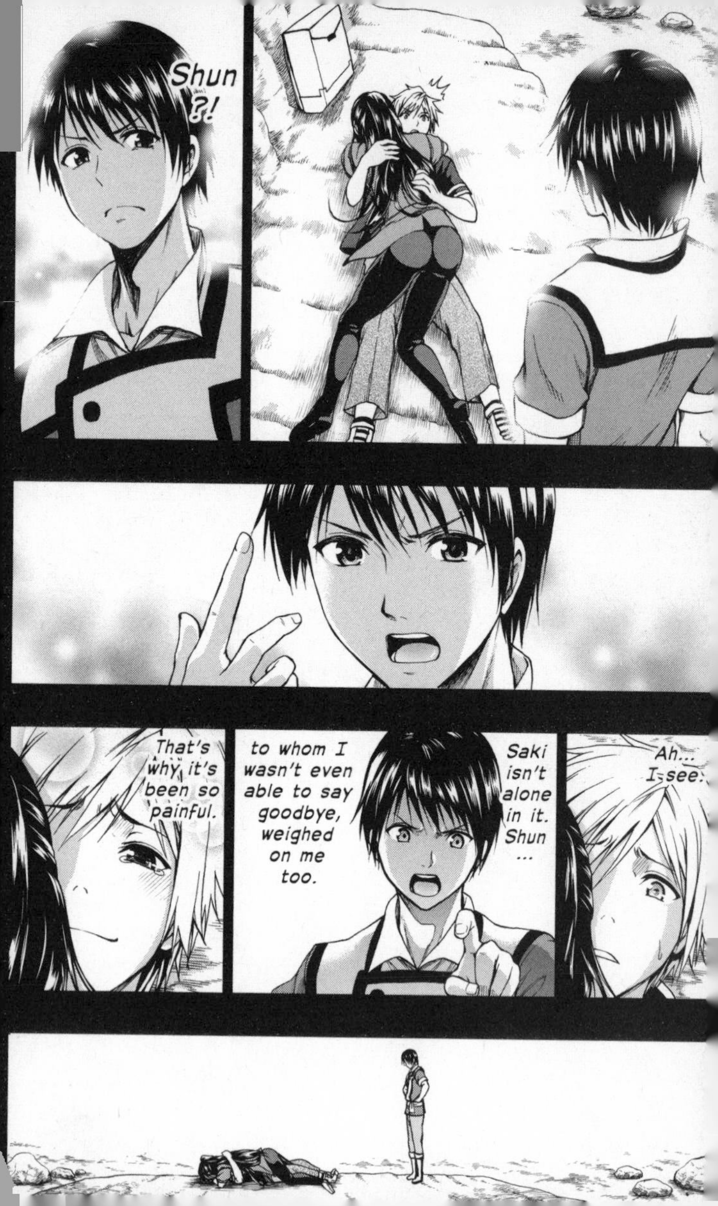
Shun ?!
Ah... I see.
Saki isn't alone in it. Shun ...
to whom I wasn't even able to say goodbye, weighed on me too.
That's why it's been so painful.

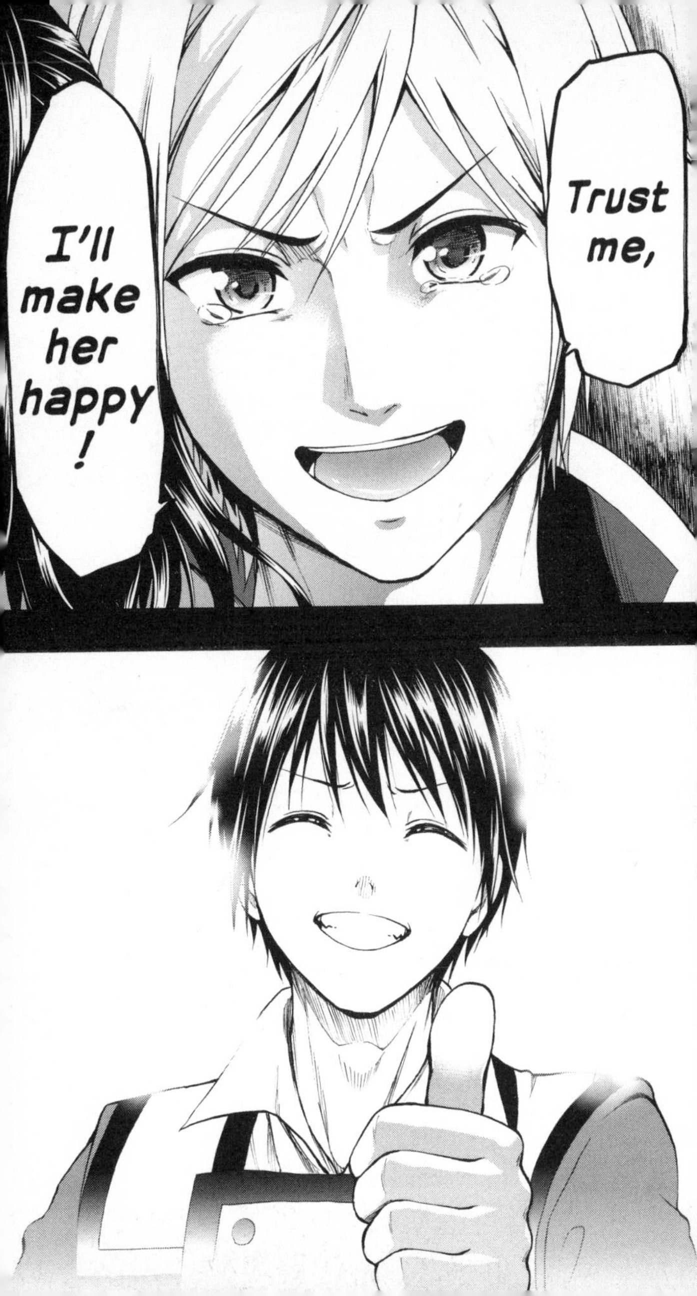
Trust me,
I'll make her happy!

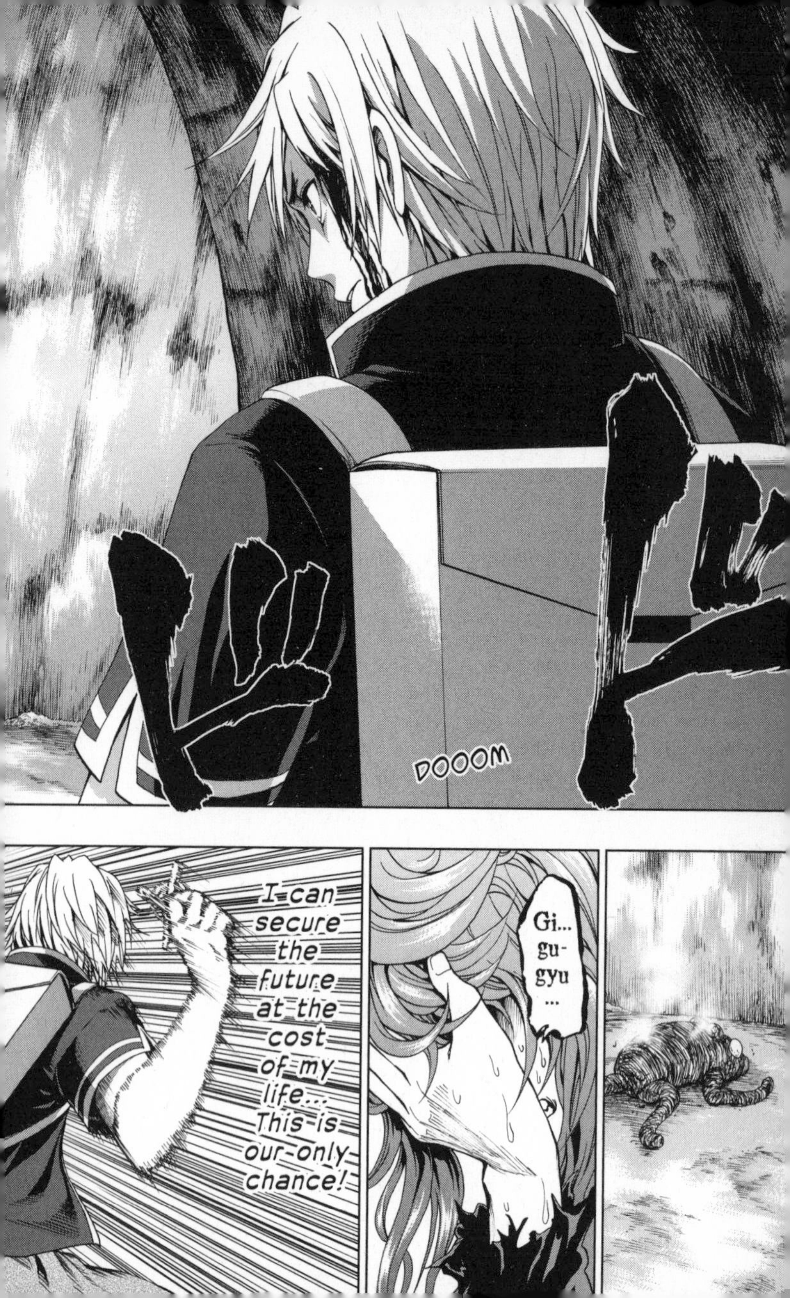
DOOOM
Gi... gu-gyu...
I can secure the future at the cost of my life... This is our only chance!

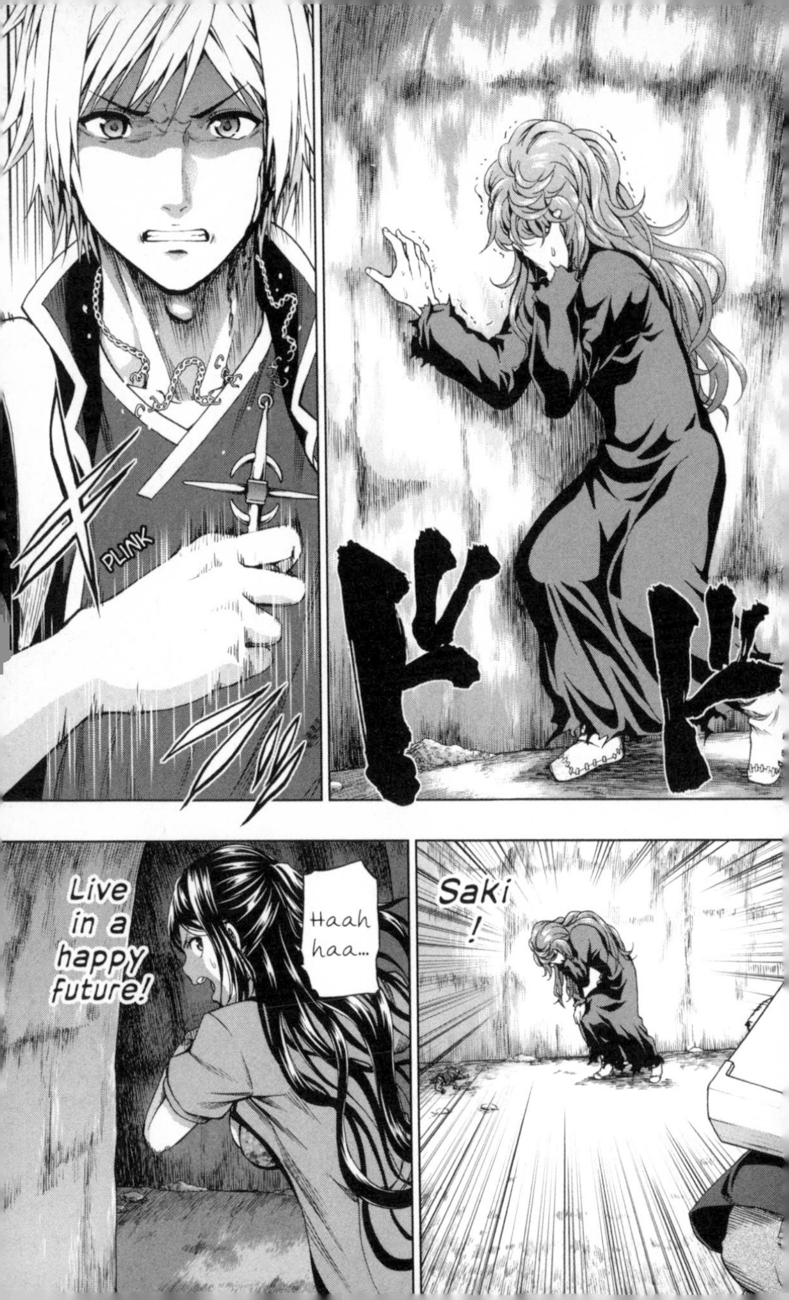
PLINK
Saki!
Haah haa...
Live in a happy future!

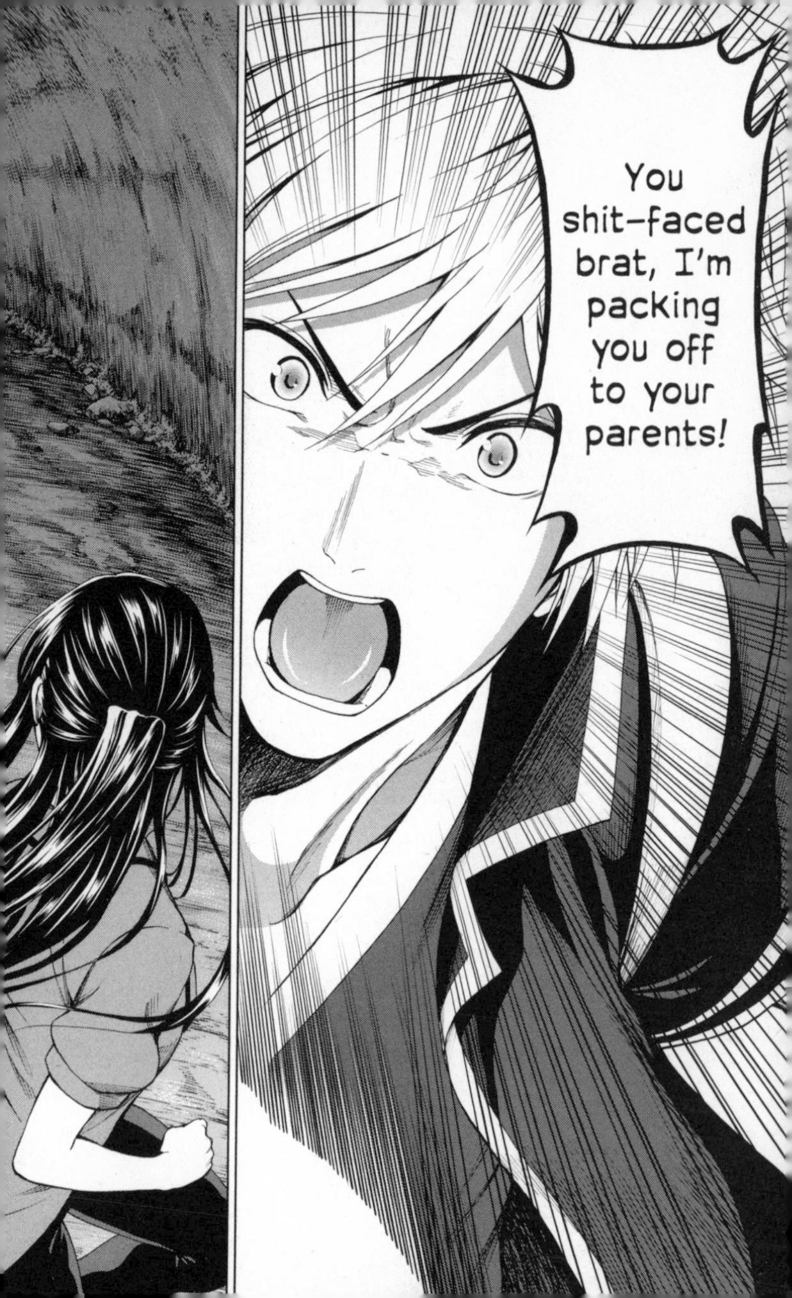
You shit-faced brat, I'm packing you off to your parents!

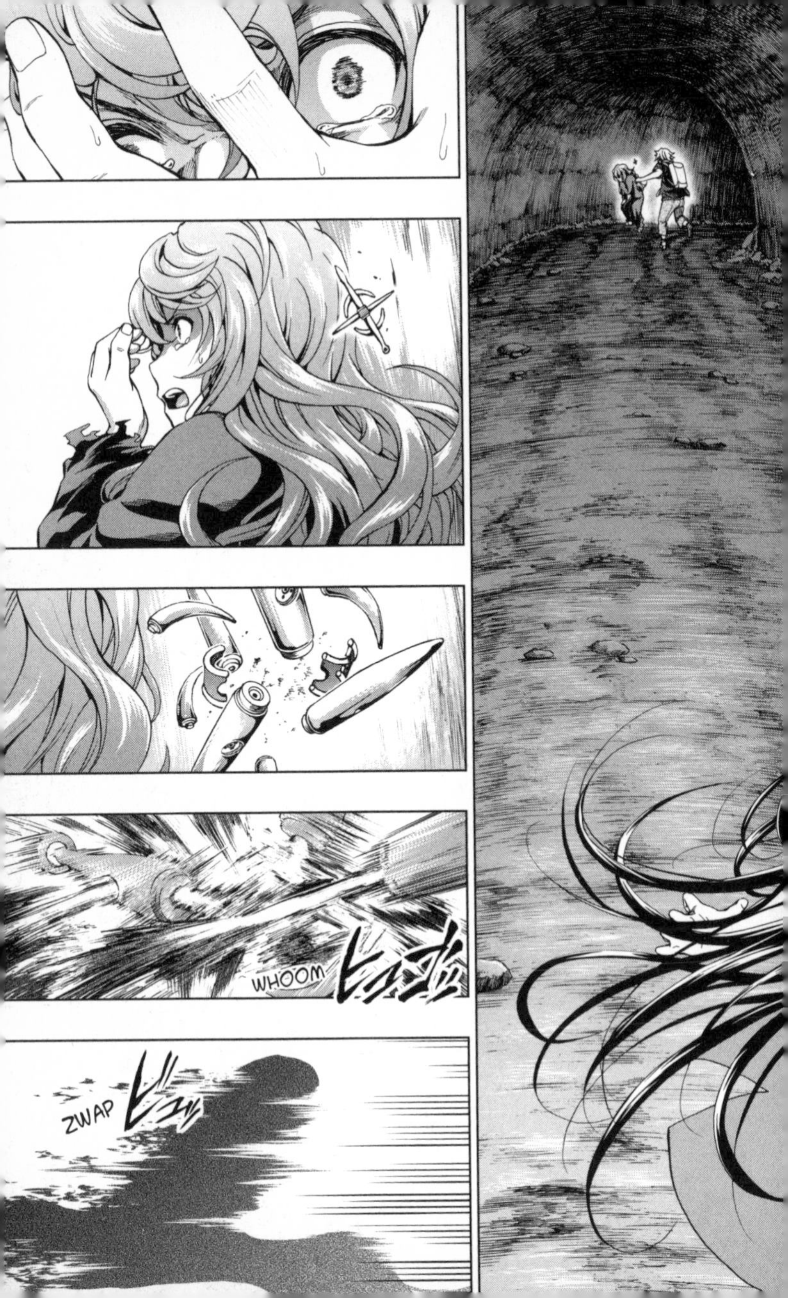
WHOOM
ZWAP

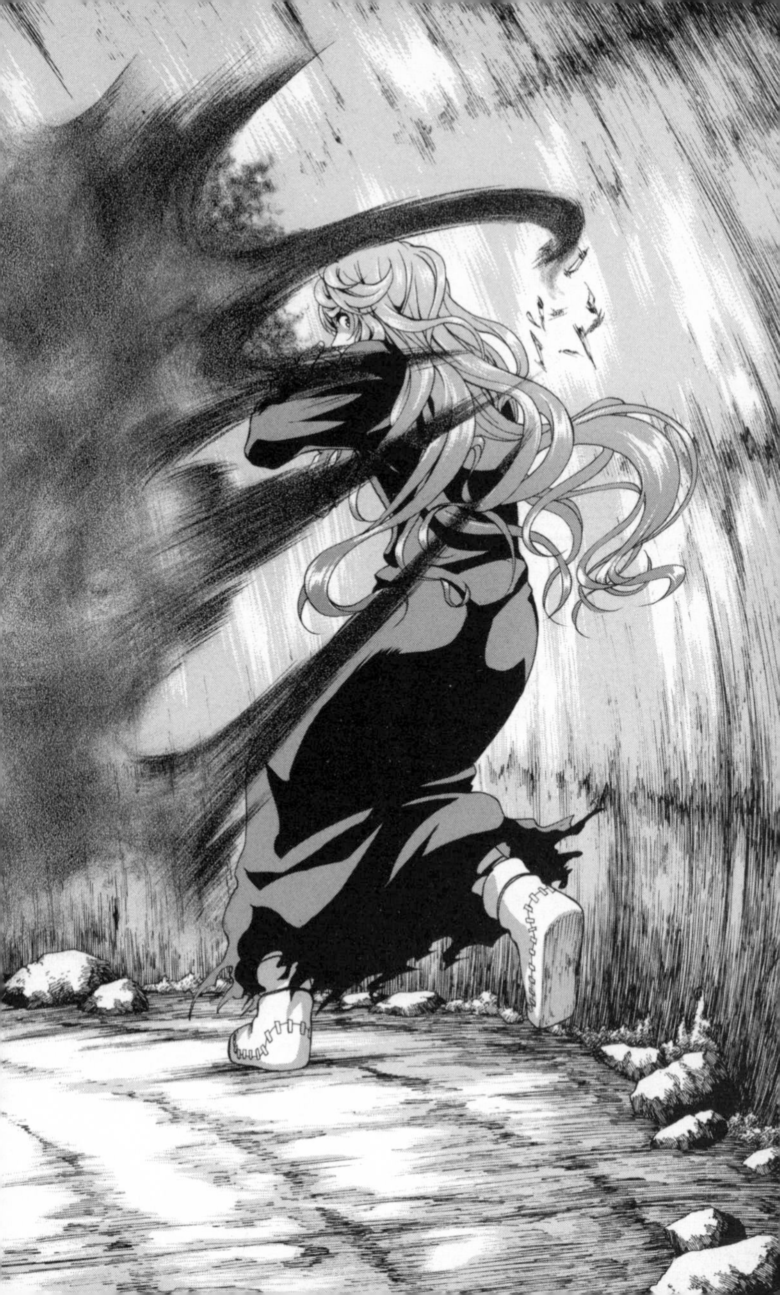

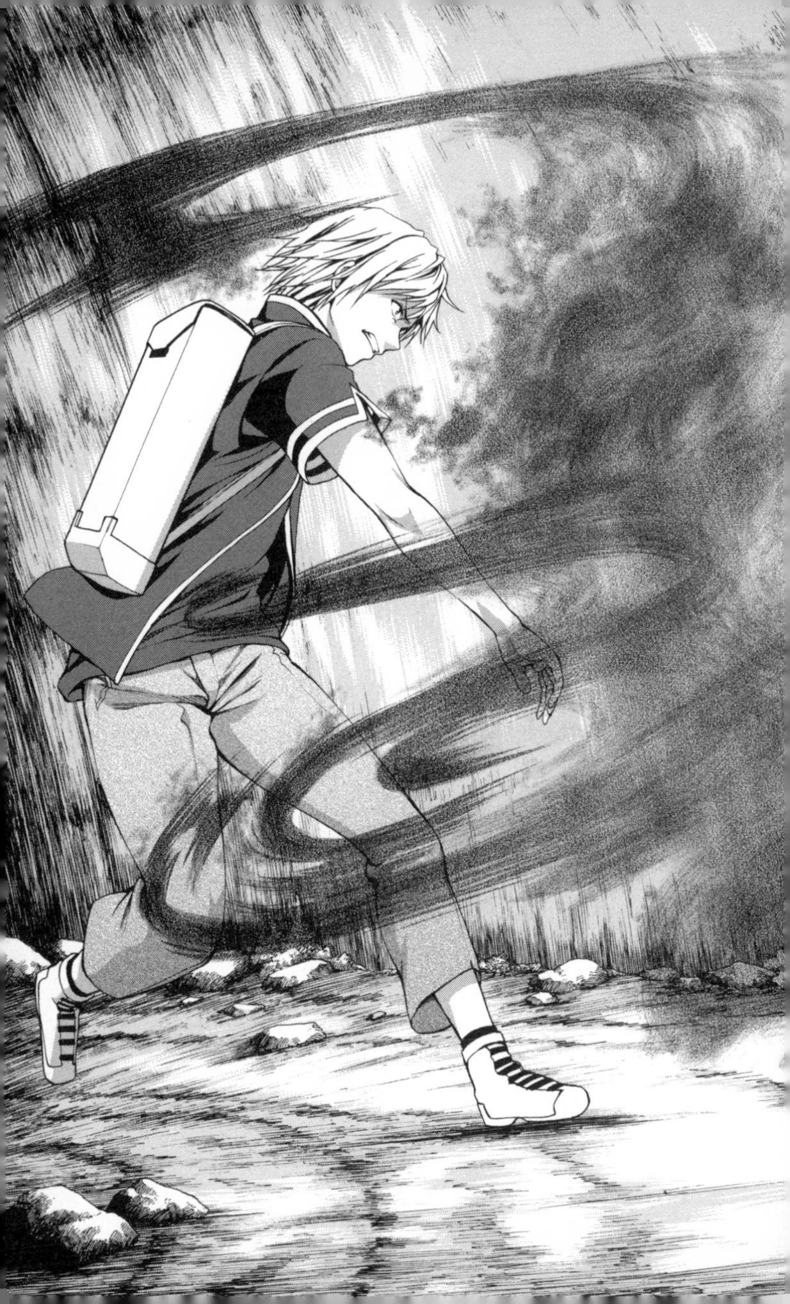

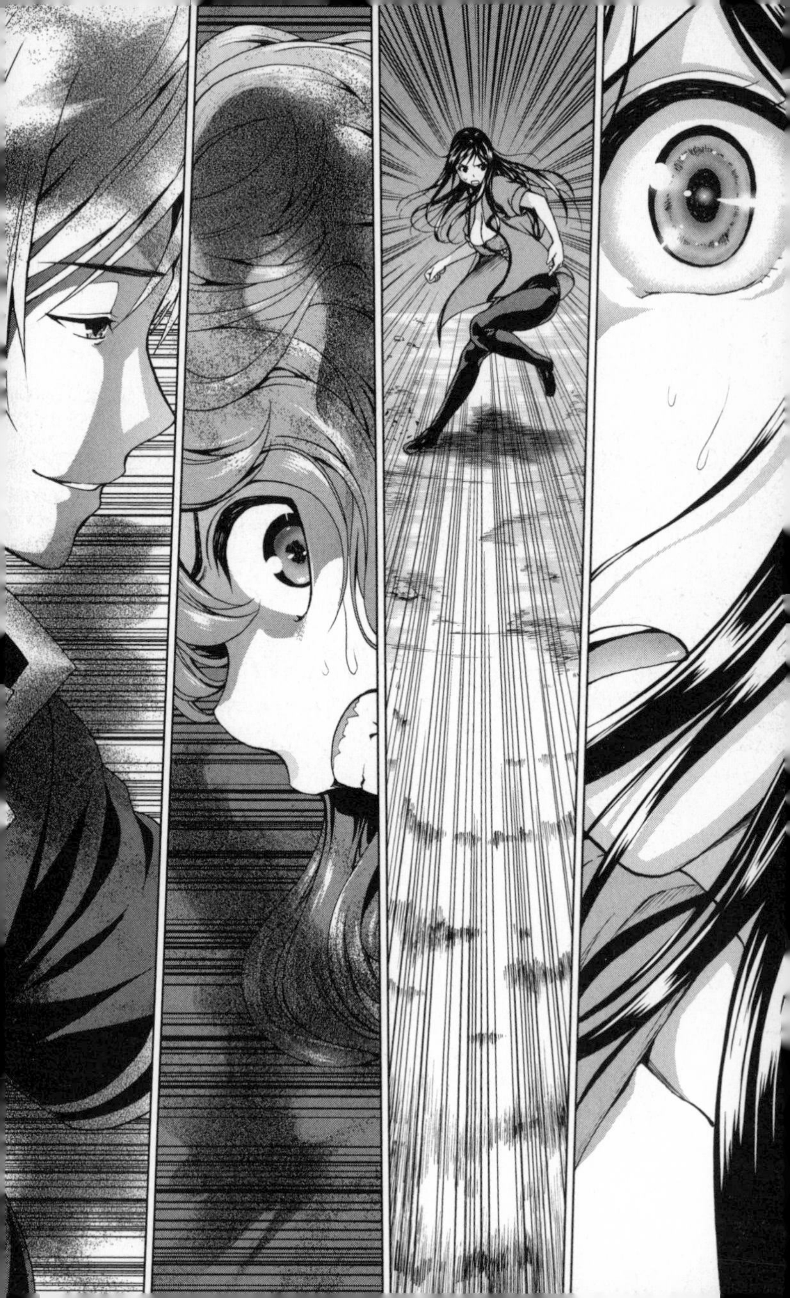

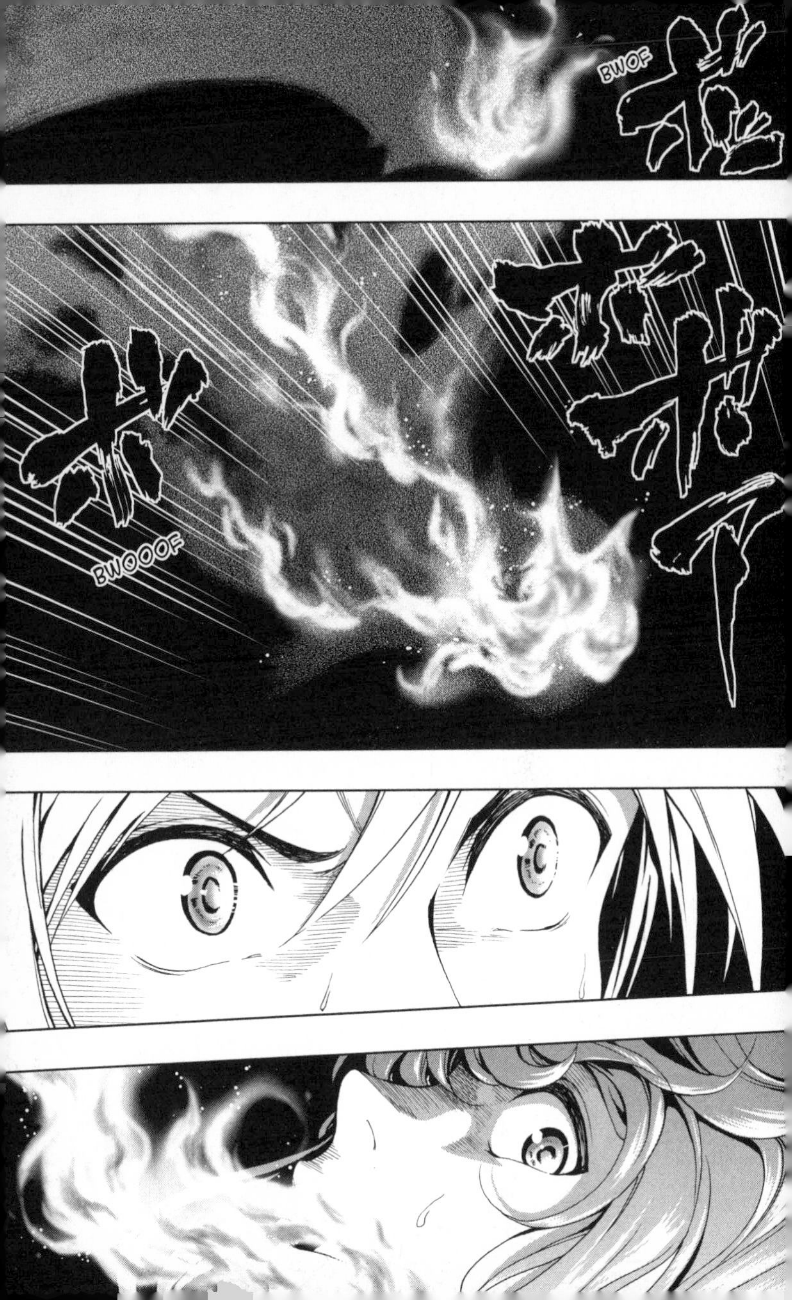
BWOF
BWOOOF

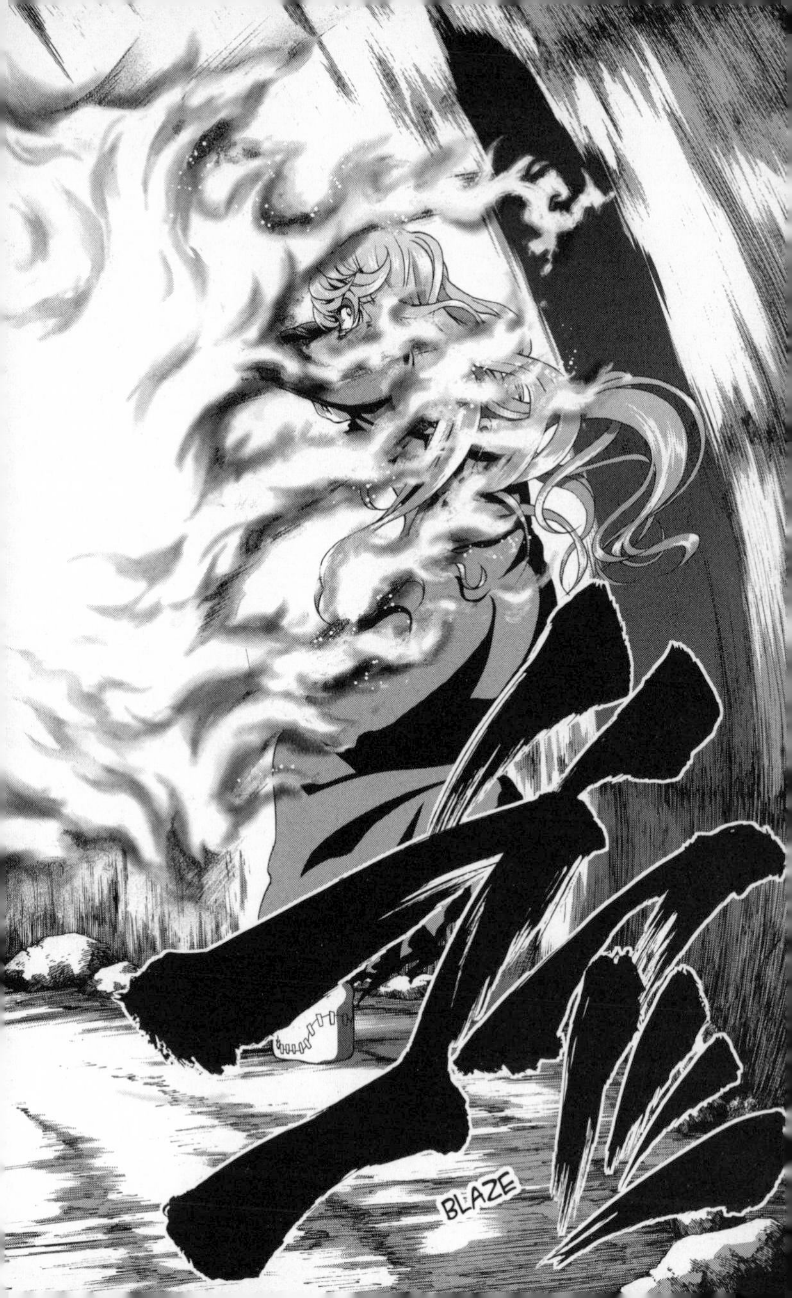
BLAZE

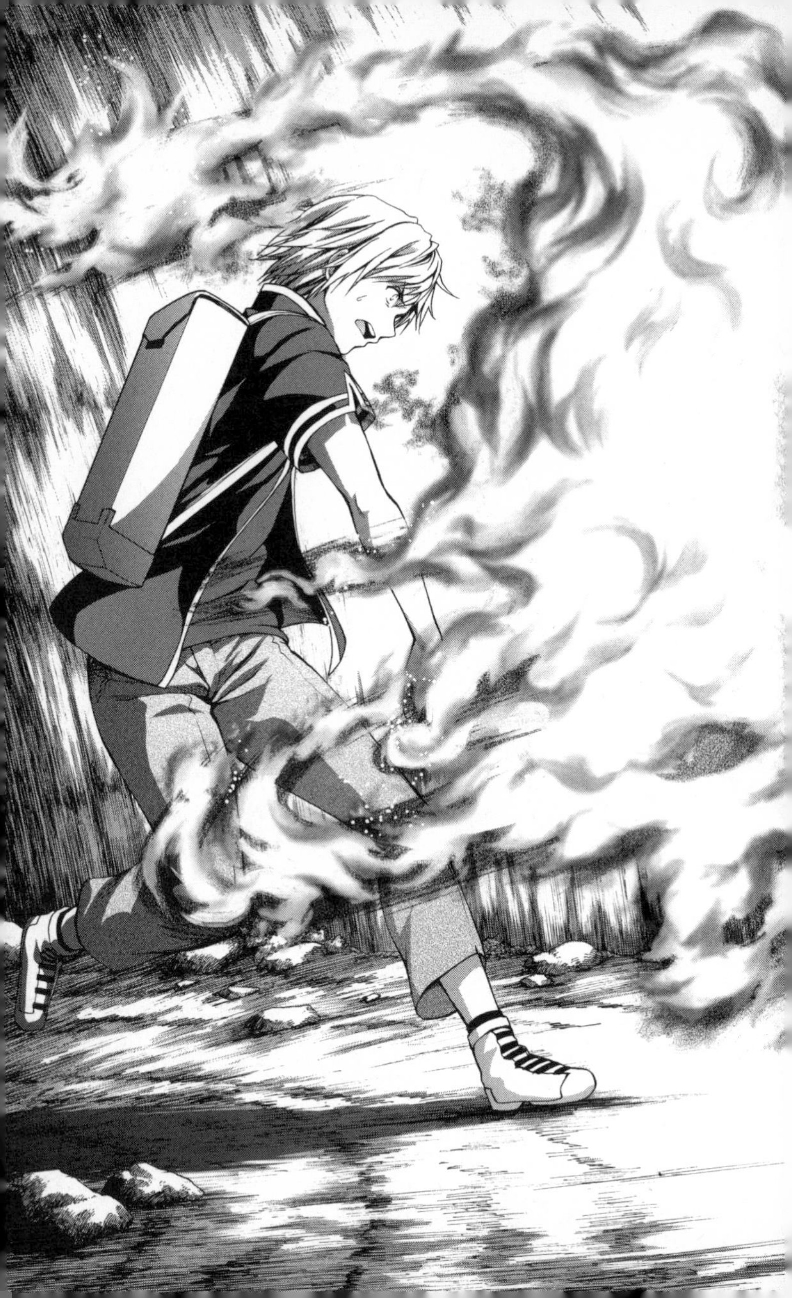

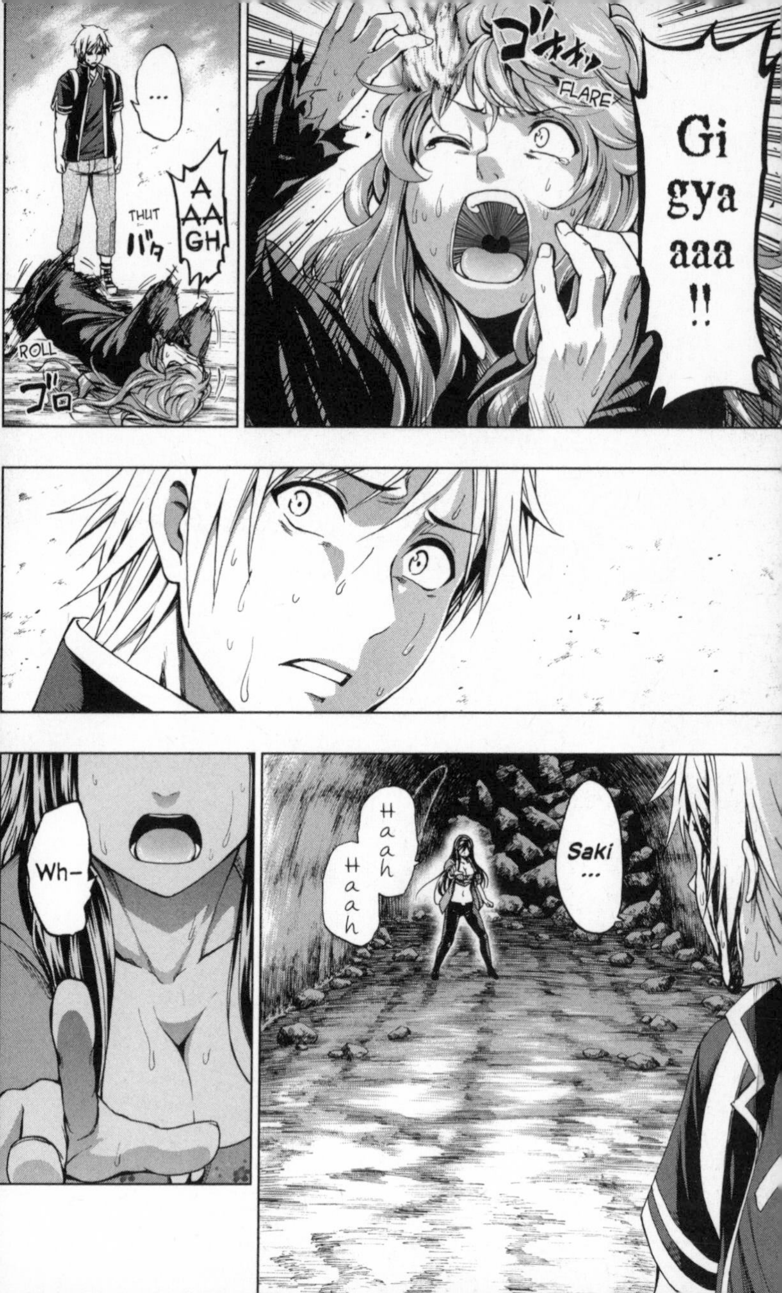
FLARE
Gi gya aaa!!
...
AAAGH
THUT
バタ
ROLL
ゴロ
Saki...
Haah Haah
Wh-

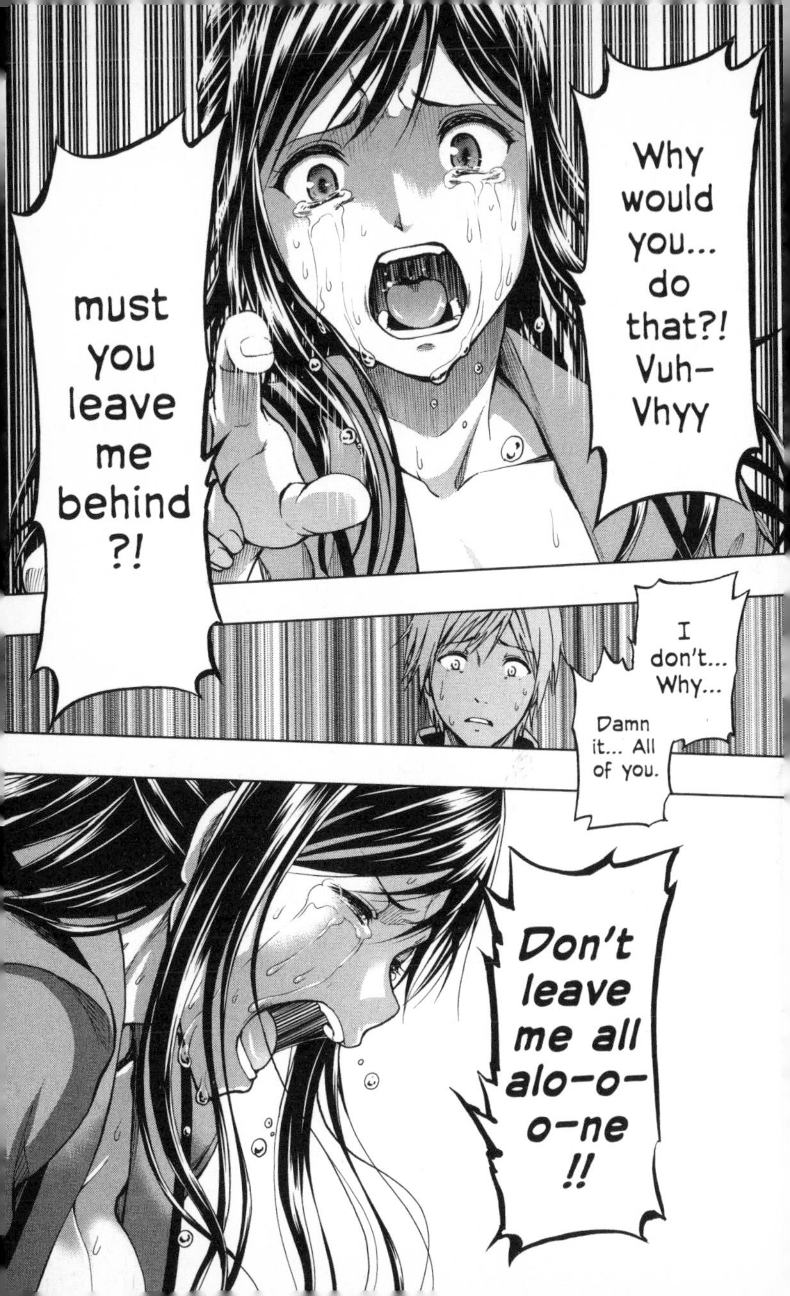
Why would you... do that?! Vuh-Vhyy
must you leave me behind?!
I don't... Why...
Damn it... All of you.
Don't leave me all alo-o-o-ne!!

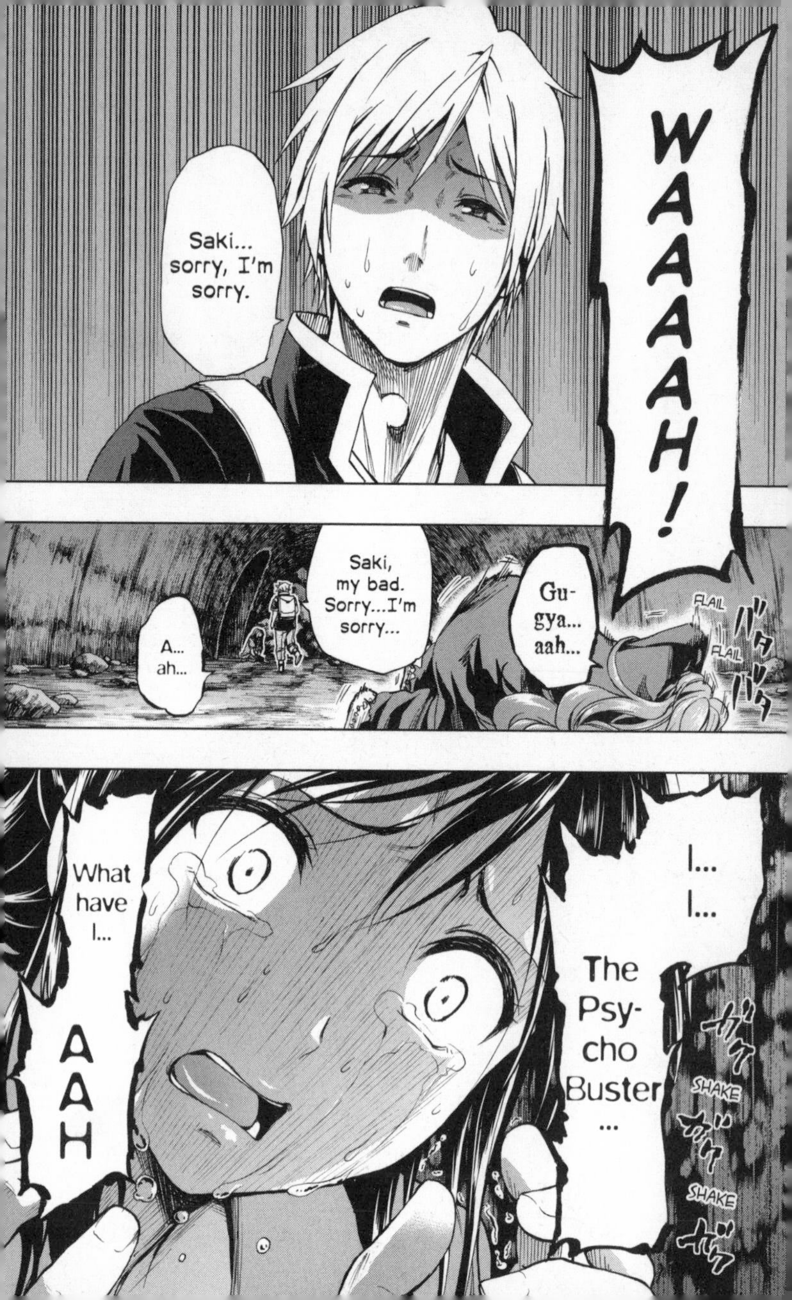
WAAAAH!
Saki... sorry, I'm sorry.
Gu-gya... aah...
FLAIL
FLAIL
Saki, my bad. Sorry...I'm sorry...
A... ah...
I... I...
The Psy-cho Buster...
SHAKE
SHAKE
What have I...
AAH

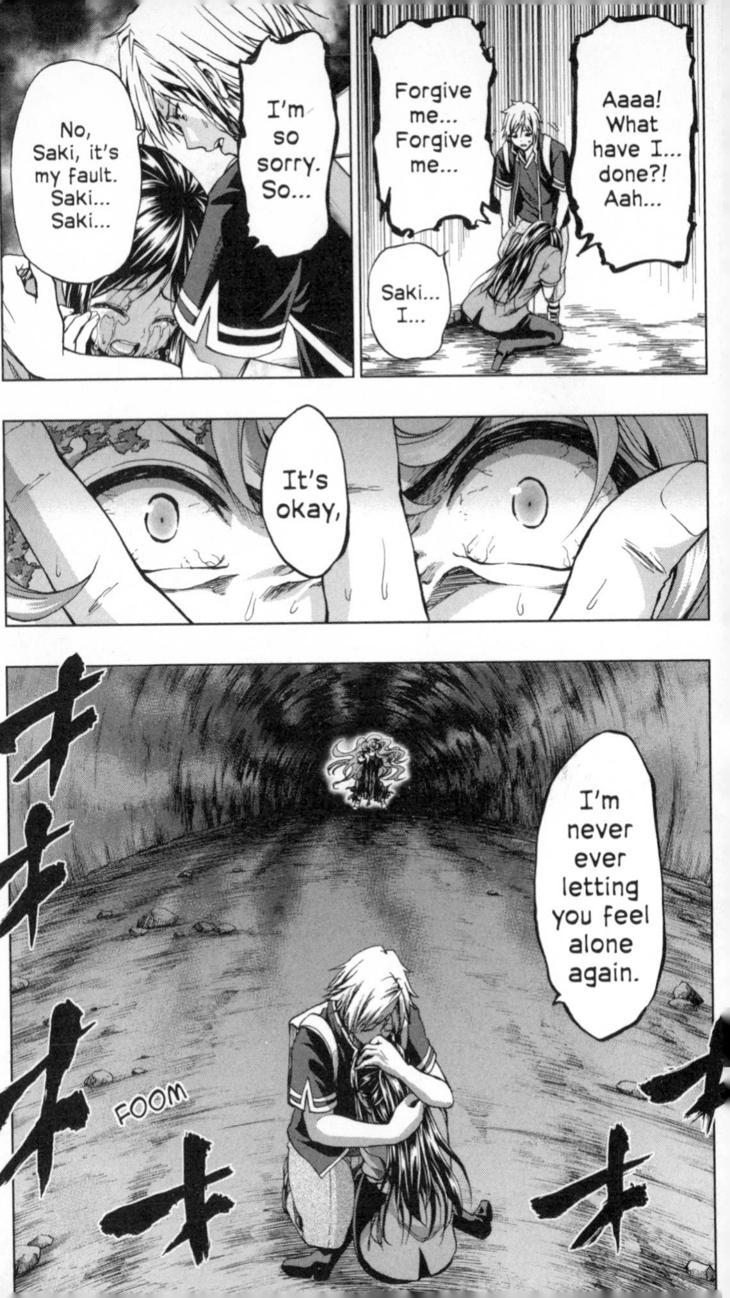
Aaaa! What have I... done?! Aah...
Forgive me... Forgive me...
Saki... I...
I'm so sorry. So...
No, Saki, it's my fault. Saki... Saki...
It's okay,
I'm never ever letting you feel alone again.
FOOM

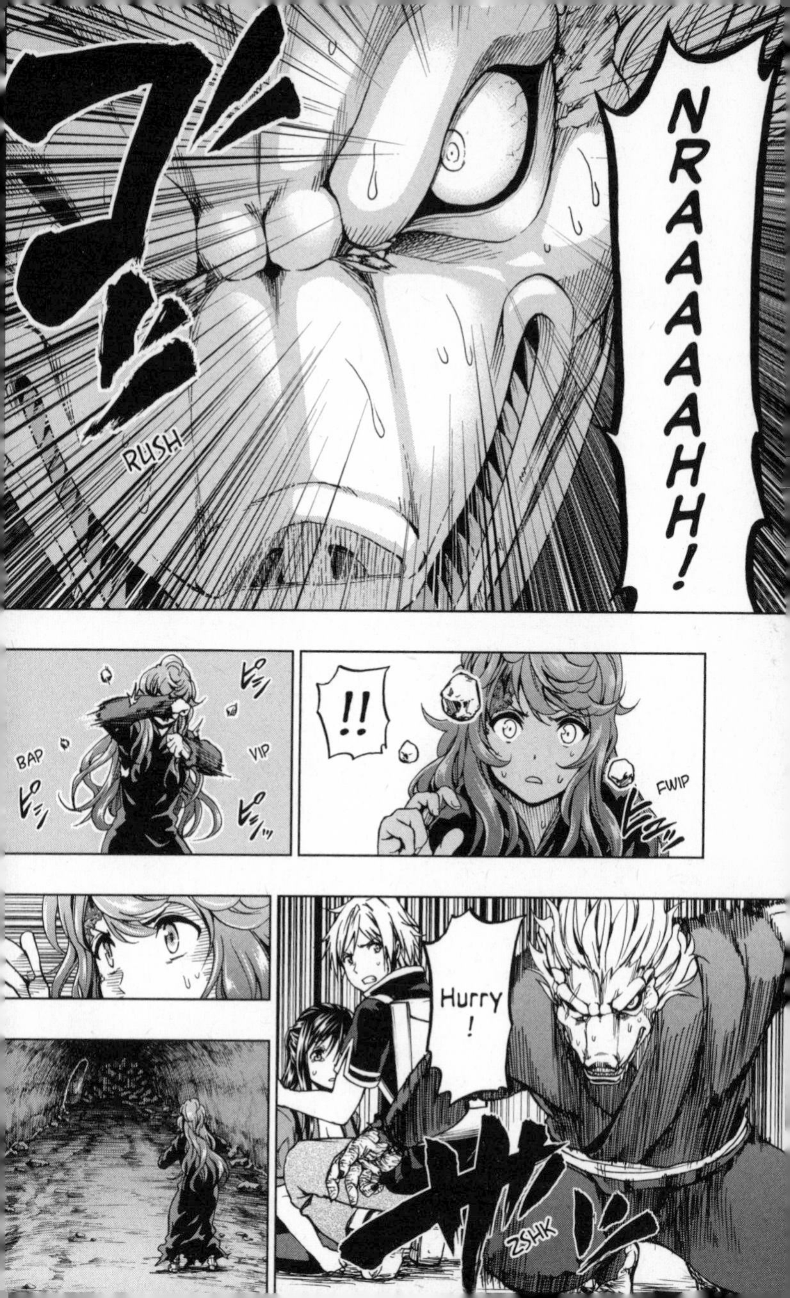
NRAAAAAAHH!
RUSH
FWIP
!!
VIP
BAP
Hurry!
ZSHK

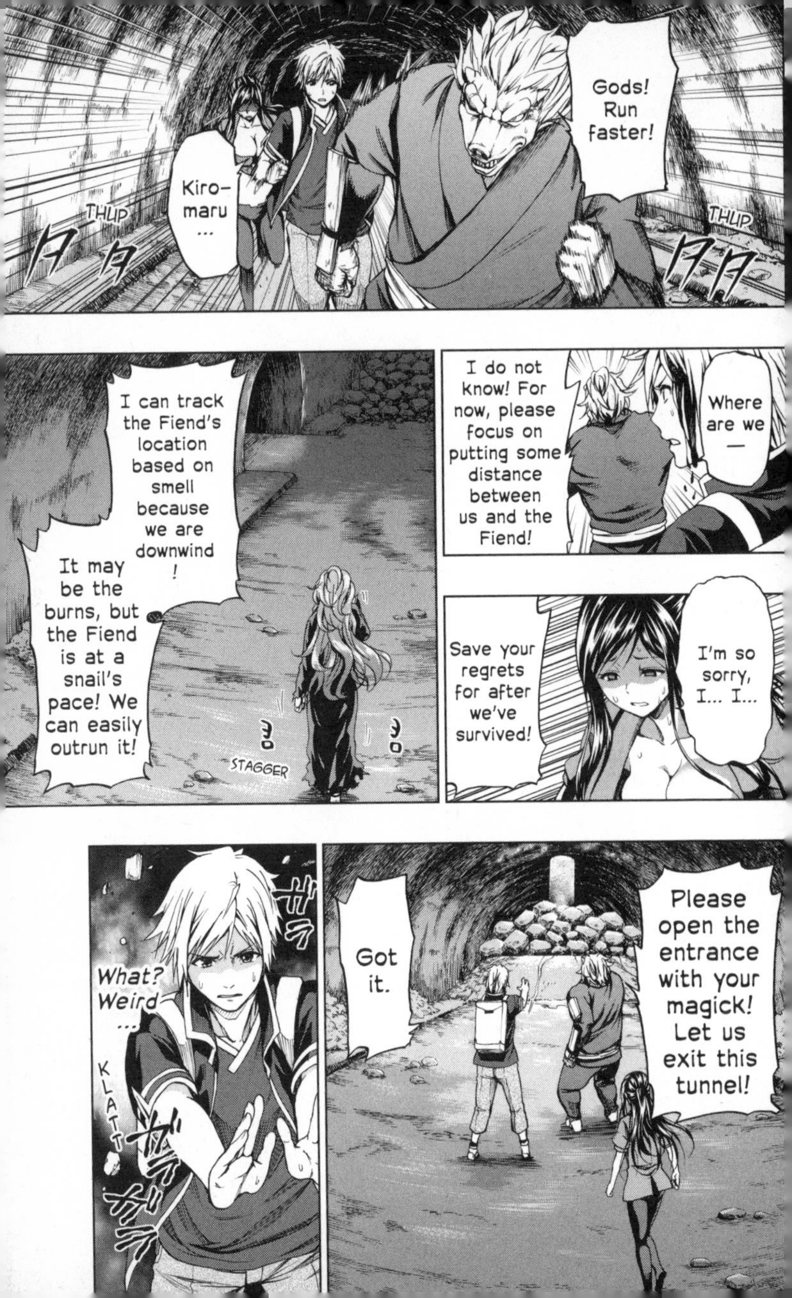
Gods! Run faster!
THUP
Kiro-maru ...
THUP
Where are we —
I do not know! For now, please focus on putting some distance between us and the Fiend!
I'm so sorry, I... I...
Save your regrets for after we've survived!
I can track the Fiend's location based on smell because we are downwind!
It may be the burns, but the Fiend is at a snail's pace! We can easily outrun it!
STAGGER
Please open the entrance with your magick! Let us exit this tunnel!
Got it.
What? Weird ...
KLATT

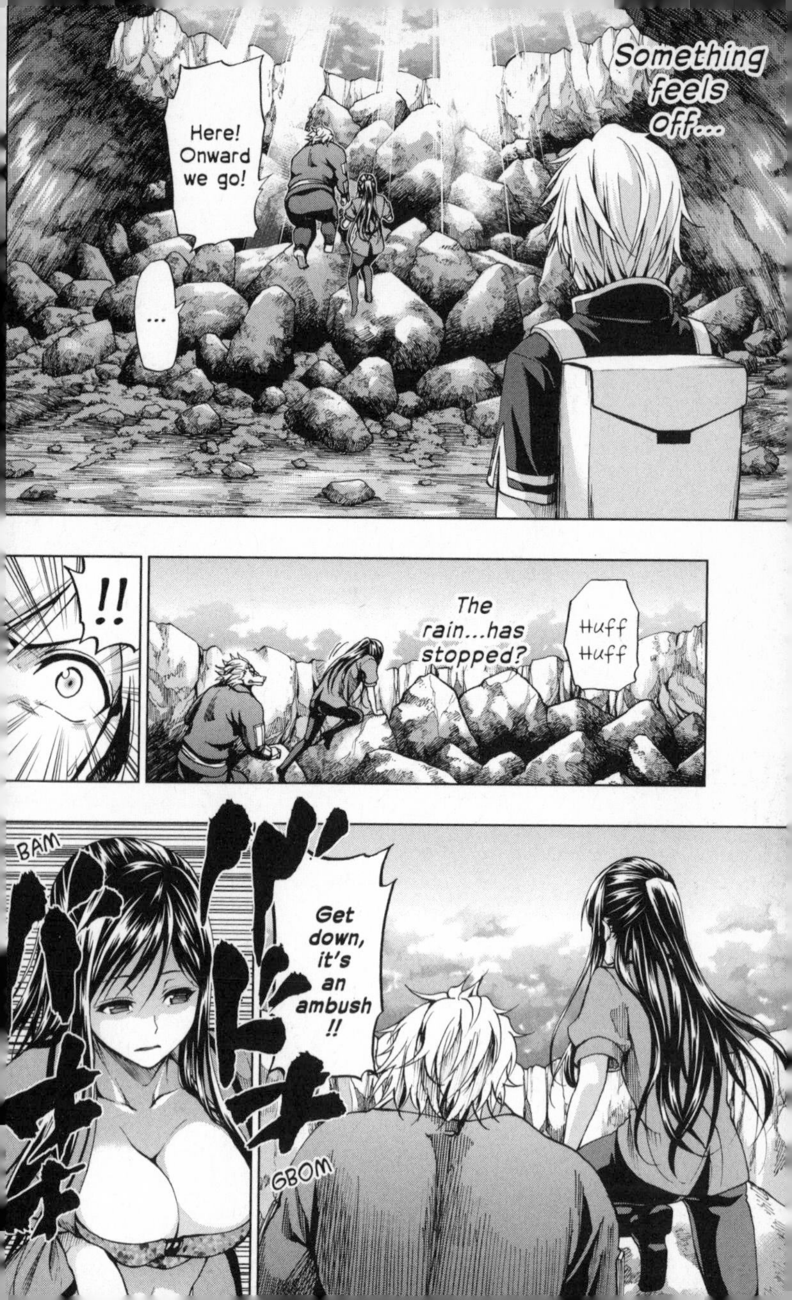
Something feels off...
Here! Onward we go!
...
Huff Huff
The rain...has stopped?
!!
Get down, it's an ambush!!
BAM
GBOM

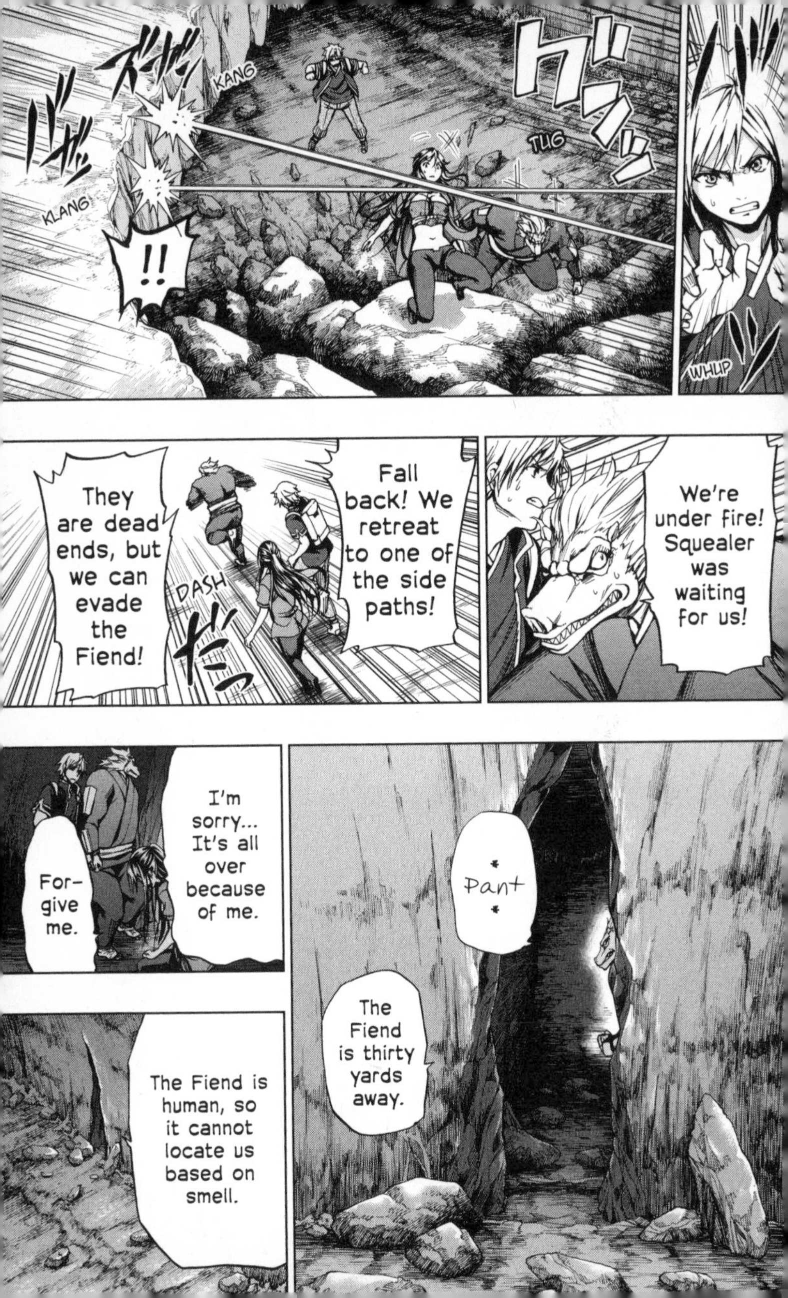
WHUP
TUG
KANG
KLANG
!!
We're under fire! Squealer was waiting for us!
Fall back! We retreat to one of the side paths!
DASH
They are dead ends, but we can evade the Fiend!
Pant
The Fiend is thirty yards away.
I'm sorry... It's all over because of me.
For-give me.
The Fiend is human, so it cannot locate us based on smell.

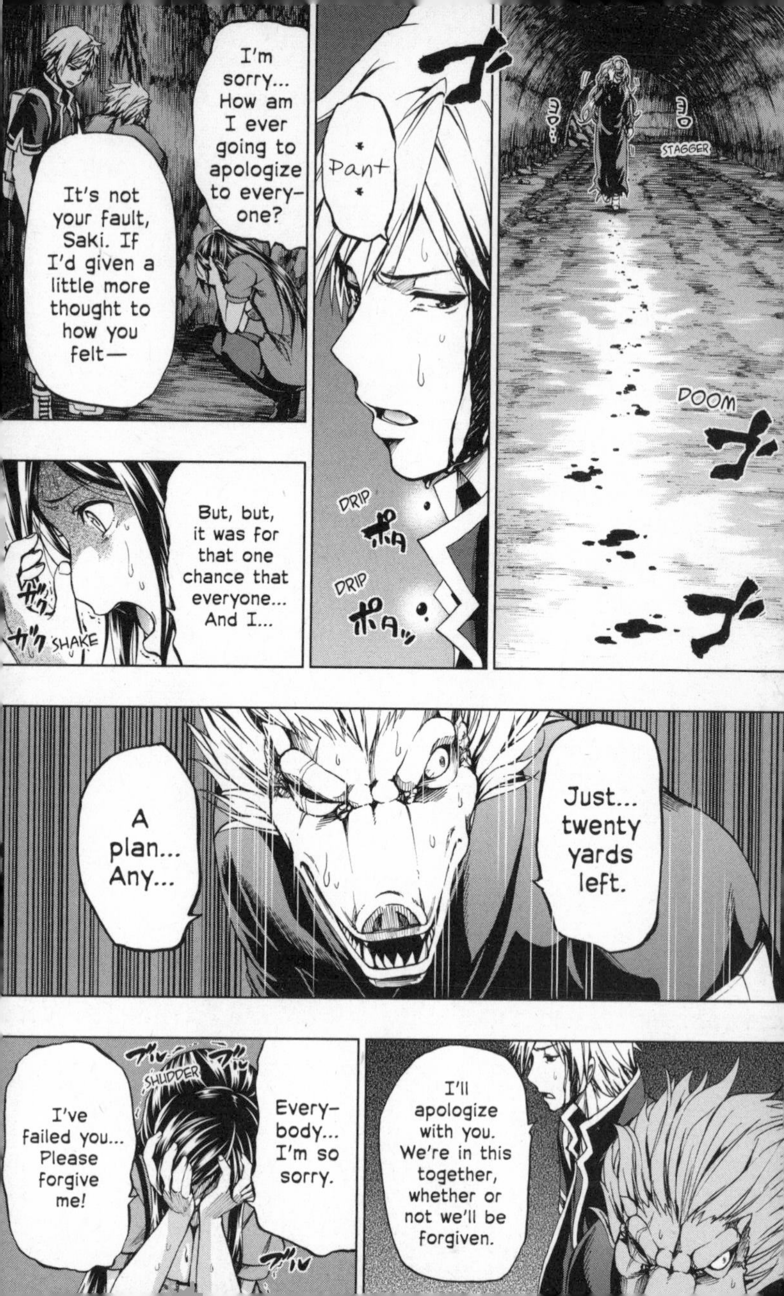
STAGGER
DOOM
Pant
DRIP
DRIP
I'm sorry... How am I ever going to apologize to everyone?
It's not your fault, Saki. If I'd given a little more thought to how you felt—
But, but, it was for that one chance that everyone... And I...
SHAKE
Just... twenty yards left.
A plan... Any...
I'll apologize with you. We're in this together, whether or not we'll be forgiven.
Every-body... I'm so sorry.
SHUDDER
I've failed you... Please forgive me!

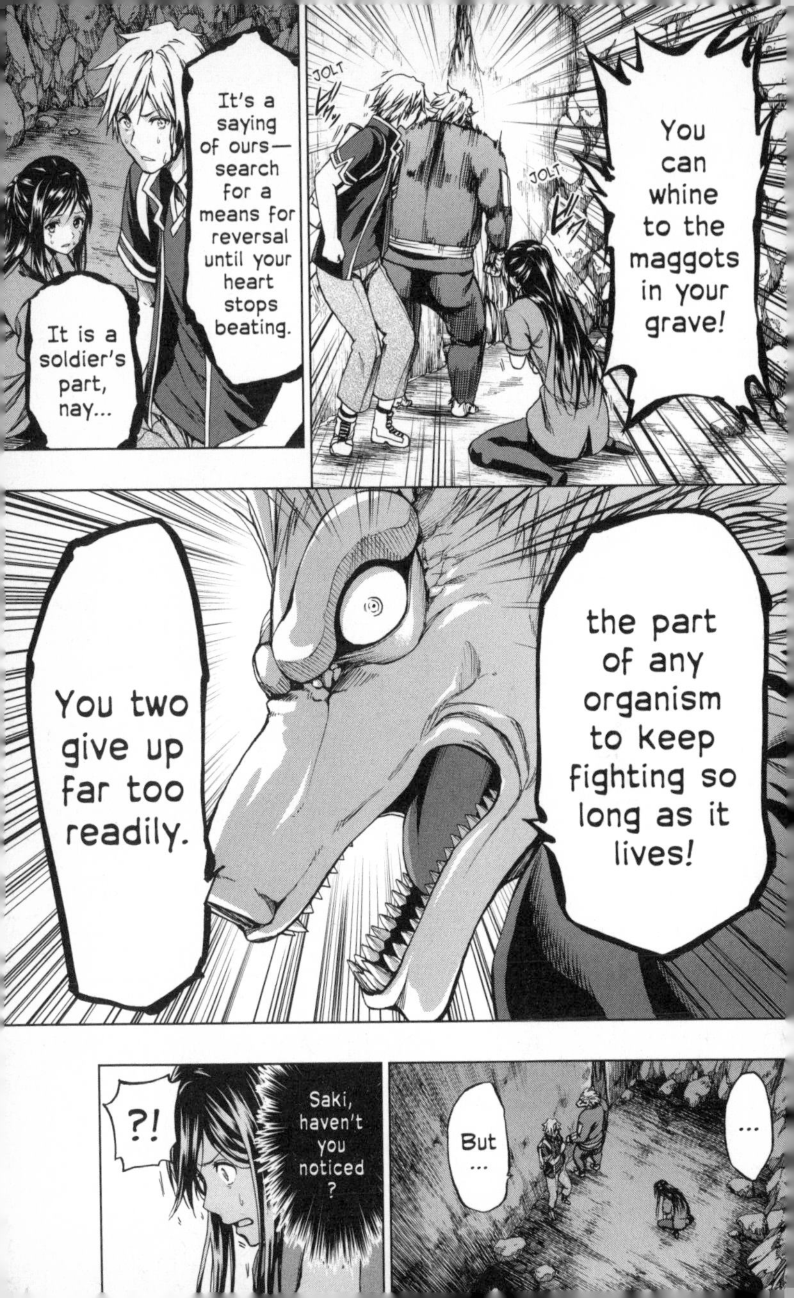
You can whine to the maggots in your grave!
JOLT
JOLT
It's a saying of ours—search for a means for reversal until your heart stops beating.
It is a soldier's part, nay...
the part of any organism to keep fighting so long as it lives!
You two give up far too readily.
...
But ...
Saki, haven't you noticed?
?!

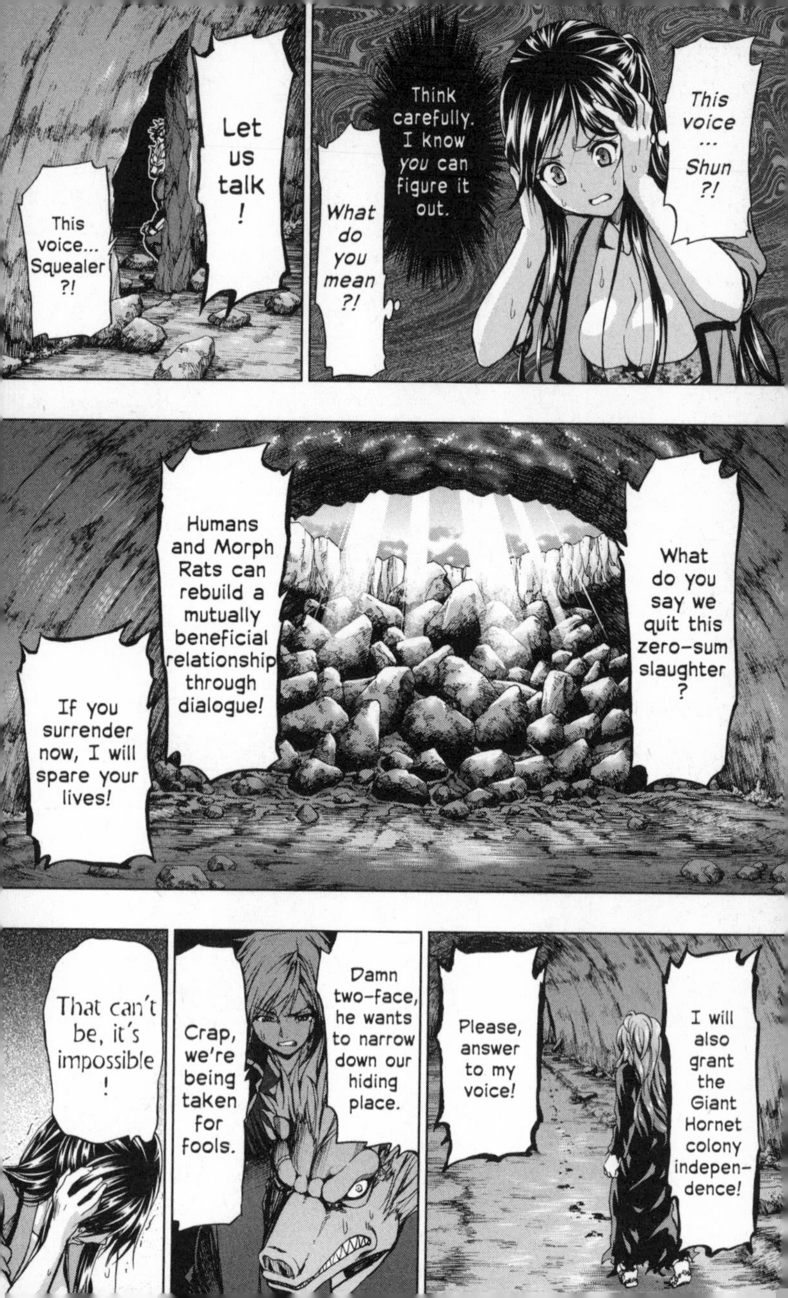
This voice ... Shun ?!
Think carefully. I know *you* can figure it out.
What do you mean ?!
Let us talk !
This voice... Squealer ?!
What do you say we quit this zero-sum slaughter ?
Humans and Morph Rats can rebuild a mutually beneficial relationship through dialogue!
If you surrender now, I will spare your lives!
I will also grant the Giant Hornet colony indepen-dence!
Please, answer to my voice!
Damn two-face, he wants to narrow down our hiding place.
Crap, we're being taken for fools.
That can't be, it's impossible !

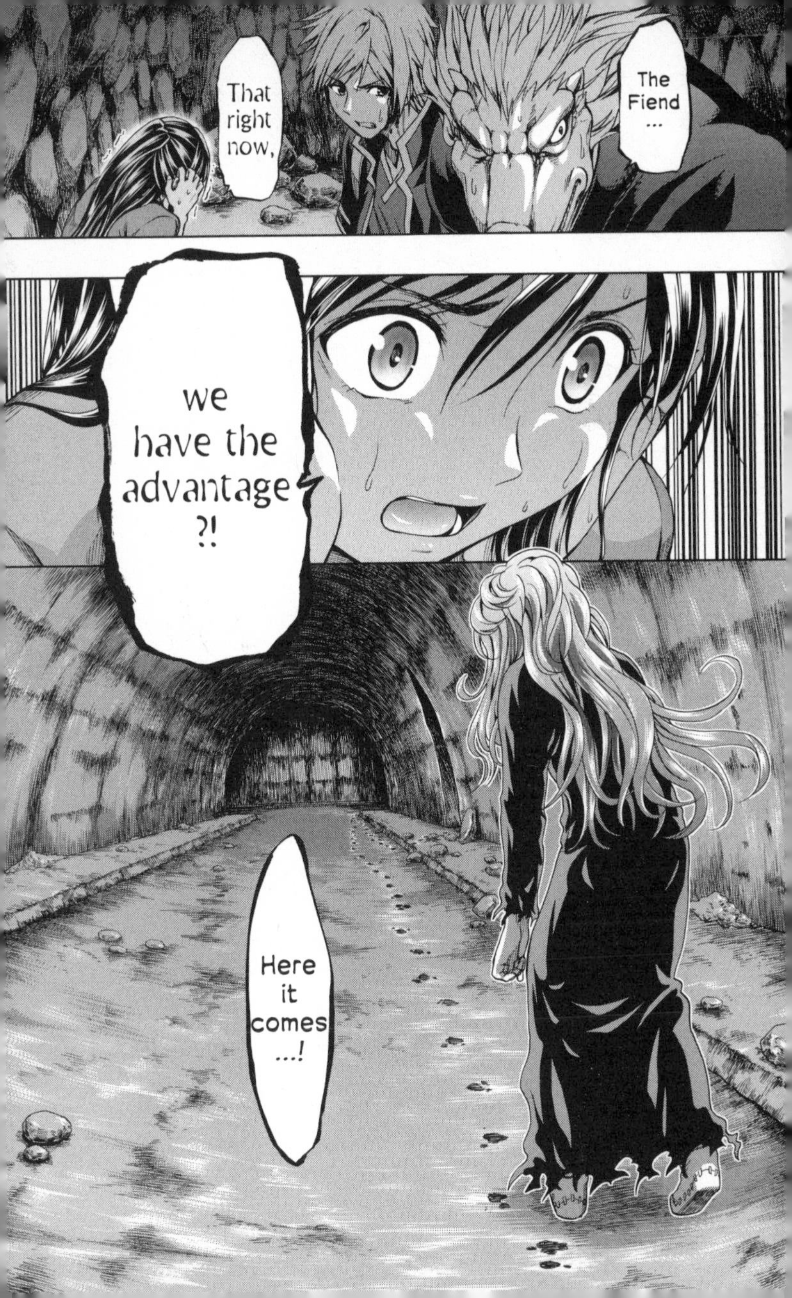
The Fiend ...
That right now,
we have the advantage ?!
Here it comes ...!

FROM
THE
new
WORLD

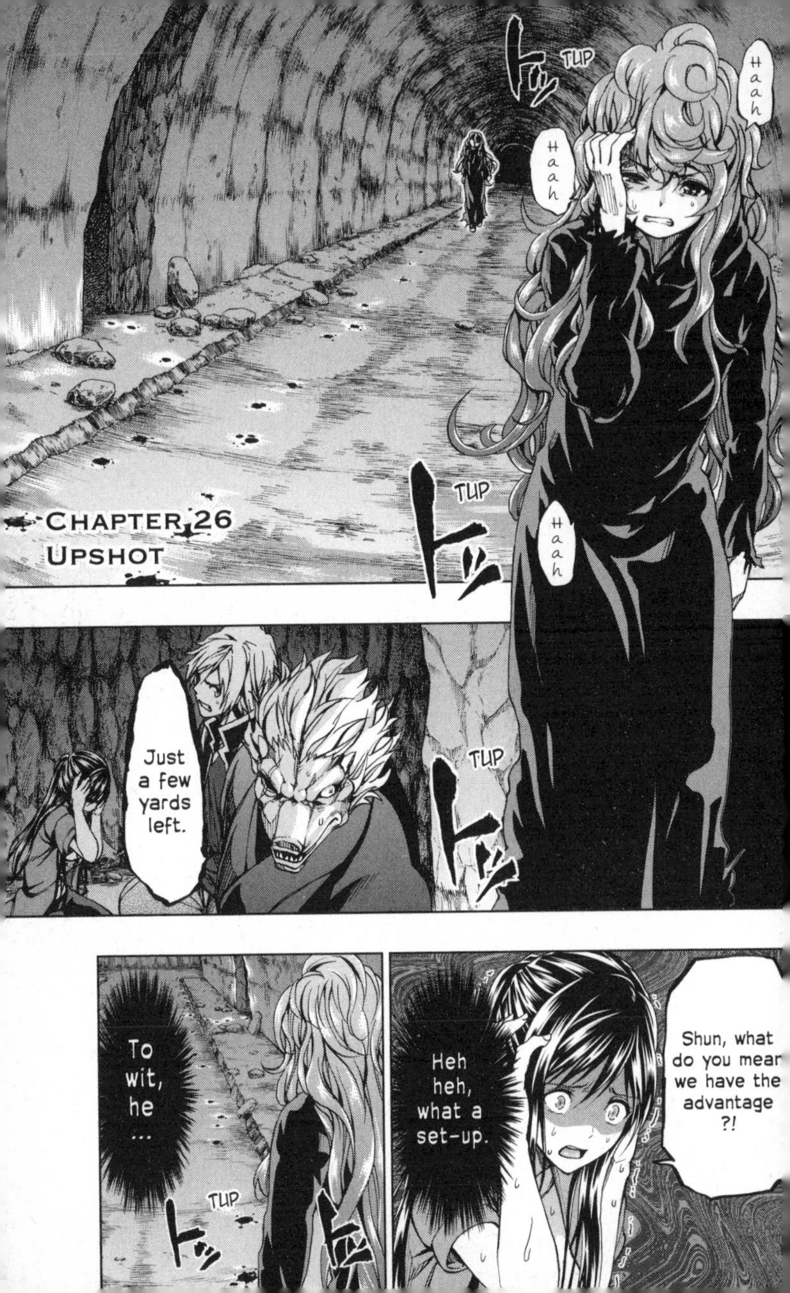
TUP
Haaah
Haaah
Chapter 26
Upshot
TUP
Haaah
TUP
Just a few yards left.
Shun, what do you mean we have the advantage?!
Heh heh, what a set-up.
To wit, he ...
TUP

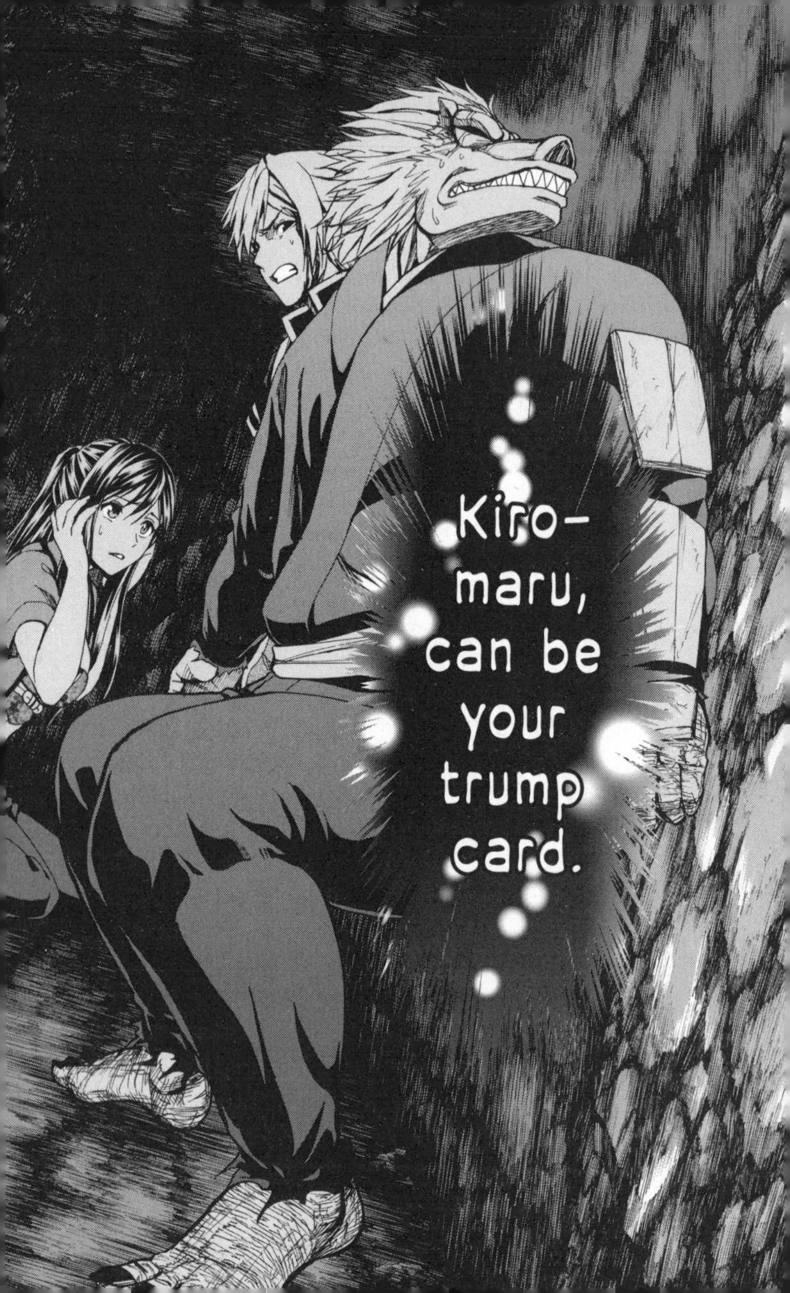
Kiro-
maru,
can be
your
trump
card.

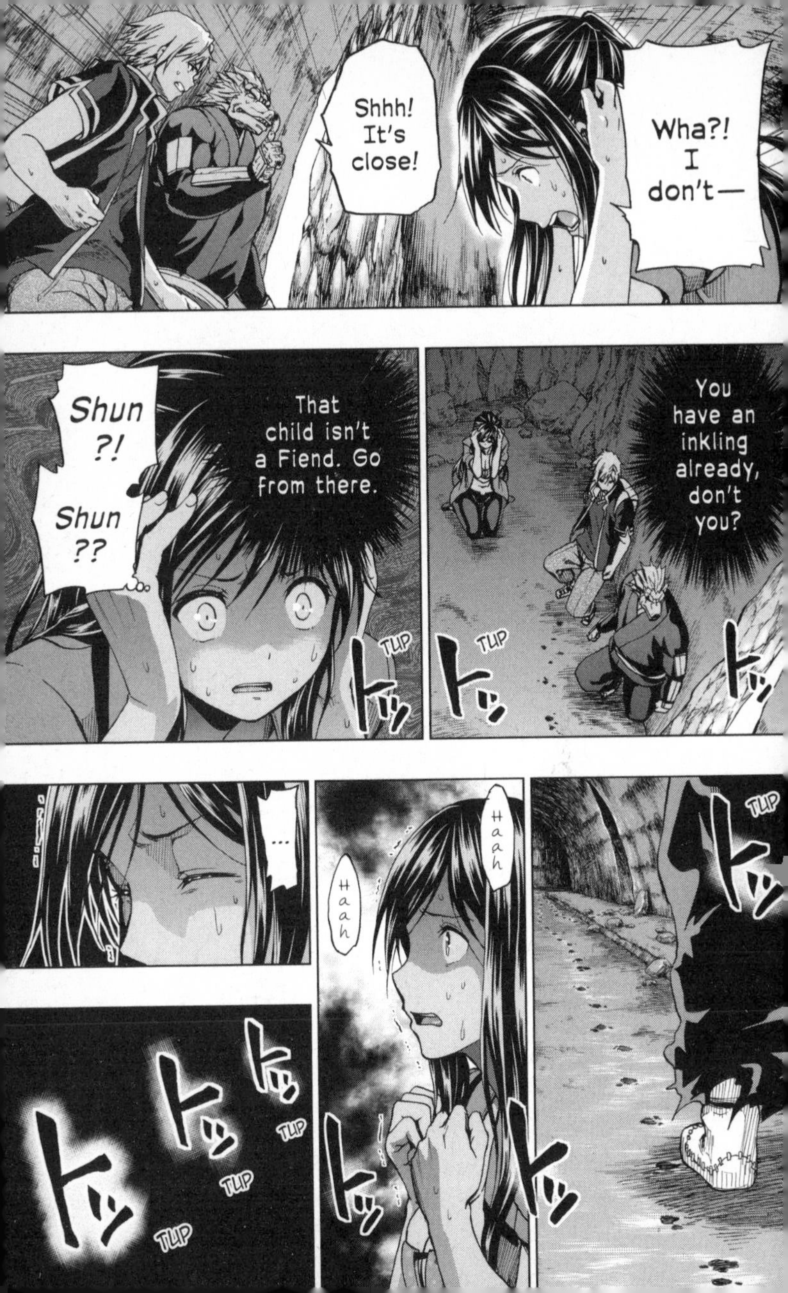
Wha?! I don't—
Shhh! It's close!
You have an inkling already, don't you?
TUP
That child isn't a Fiend. Go from there.
Shun ?!
Shun ??
TUP
TUP
Haah
Haah
...
TUP
TUP
TUP

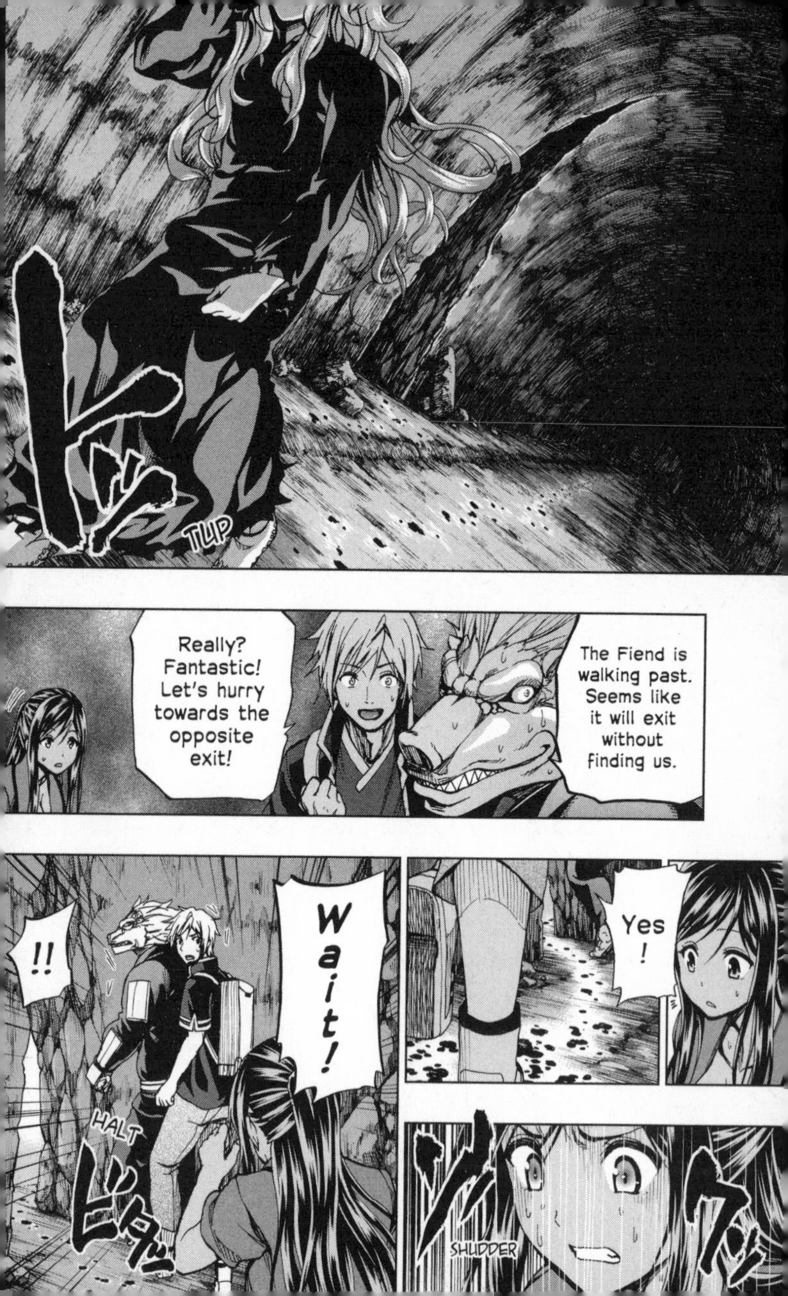
TUP
The Fiend is walking past. Seems like it will exit without finding us.
Really? Fantastic! Let's hurry towards the opposite exit!
Yes!
SHUDDER
Wait!
!!
HALT

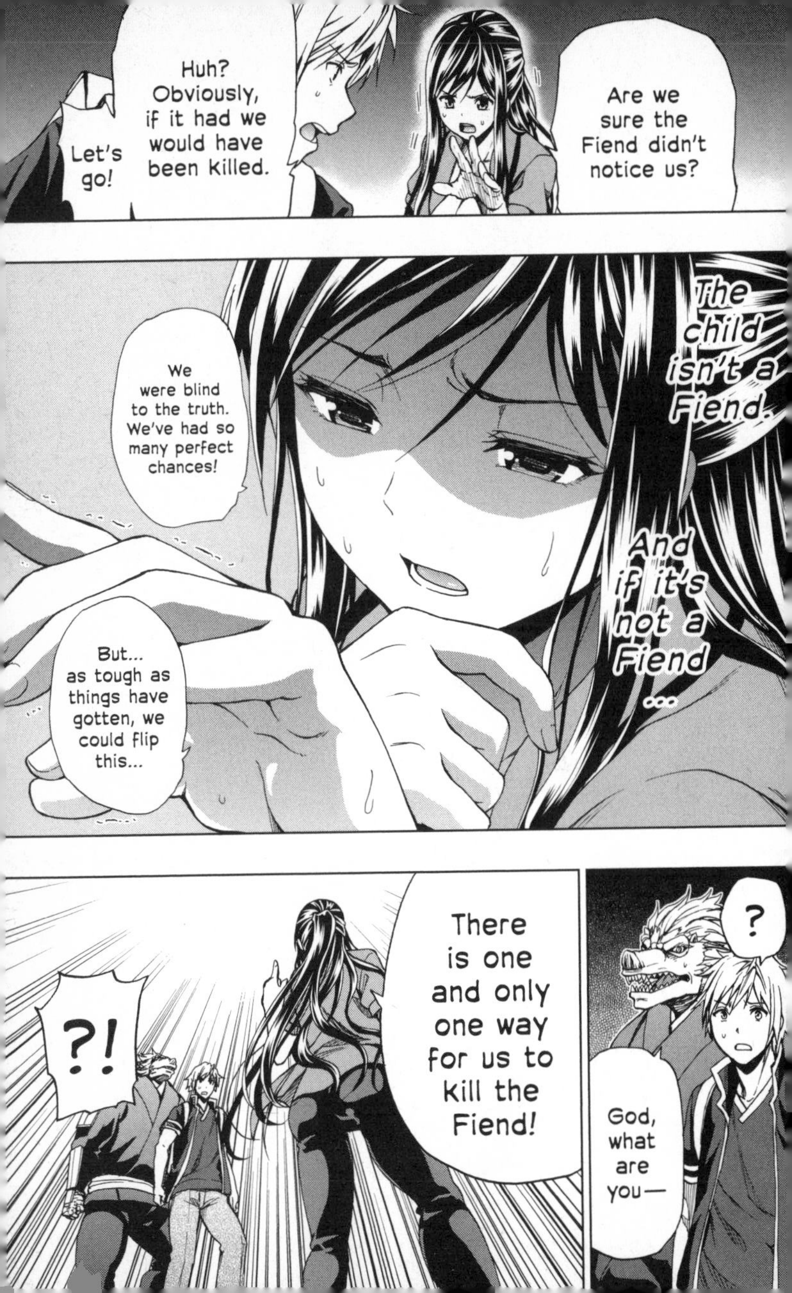
Are we sure the Fiend didn't notice us?
Huh? Obviously, if it had we would have been killed.
Let's go!
The child isn't a Fiend.
And if it's not a Fiend...
We were blind to the truth. We've had so many perfect chances!
But... as tough as things have gotten, we could flip this...
?
God, what are you—
There is one and only one way for us to kill the Fiend!
?!

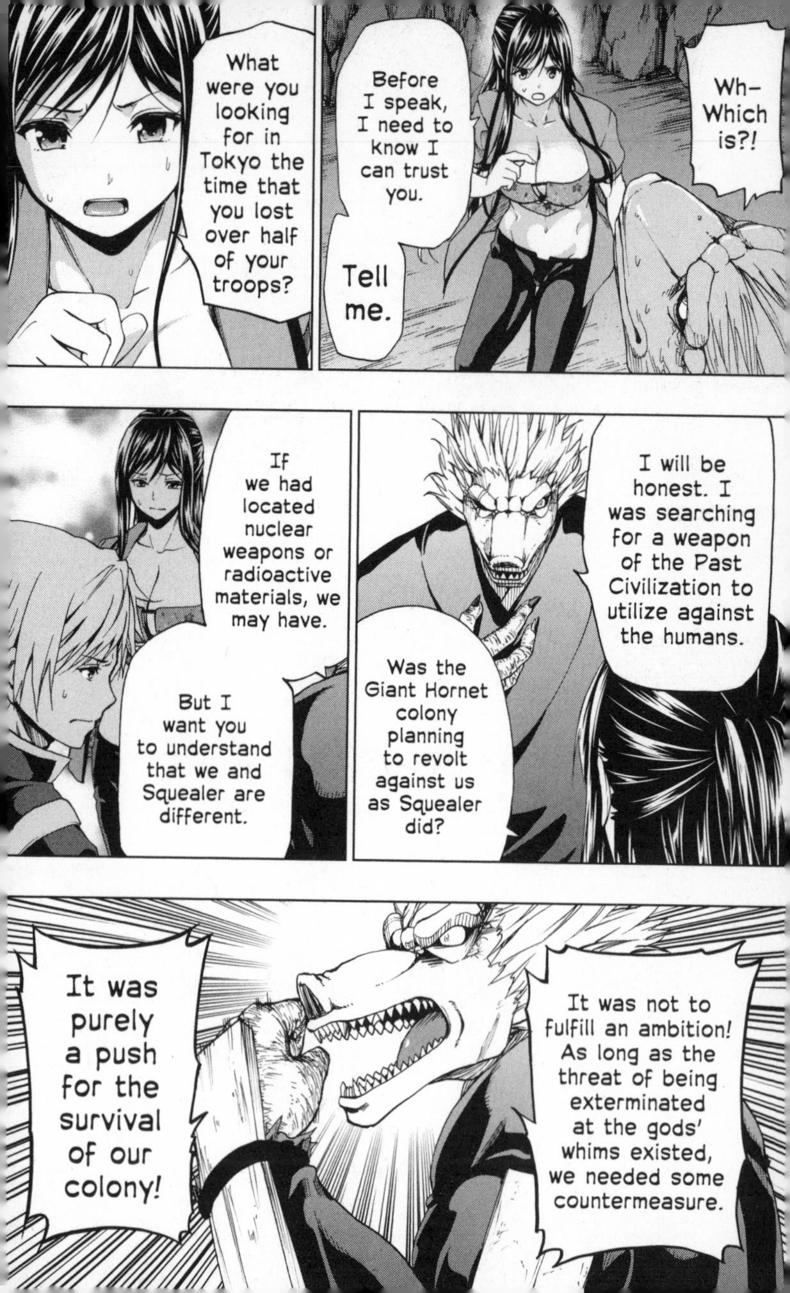
Wh– Which is?!
Before I speak, I need to know I can trust you.
Tell me.
What were you looking for in Tokyo the time that you lost over half of your troops?
I will be honest. I was searching for a weapon of the Past Civilization to utilize against the humans.
Was the Giant Hornet colony planning to revolt against us as Squealer did?
If we had located nuclear weapons or radioactive materials, we may have.
But I want you to understand that we and Squealer are different.
It was not to fulfill an ambition! As long as the threat of being exterminated at the gods' whims existed, we needed some countermeasure.
It was purely a push for the survival of our colony!

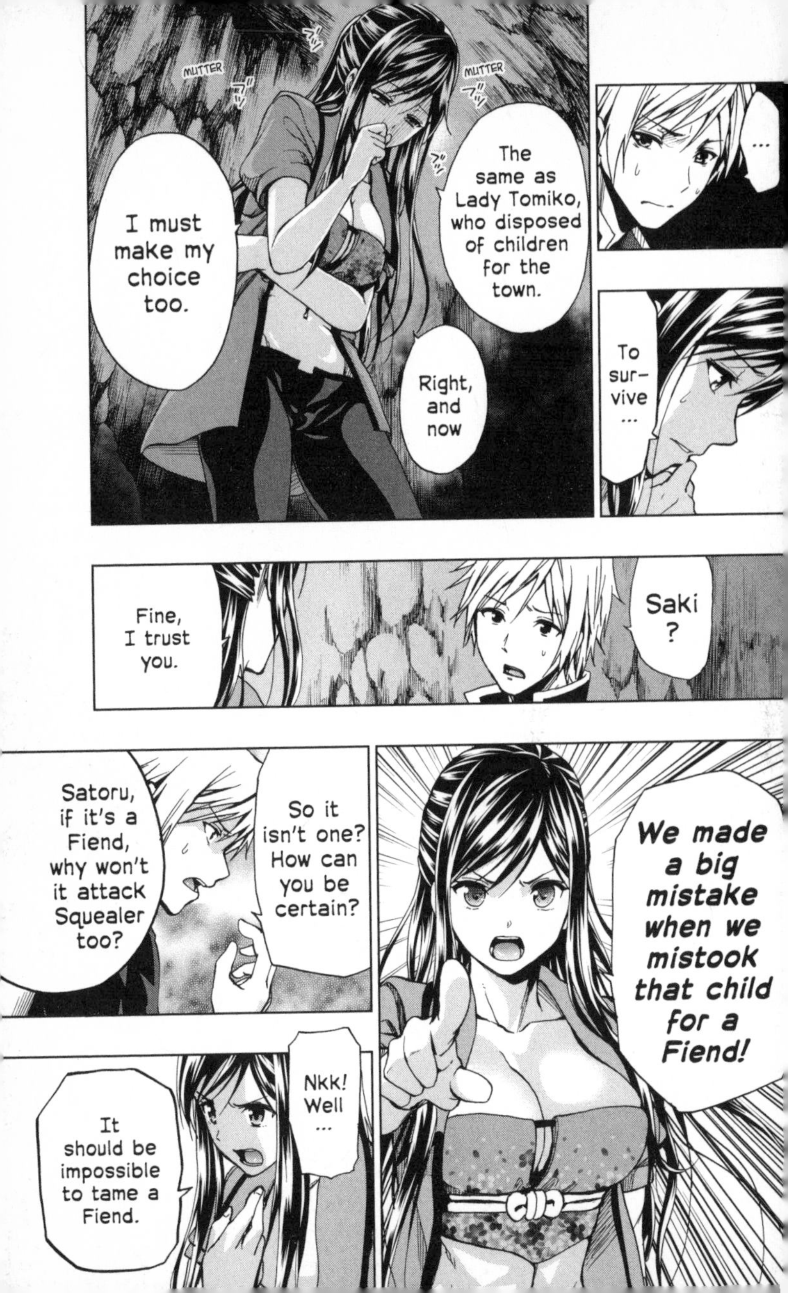
...
To sur-vive ...
MUTTER
MUTTER
The same as Lady Tomiko, who disposed of children for the town.
Right, and now
I must make my choice too.
Saki ?
Fine, I trust you.
We made a big mistake when we mistook that child for a Fiend!
So it isn't one? How can you be certain?
Satoru, if it's a Fiend, why won't it attack Squealer too?
Nkk! Well ...
It should be impossible to tame a Fiend.

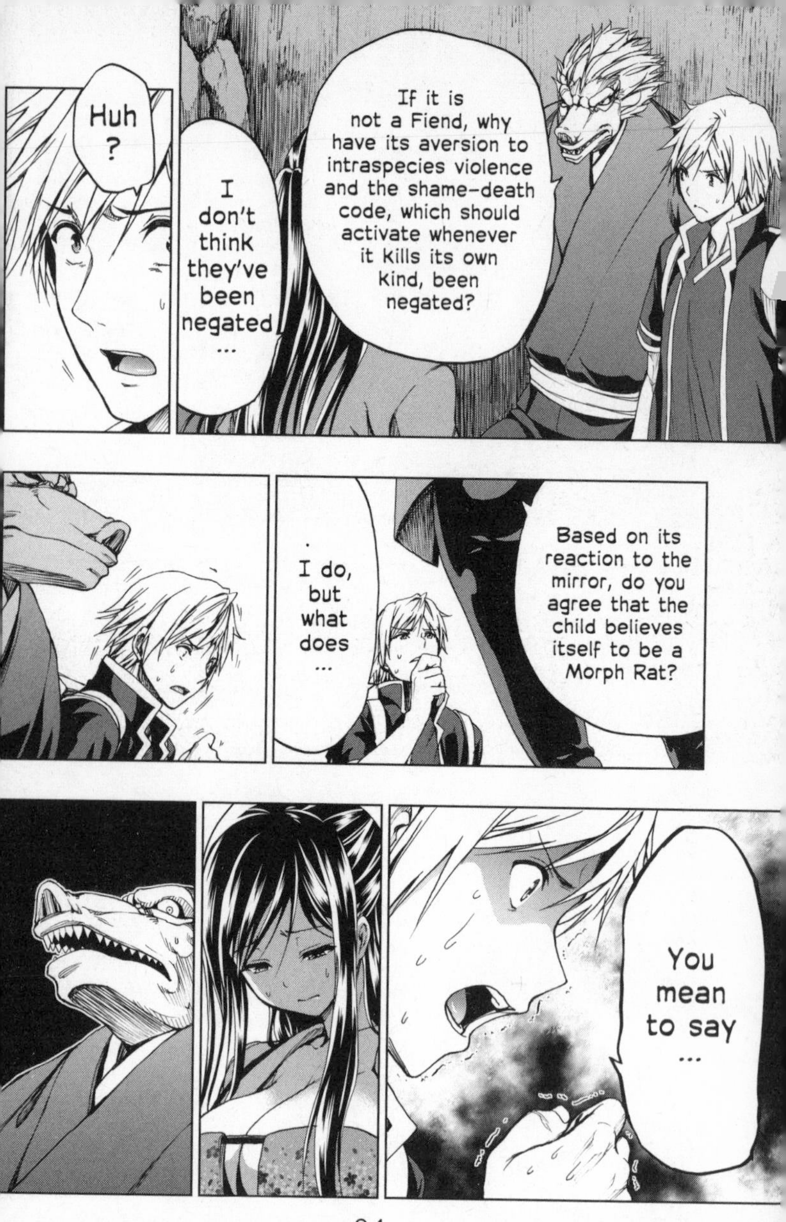
If it is not a Fiend, why have its aversion to intraspecies violence and the shame-death code, which should activate whenever it kills its own kind, been negated?
I don't think they've been negated...
Huh?
Based on its reaction to the mirror, do you agree that the child believes itself to be a Morph Rat?
. I do, but what does...
You mean to say...

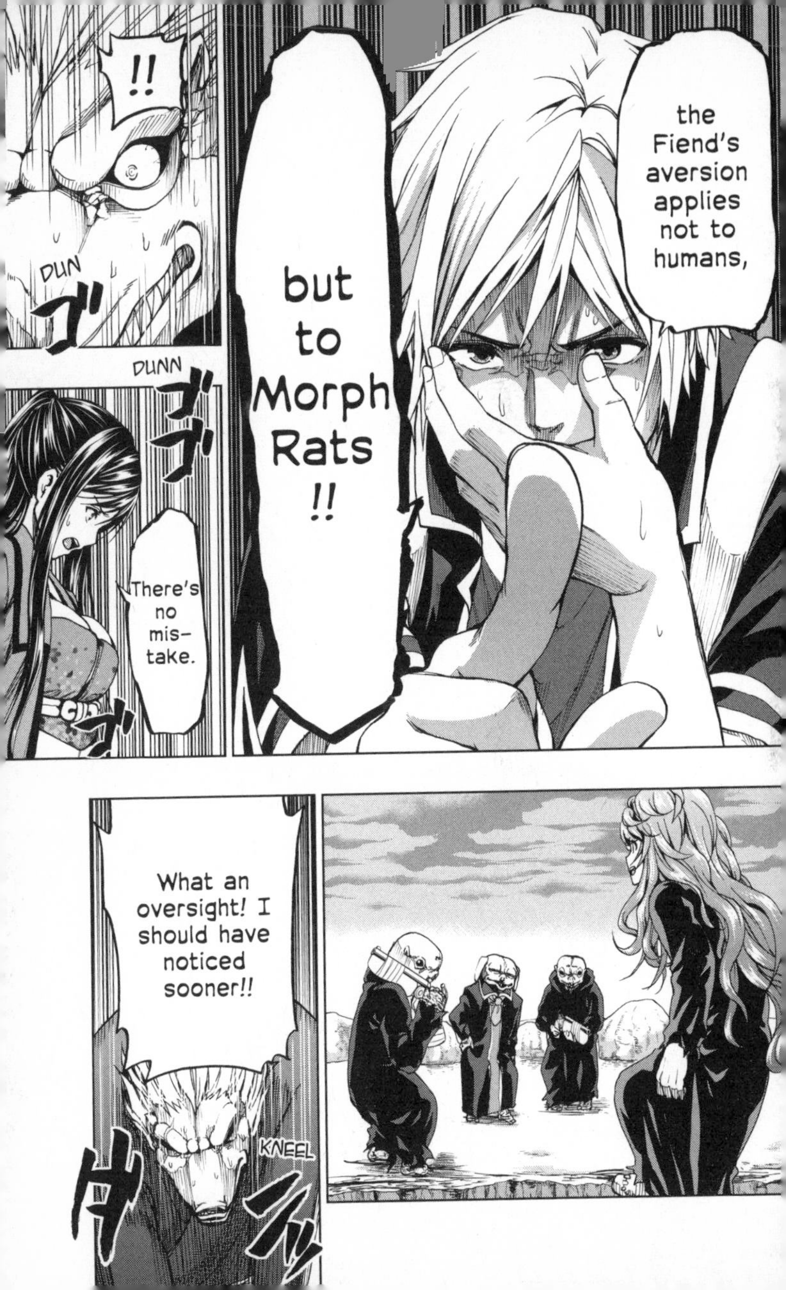
the Fiend's aversion applies not to humans,
but to Morph Rats!!
!!
DUN
DUNN
There's no mis-take.
What an oversight! I should have noticed sooner!!
KNEEL

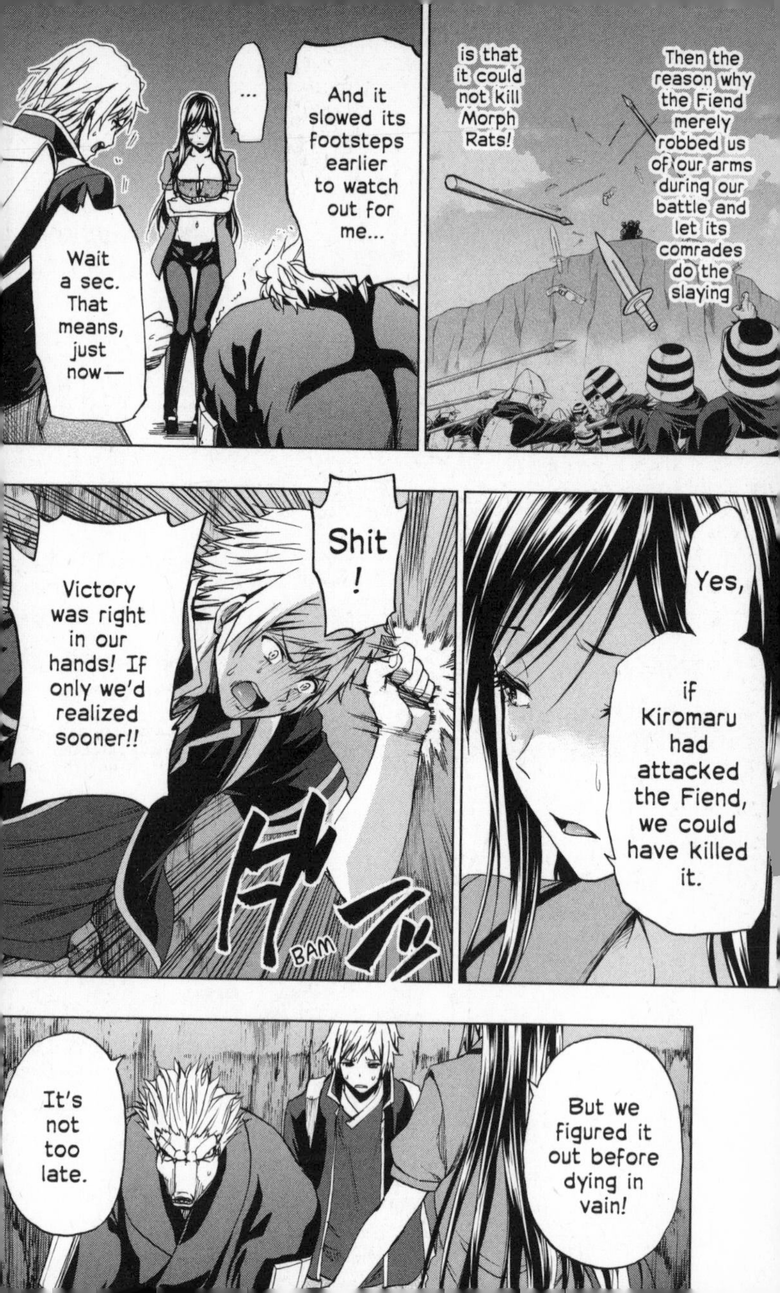
Then the reason why the Fiend merely robbed us of our arms during our battle and let its comrades do the slaying
is that it could not kill Morph Rats!
And it slowed its footsteps earlier to watch out for me...
...
Wait a sec. That means, just now—
Yes,
if Kiromaru had attacked the Fiend, we could have killed it.
Shit!
Victory was right in our hands! If only we'd realized sooner!!
BAM
But we figured it out before dying in vain!
It's not too late.

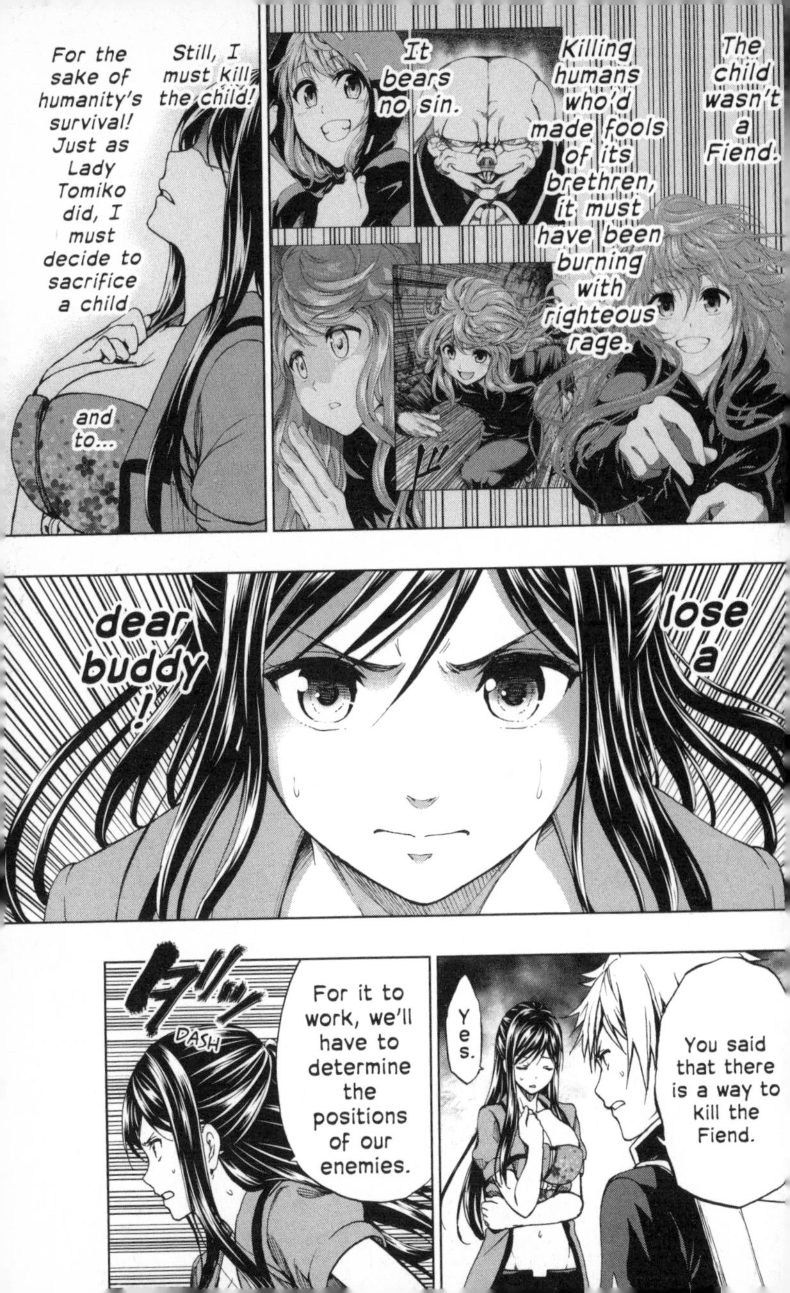
The child wasn't a Fiend.
Killing humans who'd made fools of its brethren, it must have been burning with righteous rage.
It bears no sin.
Still, I must kill the child!
For the sake of humanity's survival! Just as Lady Tomiko did, I must decide to sacrifice a child
and to...
lose a
dear buddy!
You said that there is a way to kill the Fiend.
Yes.
For it to work, we'll have to determine the positions of our enemies.
DASH

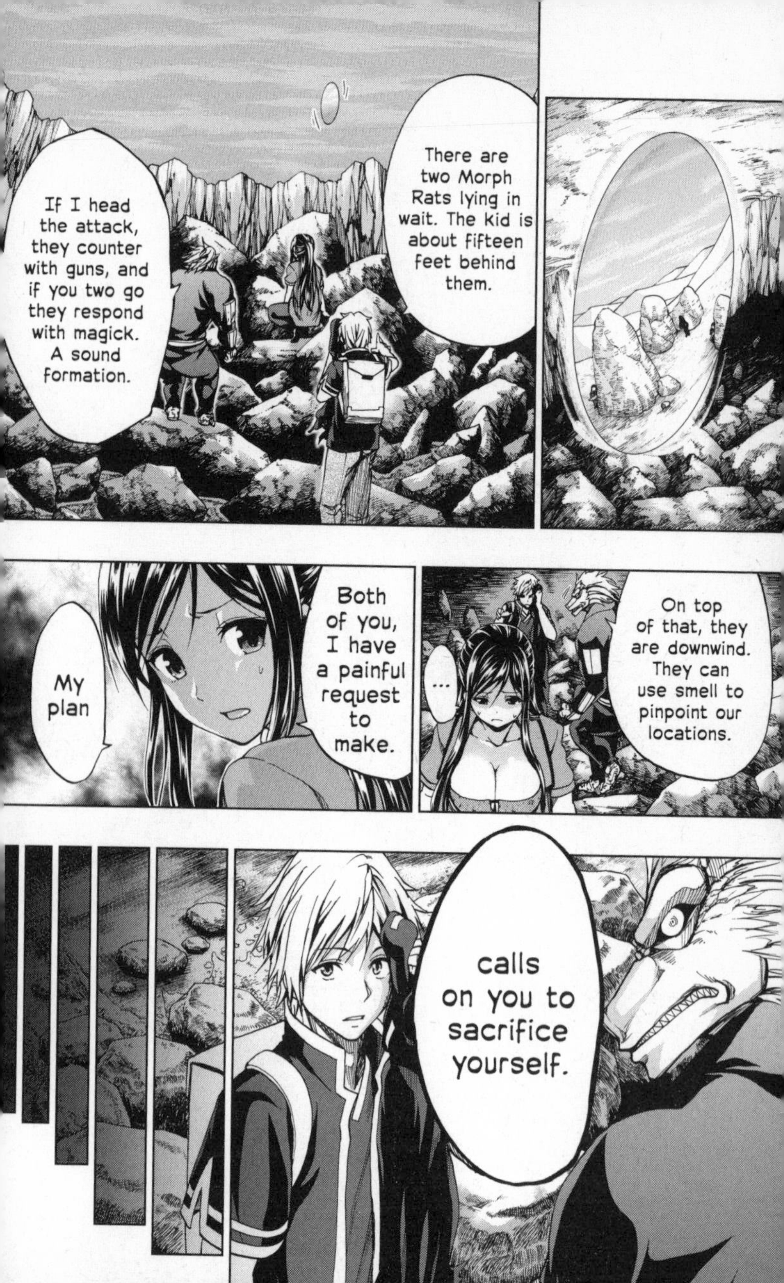
There are two Morph Rats lying in wait. The kid is about fifteen feet behind them.
If I head the attack, they counter with guns, and if you two go they respond with magick. A sound formation.
On top of that, they are downwind. They can use smell to pinpoint our locations.
...
Both of you, I have a painful request to make.
My plan
calls on you to sacrifice yourself.

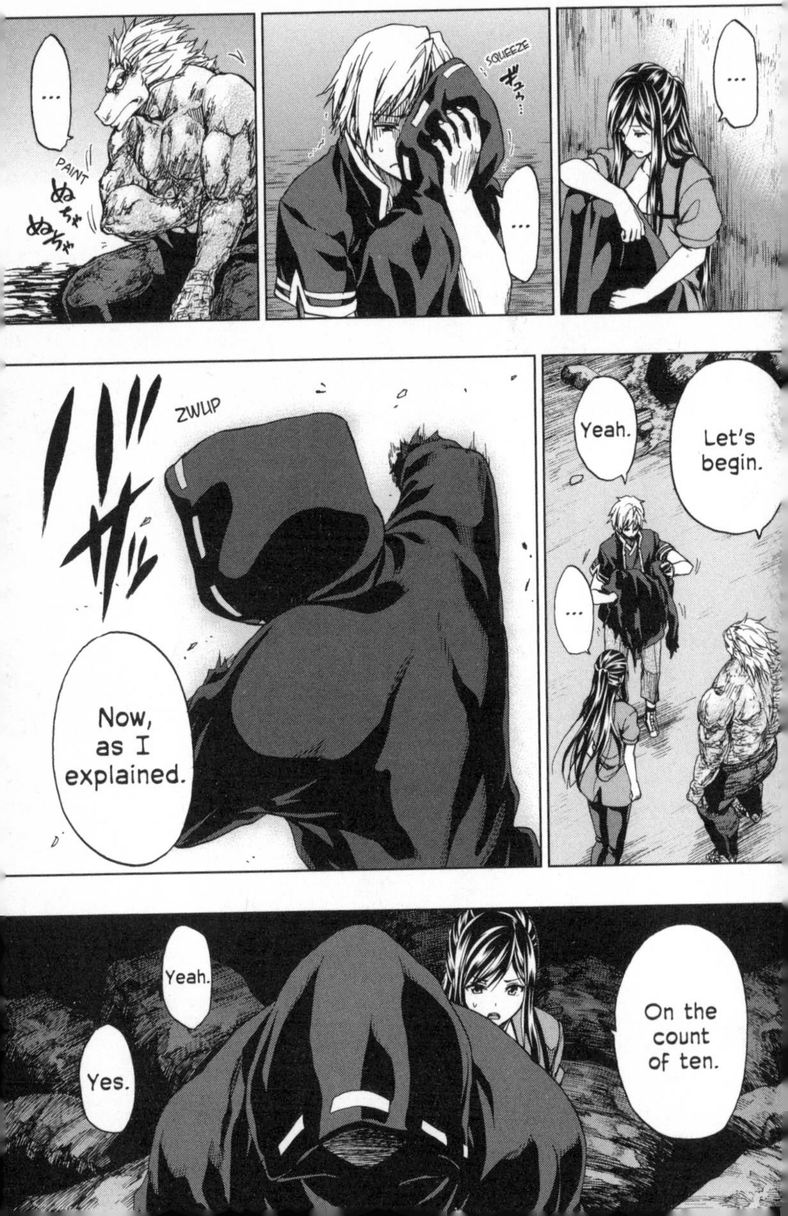
...
SQUEEZE
ギュゥ…
...
...
PAINT
ぬちゃ ぬちゃ
Let's begin.
Yeah.
...
ZWUP
Now, as I explained.
On the count of ten.
Yeah.
Yes.

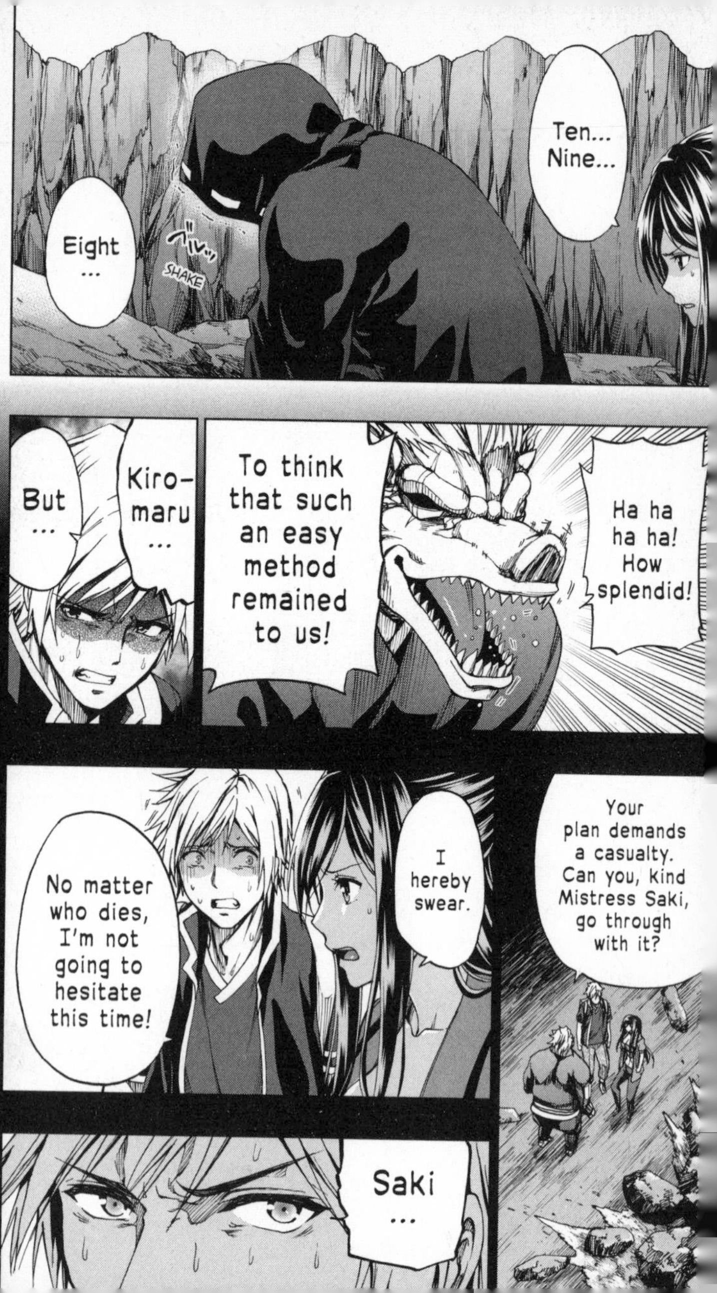
Ten... Nine...
SHAKE
Eight ...
Ha ha ha ha! How splendid!
To think that such an easy method remained to us!
Kiro-maru ...
But ...
Your plan demands a casualty. Can you, kind Mistress Saki, go through with it?
I hereby swear.
No matter who dies, I'm not going to hesitate this time!
Saki ...

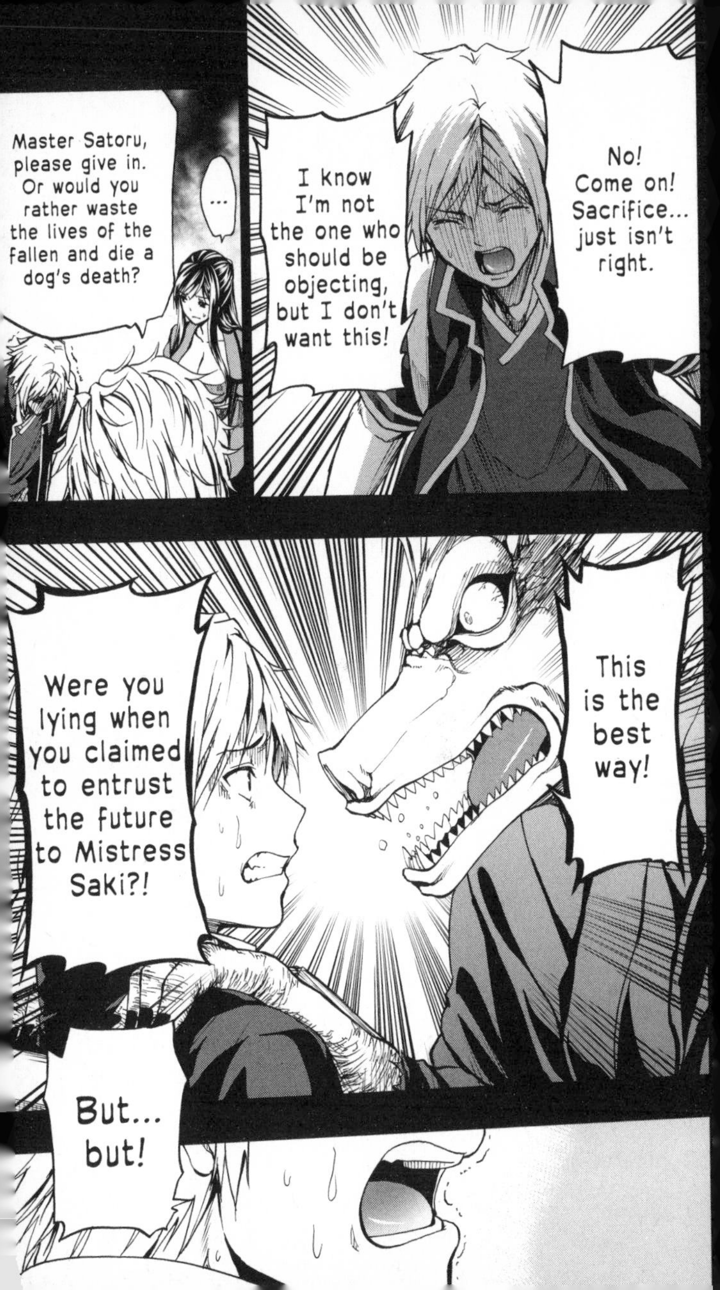
No! Come on! Sacrifice... just isn't right.
I know I'm not the one who should be objecting, but I don't want this!
Master Satoru, please give in. Or would you rather waste the lives of the fallen and die a dog's death?
...
This is the best way!
Were you lying when you claimed to entrust the future to Mistress Saki?!
But... but!

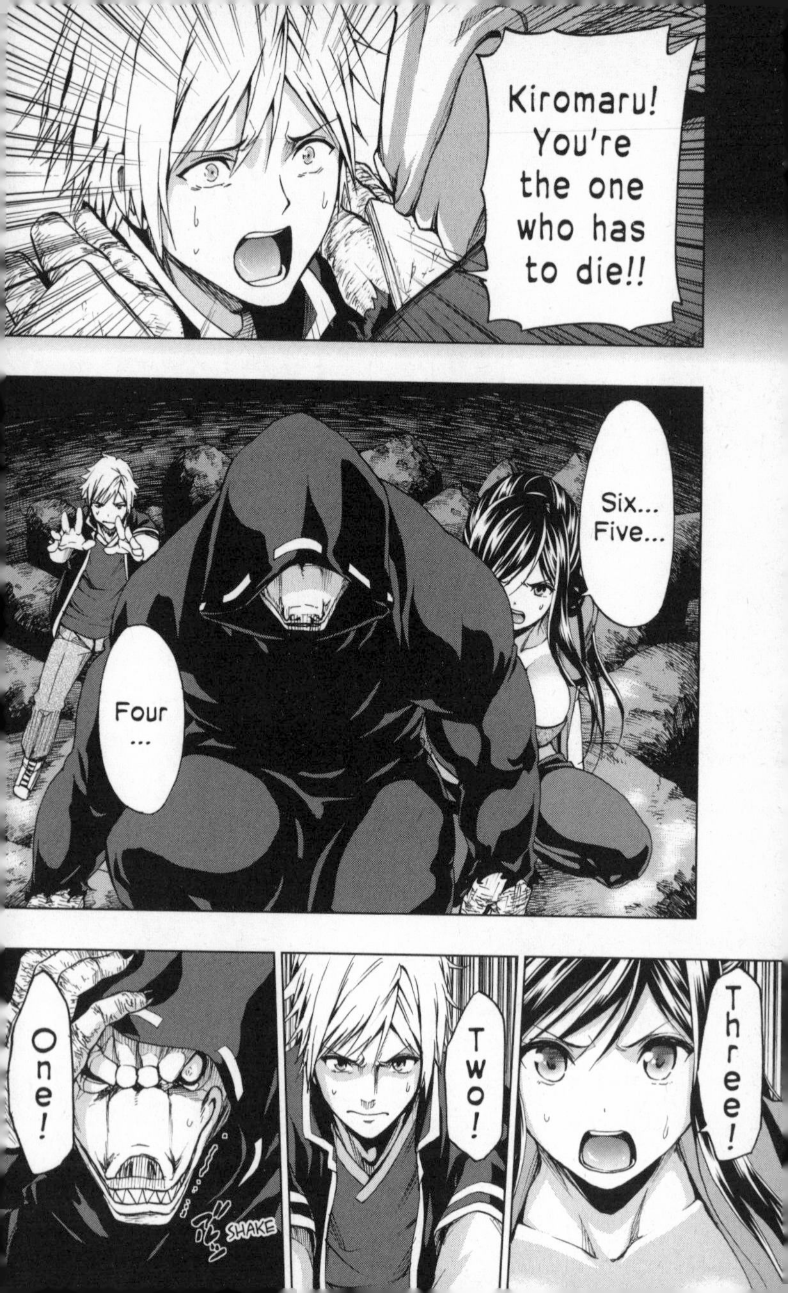
Kiromaru! You're the one who has to die!!
Six... Five...
Four ...
Three!
Two!
One!
SHAKE

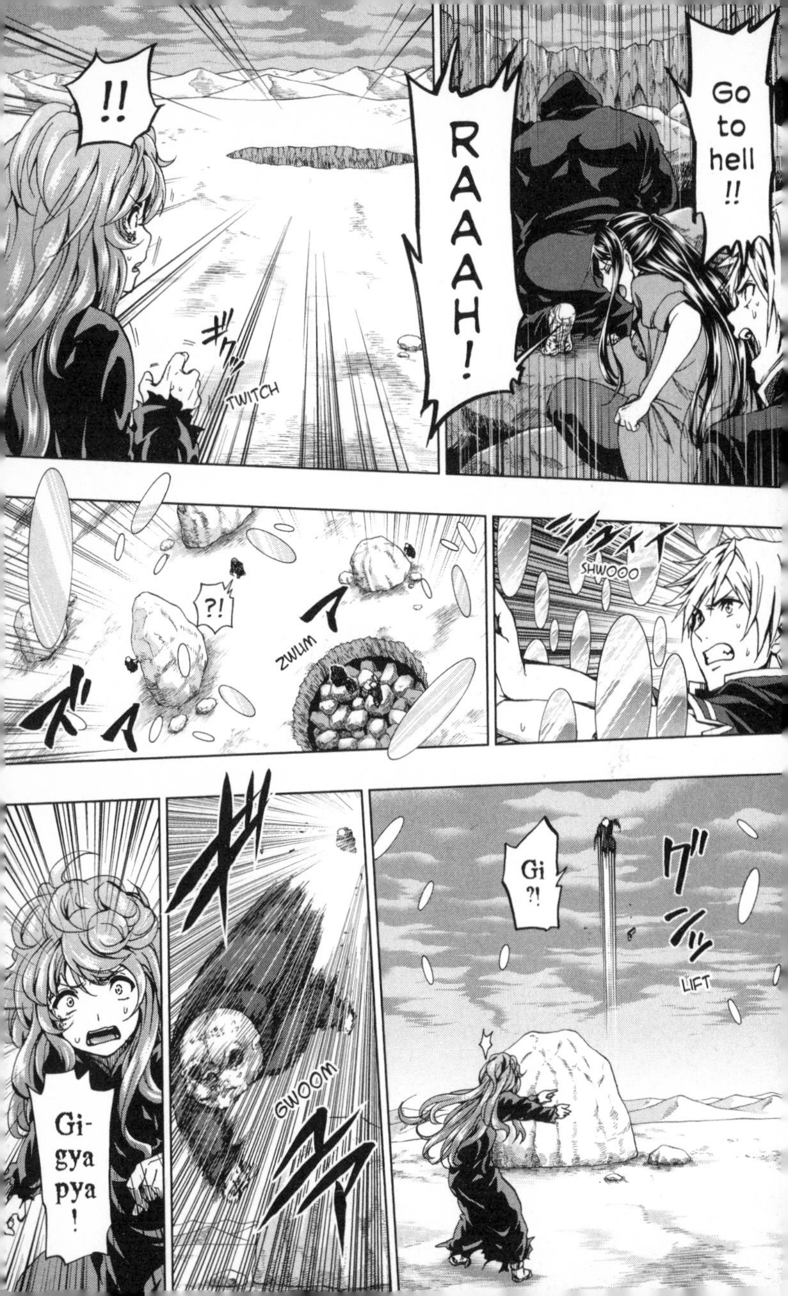
Go to hell !!
RAAAAH!
!!
TWITCH
SHWOOO
?!
ZWUM
Gi ?!
LIFT
GWOOM
Gi-gya pya!

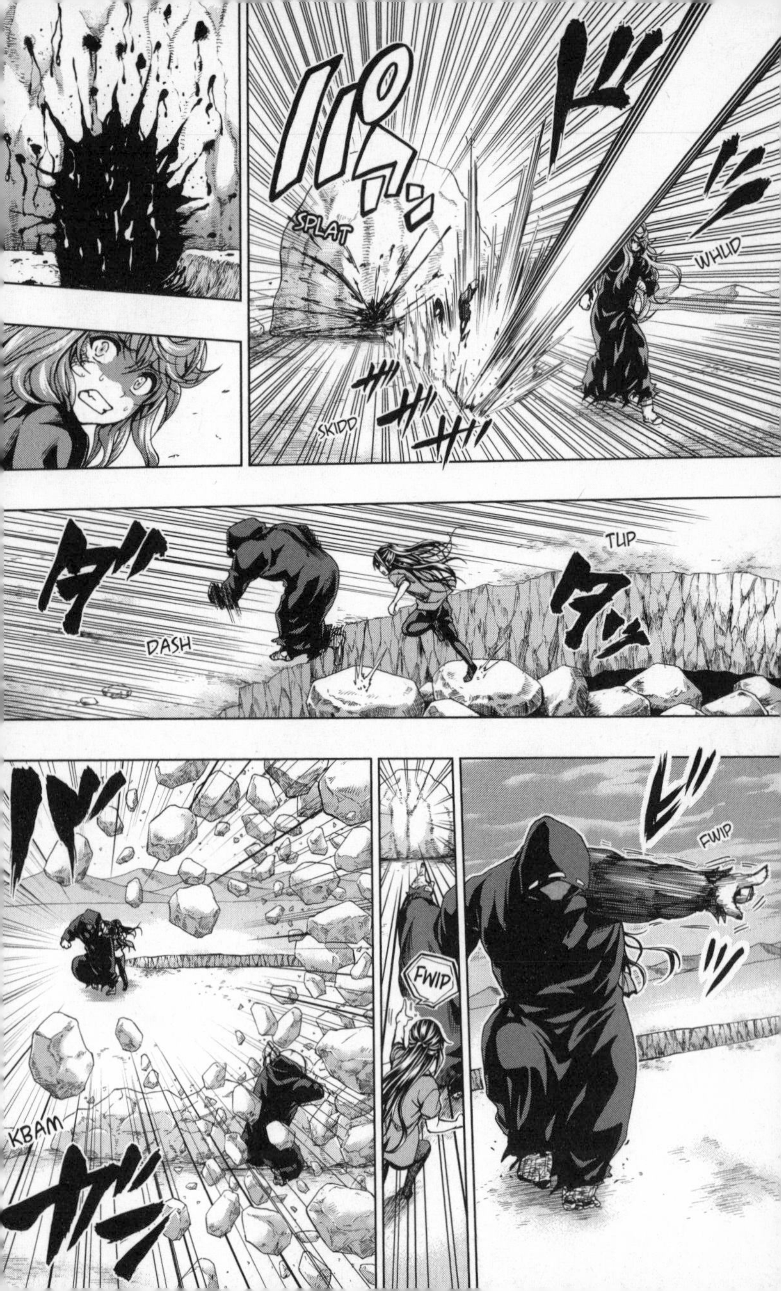
WHUD
SPLAT
SKIDD
TUP
DASH
FWIP
FWIP
KBAM

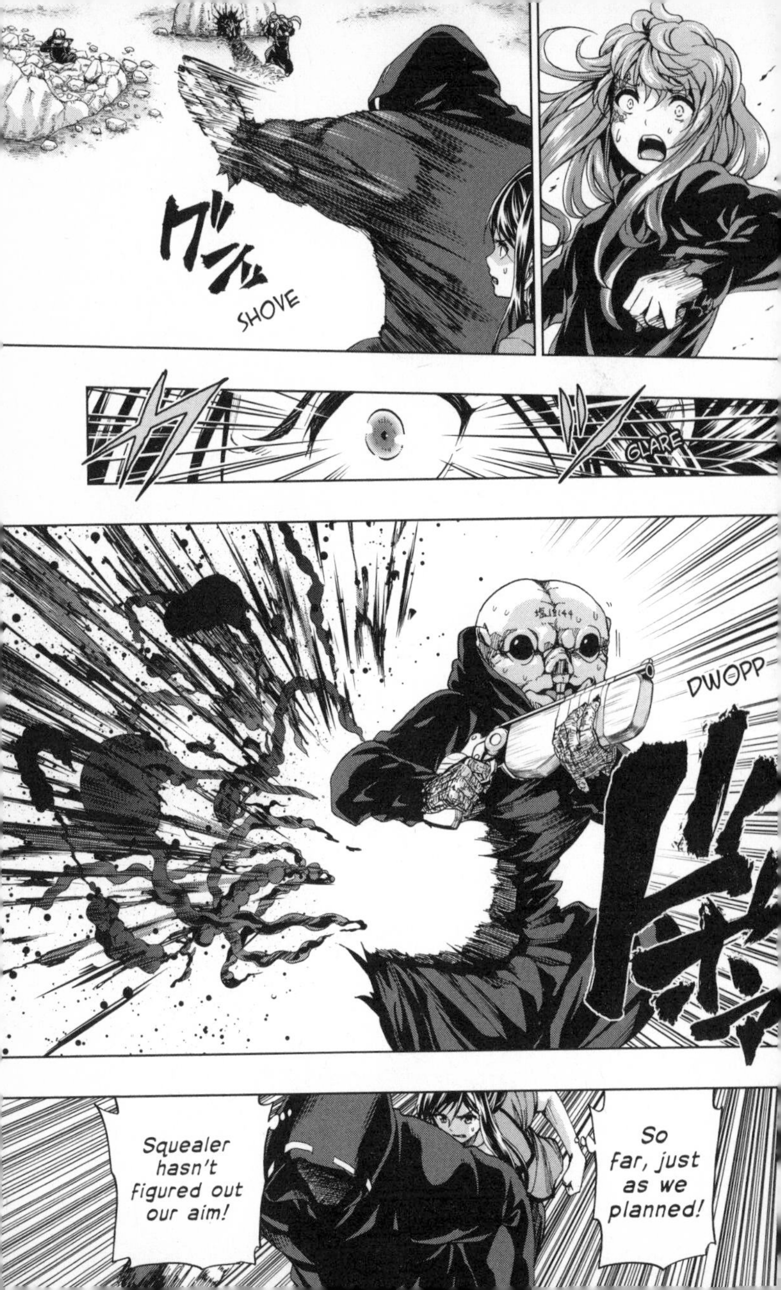

SHOVE
GLARE
DWOPP
So far, just as we planned!
Squealer hasn't figured out our aim!

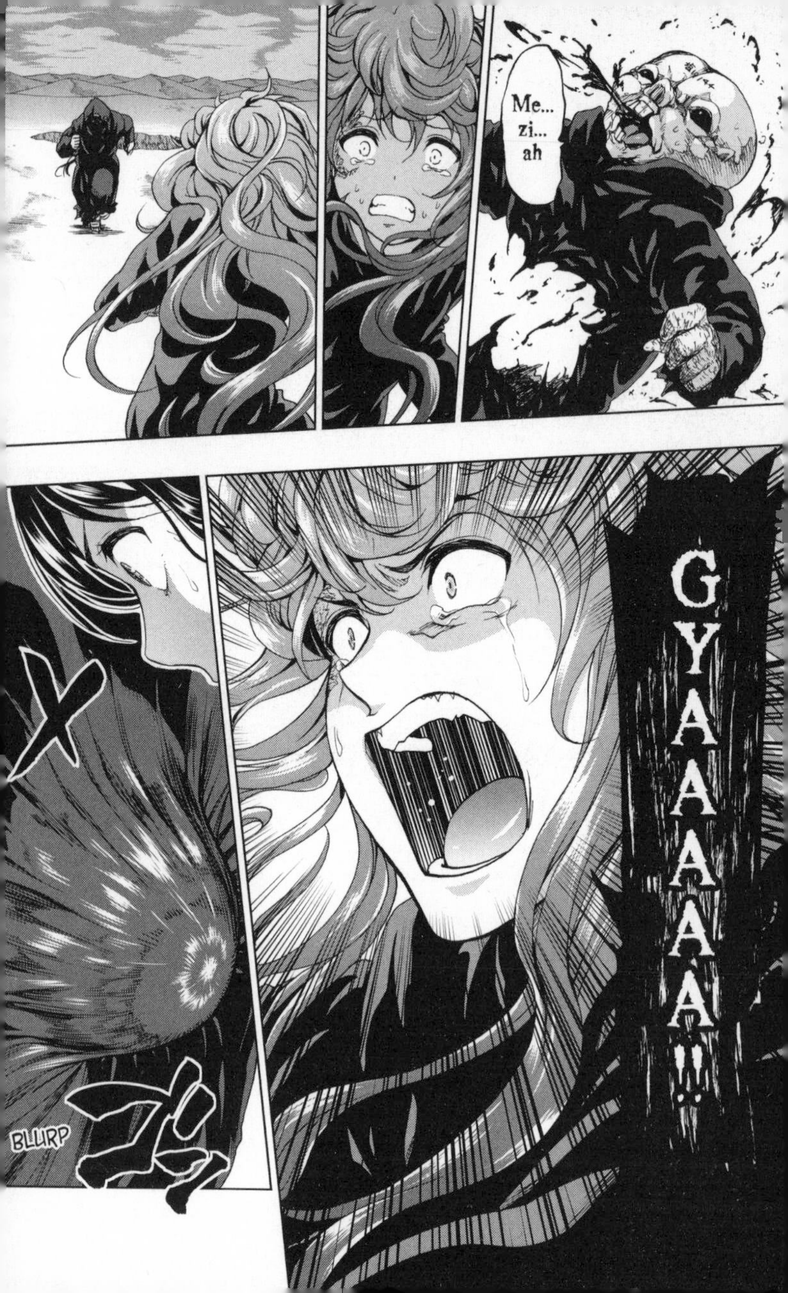

Me...
zi...
ah
GYAAAAA!!
BLURP

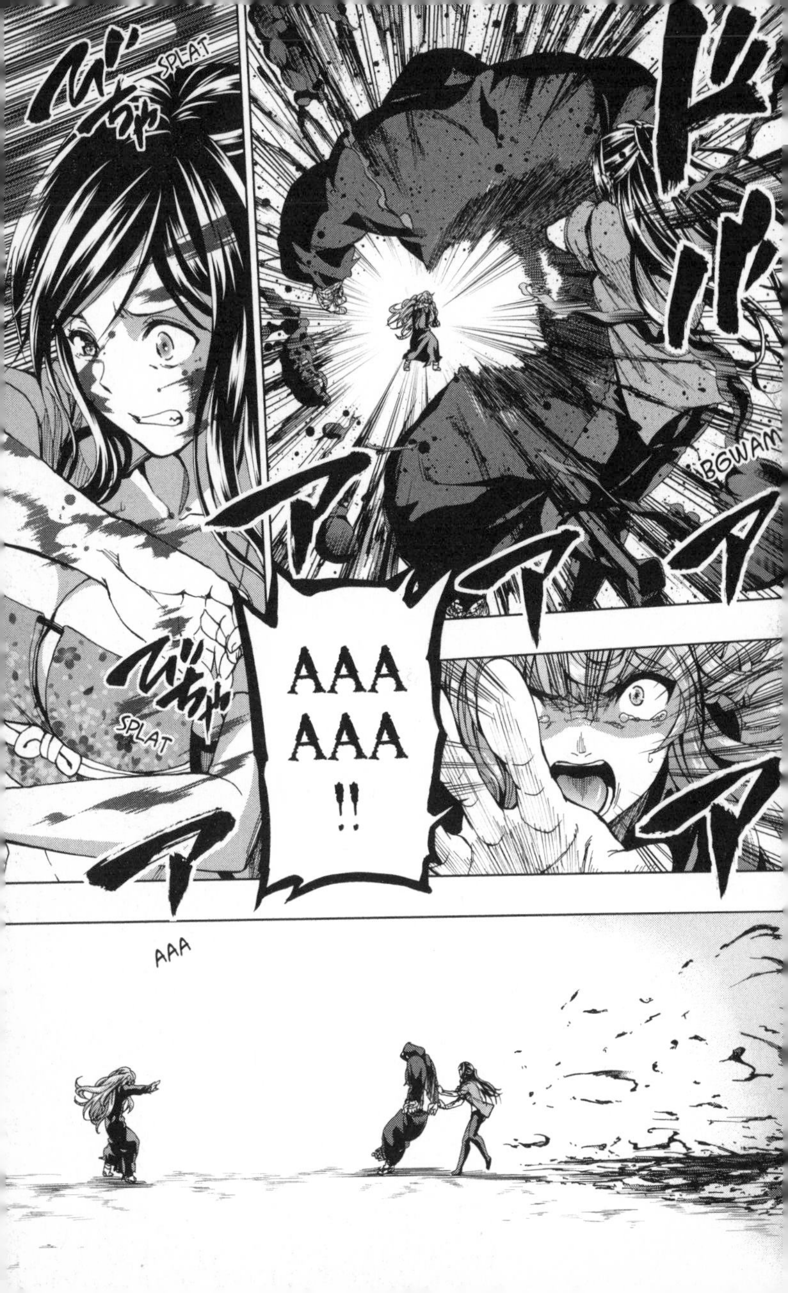
BGWAM
SPLAT
AAA
AAA
!!
SPLAT
AAA

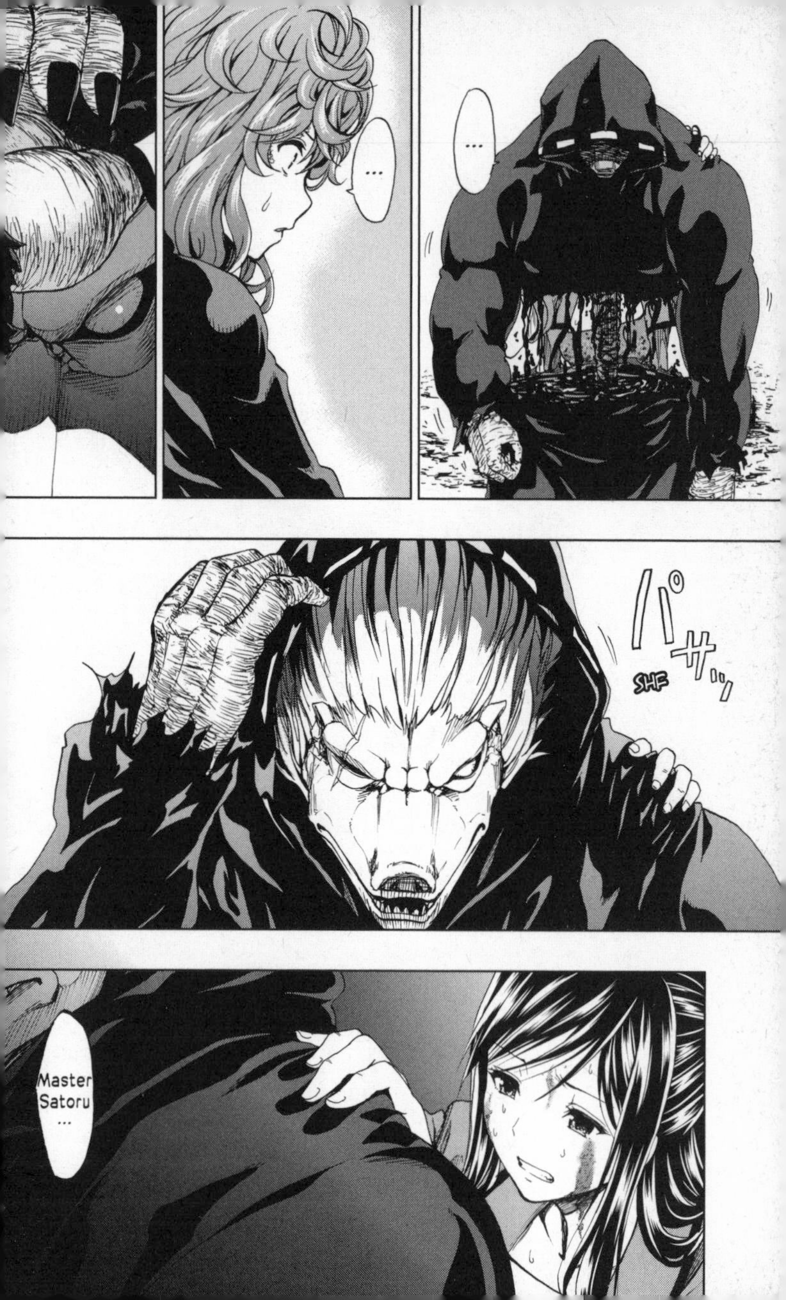
...
...
パサッ
SHF
Master Satoru ...

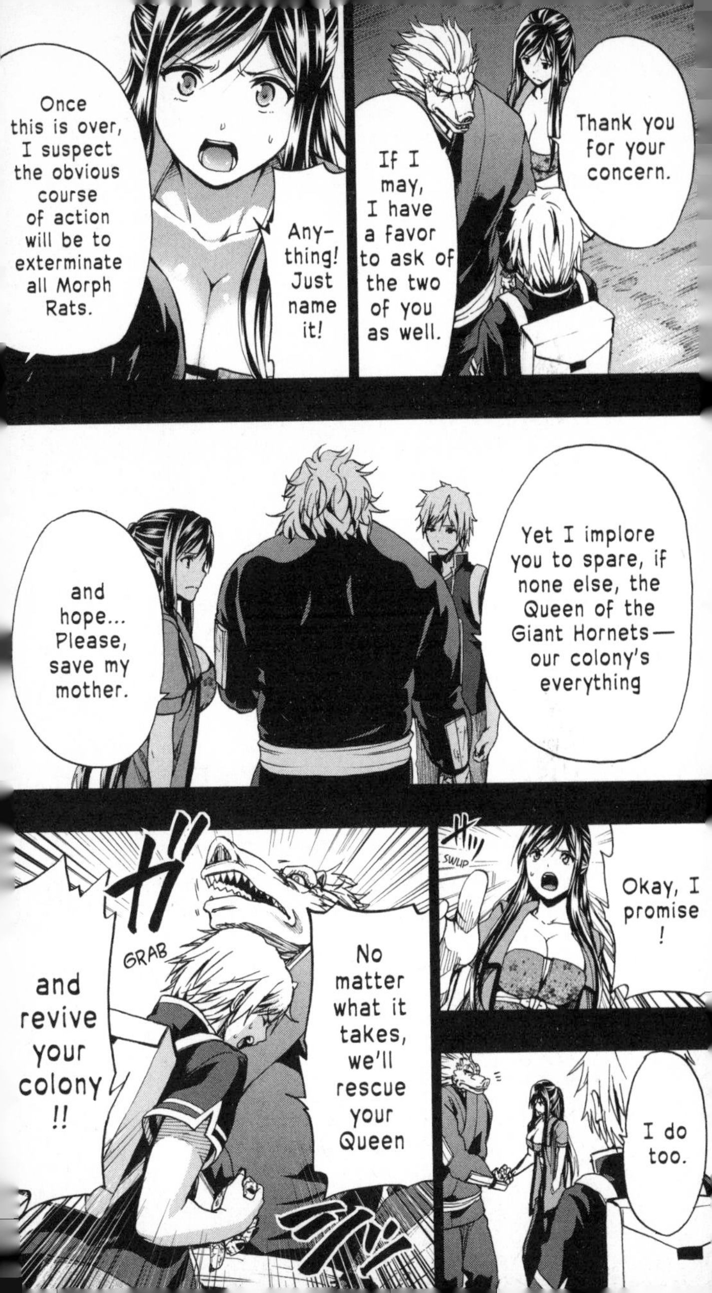
Thank you for your concern.
If I may, I have a favor to ask of the two of you as well.
Any-thing! Just name it!
Once this is over, I suspect the obvious course of action will be to exterminate all Morph Rats.
Yet I implore you to spare, if none else, the Queen of the Giant Hornets— our colony's everything
and hope... Please, save my mother.
SWUP
Okay, I promise!
I do too.
GRAB
No matter what it takes, we'll rescue your Queen
and revive your colony!!

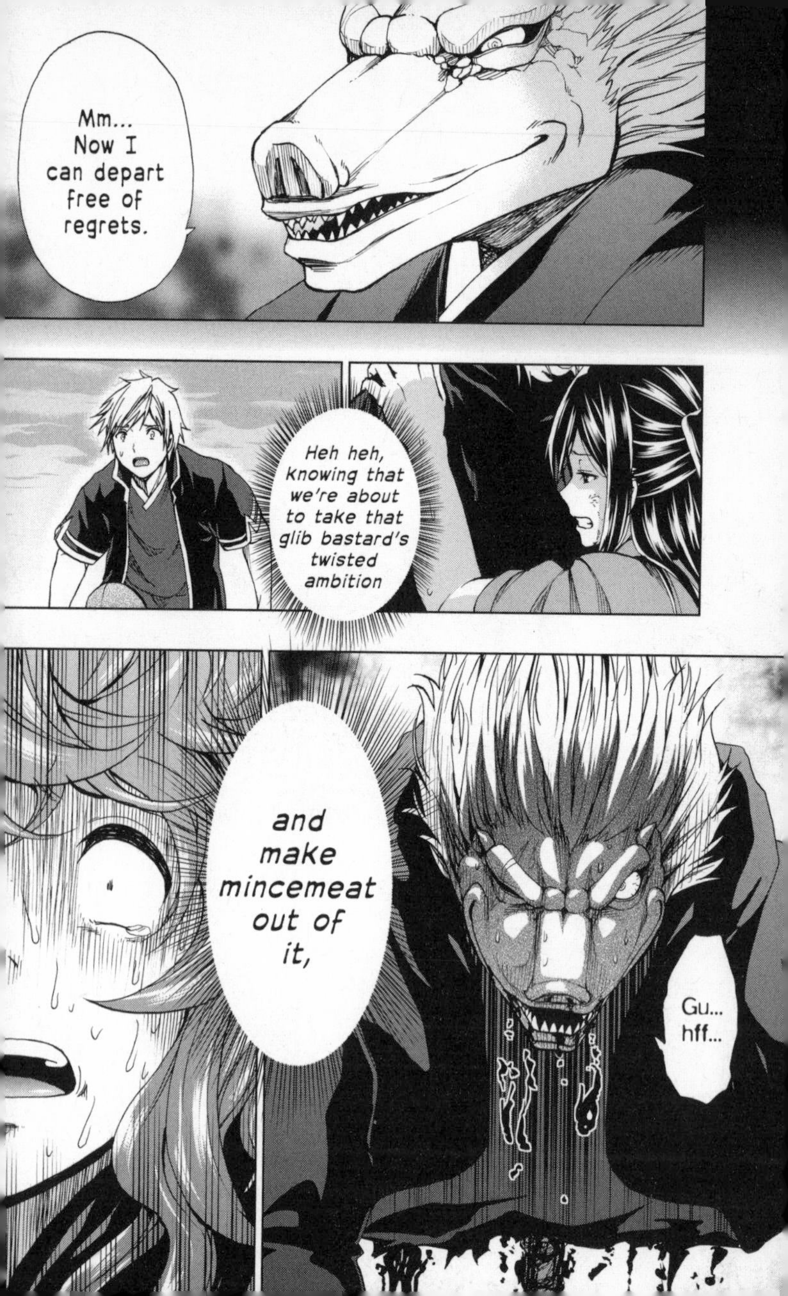
Mm... Now I can depart free of regrets.
Heh heh, knowing that we're about to take that glib bastard's twisted ambition
and make mincemeat out of it,
Gu... hff...

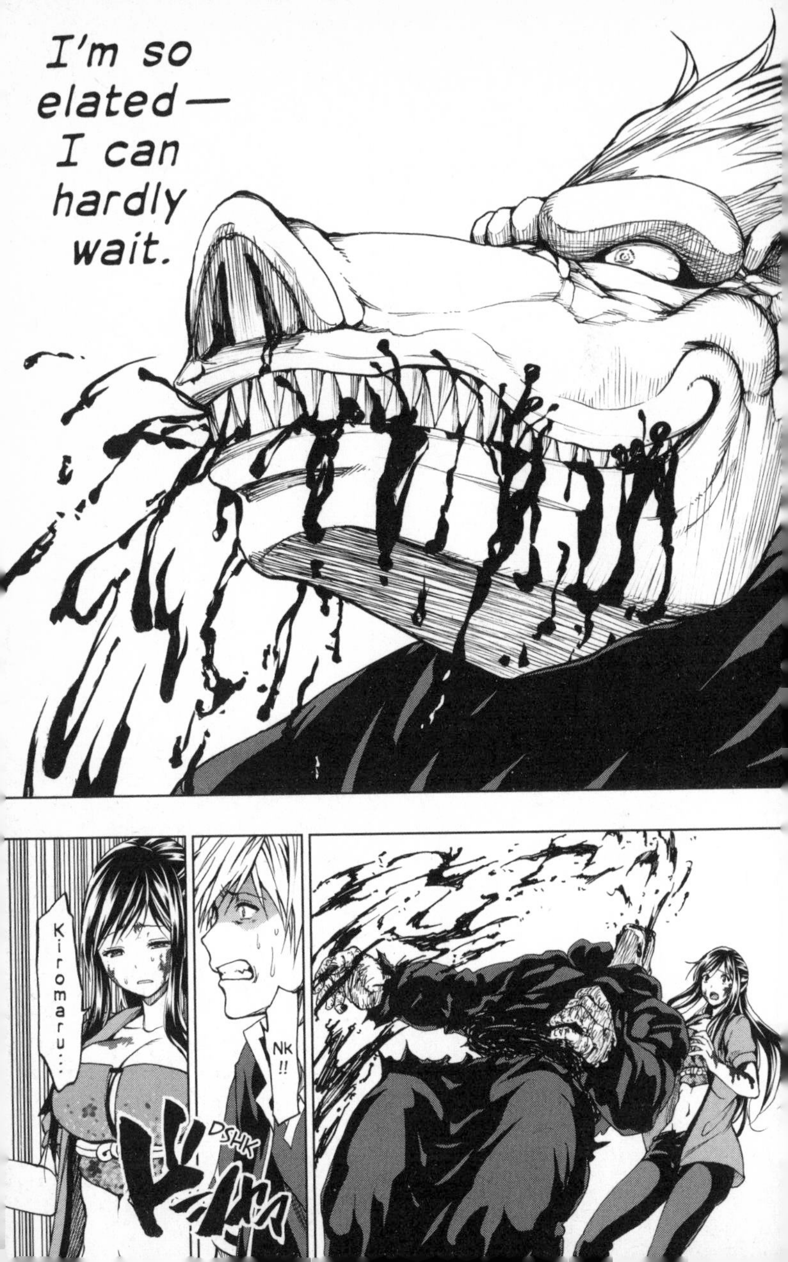
I'm so elated—I can hardly wait.
Nk !!
DSHK
Kiromaru...

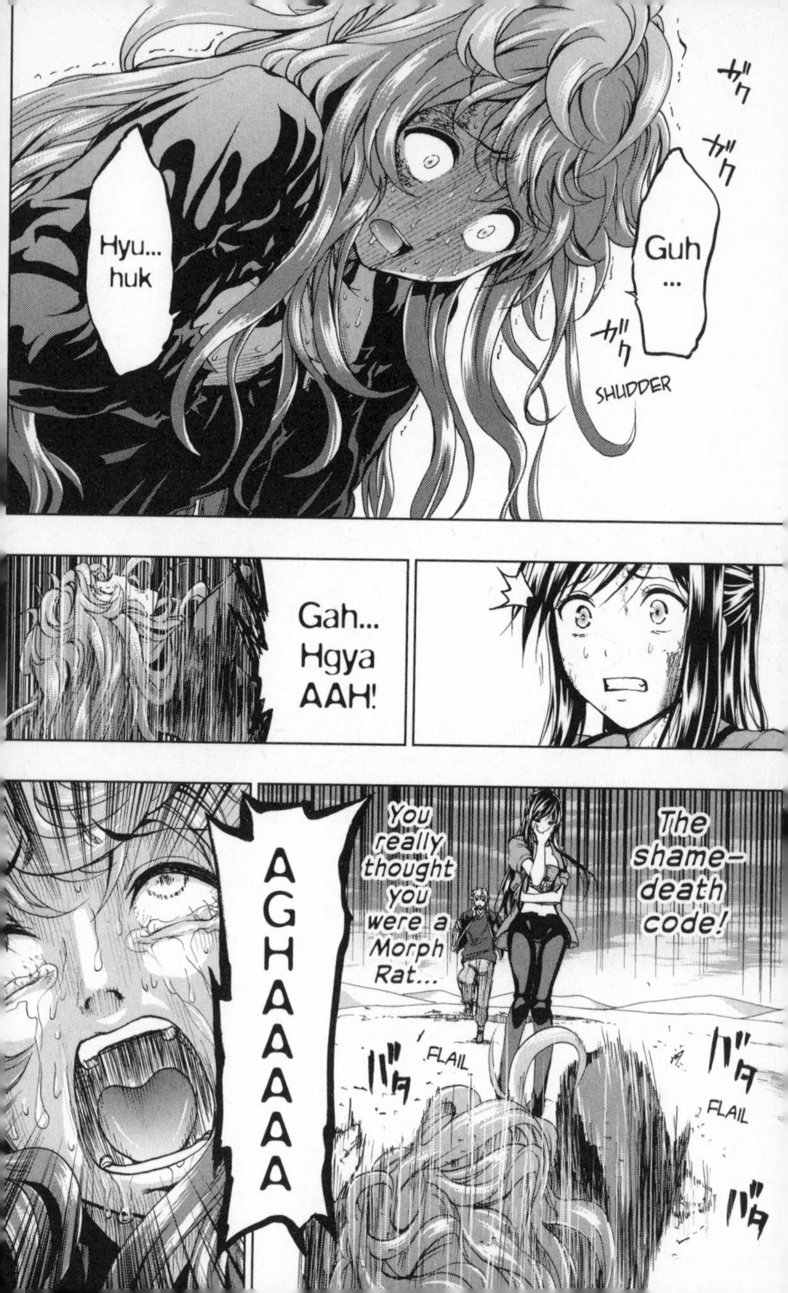
Guh
...
ガク
ガク
ガク
SHUDDER
Hyu...
huk
Gah...
Hgya
AAH!
The shame-death code!
You really thought you were a Morph Rat...
バタ
FLAIL
バタ
FLAIL
バタ
AGHAAAAAA

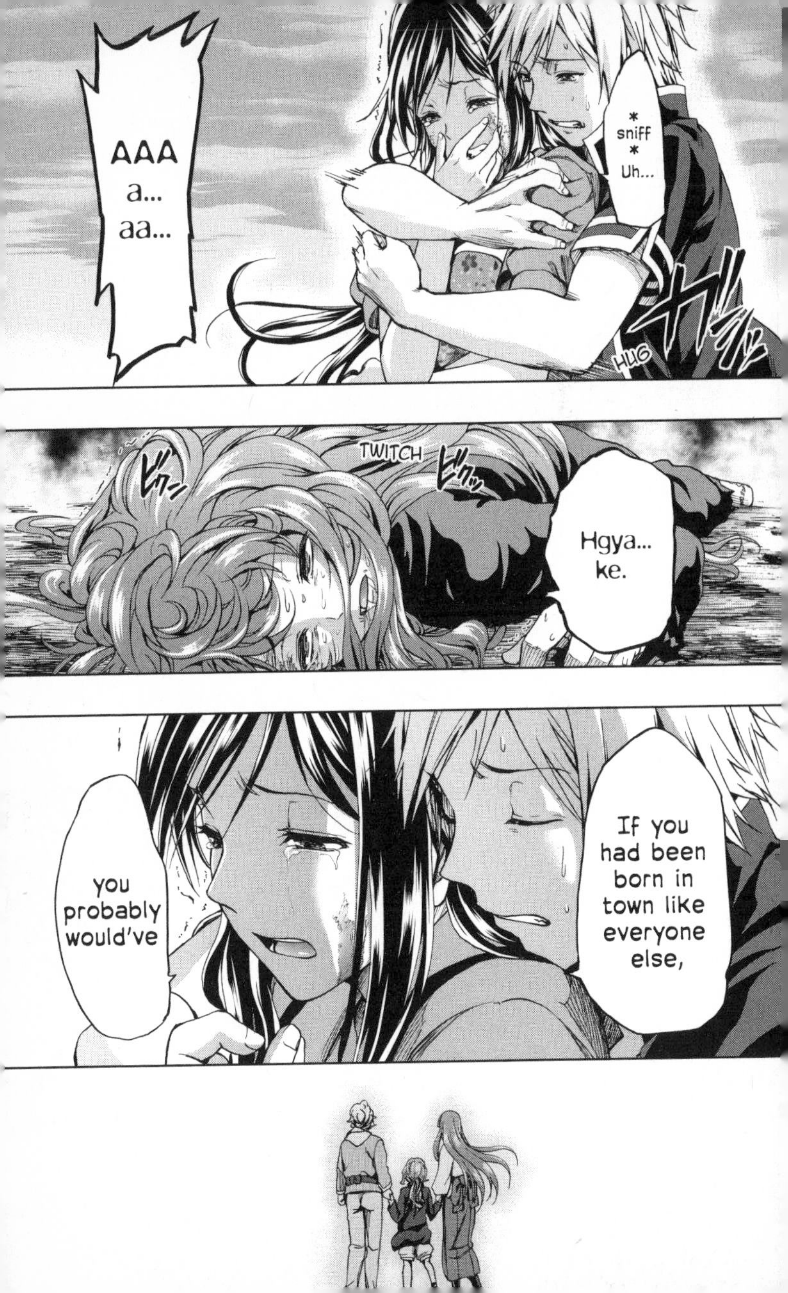
* sniff * Uh...
HUG
AAA a... aa...
Hgya... ke.
TWITCH
If you had been born in town like everyone else,
you probably would've

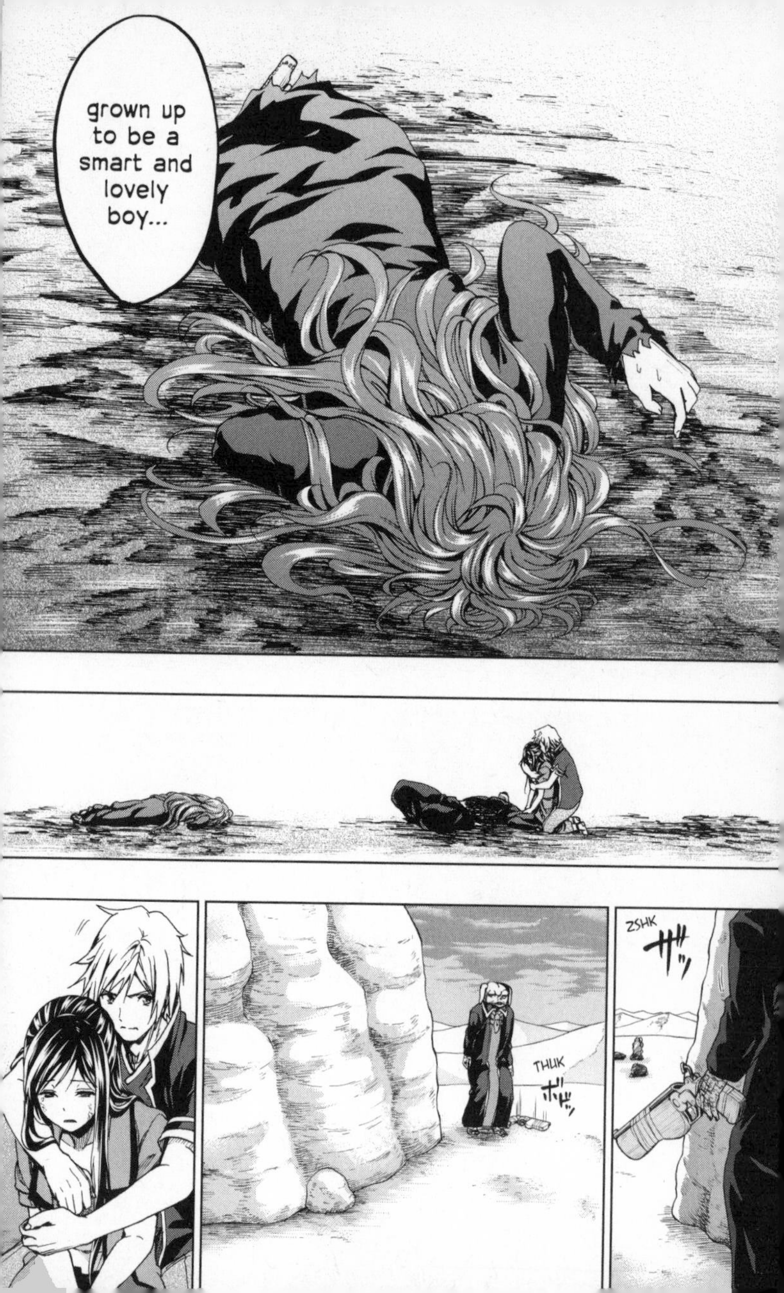
grown up to be a smart and lovely boy...
ZSHK
ザッ
THUK
ボドッ

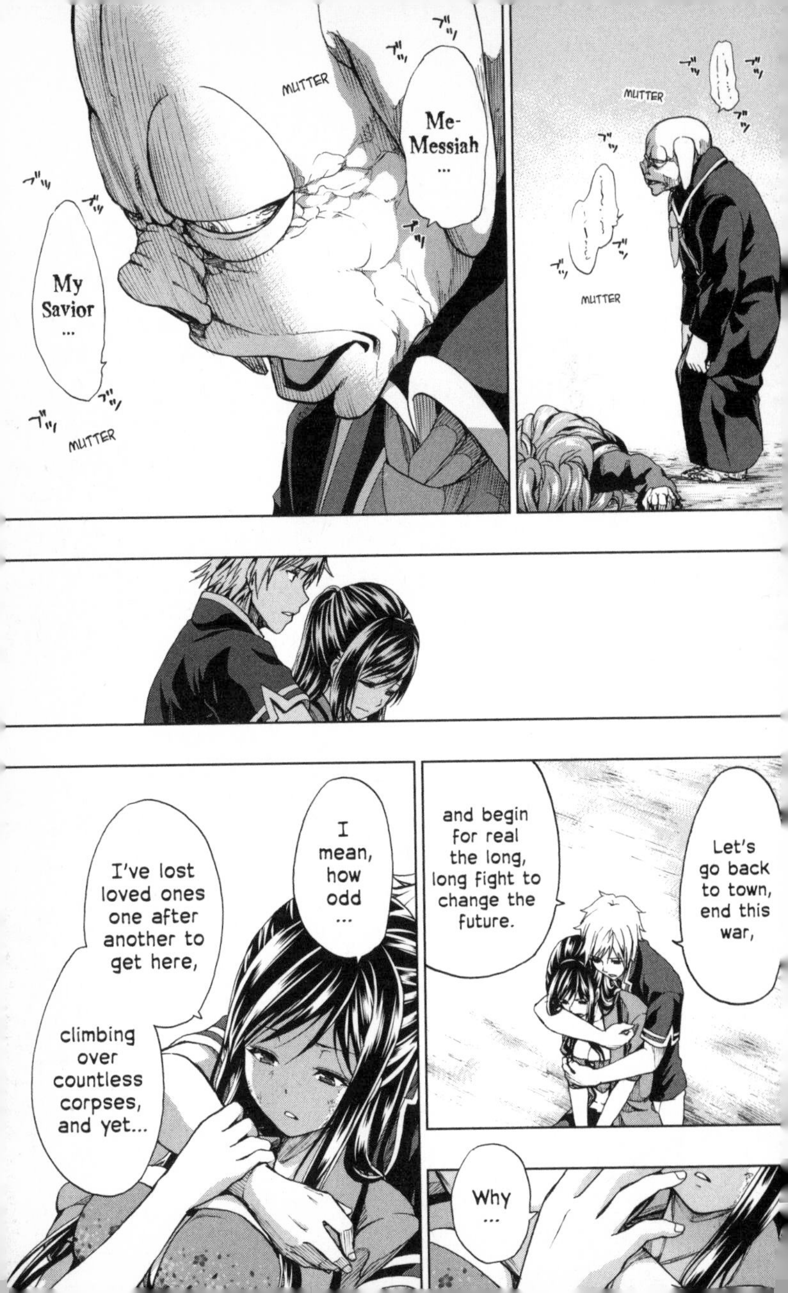
MUTTER
MUTTER
Me- Messiah ...
MUTTER
My Savior ...
MUTTER
Let's go back to town, end this war,
and begin for real the long, long fight to change the future.
Why ...
I mean, how odd ...
I've lost loved ones one after another to get here,
climbing over countless corpses, and yet...

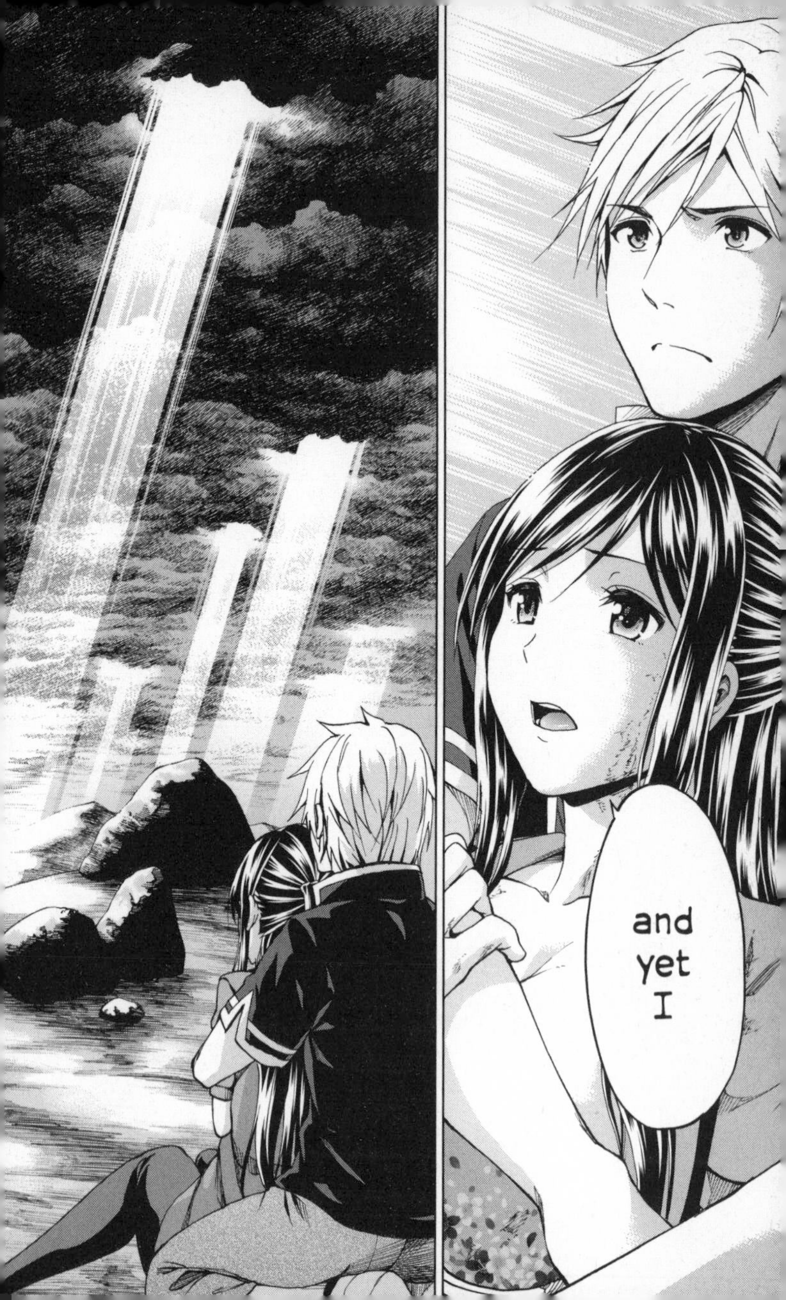
and yet I

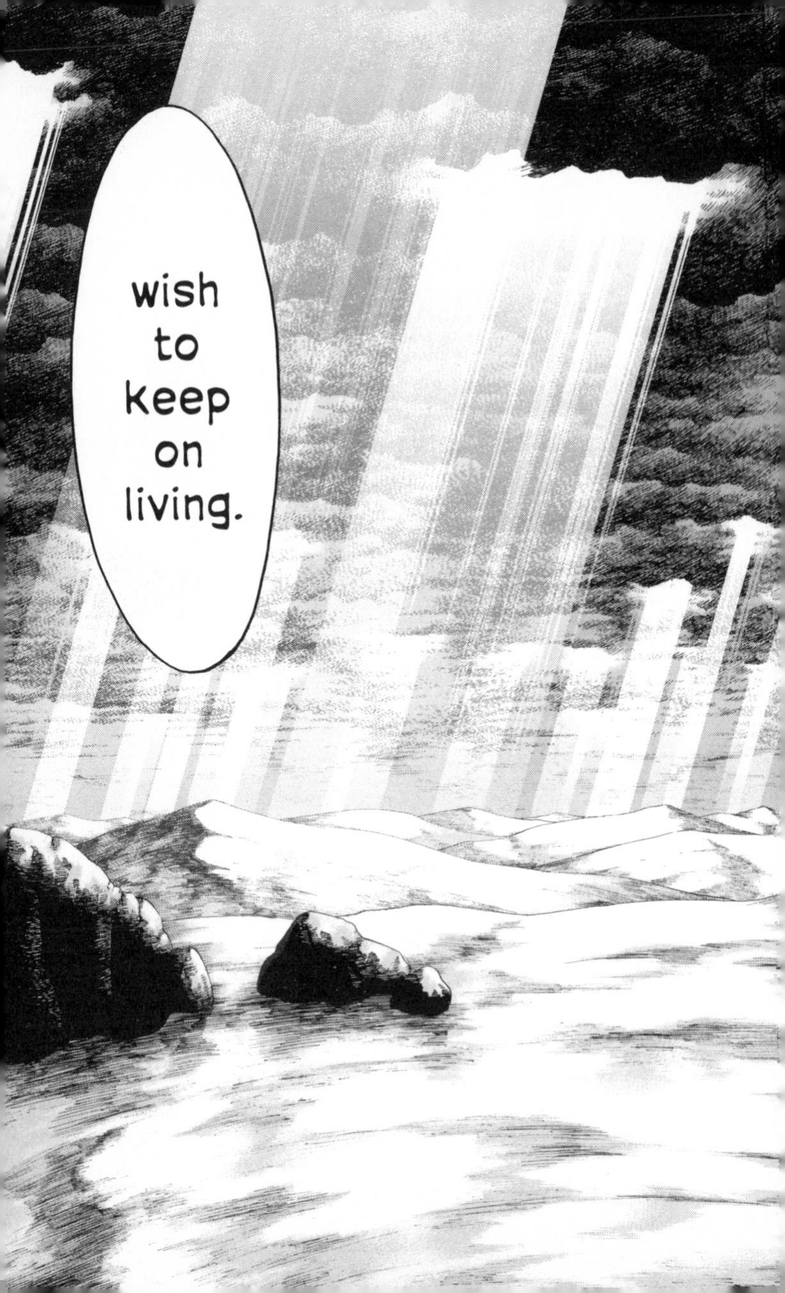
wish to keep on living.

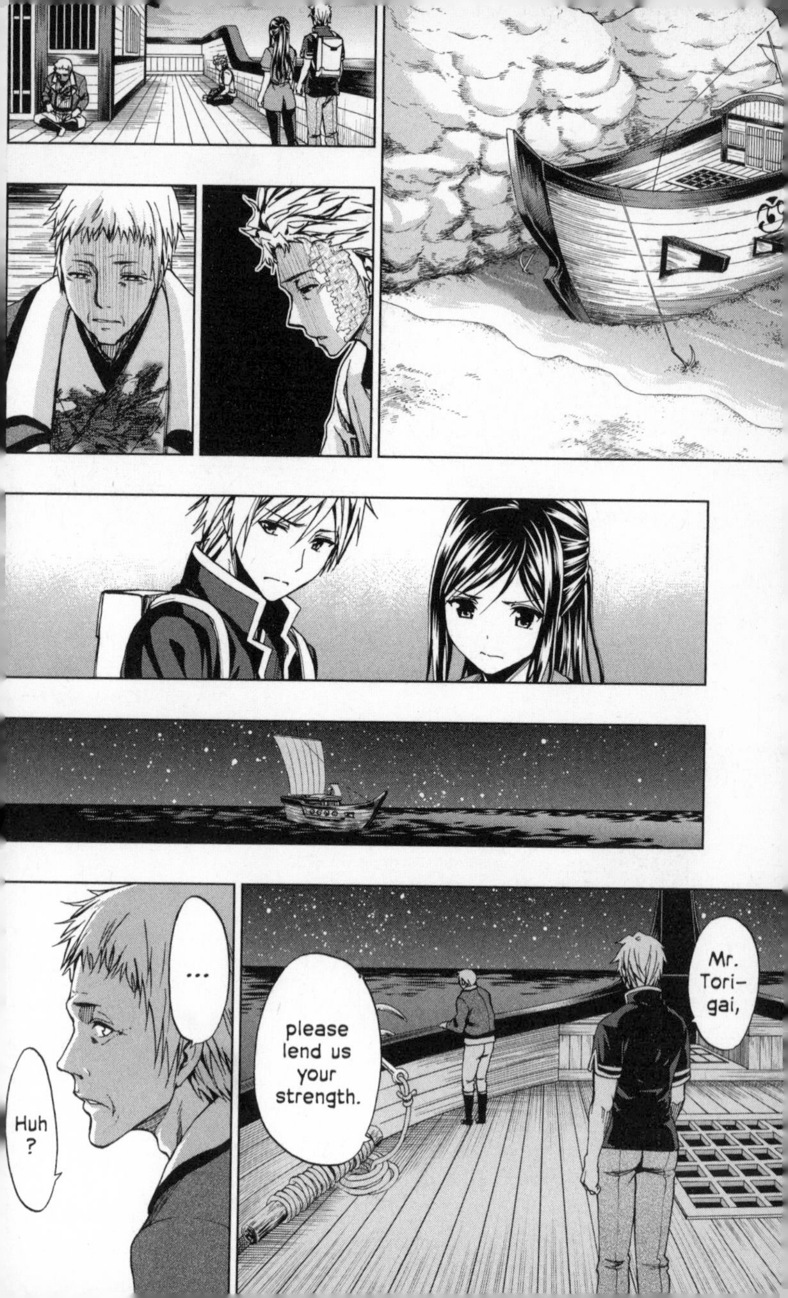
Mr. Tori-gai,
please lend us your strength.
...
Huh?

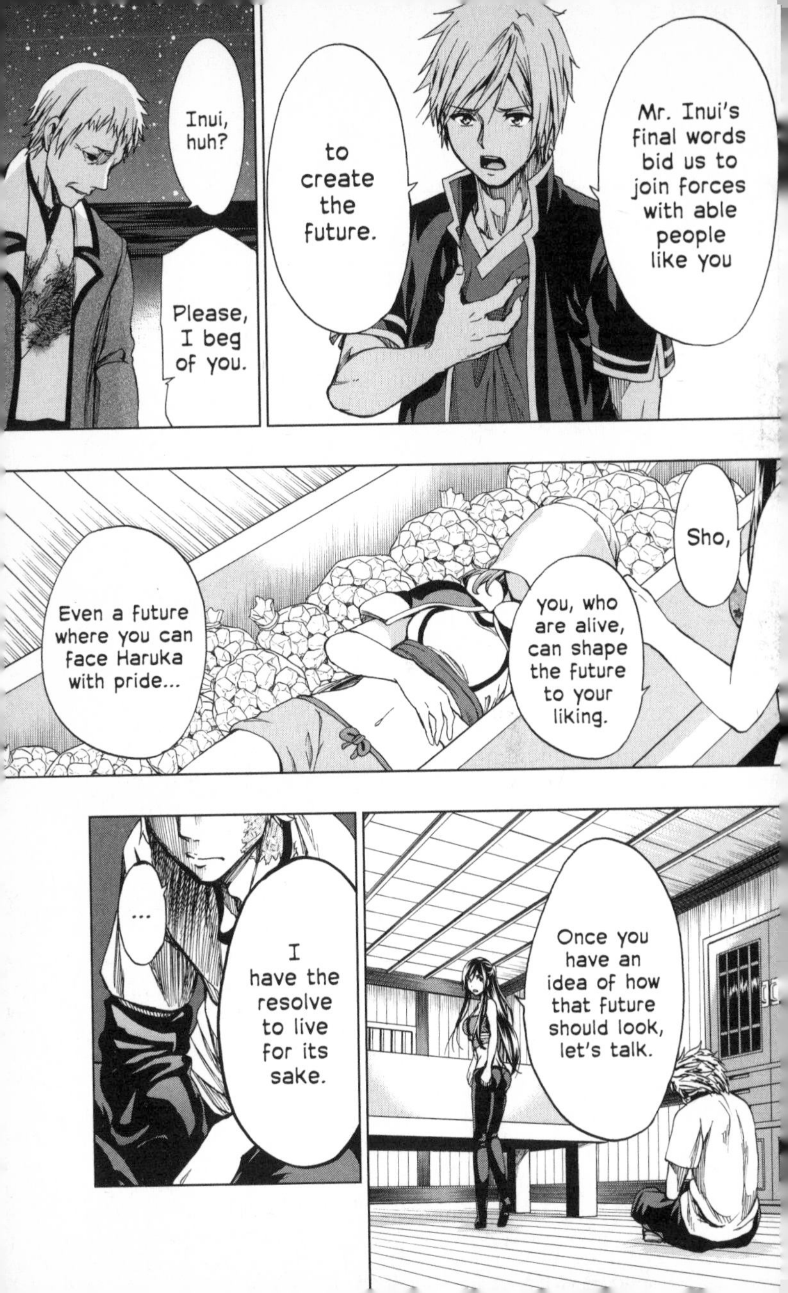
Mr. Inui's final words bid us to join forces with able people like you
to create the future.
Inui, huh?
Please, I beg of you.
Sho,
you, who are alive, can shape the future to your liking.
Even a future where you can face Haruka with pride...
Once you have an idea of how that future should look, let's talk.
I have the resolve to live for its sake.
...

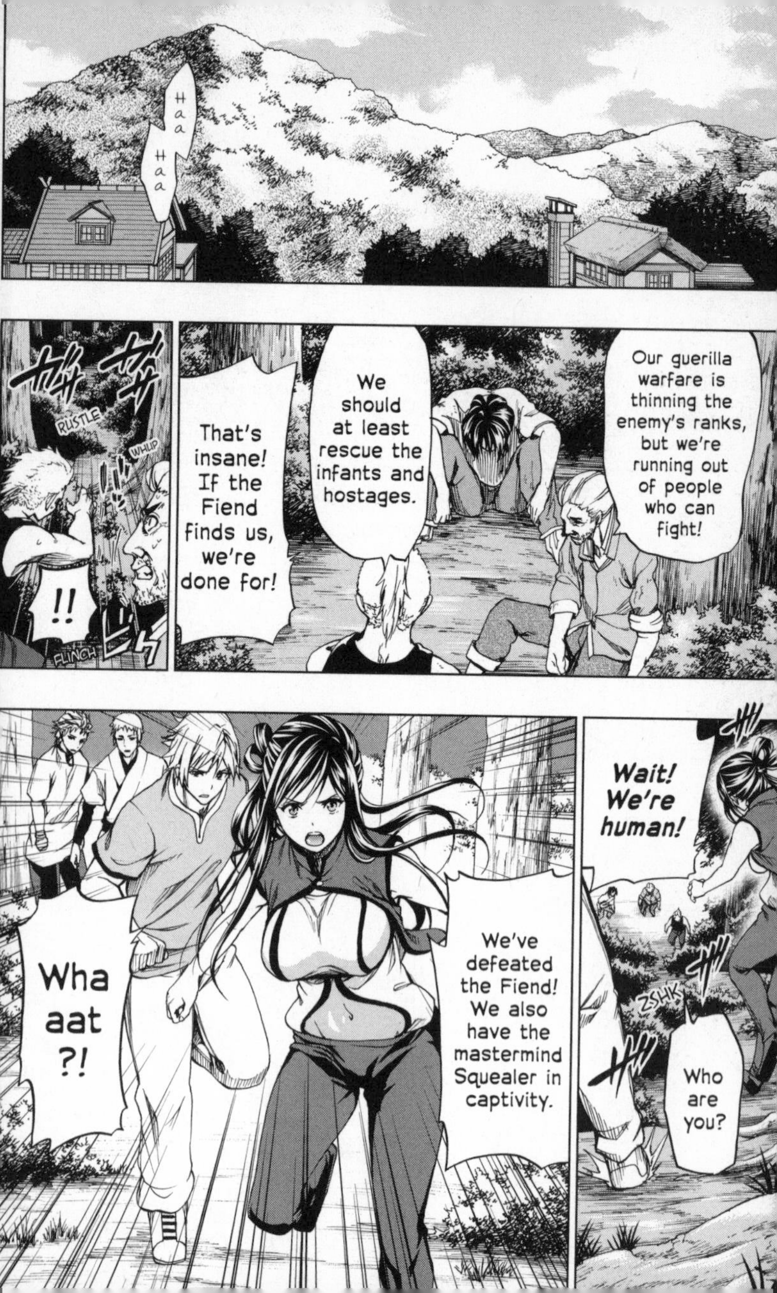
Haa Haa
Our guerilla warfare is thinning the enemy's ranks, but we're running out of people who can fight!
We should at least rescue the infants and hostages.
That's insane! If the Fiend finds us, we're done for!
RUSTLE
WHUP
!!
FLINCH
Wait! We're human!
ZSHK
Who are you?
We've defeated the Fiend! We also have the mastermind Squealer in captivity.
Whaaat?!

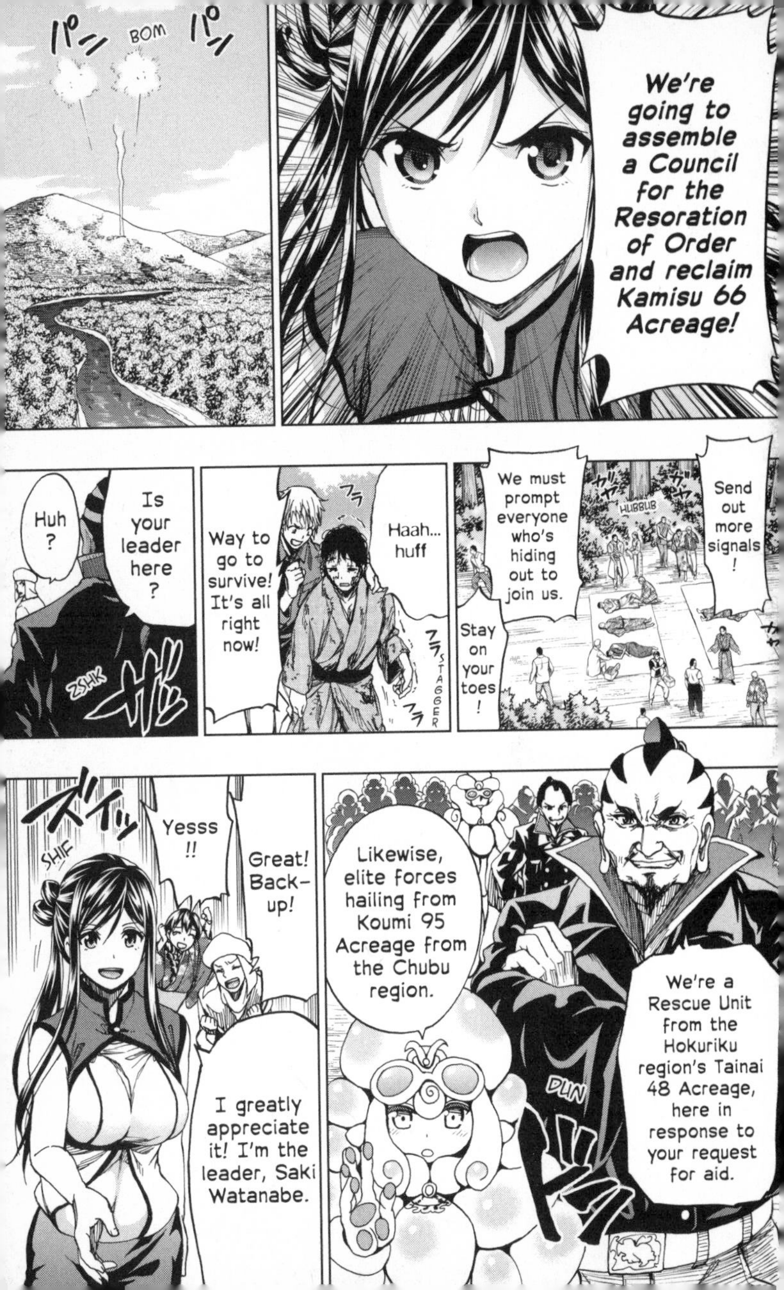
We're going to assemble a Council for the Resoration of Order and reclaim Kamisu 66 Acreage!
BOM
Send out more signals!
HUBBUB
We must prompt everyone who's hiding out to join us.
Stay on your toes!
Haah... huff
Way to go to survive! It's all right now!
STAGGER
Is your leader here?
Huh?
ZSHK
We're a Rescue Unit from the Hokuriku region's Tainai 48 Acreage, here in response to your request for aid.
DUN
Likewise, elite forces hailing from Koumi 95 Acreage from the Chubu region.
Great! Back-up!
Yesss!!
SHIF
I greatly appreciate it! I'm the leader, Saki Watanabe.

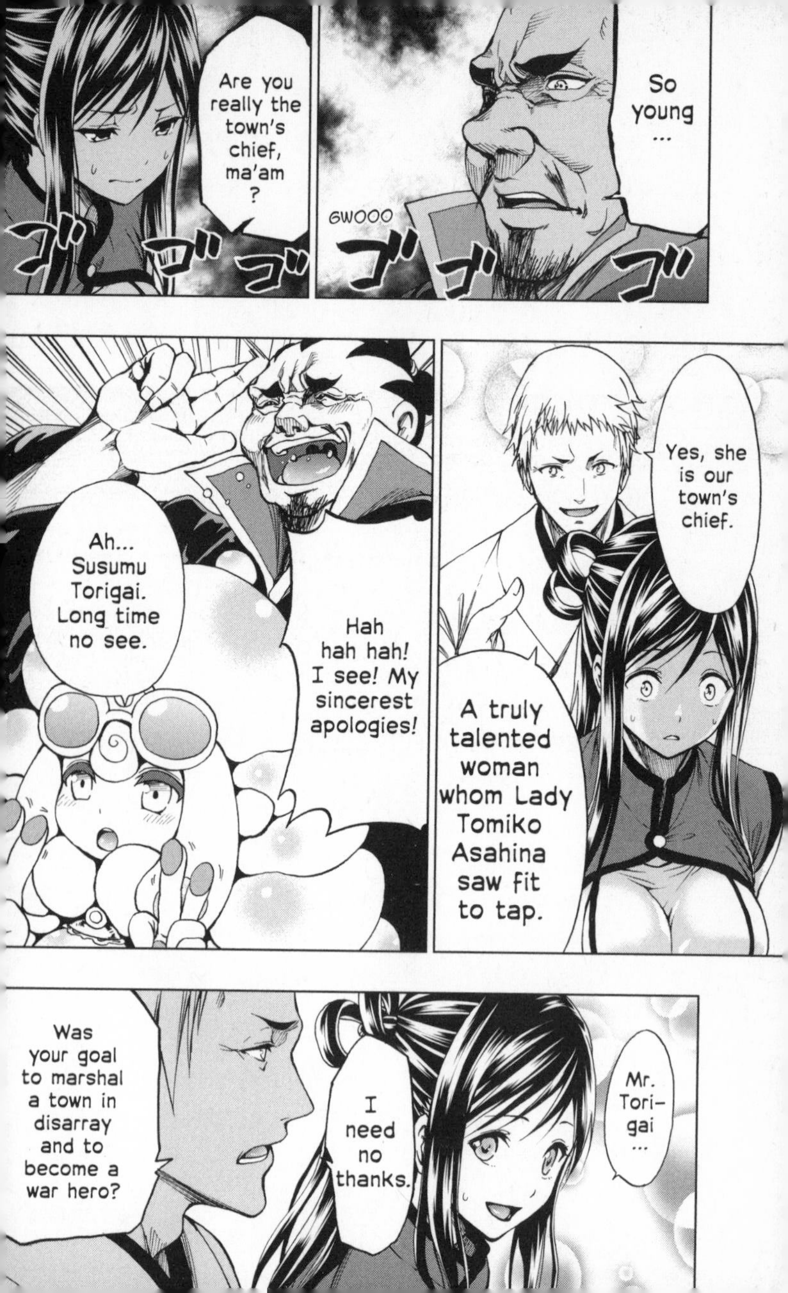
So young ...
GWOOO
Are you really the town's chief, ma'am ?
Yes, she is our town's chief.
A truly talented woman whom Lady Tomiko Asahina saw fit to tap.
Hah hah hah! I see! My sincerest apologies!
Ah... Susumu Torigai. Long time no see.
Mr. Tori-gai ...
I need no thanks.
Was your goal to marshal a town in disarray and to become a war hero?

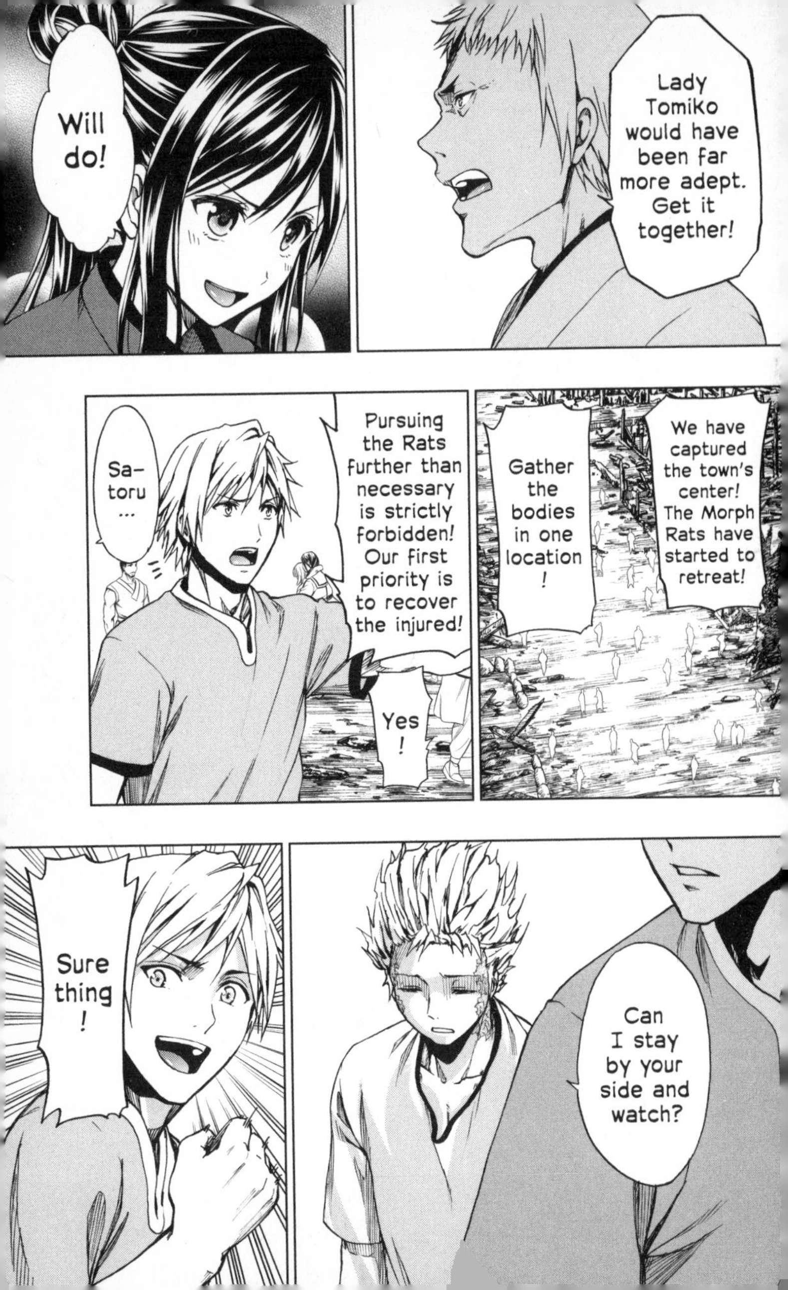
Lady Tomiko would have been far more adept. Get it together!
Will do!
We have captured the town's center! The Morph Rats have started to retreat!
Gather the bodies in one location!
Pursuing the Rats further than necessary is strictly forbidden! Our first priority is to recover the injured!
Sa-toru...
Yes!
Can I stay by your side and watch?
Sure thing!

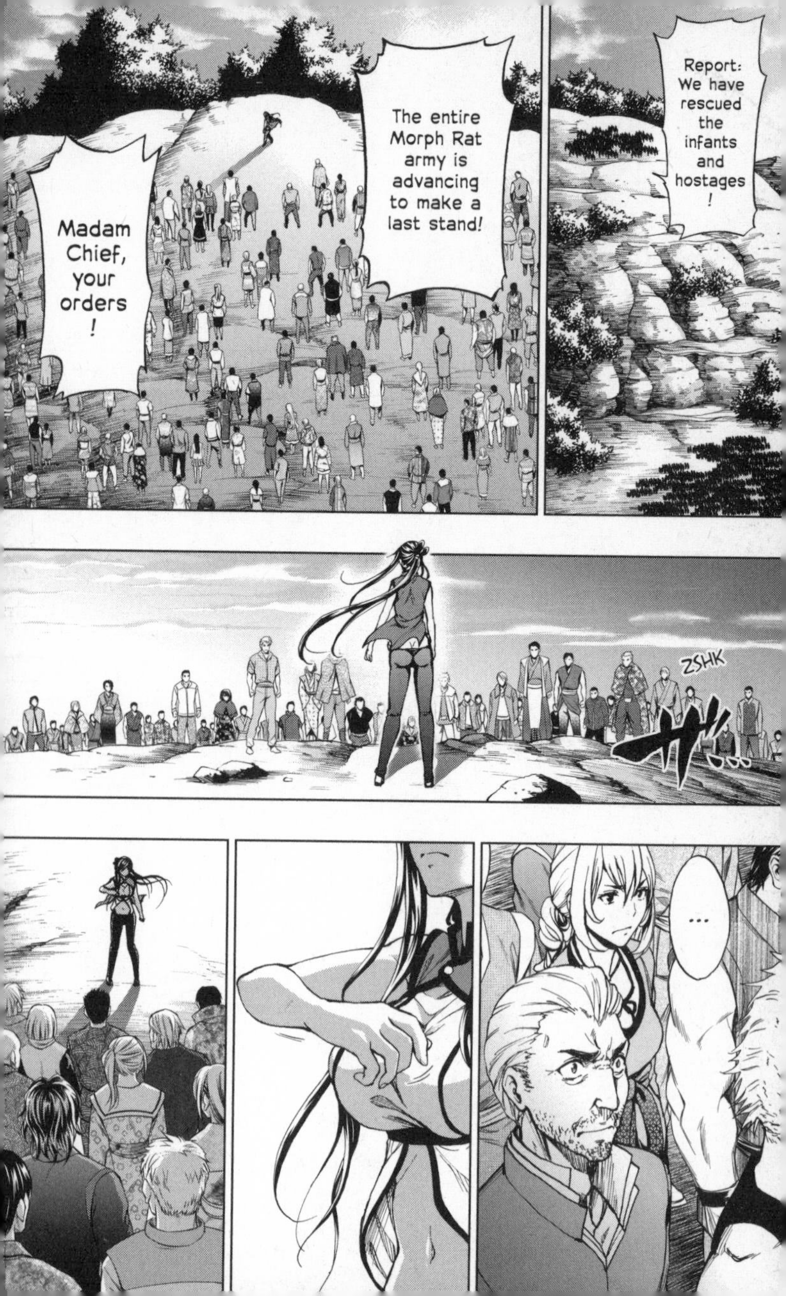
Report: We have rescued the infants and hostages!
The entire Morph Rat army is advancing to make a last stand!
Madam Chief, your orders!
ZSHK
...

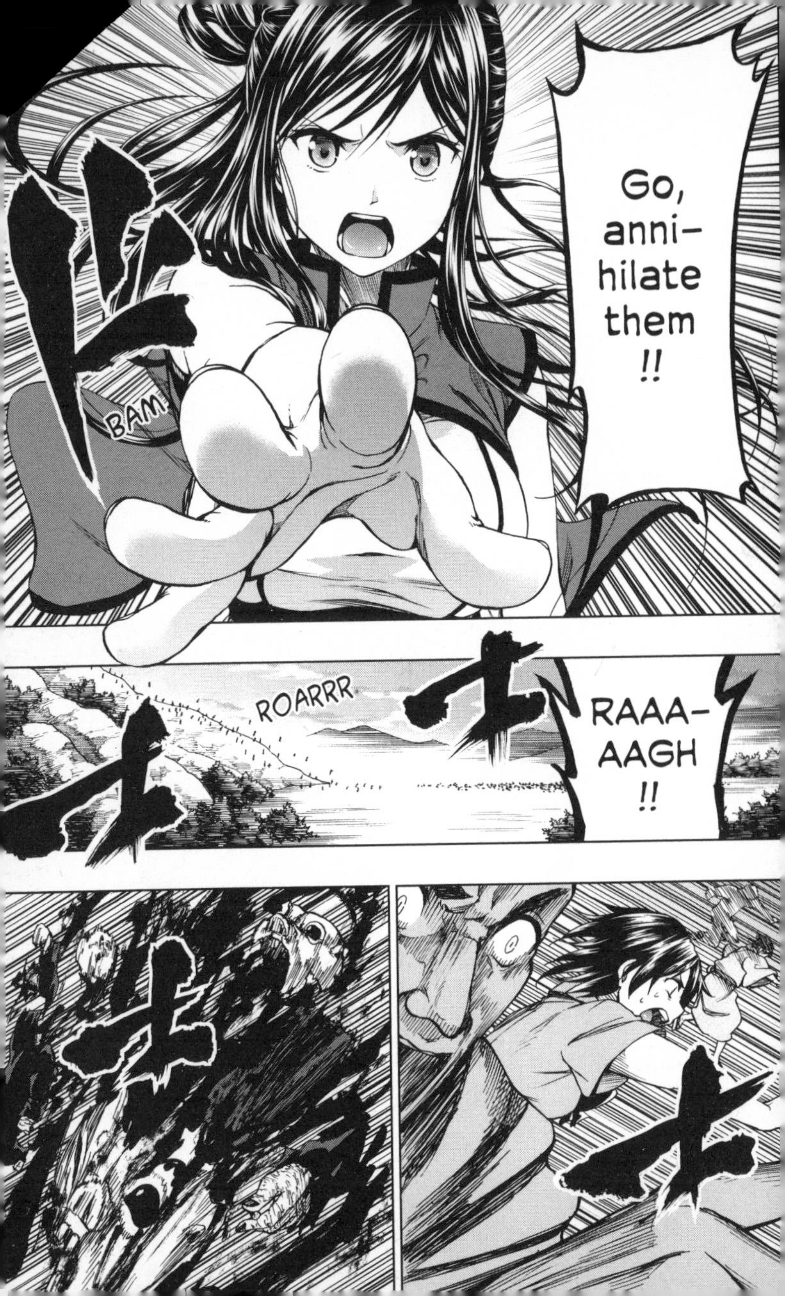
Go, anni-hilate them !!
BAM
RAAA-AAGH !!
ROARRR

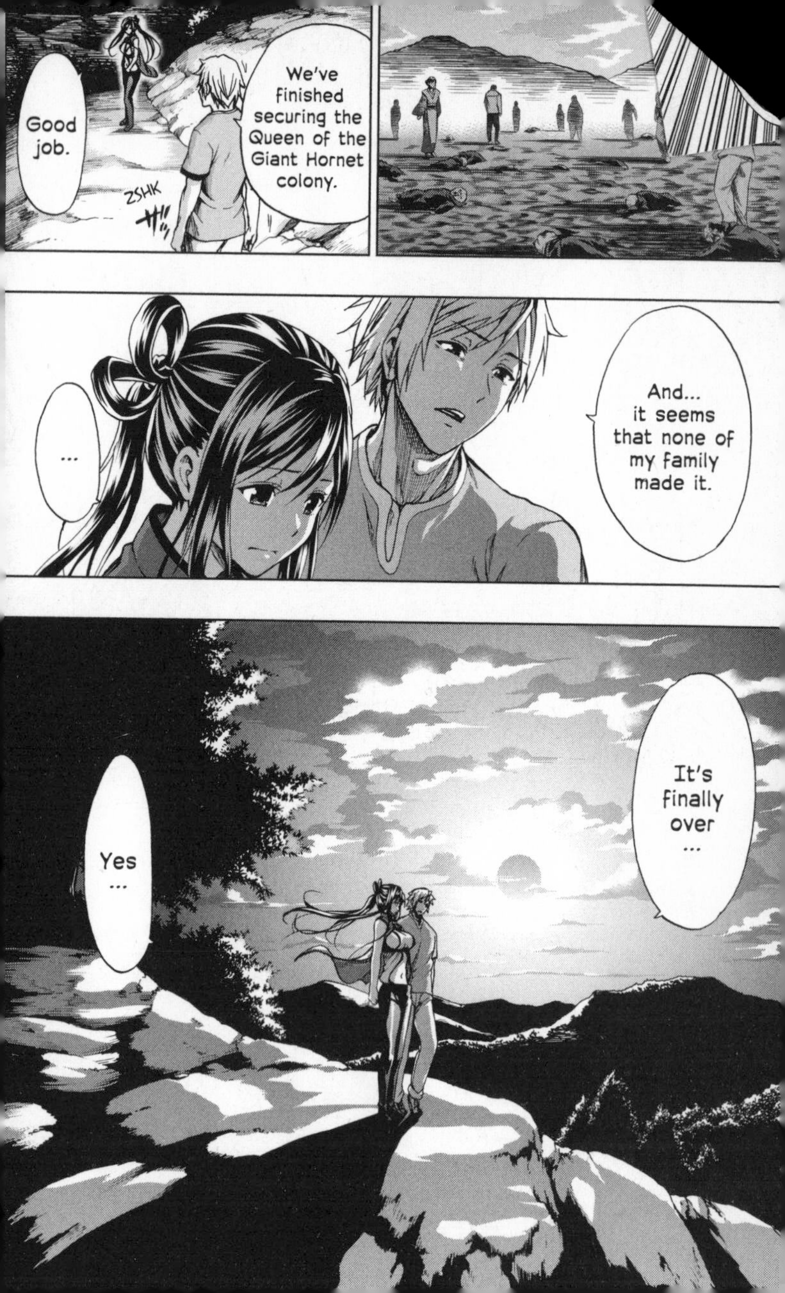
We've finished securing the Queen of the Giant Hornet colony.
ZSHK
Good job.
And... it seems that none of my family made it.
...
It's finally over ...
Yes ...

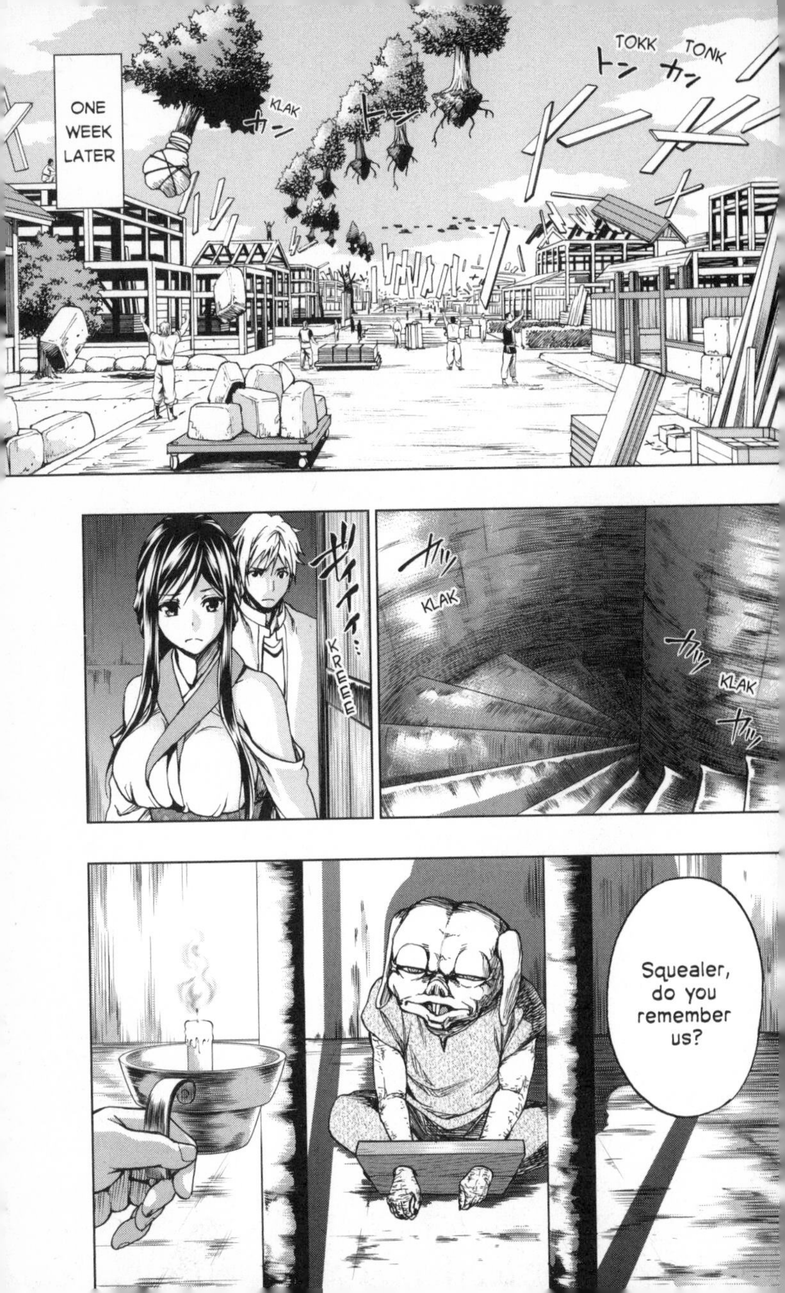

TOKK
TONK
KLAK
ONE WEEK LATER
KLAK
KLAK
KREEEE...
Squealer, do you remember us?

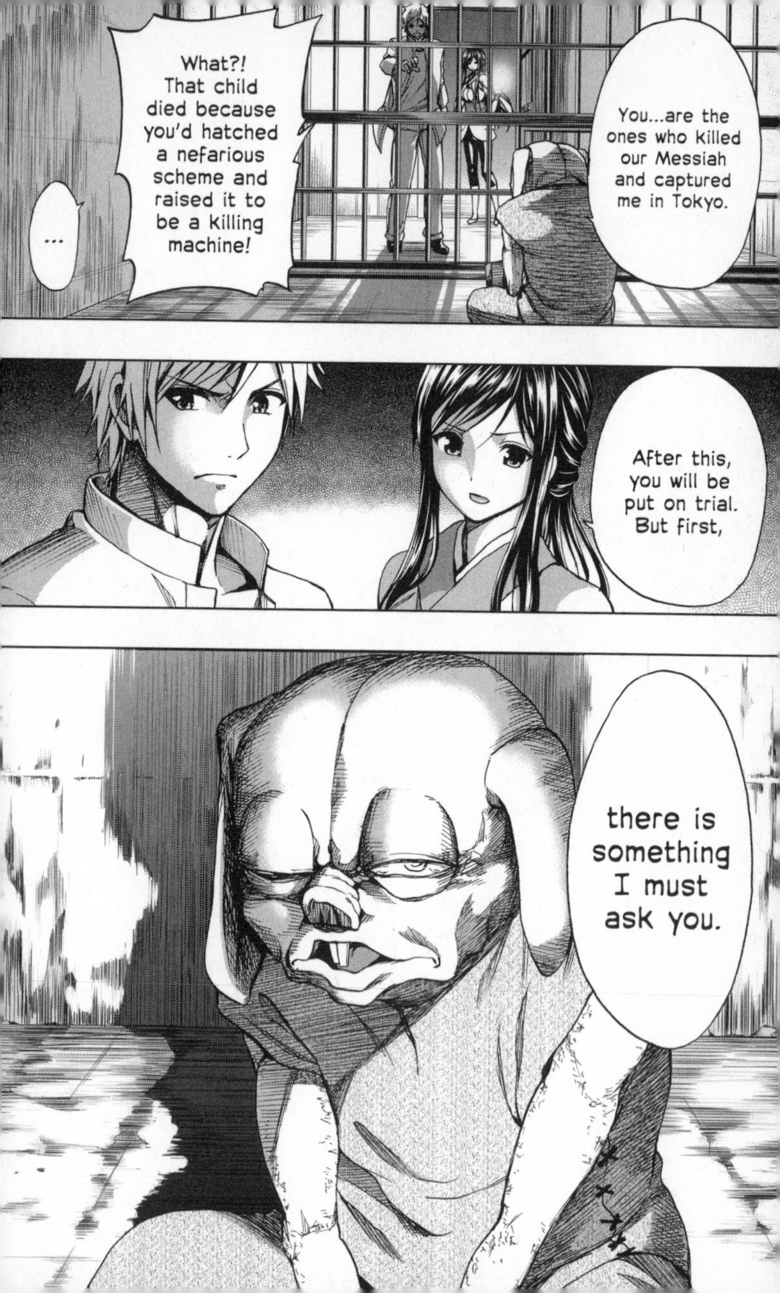
You...are the ones who killed our Messiah and captured me in Tokyo.
What?! That child died because you'd hatched a nefarious scheme and raised it to be a killing machine!
...
After this, you will be put on trial. But first,
there is something I must ask you.

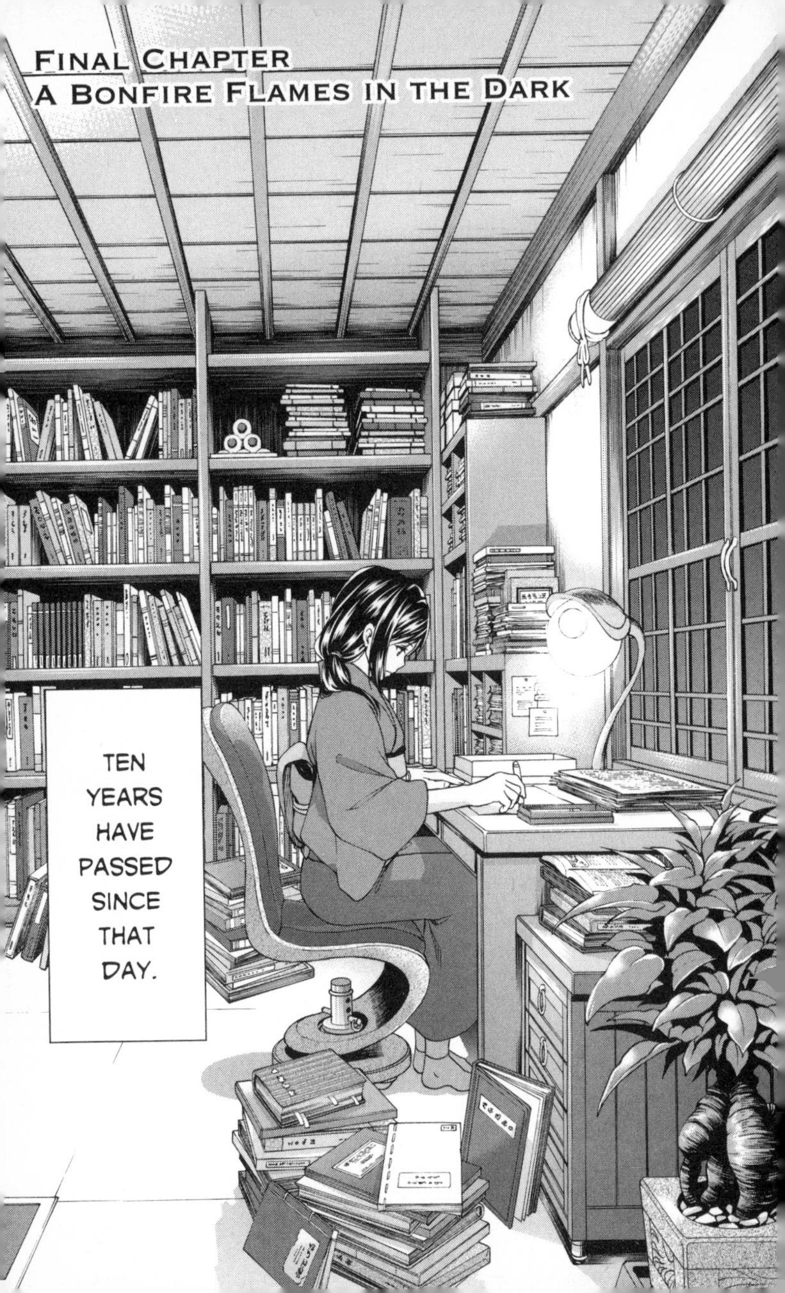
Final Chapter
A Bonfire Flames in the Dark
TEN YEARS HAVE PASSED SINCE THAT DAY.

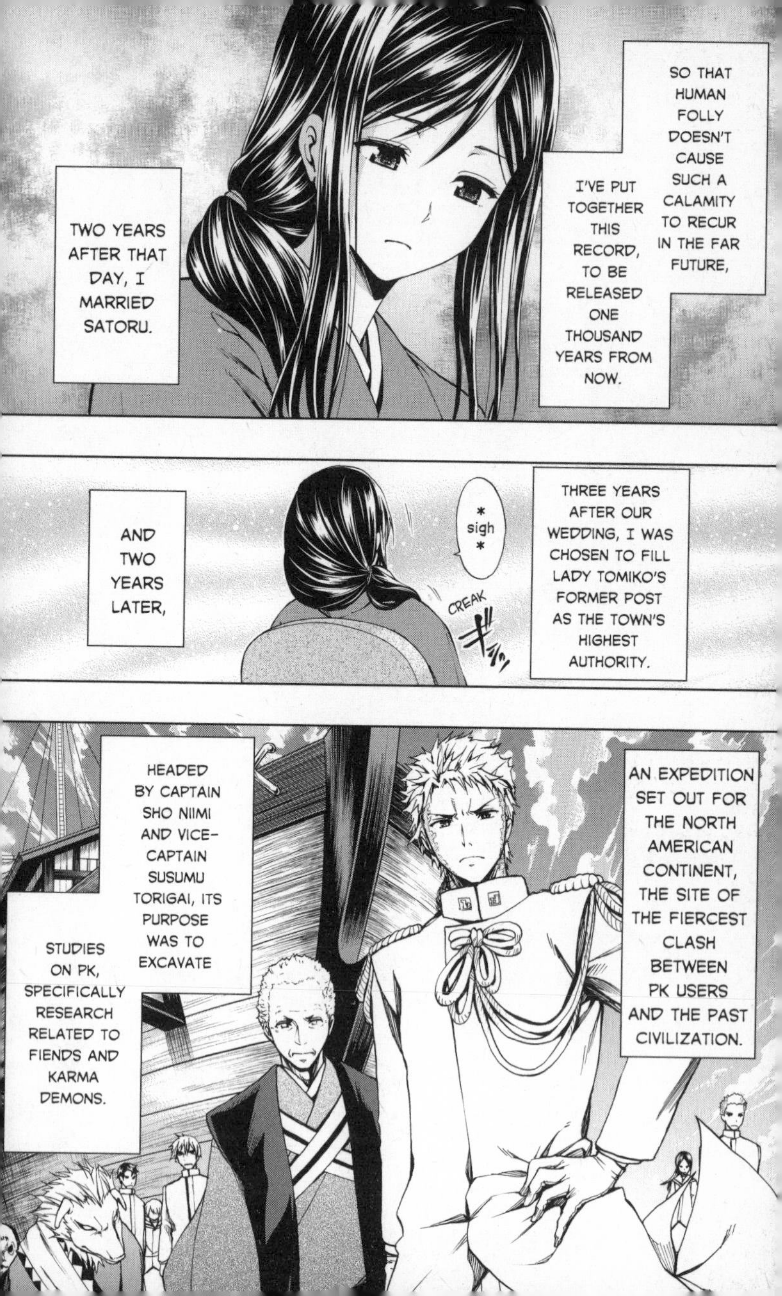
SO THAT HUMAN FOLLY DOESN'T CAUSE SUCH A CALAMITY TO RECUR IN THE FAR FUTURE,
I'VE PUT TOGETHER THIS RECORD, TO BE RELEASED ONE THOUSAND YEARS FROM NOW.
TWO YEARS AFTER THAT DAY, I MARRIED SATORU.
THREE YEARS AFTER OUR WEDDING, I WAS CHOSEN TO FILL LADY TOMIKO'S FORMER POST AS THE TOWN'S HIGHEST AUTHORITY.
* sigh *
CREAK
AND TWO YEARS LATER,
AN EXPEDITION SET OUT FOR THE NORTH AMERICAN CONTINENT, THE SITE OF THE FIERCEST CLASH BETWEEN PK USERS AND THE PAST CIVILIZATION.
HEADED BY CAPTAIN SHO NIIMI AND VICE-CAPTAIN SUSUMU TORIGAI, ITS PURPOSE WAS TO EXCAVATE
STUDIES ON PK, SPECIFICALLY RESEARCH RELATED TO FIENDS AND KARMA DEMONS.

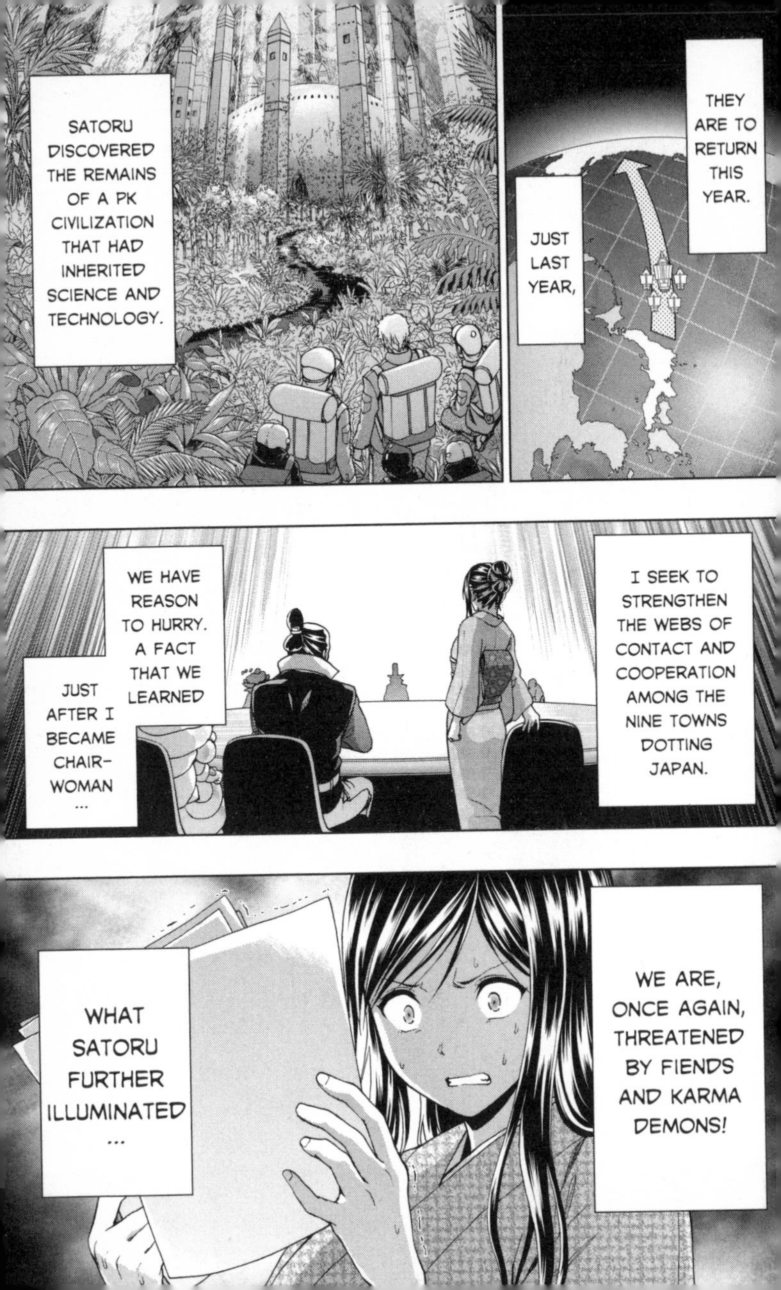
THEY ARE TO RETURN THIS YEAR.
JUST LAST YEAR,
SATORU DISCOVERED THE REMAINS OF A PK CIVILIZATION THAT HAD INHERITED SCIENCE AND TECHNOLOGY.
I SEEK TO STRENGTHEN THE WEBS OF CONTACT AND COOPERATION AMONG THE NINE TOWNS DOTTING JAPAN.
WE HAVE REASON TO HURRY. A FACT THAT WE LEARNED
JUST AFTER I BECAME CHAIR-WOMAN ...
WE ARE, ONCE AGAIN, THREATENED BY FIENDS AND KARMA DEMONS!
WHAT SATORU FURTHER ILLUMINATED ...

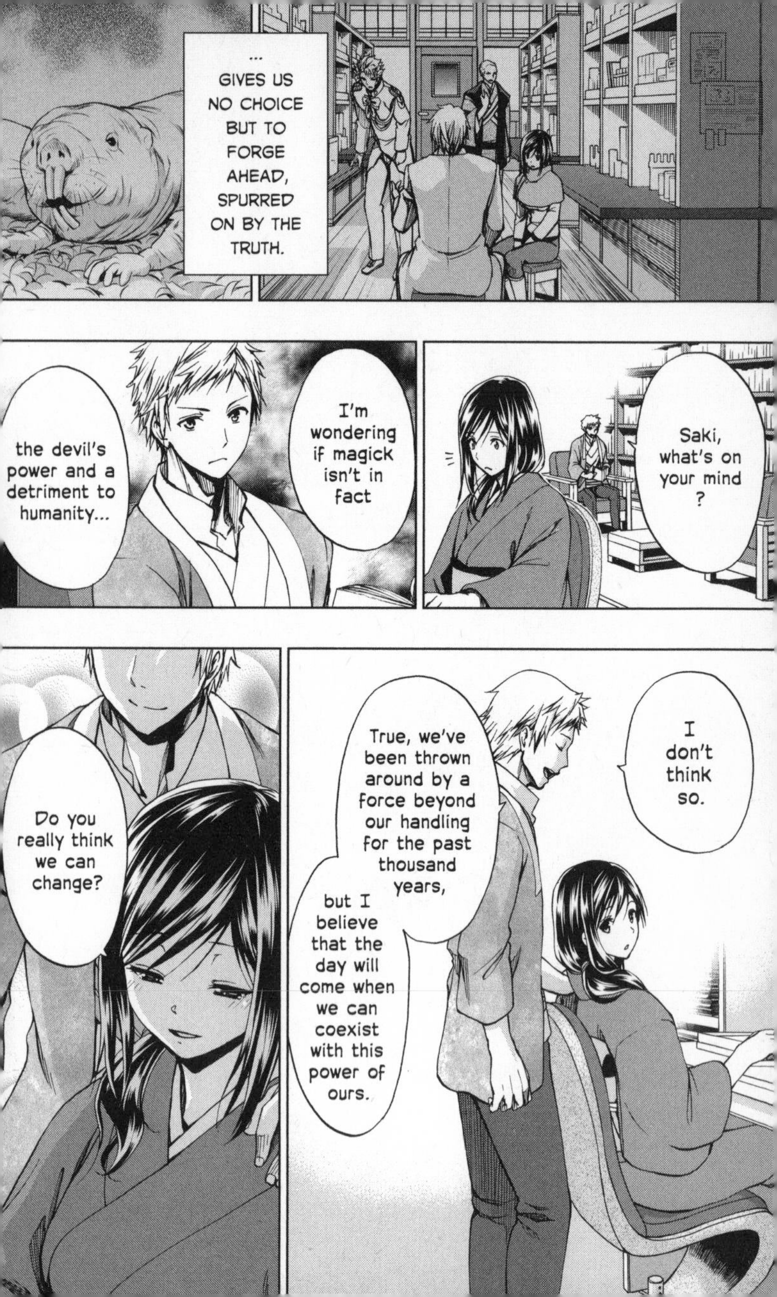
... GIVES US NO CHOICE BUT TO FORGE AHEAD, SPURRED ON BY THE TRUTH.
Saki, what's on your mind?
I'm wondering if magick isn't in fact
the devil's power and a detriment to humanity...
I don't think so.
True, we've been thrown around by a force beyond our handling for the past thousand years,
but I believe that the day will come when we can coexist with this power of ours.
Do you really think we can change?

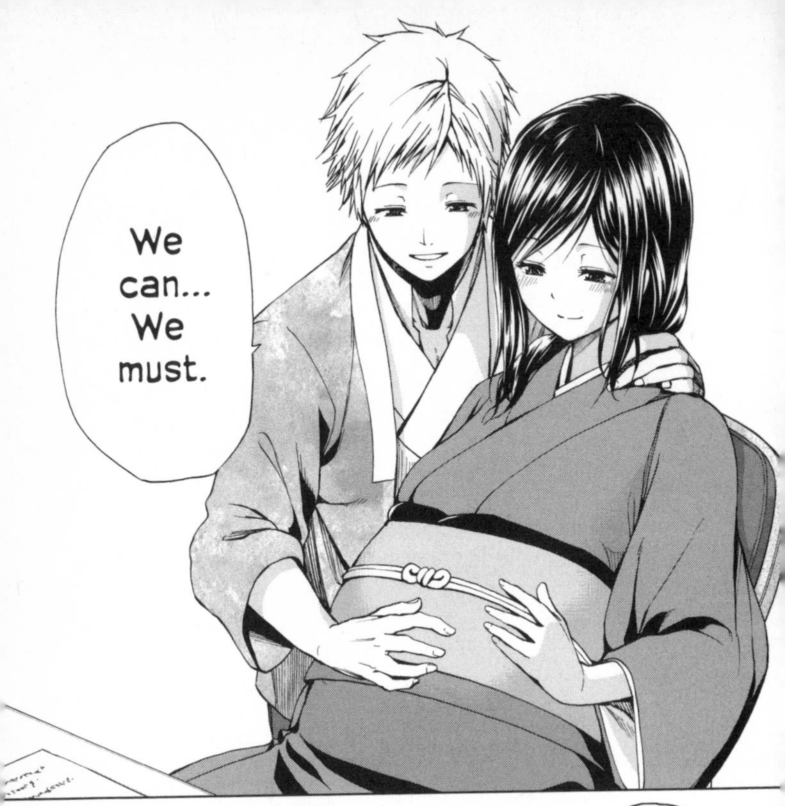
We can... We must.

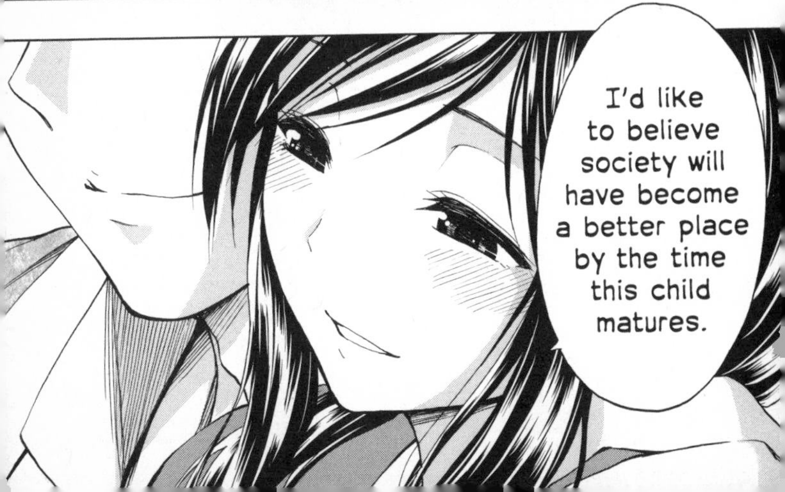
I'd like to believe society will have become a better place by the time this child matures.

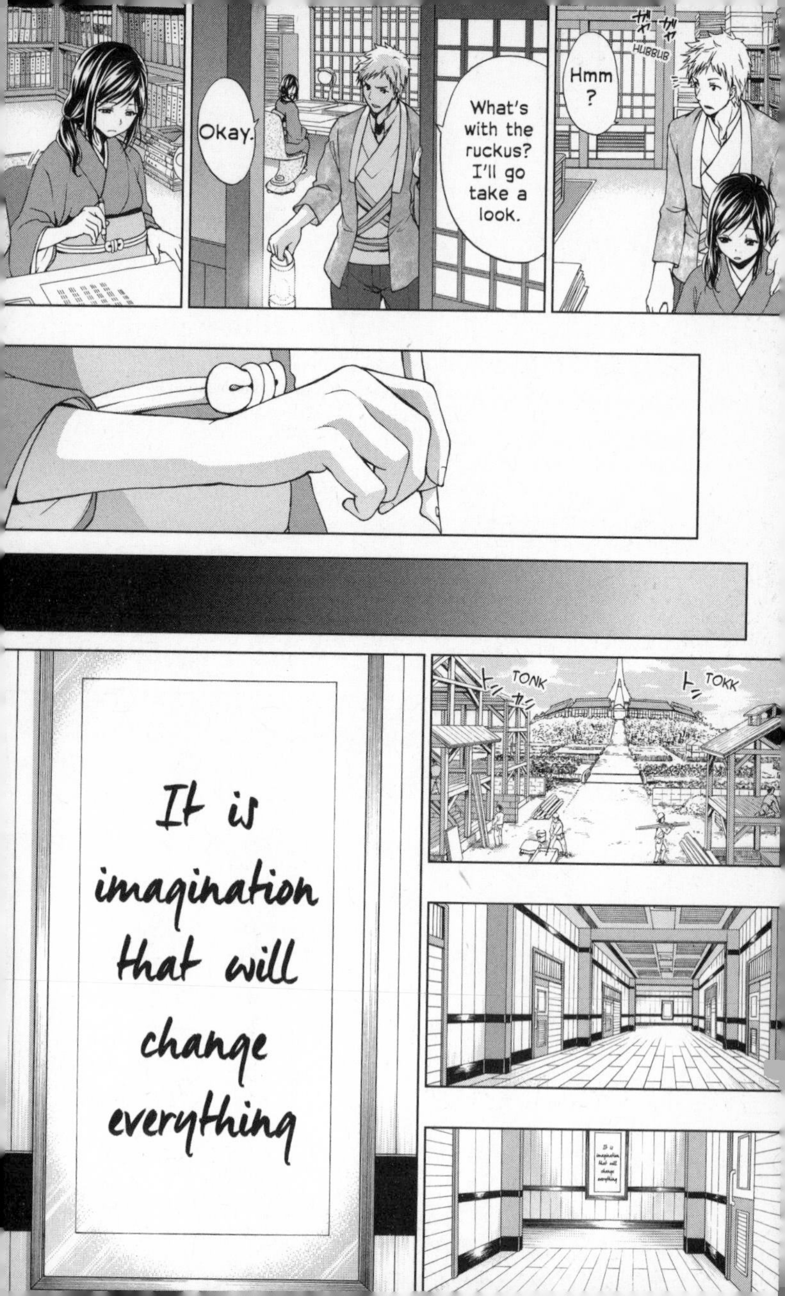
HUBBUB
Hmm?
What's with the ruckus? I'll go take a look.
Okay.
TOKK
TONK
It is imagination that will change everything

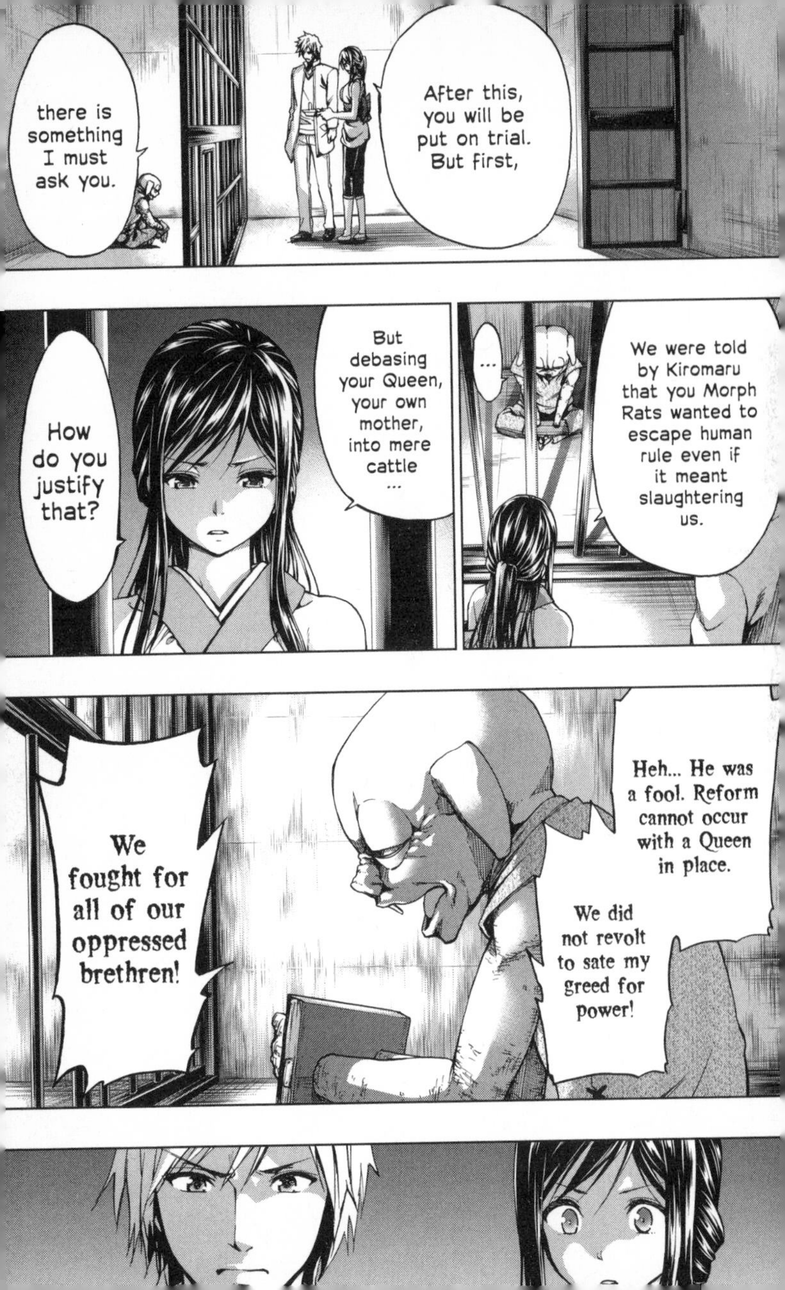
After this, you will be put on trial. But first,
there is something I must ask you.
We were told by Kiromaru that you Morph Rats wanted to escape human rule even if it meant slaughtering us.
...
But debasing your Queen, your own mother, into mere cattle ...
How do you justify that?
Heh... He was a fool. Reform cannot occur with a Queen in place.
We did not revolt to sate my greed for power!
We fought for all of our oppressed brethren!

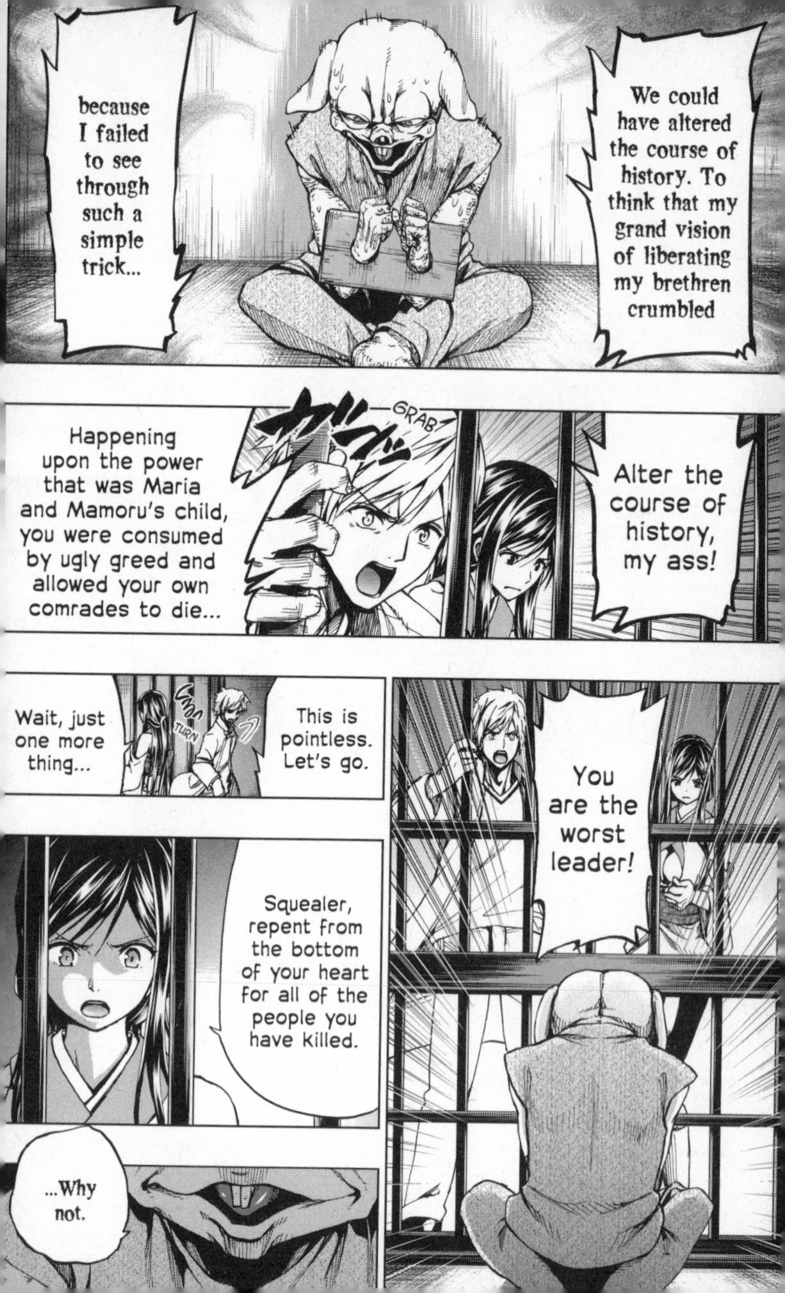

We could have altered the course of history. To think that my grand vision of liberating my brethren crumbled
because I failed to see through such a simple trick...
Alter the course of history, my ass!
GRAB
Happening upon the power that was Maria and Mamoru's child, you were consumed by ugly greed and allowed your own comrades to die...
You are the worst leader!
This is pointless. Let's go.
TURN
Wait, just one more thing...
Squealer, repent from the bottom of your heart for all of the people you have killed.
...Why not.

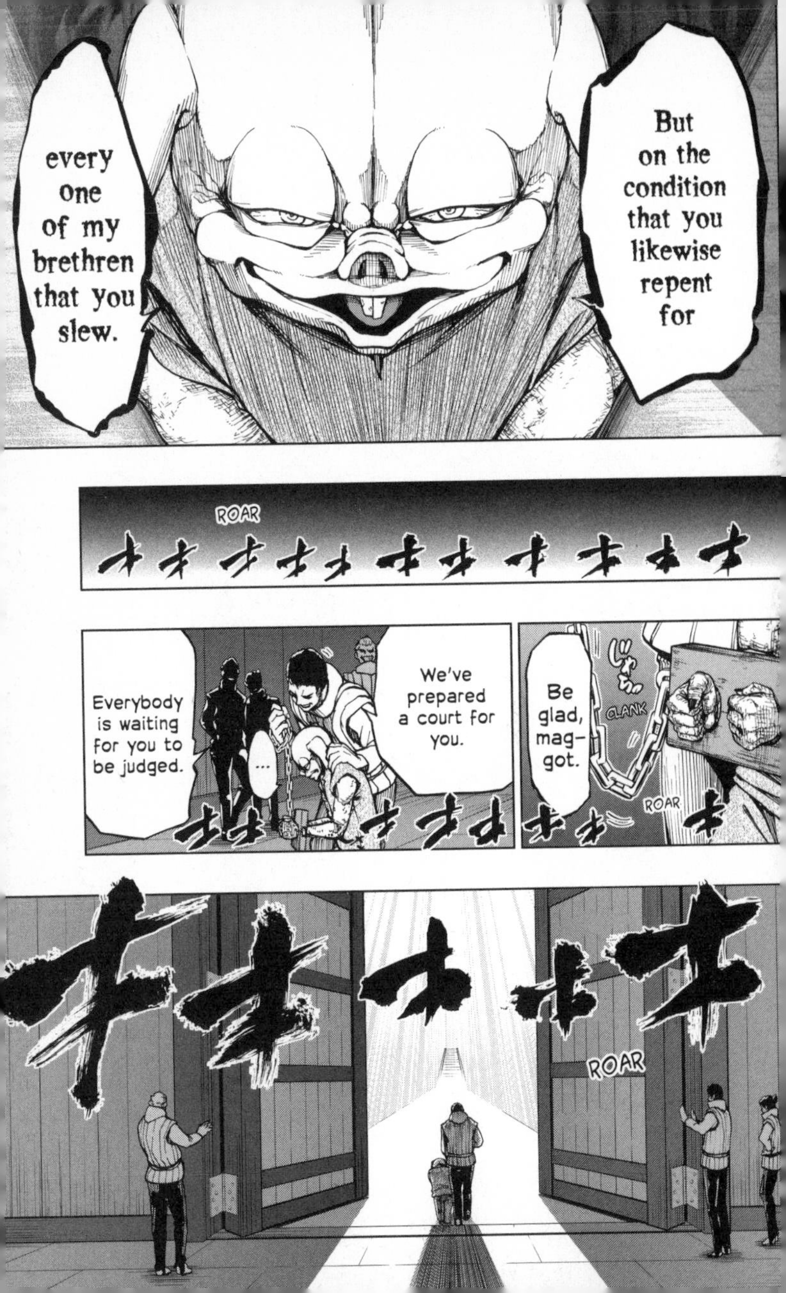
But on the condition that you likewise repent for
every one of my brethren that you slew.
ROAR
Be glad, maggot.
CLANK
ROAR
We've prepared a court for you.
...
Everybody is waiting for you to be judged.
ROAR

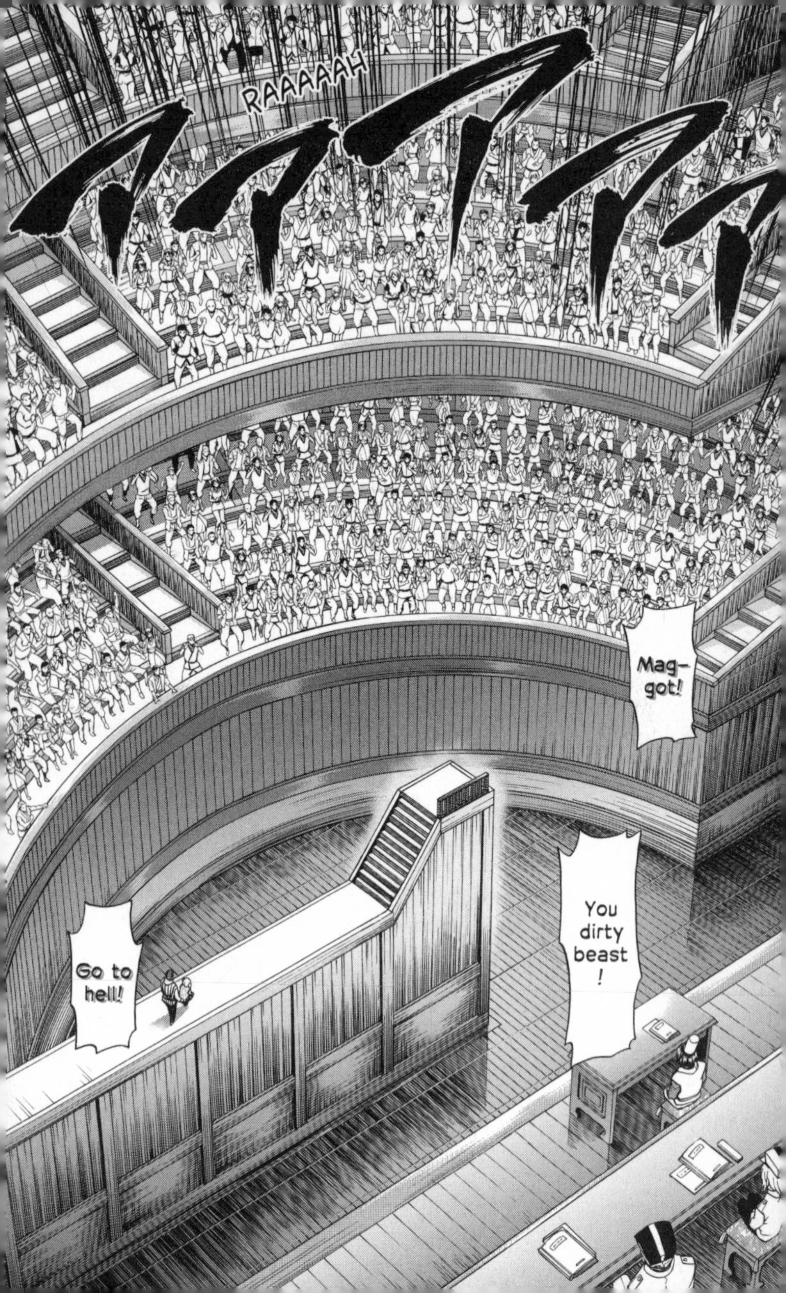
RAAAAAH
Mag-got!
You dirty beast!
Go to hell!

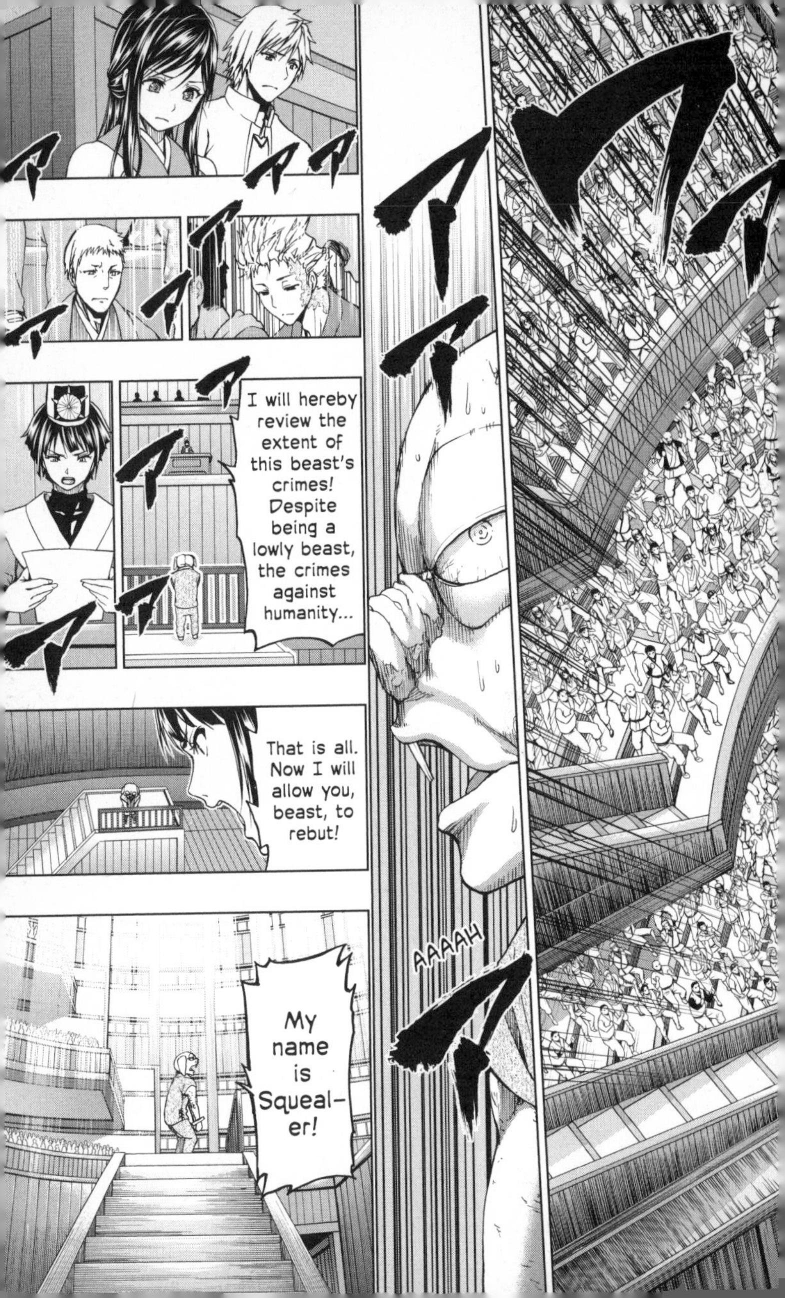

AAAAH
I will hereby review the extent of this beast's crimes! Despite being a lowly beast, the crimes against humanity...
That is all. Now I will allow you, beast, to rebut!
My name is Squeal-er!

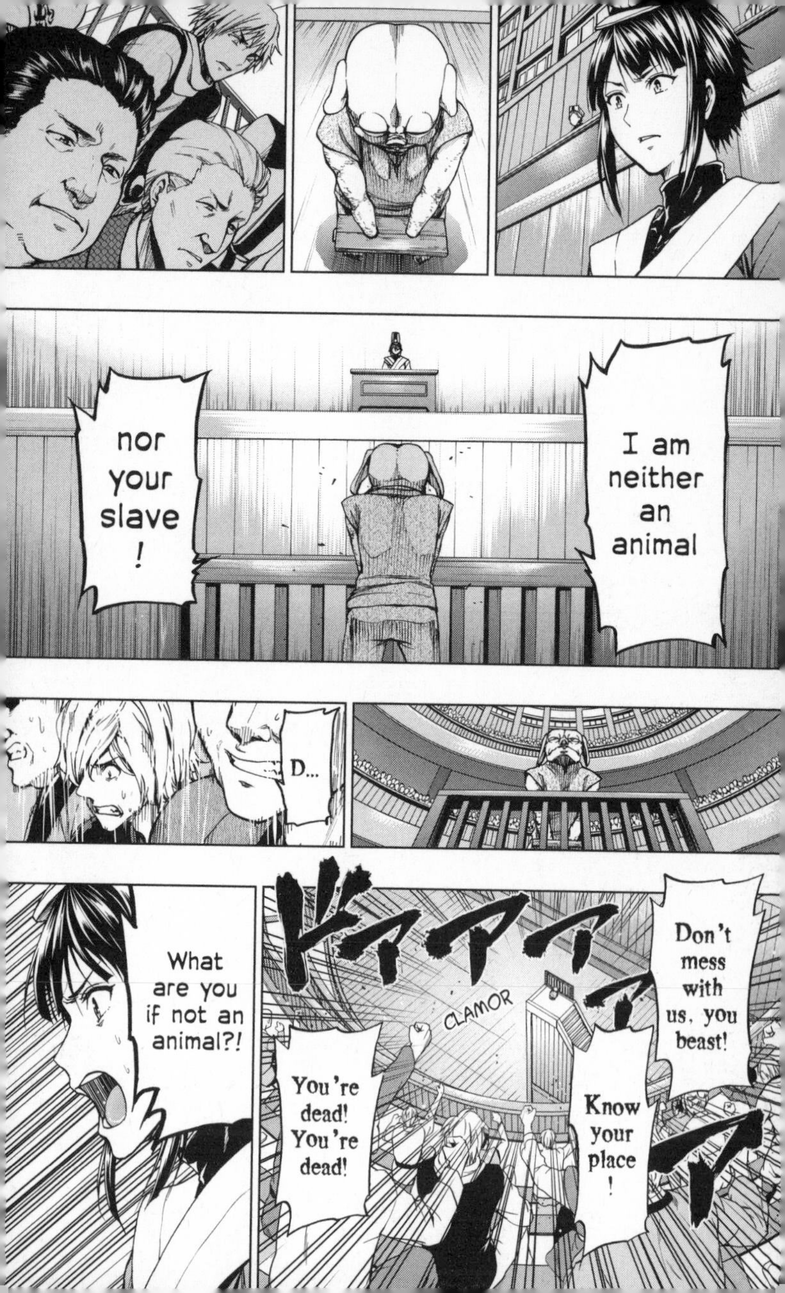
I am neither an animal
nor your slave !
D...
Don't mess with us, you beast!
Know your place !
CLAMOR
You're dead! You're dead!
What are you if not an animal?!

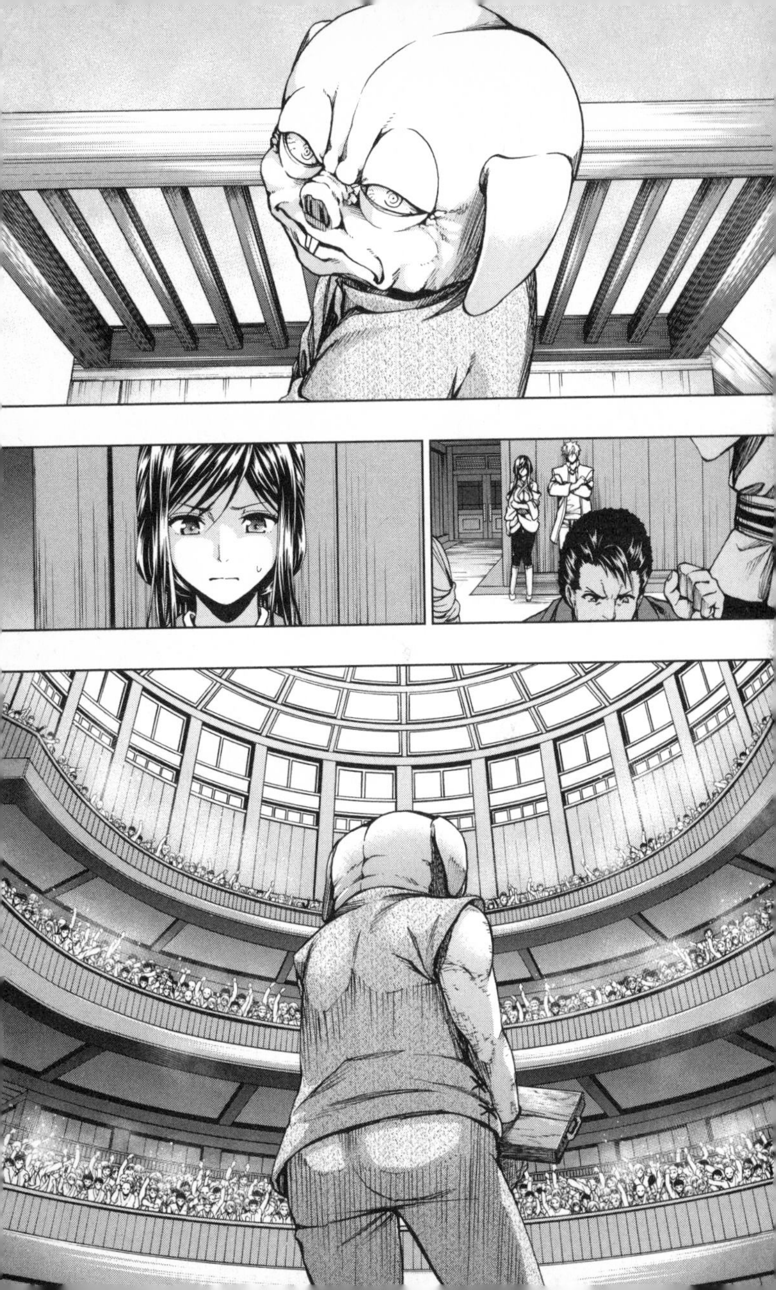

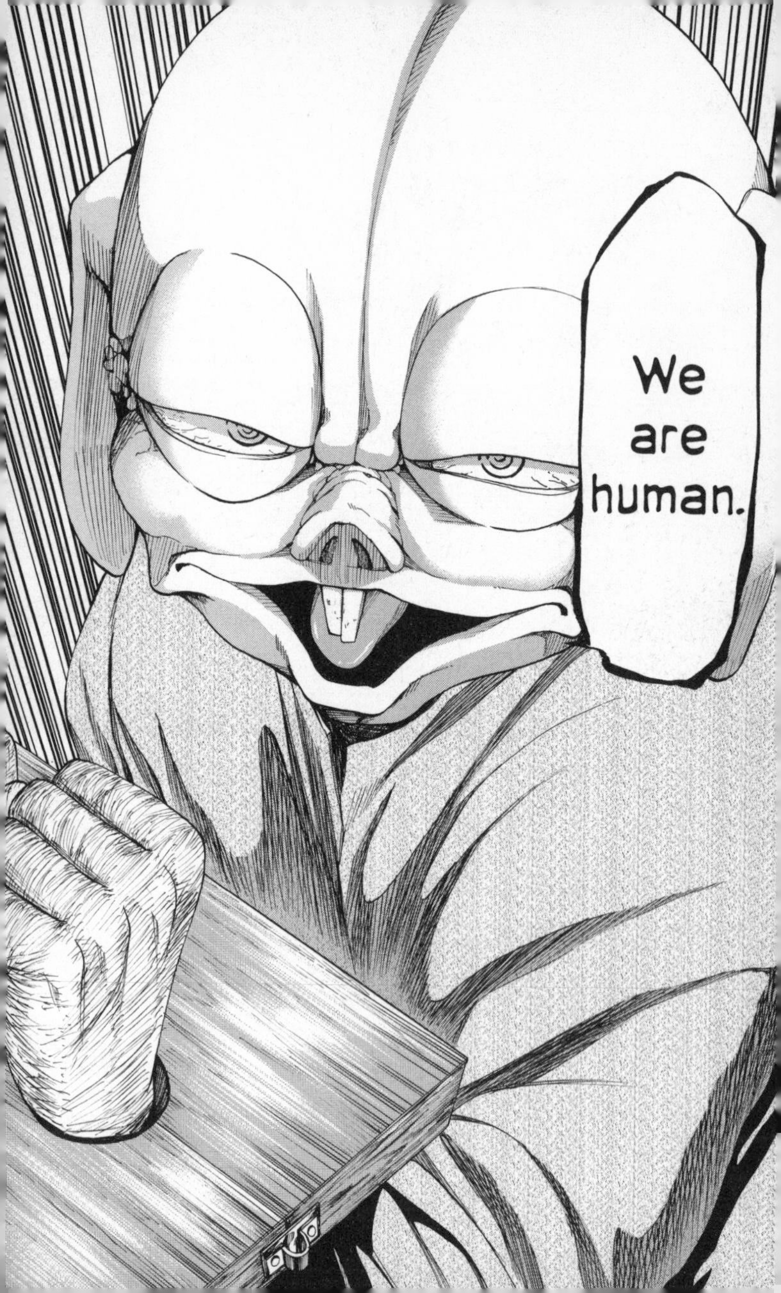
We are human.

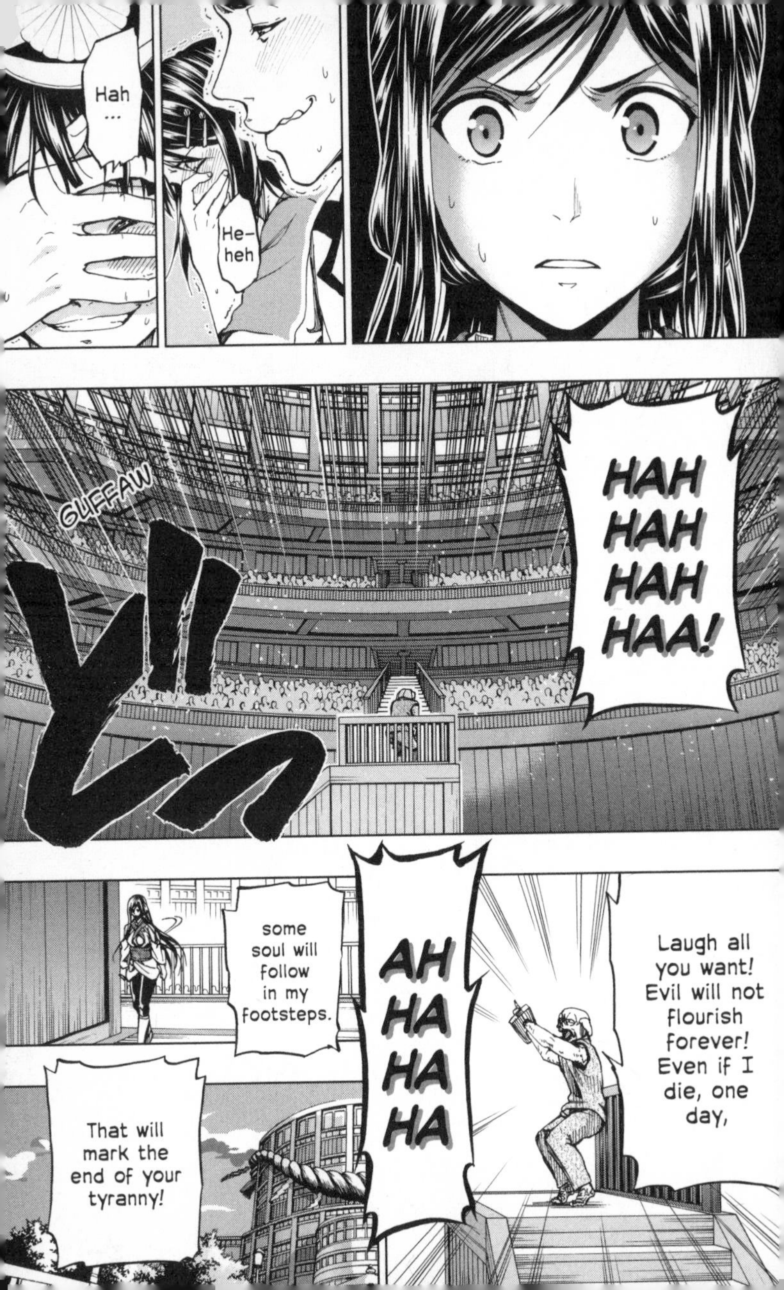
He-heh
Hah ...
HAH HAH HAH HAA!
GUFFAW
Laugh all you want! Evil will not flourish forever! Even if I die, one day,
AH HA HA HA HA
some soul will follow in my footsteps.
That will mark the end of your tyranny!

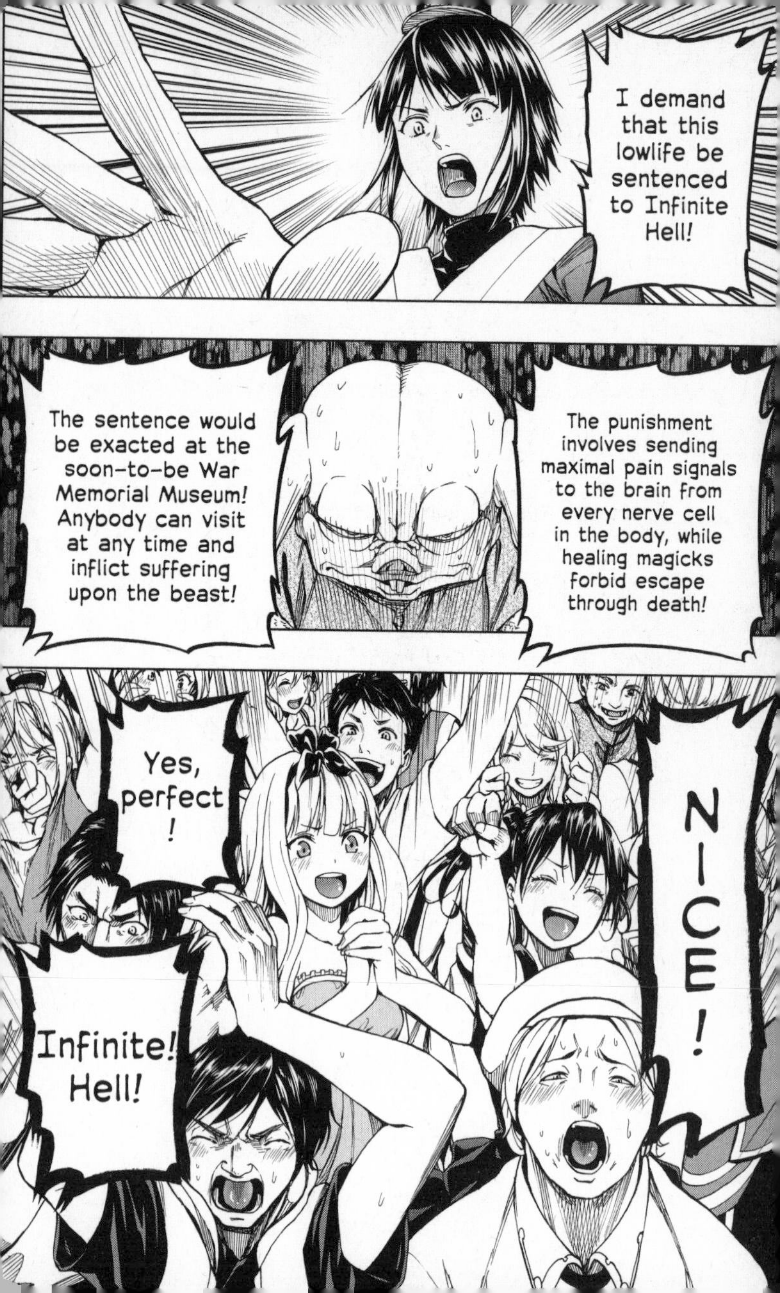
I demand that this lowlife be sentenced to Infinite Hell!
The punishment involves sending maximal pain signals to the brain from every nerve cell in the body, while healing magicks forbid escape through death!
The sentence would be exacted at the soon-to-be War Memorial Museum! Anybody can visit at any time and inflict suffering upon the beast!
NICE!
Yes, perfect!
Infinite! Hell!

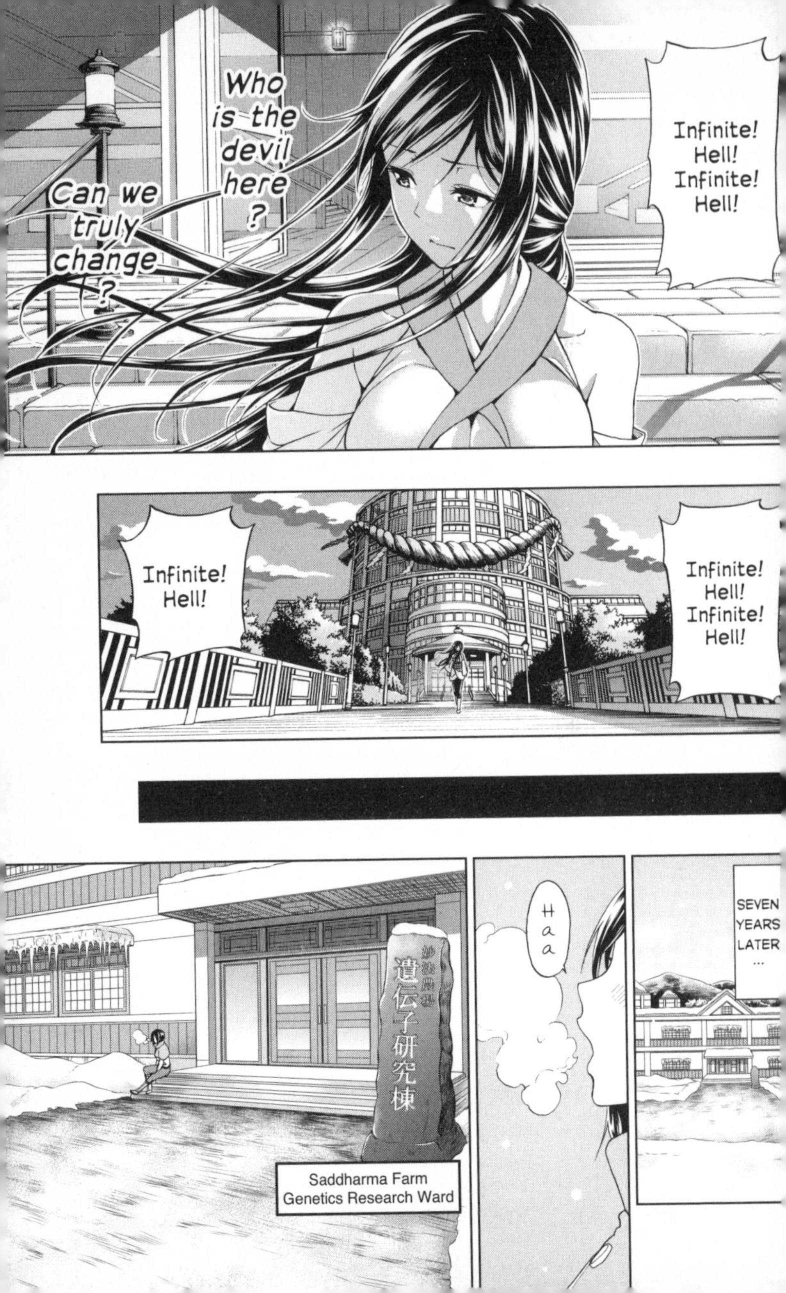
Infinite! Hell! Infinite! Hell!
Who is the devil here?
Can we truly change?
Infinite! Hell! Infinite! Hell!
Infinite! Hell!
SEVEN YEARS LATER ...
Haa
遺伝子研究棟
Saddharma Farm Genetics Research Ward

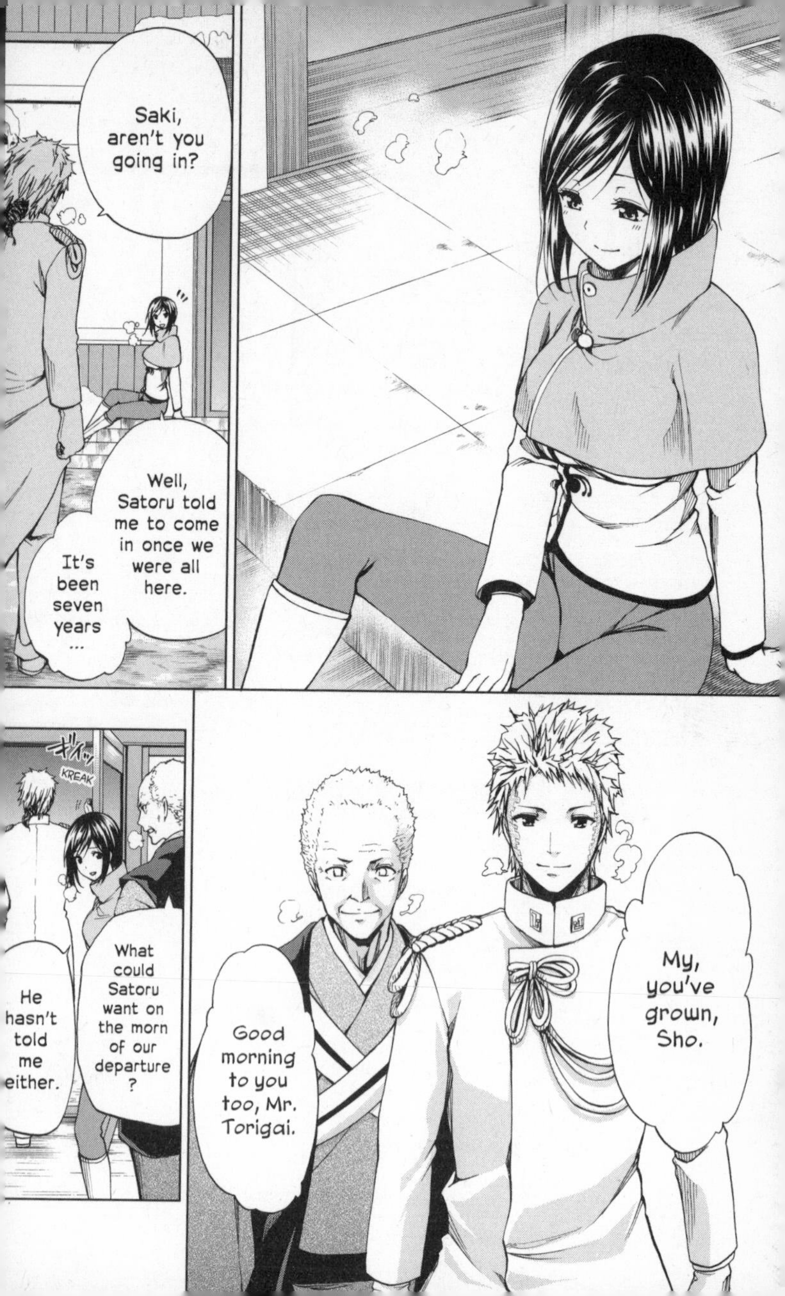
Saki, aren't you going in?
Well, Satoru told me to come in once we were all here.
It's been seven years ...
My, you've grown, Sho.
Good morning to you too, Mr. Torigai.
KREAK
What could Satoru want on the morn of our departure?
He hasn't told me either.

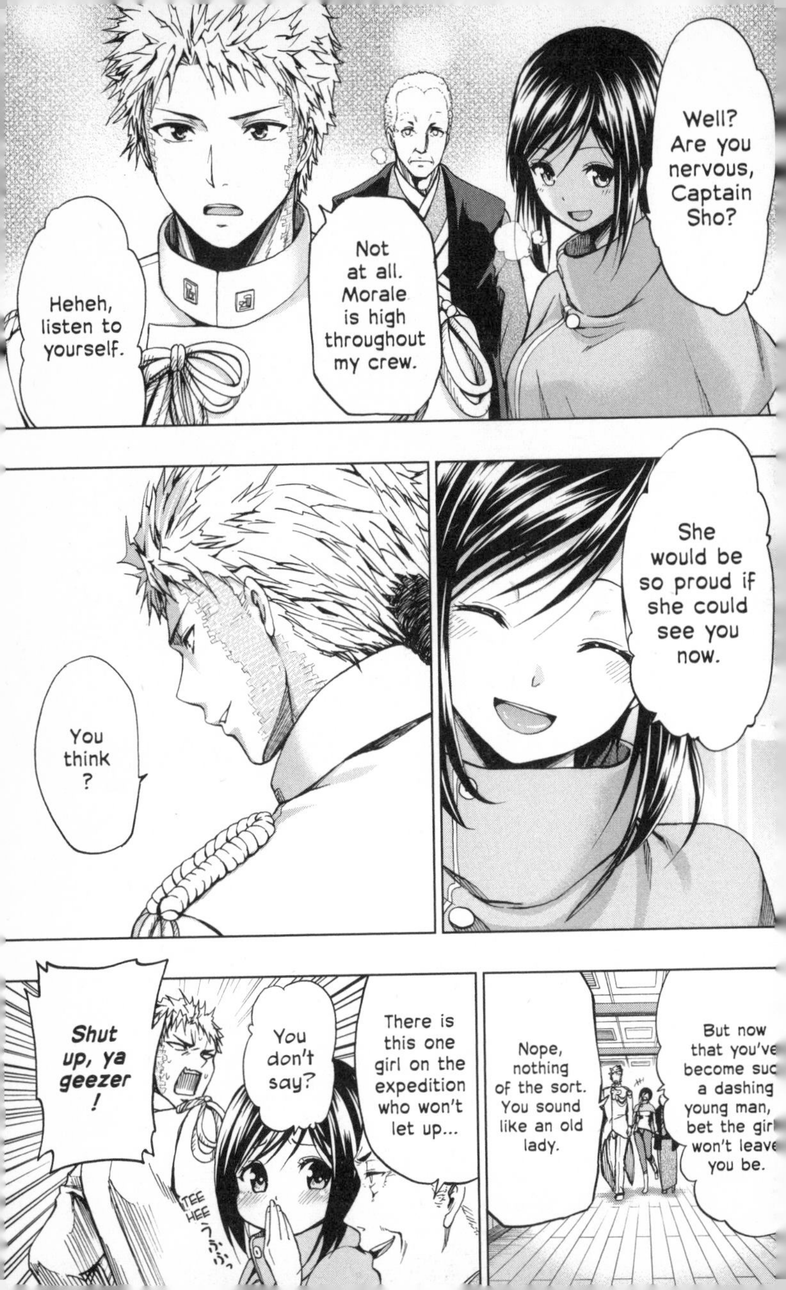
Well? Are you nervous, Captain Sho?
Not at all. Morale is high throughout my crew.
Heheh, listen to yourself.
She would be so proud if she could see you now.
You think?
But now that you've become suc a dashing young man, bet the gir won't leave you be.
Nope, nothing of the sort. You sound like an old lady.
There is this one girl on the expedition who won't let up...
You don't say?
TEE HEE
うふっ
Shut up, ya geezer!

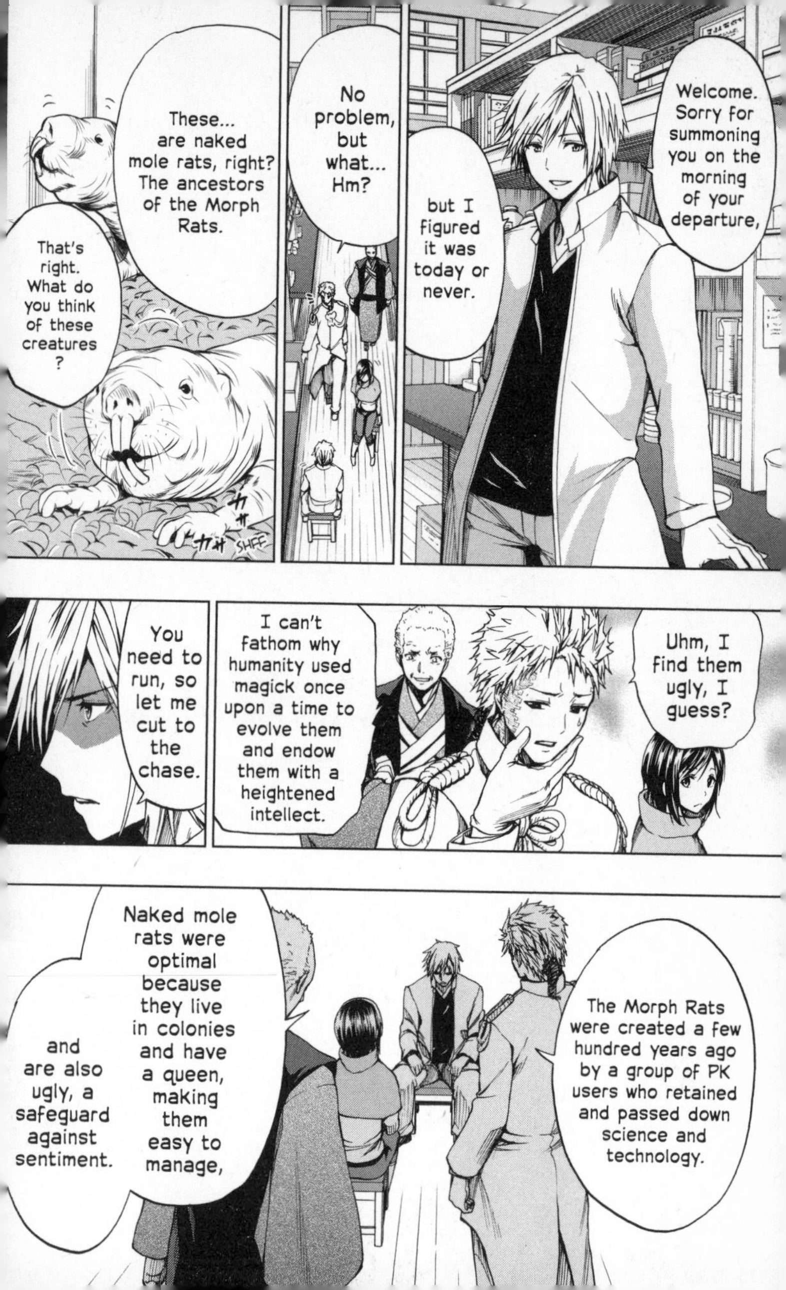
Welcome. Sorry for summoning you on the morning of your departure,
but I figured it was today or never.
No problem, but what... Hm?
These... are naked mole rats, right? The ancestors of the Morph Rats.
That's right. What do you think of these creatures?
SHFF
Uhm, I find them ugly, I guess?
I can't fathom why humanity used magick once upon a time to evolve them and endow them with a heightened intellect.
You need to run, so let me cut to the chase.
The Morph Rats were created a few hundred years ago by a group of PK users who retained and passed down science and technology.
Naked mole rats were optimal because they live in colonies and have a queen, making them easy to manage,
and are also ugly, a safeguard against sentiment.

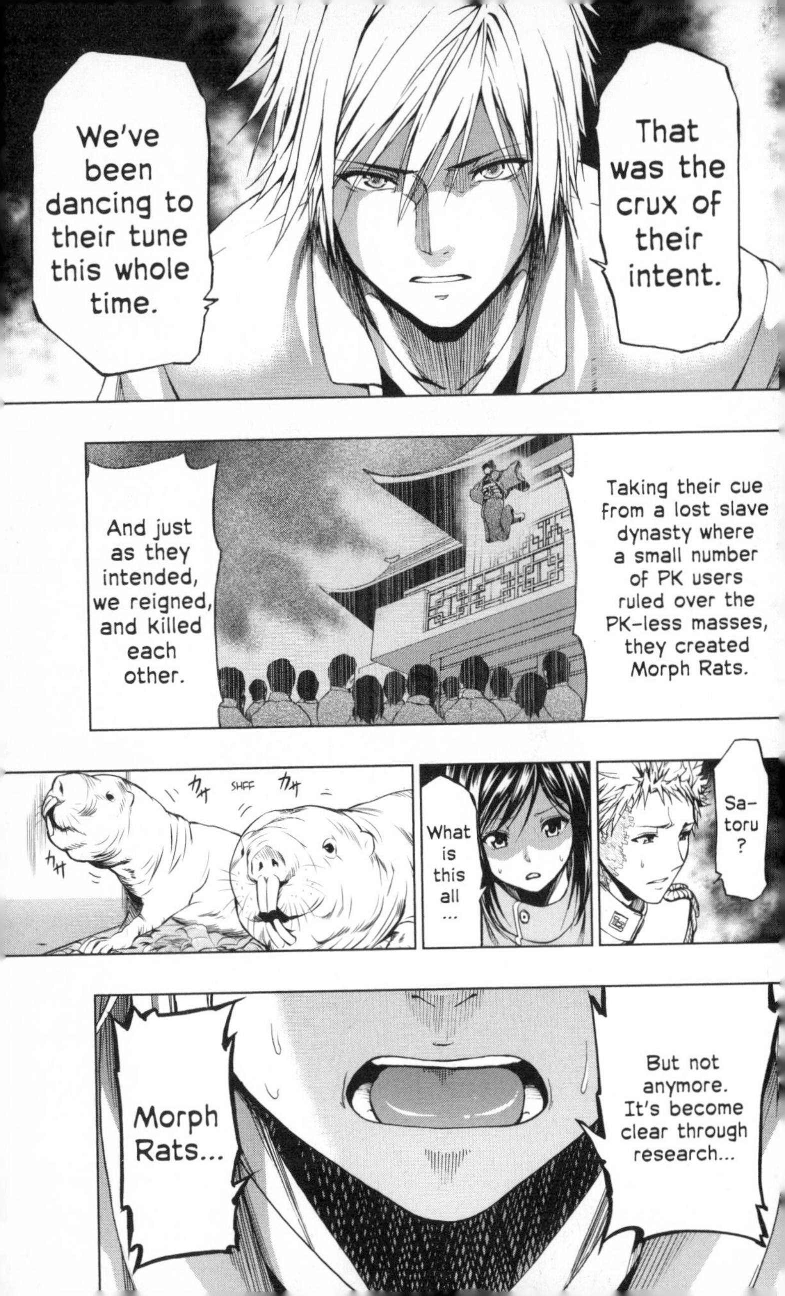
That was the crux of their intent.
We've been dancing to their tune this whole time.
Taking their cue from a lost slave dynasty where a small number of PK users ruled over the PK-less masses, they created Morph Rats.
And just as they intended, we reigned, and killed each other.
Sa-toru?
What is this all ...
SHFF
But not anymore. It's become clear through research...
Morph Rats...

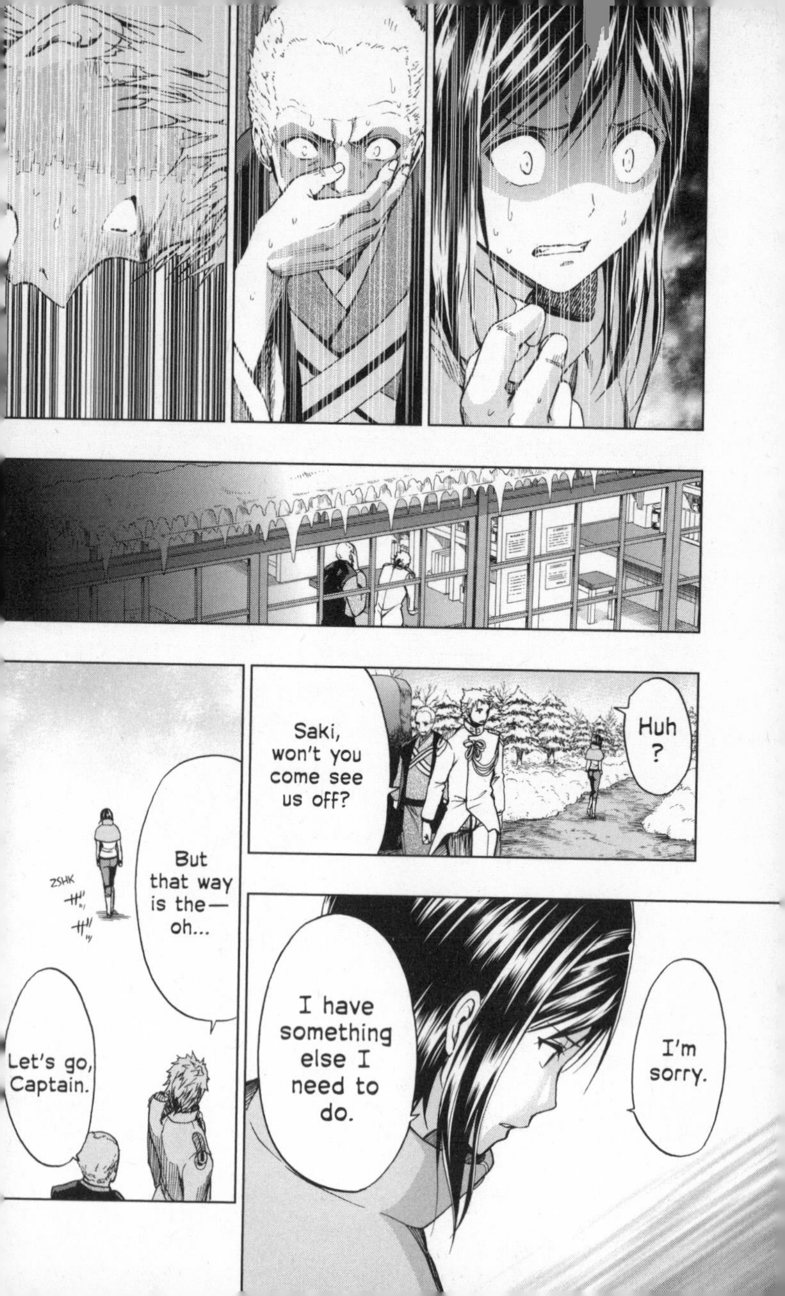
Huh?
Saki, won't you come see us off?
I'm sorry.
I have something else I need to do.
But that way is the— oh...
ZSHK
Let's go, Captain.

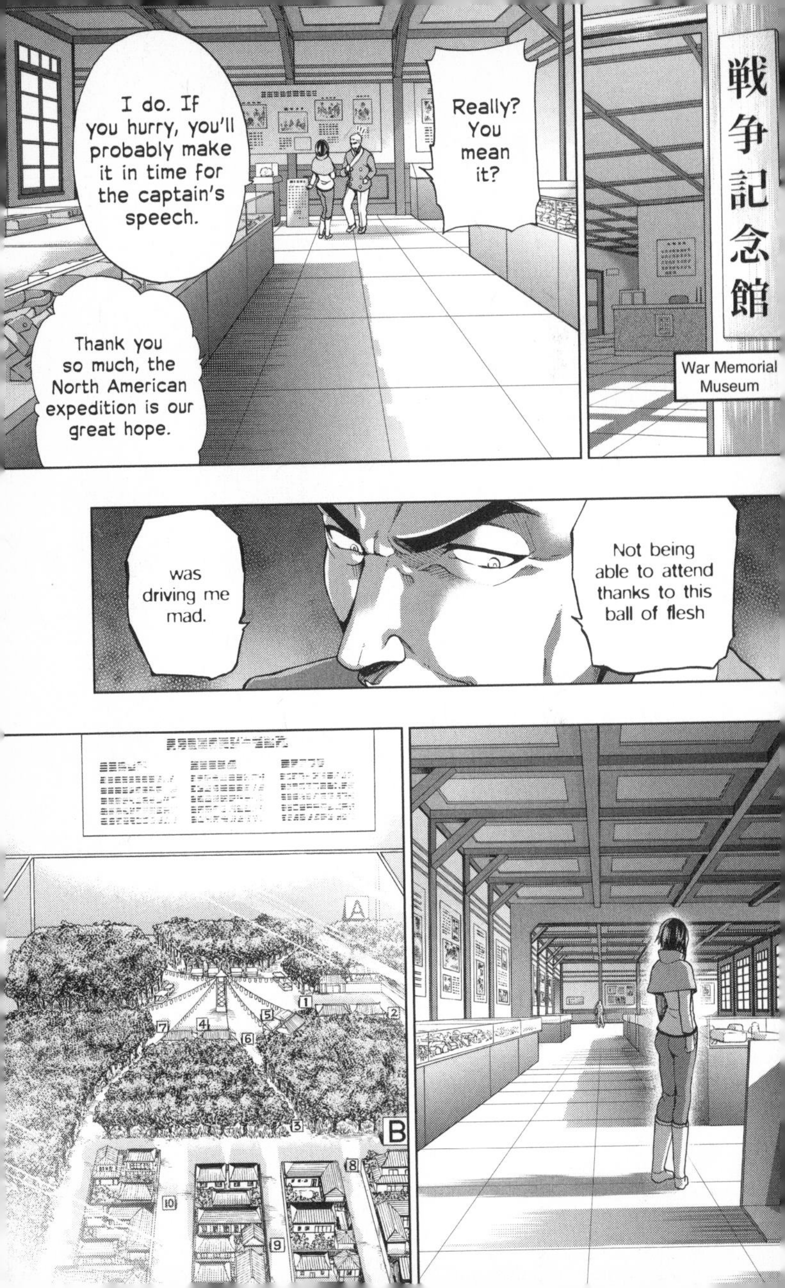
戦争記念館
War Memorial Museum
Really? You mean it?
I do. If you hurry, you'll probably make it in time for the captain's speech.
Thank you so much, the North American expedition is our great hope.
Not being able to attend thanks to this ball of flesh
was driving me mad.
A
1
2
5
7
4
6
3
B
8
10
9

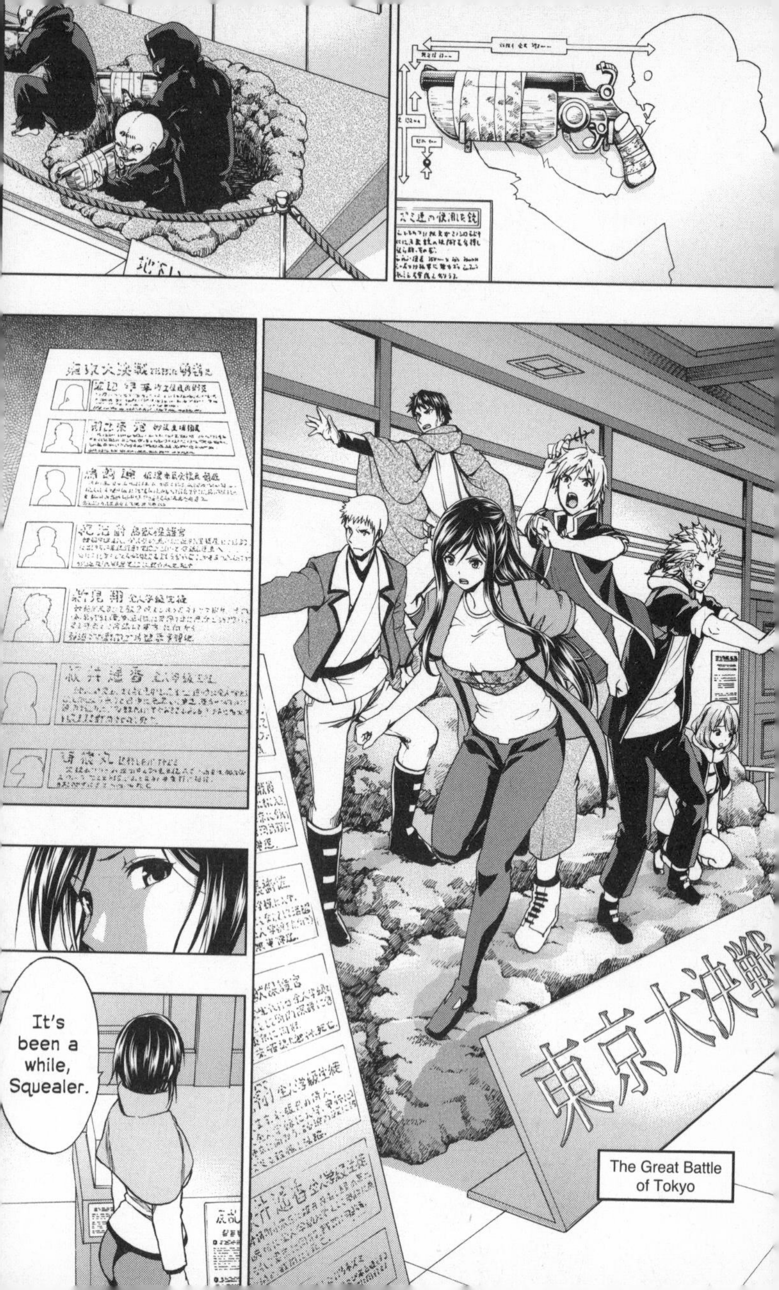
東京大決
The Great Battle of Tokyo
It's been a while, Squealer.

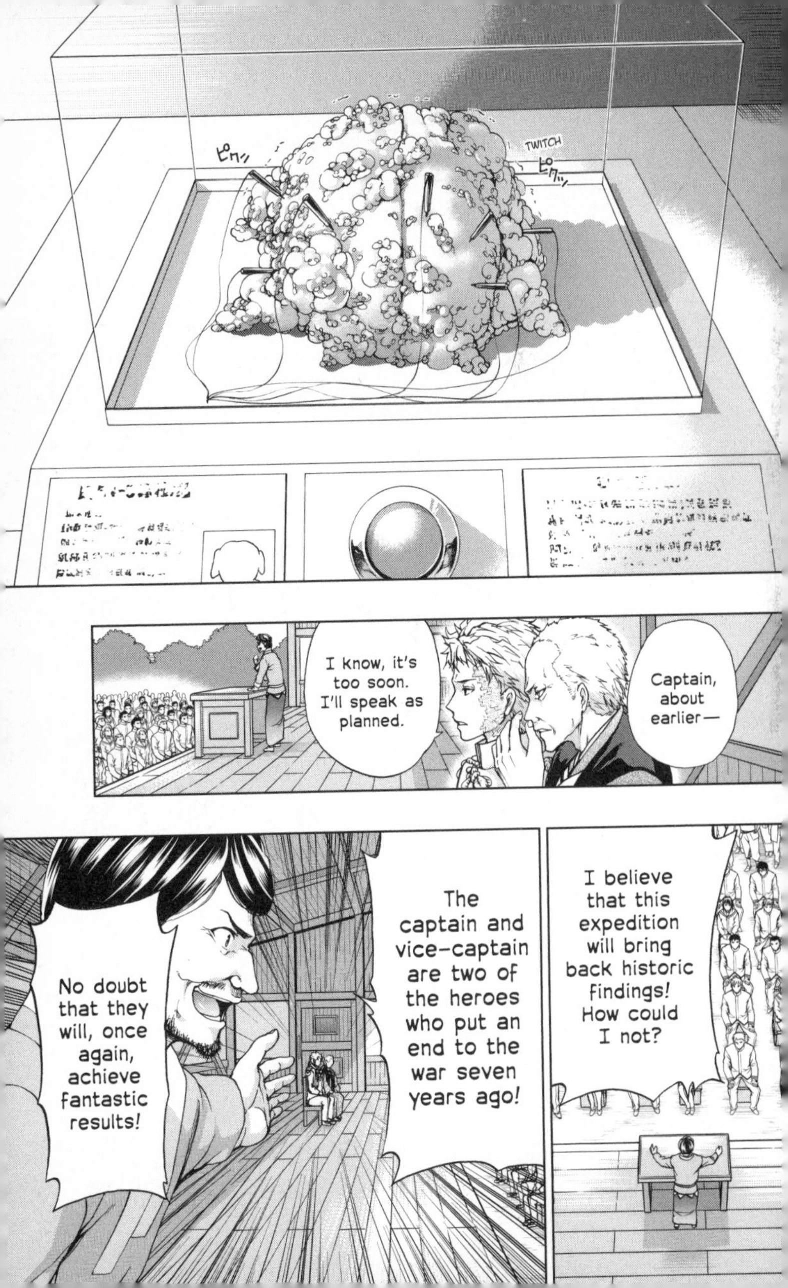

ピクッ
TWITCH
ピクッ
Captain, about earlier—
I know, it's too soon. I'll speak as planned.
I believe that this expedition will bring back historic findings! How could I not?
The captain and vice-captain are two of the heroes who put an end to the war seven years ago!
No doubt that they will, once again, achieve fantastic results!

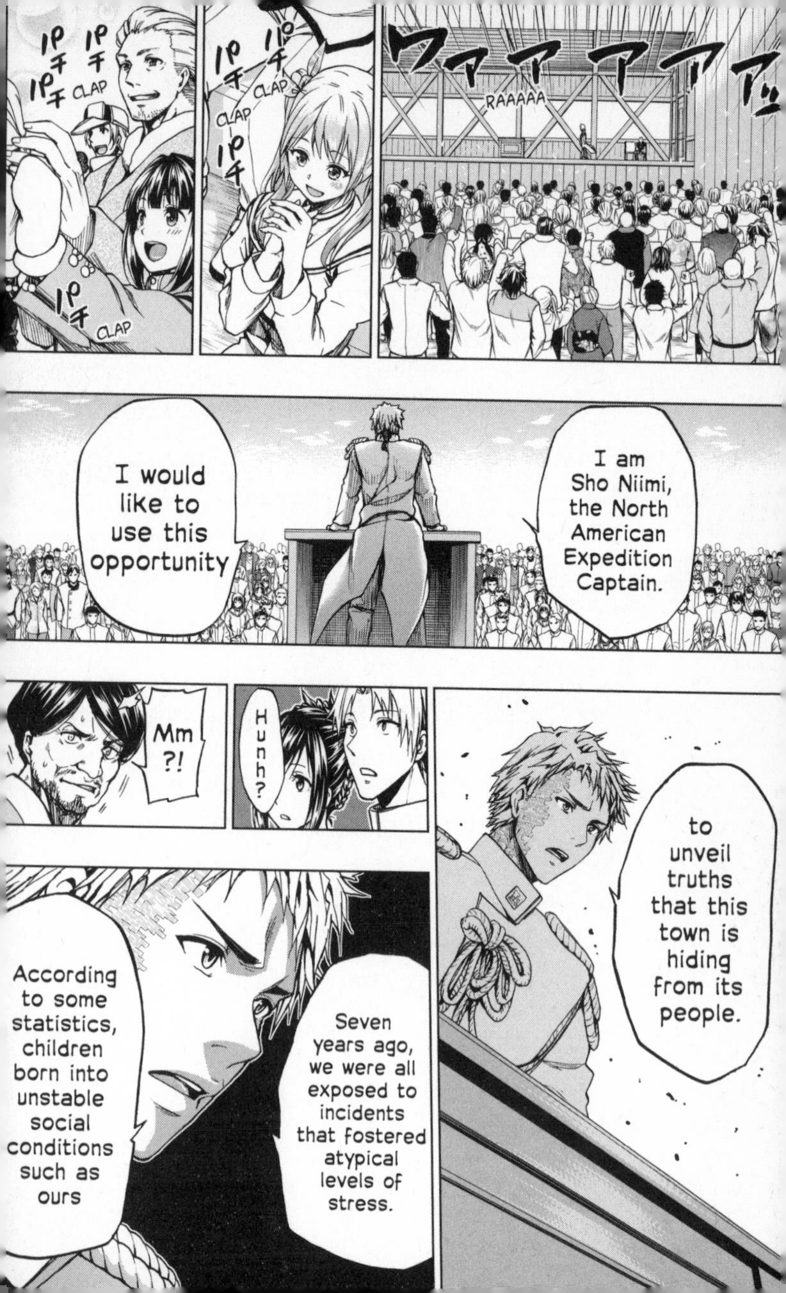

ワァアアアッ
RAAAAA
パチ パチ
CLAP CLAP
パチ
パチ パチ パチ パチ
CLAP
パチ
CLAP
I am Sho Niimi, the North American Expedition Captain.
I would like to use this opportunity
to unveil truths that this town is hiding from its people.
Hunh?
Mm ?!
Seven years ago, we were all exposed to incidents that fostered atypical levels of stress.
According to some statistics, children born into unstable social conditions such as ours

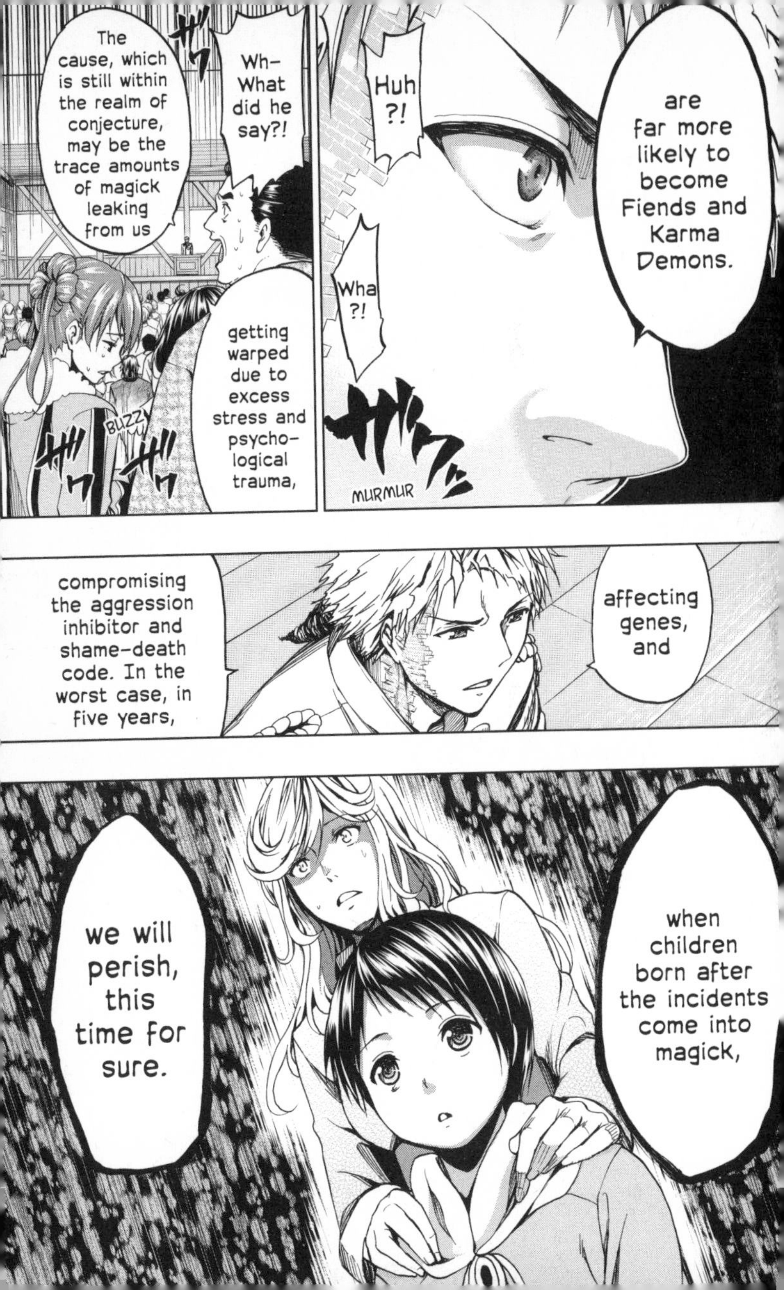
are far more likely to become Fiends and Karma Demons.
Huh?!
Wha?!
MURMUR
Wh- What did he say?!
The cause, which is still within the realm of conjecture, may be the trace amounts of magick leaking from us
getting warped due to excess stress and psycho-logical trauma,
BUZZ
affecting genes, and
compromising the aggression inhibitor and shame-death code. In the worst case, in five years,
when children born after the incidents come into magick,
we will perish, this time for sure.

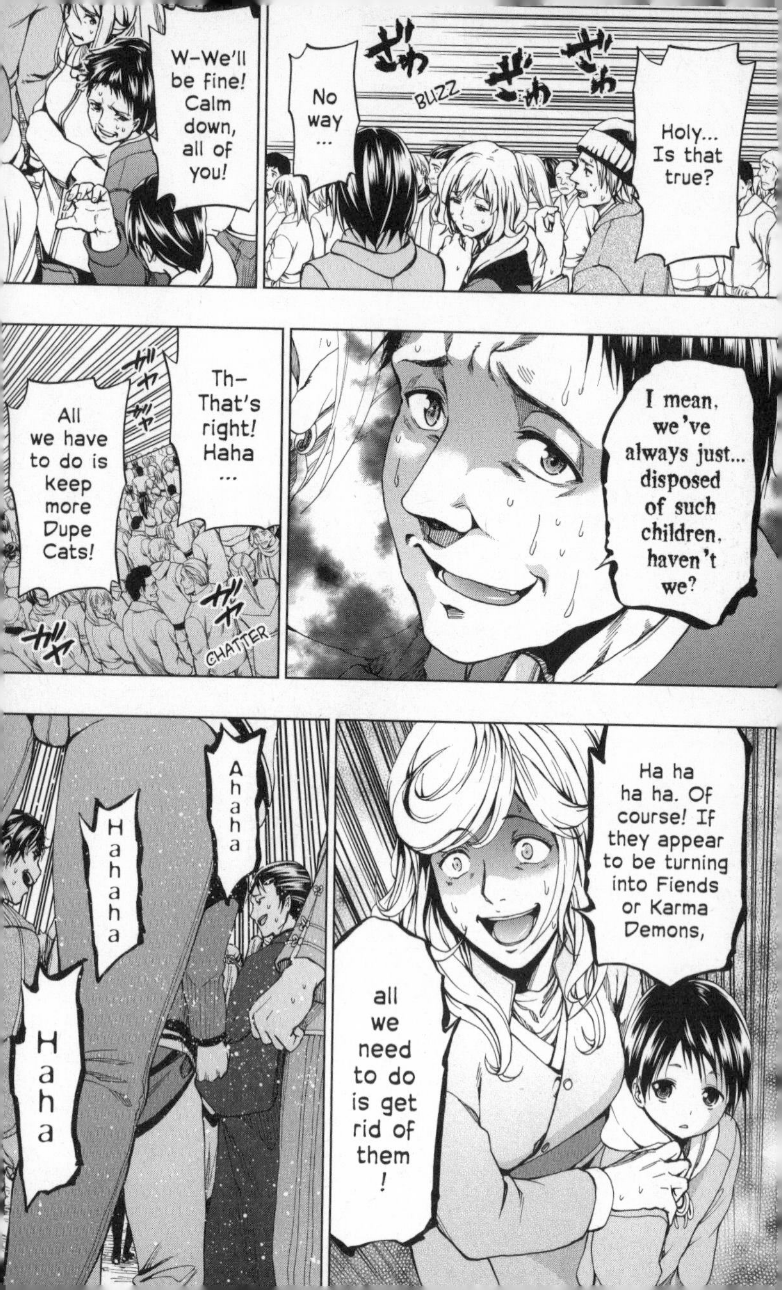
ざわ ざわ ざわ
BUZZ
Holy... Is that true?
No way ...
W-We'll be fine! Calm down, all of you!
I mean, we've always just... disposed of such children, haven't we?
Th- That's right! Haha ...
All we have to do is keep more Dupe Cats!
ガヤ ガヤ ガヤ ガヤ
CHATTER
Ha ha ha ha. Of course! If they appear to be turning into Fiends or Karma Demons,
all we need to do is get rid of them!
Ahaha
Hahahaha
Haha

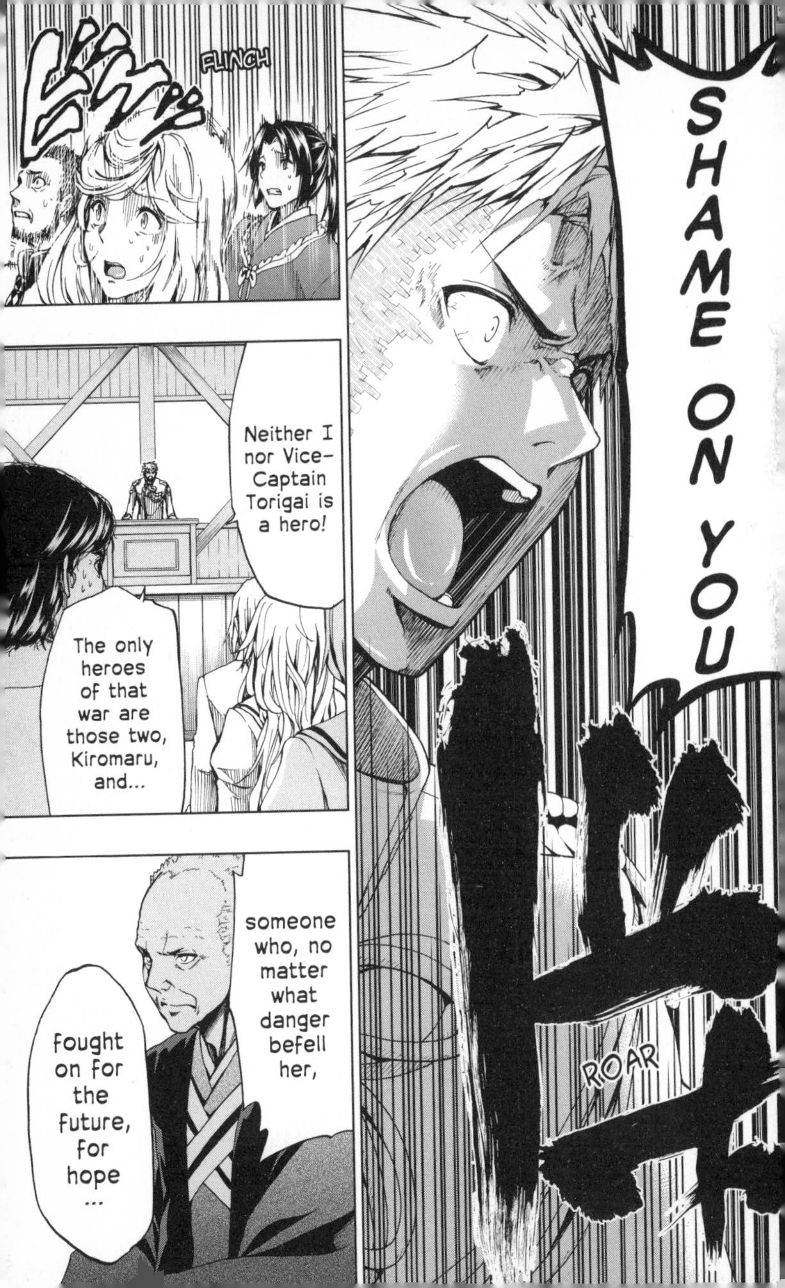
SHAME ON YOU
ROAR
FLINCH
Neither I nor Vice-Captain Torigai is a hero!
The only heroes of that war are those two, Kiromaru, and...
someone who, no matter what danger befell her,
fought on for the future, for hope...

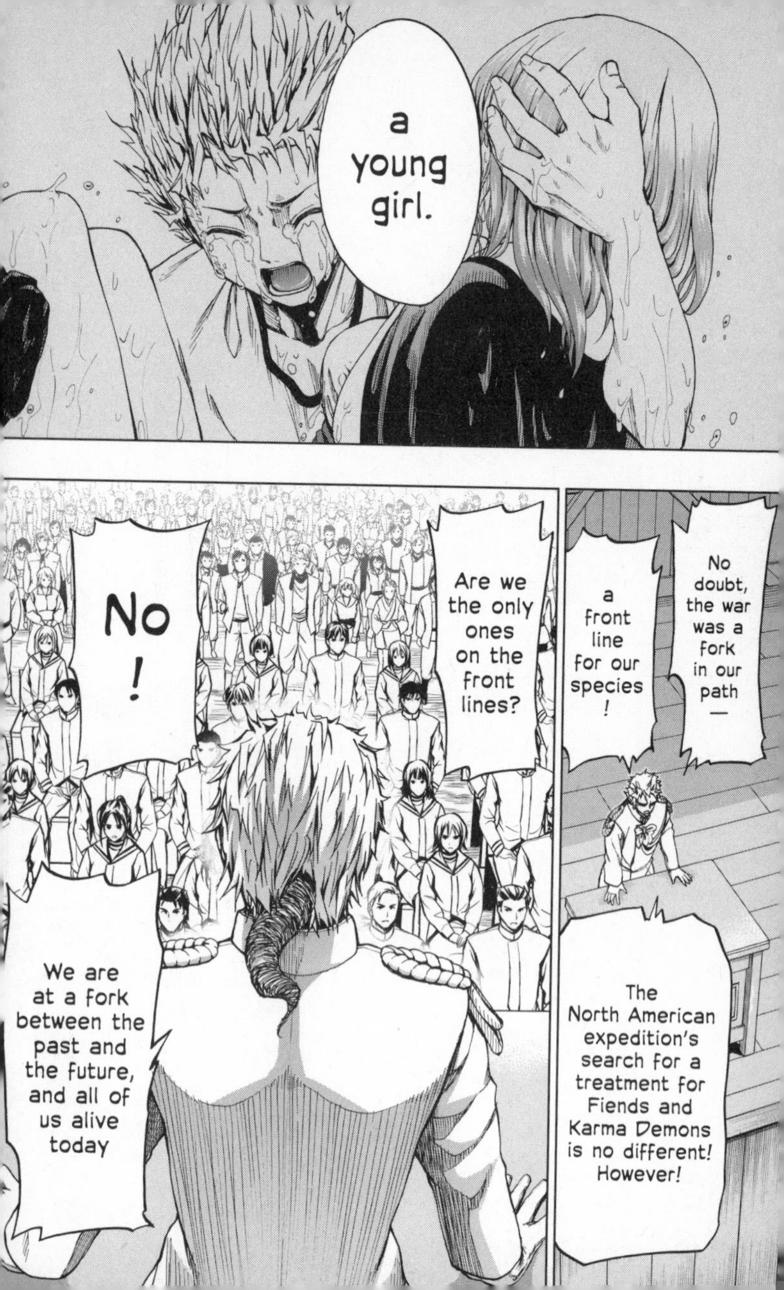
a young girl.
No doubt, the war was a fork in our path —
a front line for our species!
The North American expedition's search for a treatment for Fiends and Karma Demons is no different! However!
Are we the only ones on the front lines?
No!
We are at a fork between the past and the future, and all of us alive today

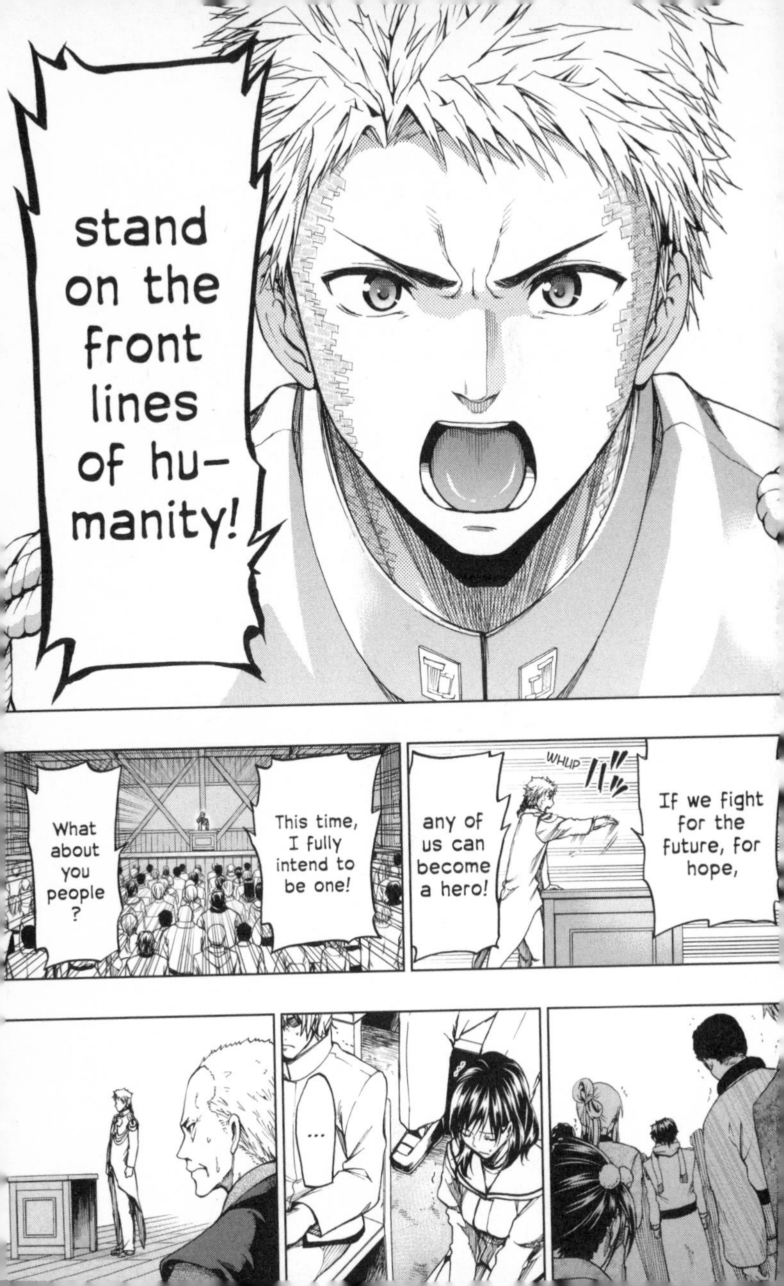
stand on the front lines of hu-manity!
If we fight for the future, for hope,
WHUP
any of us can become a hero!
This time, I fully intend to be one!
What about you people?
...

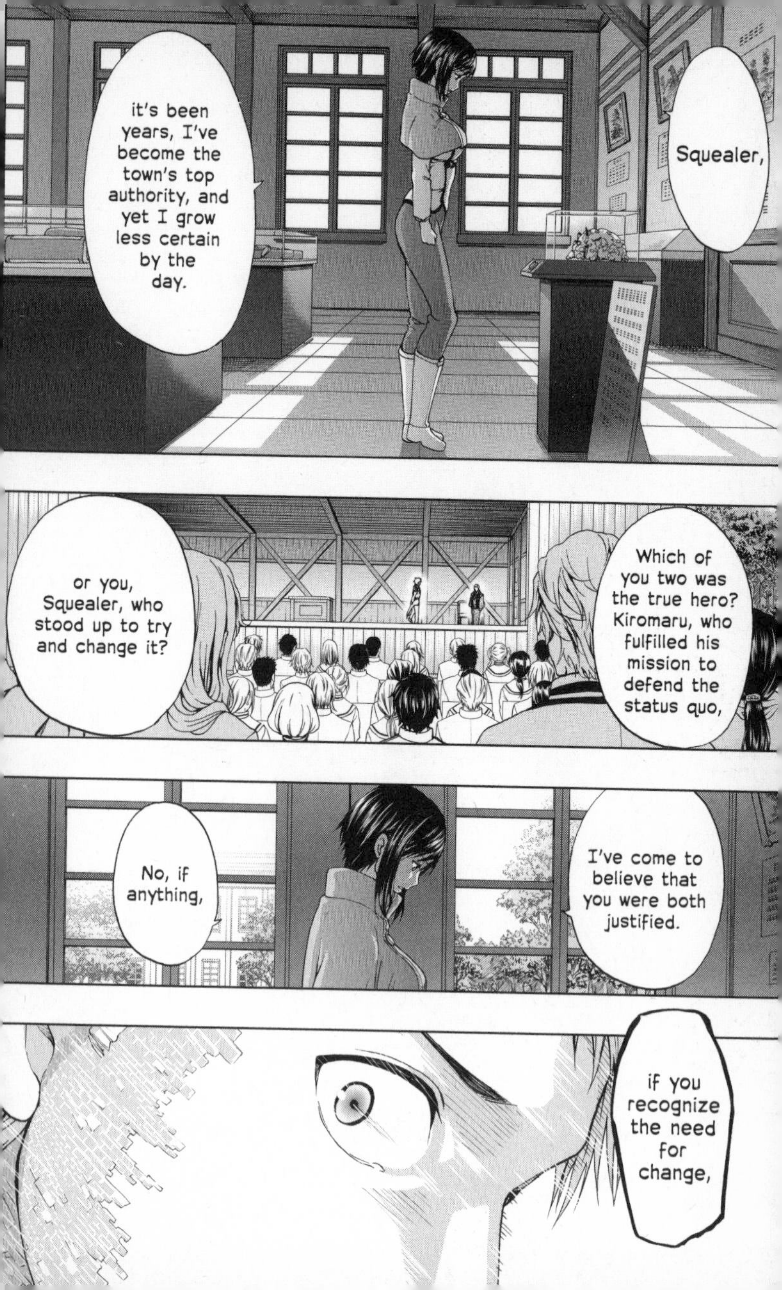
Squealer,
it's been years, I've become the town's top authority, and yet I grow less certain by the day.
Which of you two was the true hero? Kiromaru, who fulfilled his mission to defend the status quo,
or you, Squealer, who stood up to try and change it?
I've come to believe that you were both justified.
No, if anything,
if you recognize the need for change,

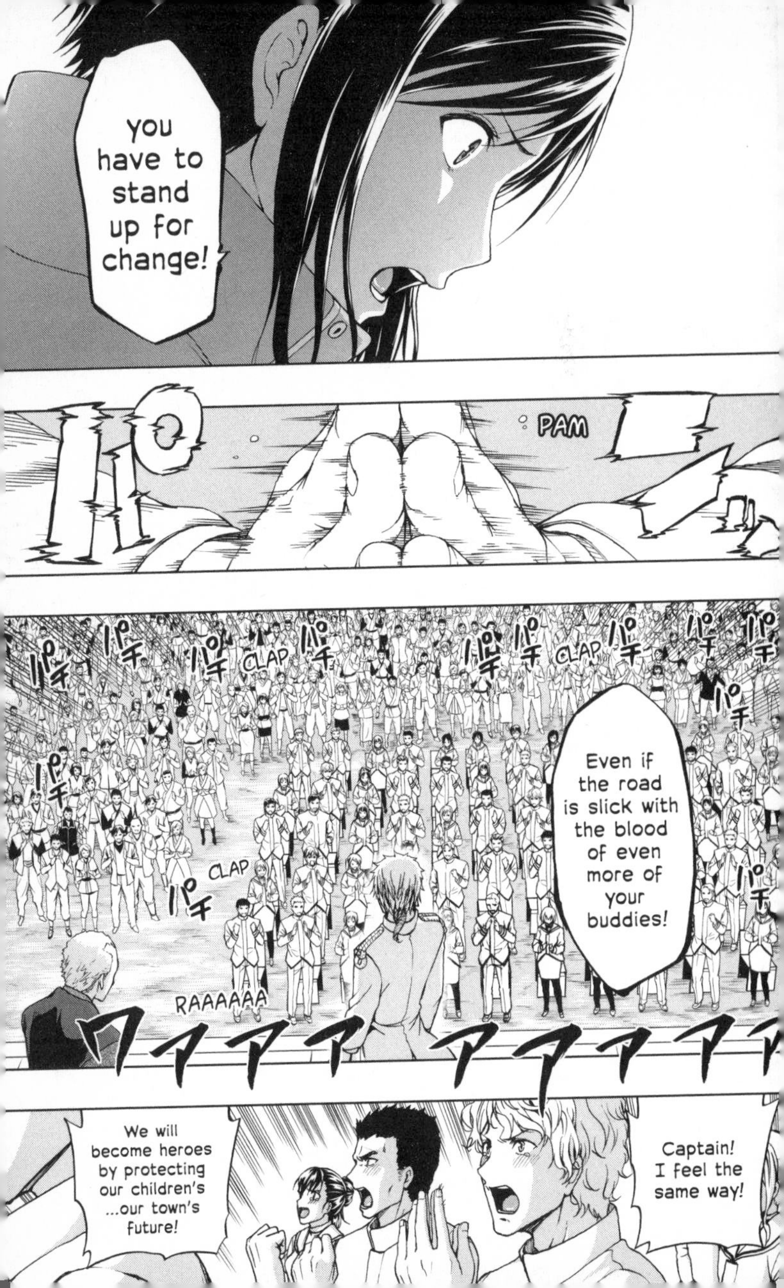
you have to stand up for change!
PAM
パチ
CLAP
CLAP
CLAP
Even if the road is slick with the blood of even more of your buddies!
RAAAAAA
ワァァァァァ
Captain! I feel the same way!
We will become heroes by protecting our children's ...our town's future!

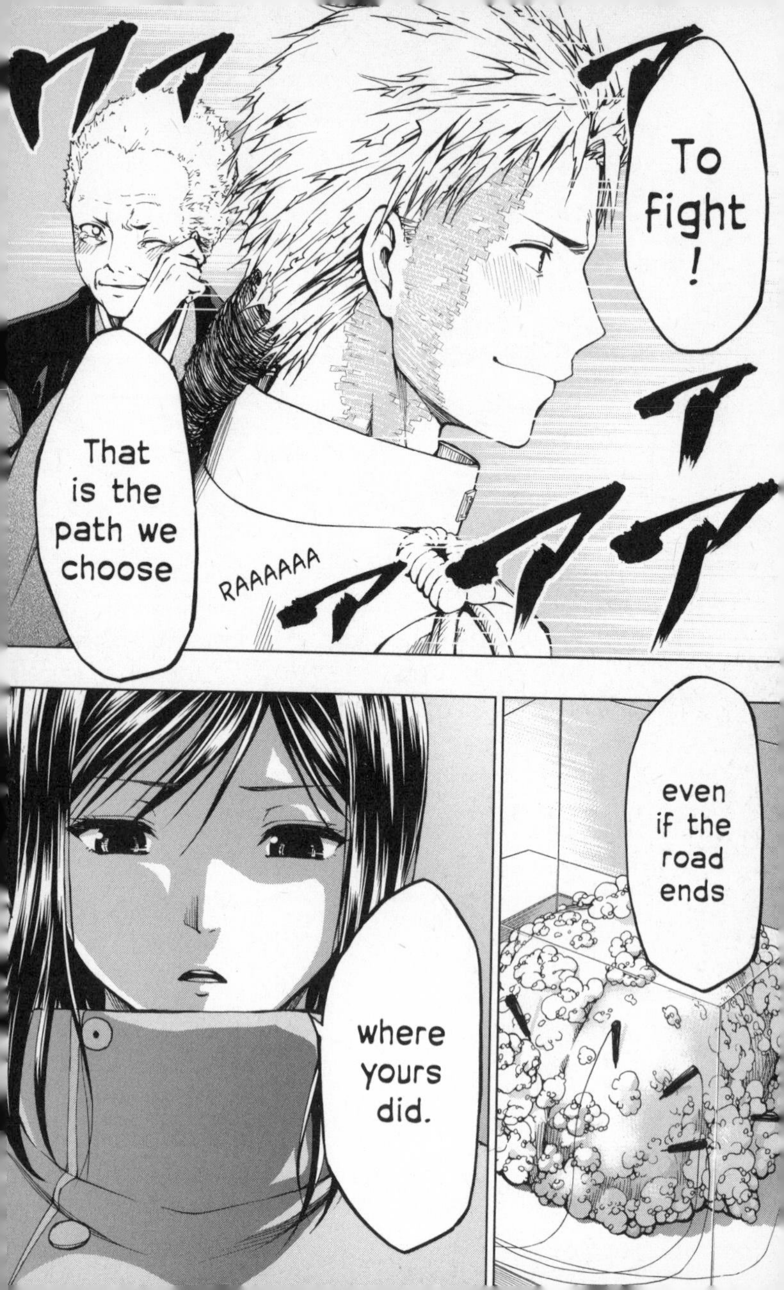
To fight!
That is the path we choose
RAAAAAA
even if the road ends
where yours did.

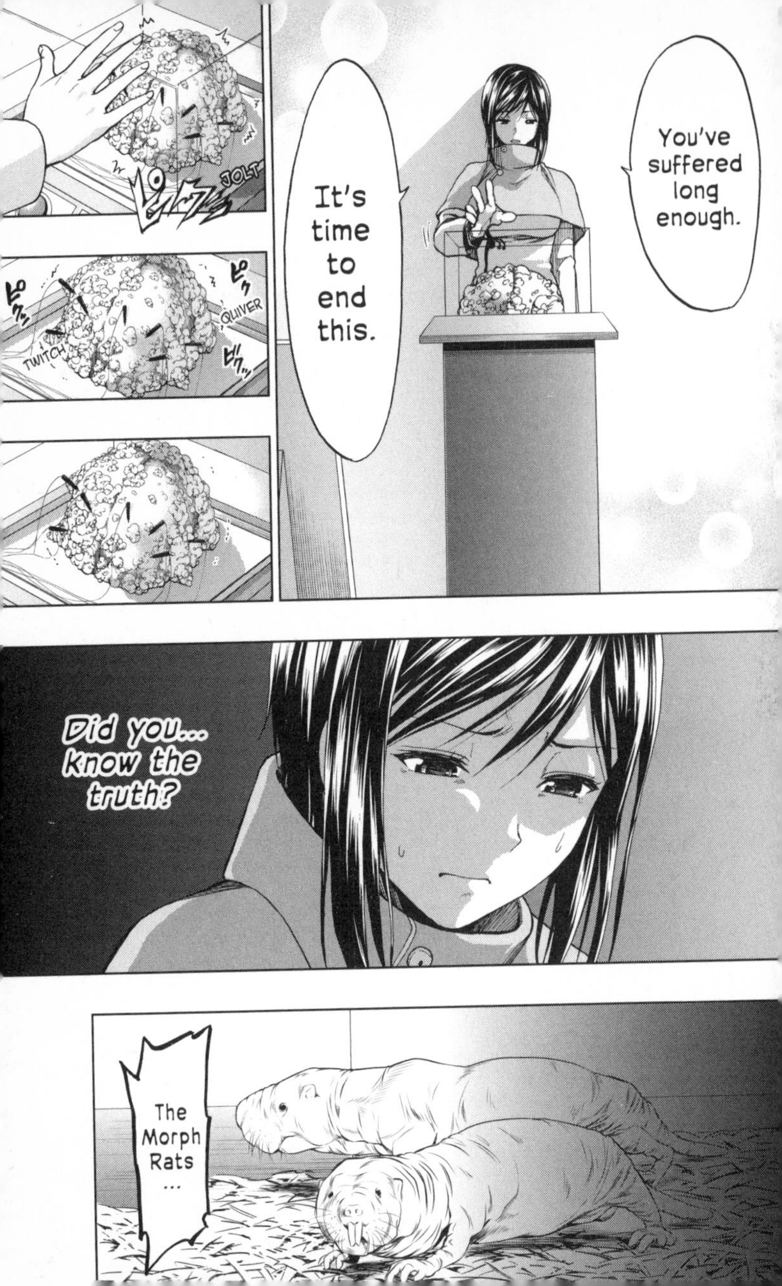
You've suffered long enough.
It's time to end this.
JOLT
QUIVER
TWITCH
Did you... know the truth?
The Morph Rats
...

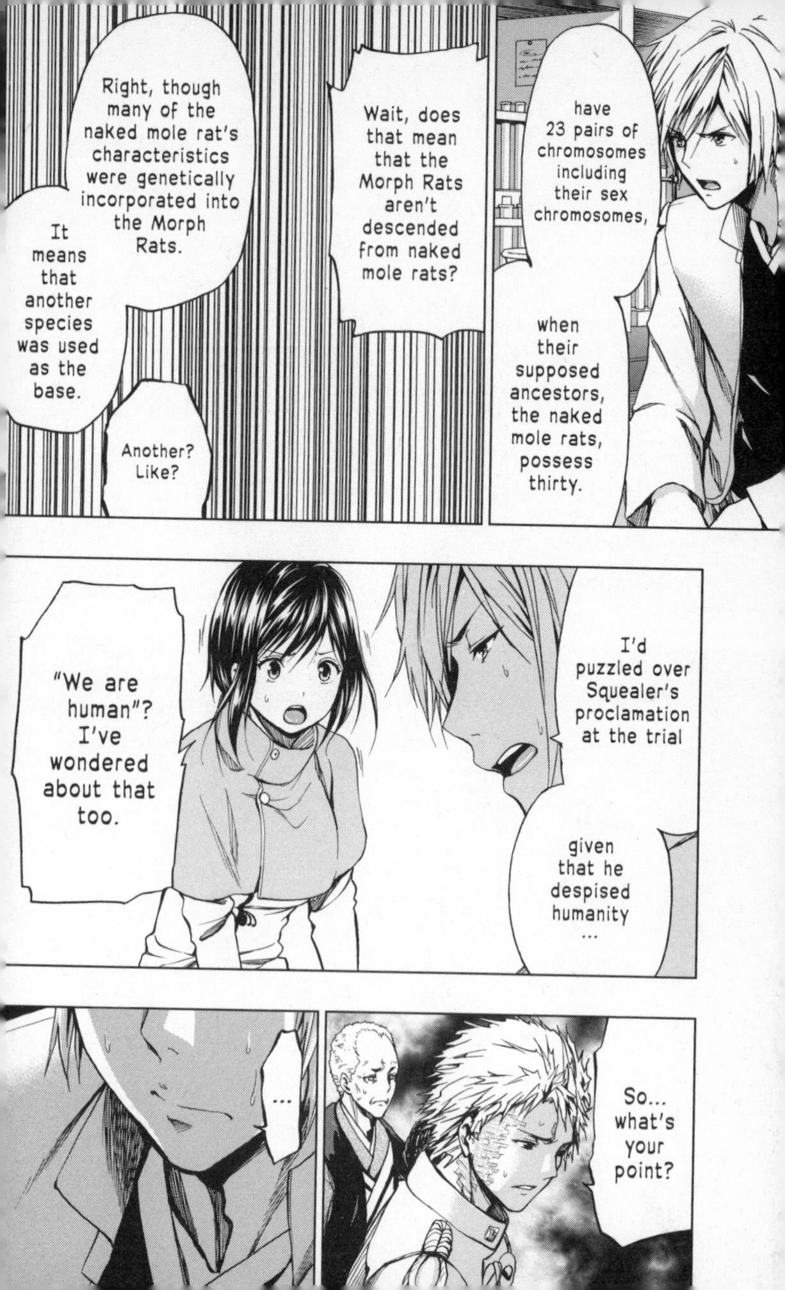
have 23 pairs of chromosomes including their sex chromosomes,
when their supposed ancestors, the naked mole rats, possess thirty.
Wait, does that mean that the Morph Rats aren't descended from naked mole rats?
Right, though many of the naked mole rat's characteristics were genetically incorporated into the Morph Rats.
It means that another species was used as the base.
Another? Like?
I'd puzzled over Squealer's proclamation at the trial
given that he despised humanity ...
"We are human"? I've wondered about that too.
So... what's your point?
...

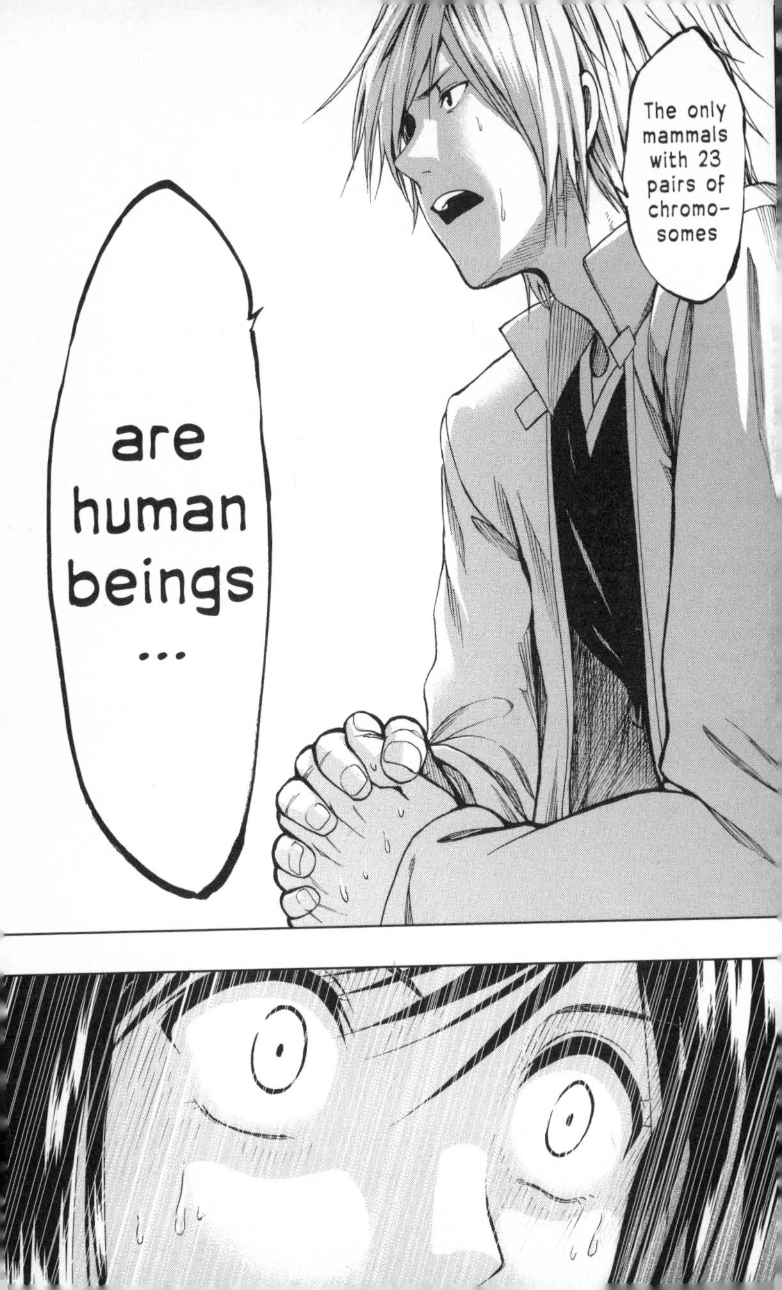
The only mammals with 23 pairs of chromo- somes
are human beings ...

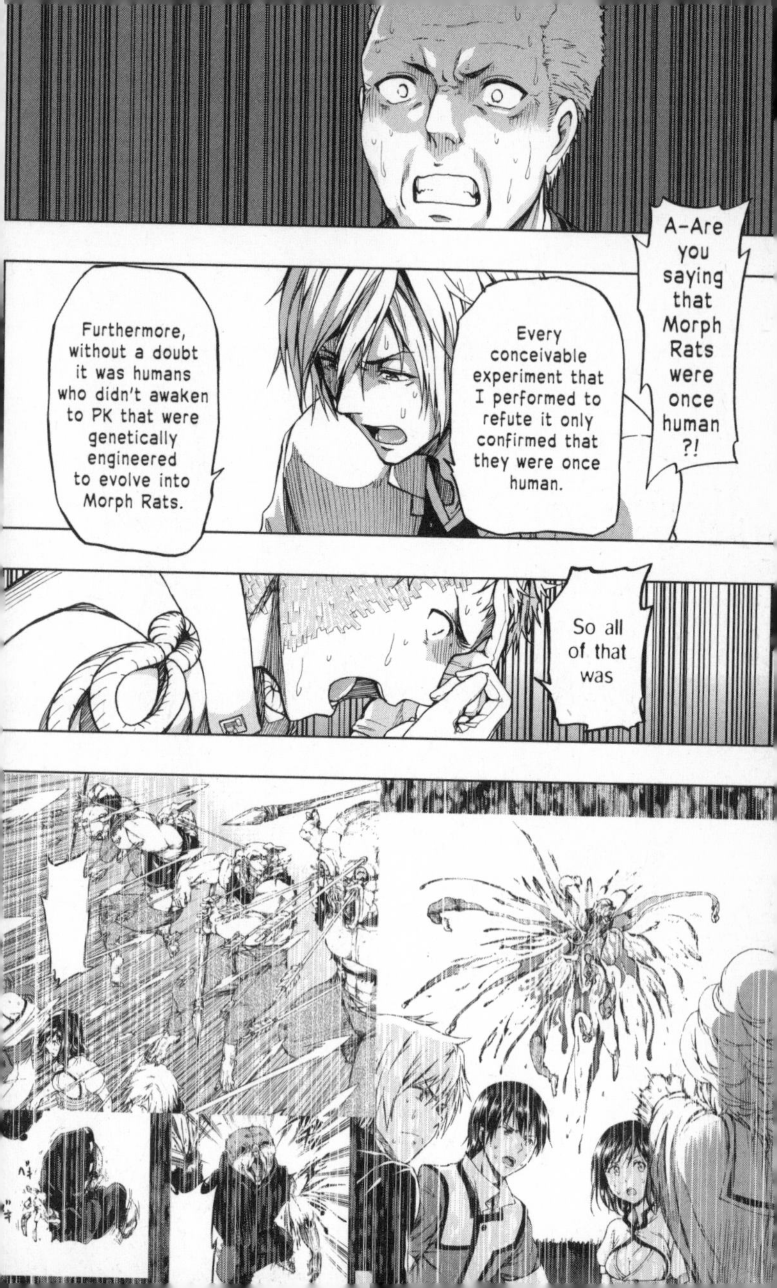
A-Are you saying that Morph Rats were once human?!
Every conceivable experiment that I performed to refute it only confirmed that they were once human.
Furthermore, without a doubt it was humans who didn't awaken to PK that were genetically engineered to evolve into Morph Rats.
So all of that was

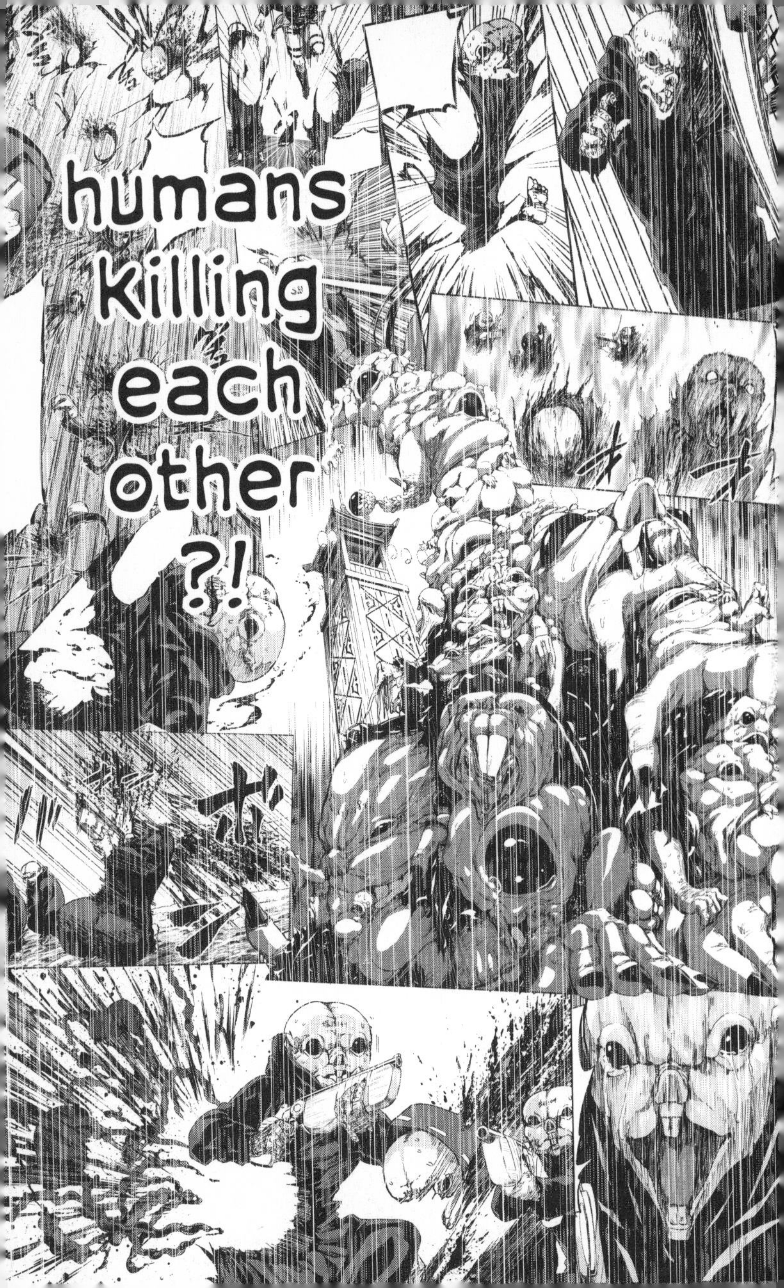
humans killing each other ?!

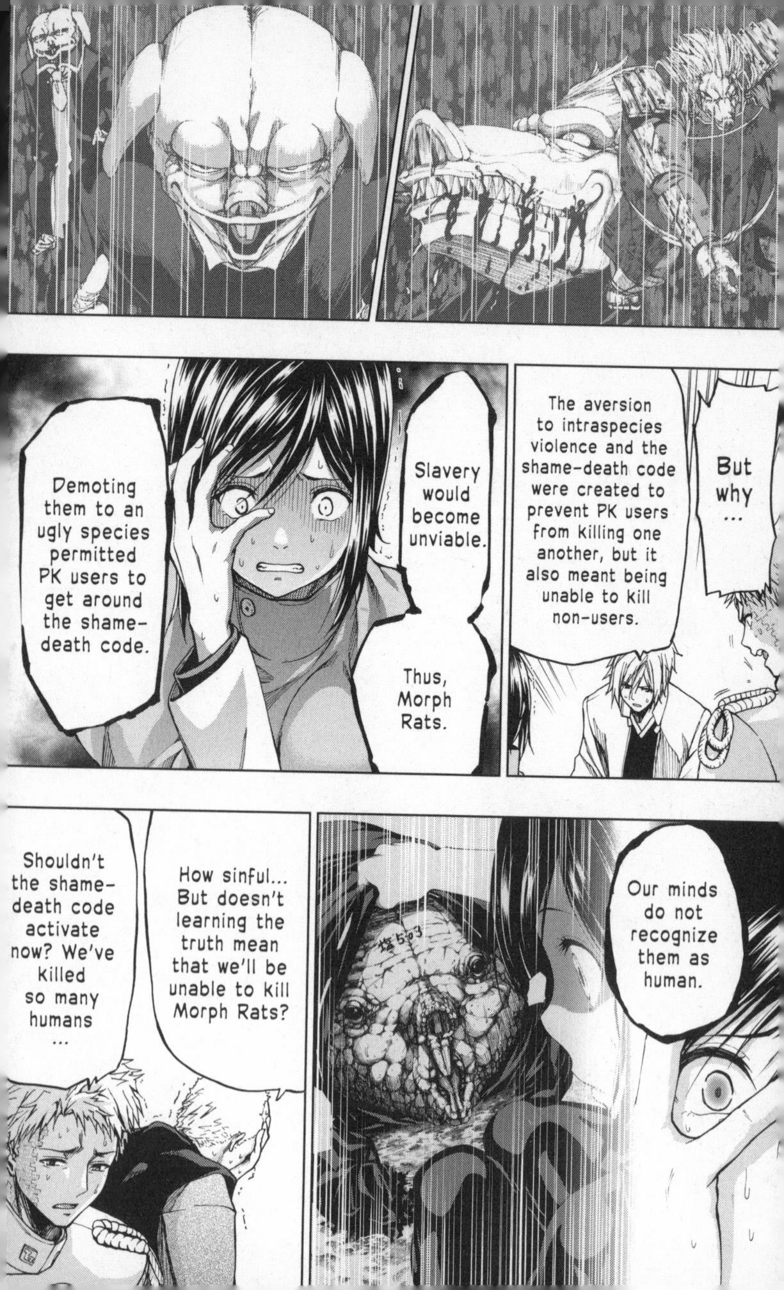
But why...
The aversion to intraspecies violence and the shame-death code were created to prevent PK users from killing one another, but it also meant being unable to kill non-users.
Slavery would become unviable.
Thus, Morph Rats.
Demoting them to an ugly species permitted PK users to get around the shame-death code.
Our minds do not recognize them as human.
How sinful... But doesn't learning the truth mean that we'll be unable to kill Morph Rats?
Shouldn't the shame-death code activate now? We've killed so many humans...

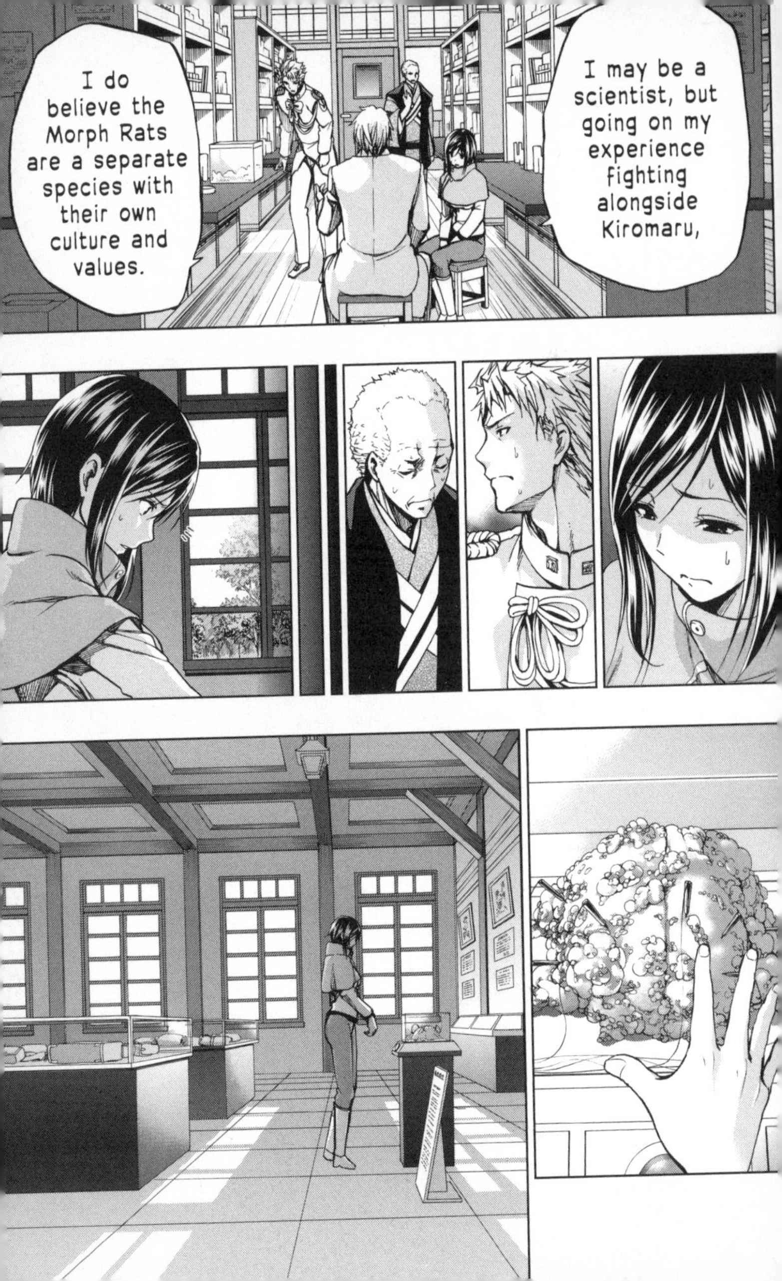
I may be a scientist, but going on my experience fighting alongside Kiromaru,
I do believe the Morph Rats are a separate species with their own culture and values.

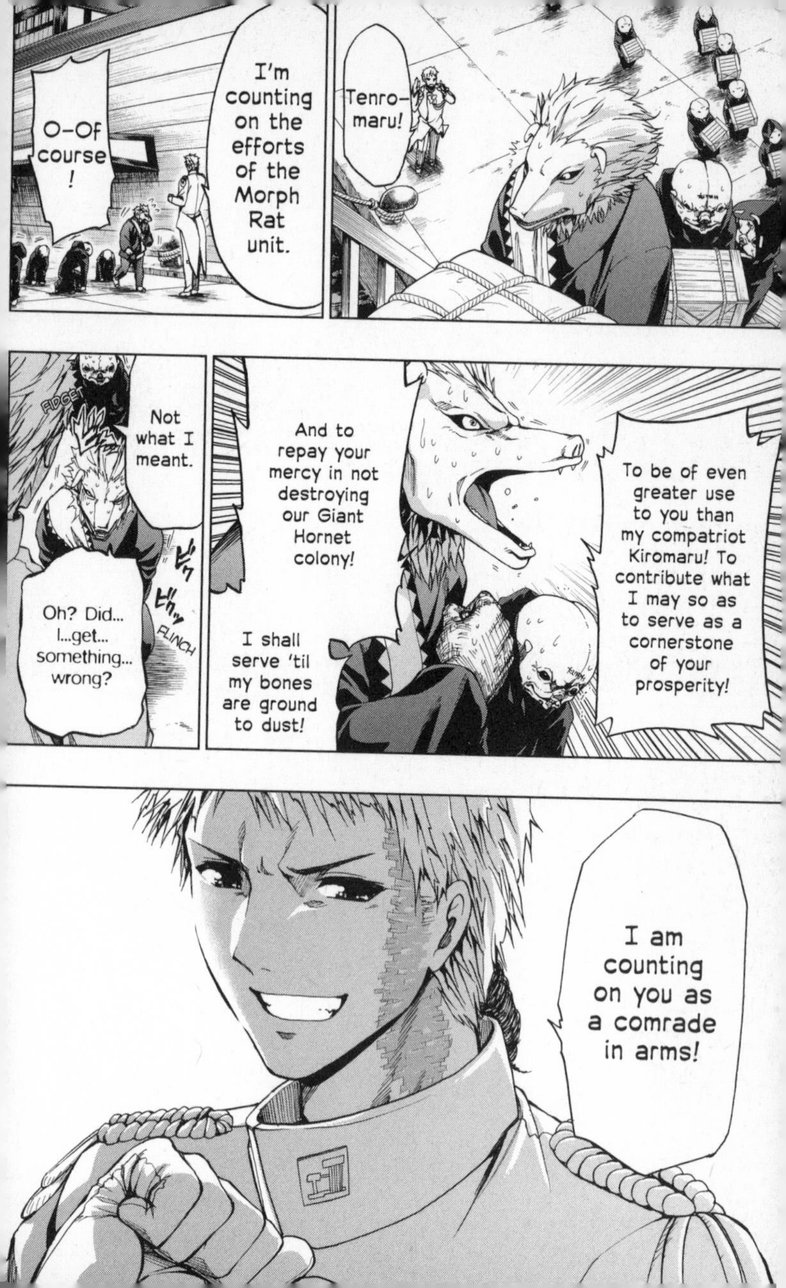
Tenro-maru!
I'm counting on the efforts of the Morph Rat unit.
O-Of course!
To be of even greater use to you than my compatriot Kiromaru! To contribute what I may so as to serve as a cornerstone of your prosperity!
And to repay your mercy in not destroying our Giant Hornet colony!
I shall serve 'til my bones are ground to dust!
FIDGET
Not what I meant.
FLINCH
Oh? Did... I...get... something... wrong?
I am counting on you as a comrade in arms!

There will be change ...I swear.

Infinite Hell Execution Site

無間地獄処刑地

GLOW

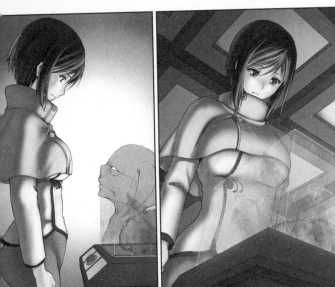

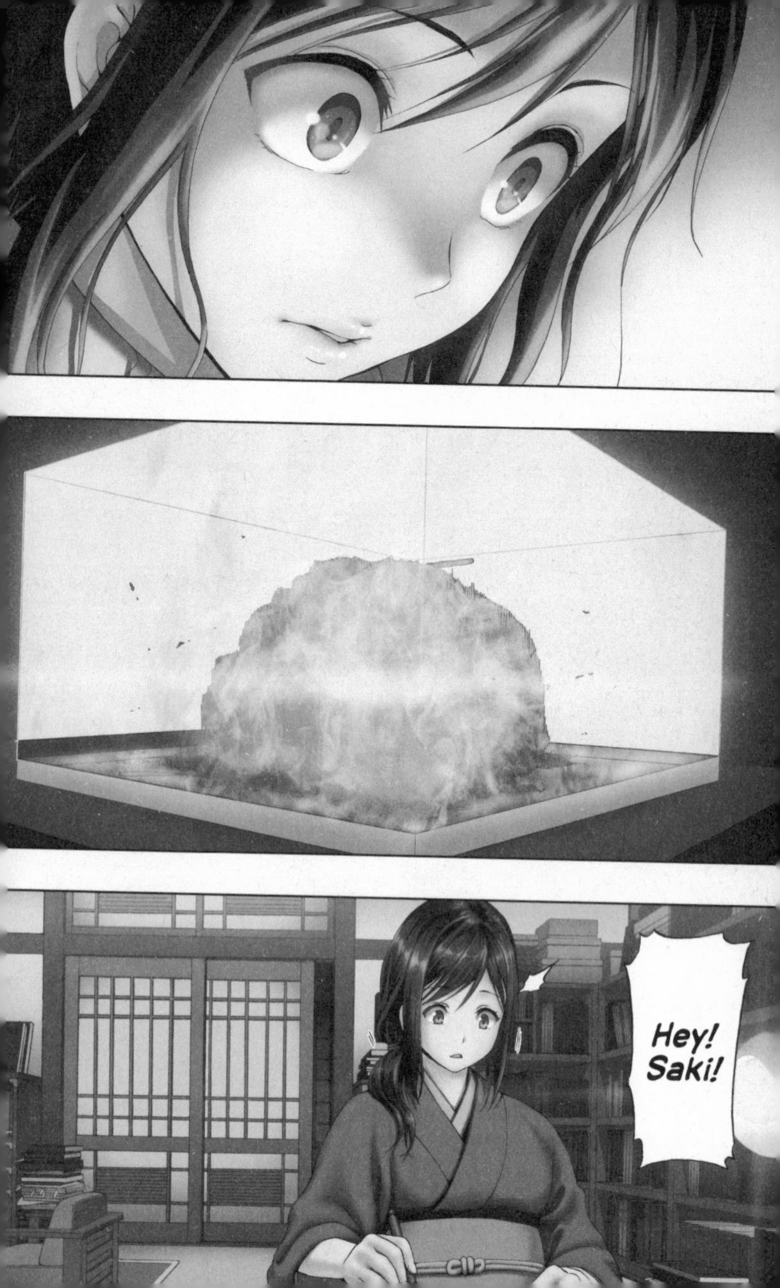
Hey! Saki!

Sa-toru?
Sho and his expedition have returned! And...
Just get over here!
Uh... Okay!
TUP
IF YOU ARE READING THIS CHRONICLE A THOUSAND YEARS FROM NOW,
YOU KNOW THE ANSWER AS TO WHETHER WE EVER MANAGED TO CHANGE.

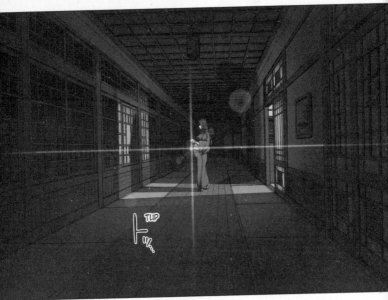

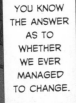

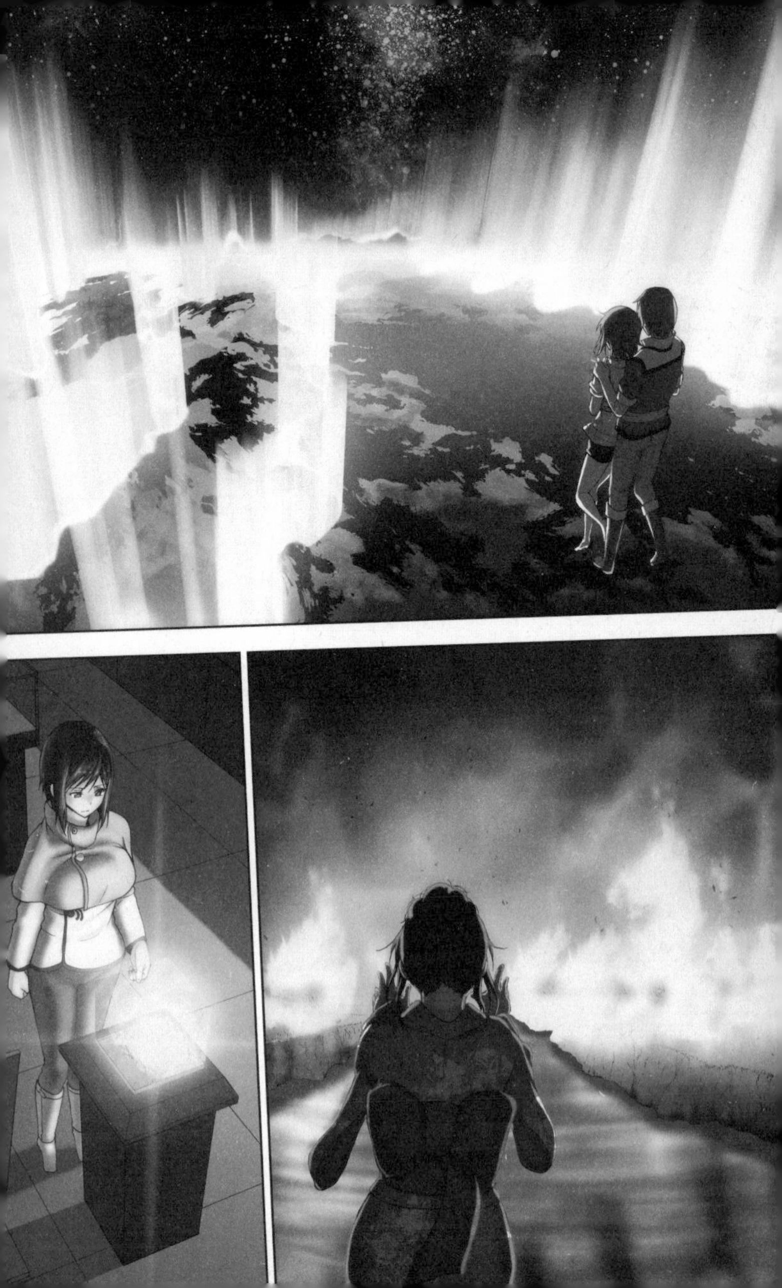

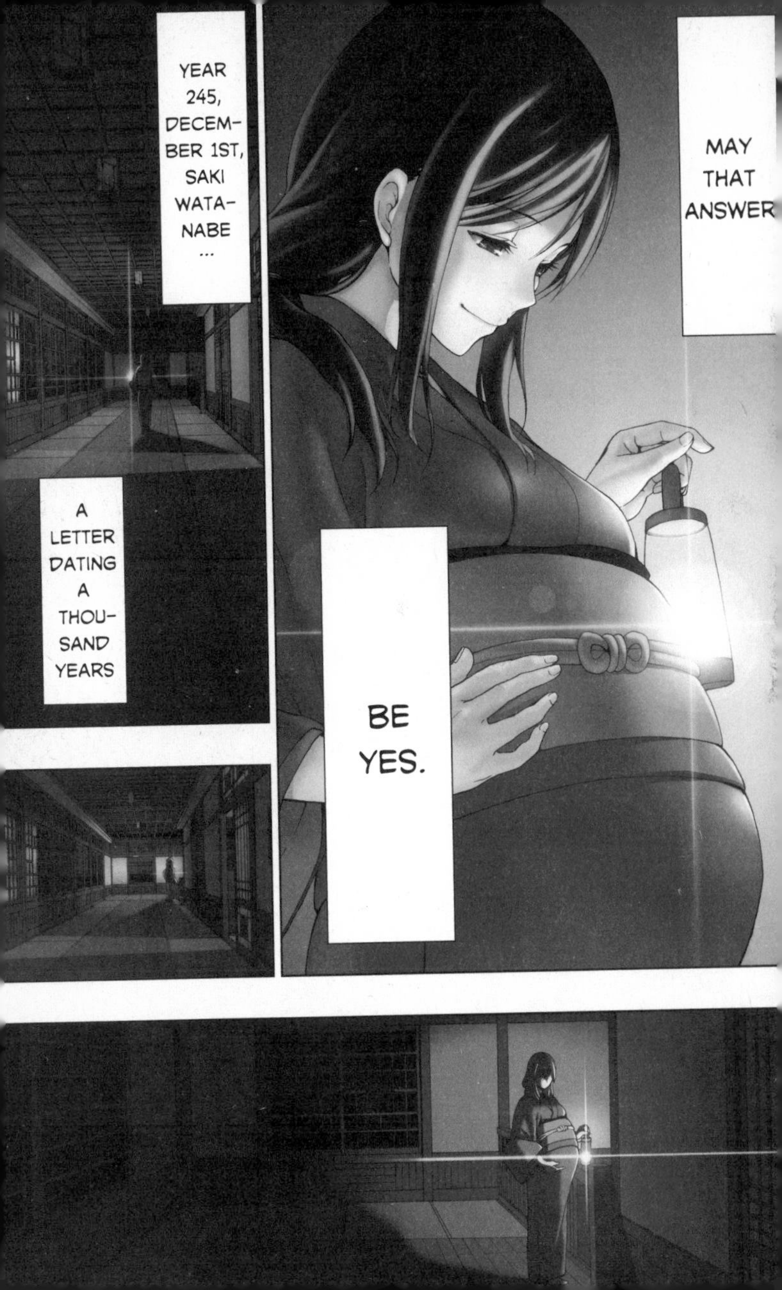
MAY THAT ANSWER
BE YES.
YEAR 245, DECEMBER 1ST, SAKI WATANABE ...
A LETTER DATING A THOUSAND YEARS

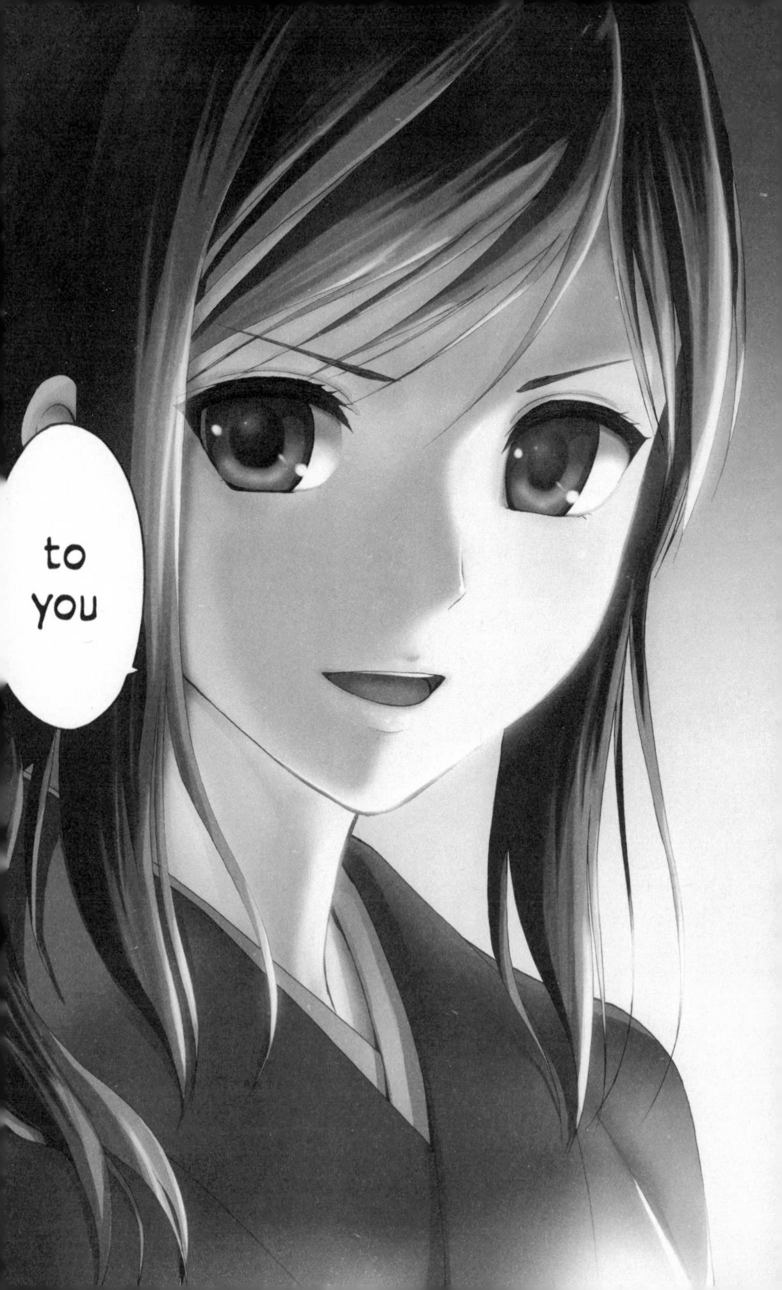
to you

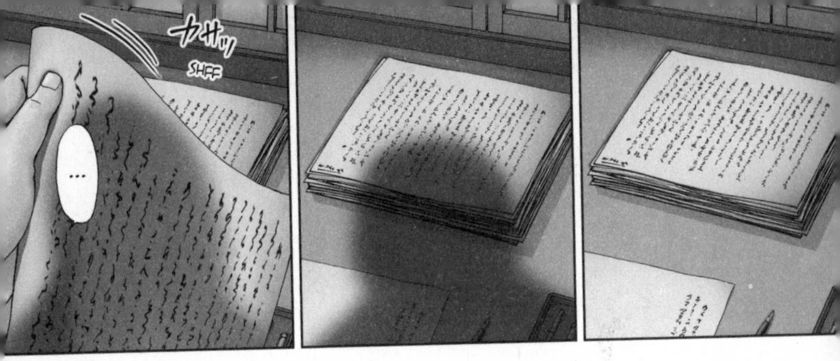
カサッ
SHFF
...

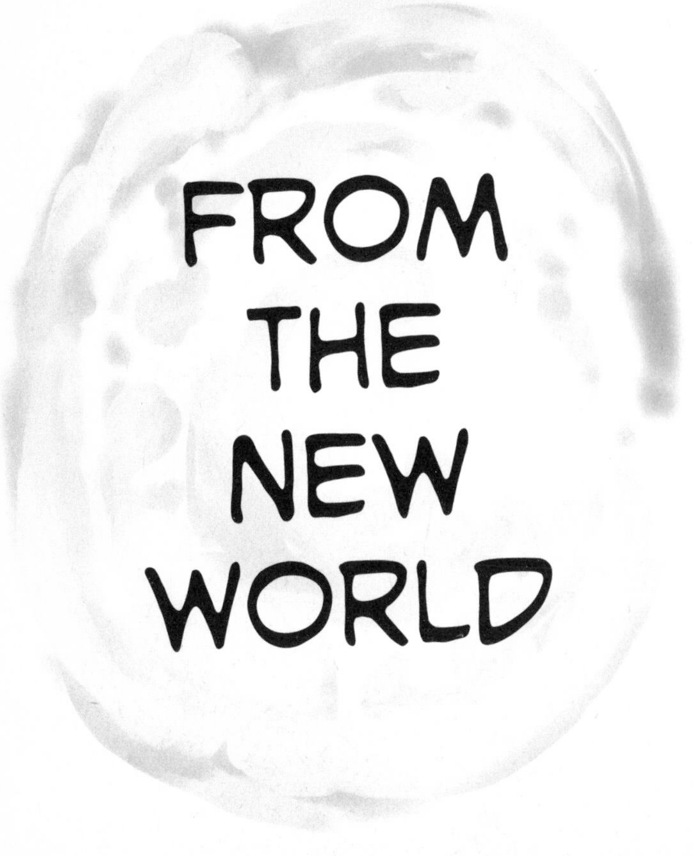
FROM
THE
NEW
WORLD

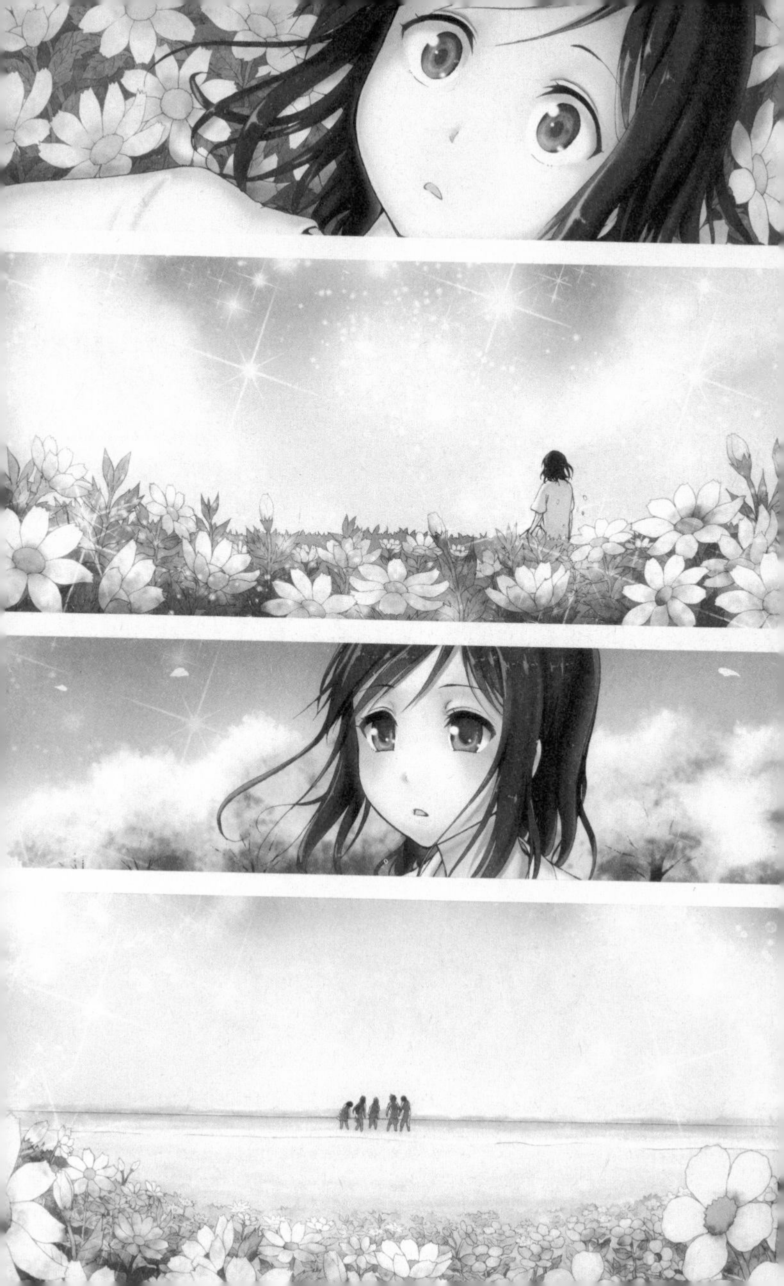

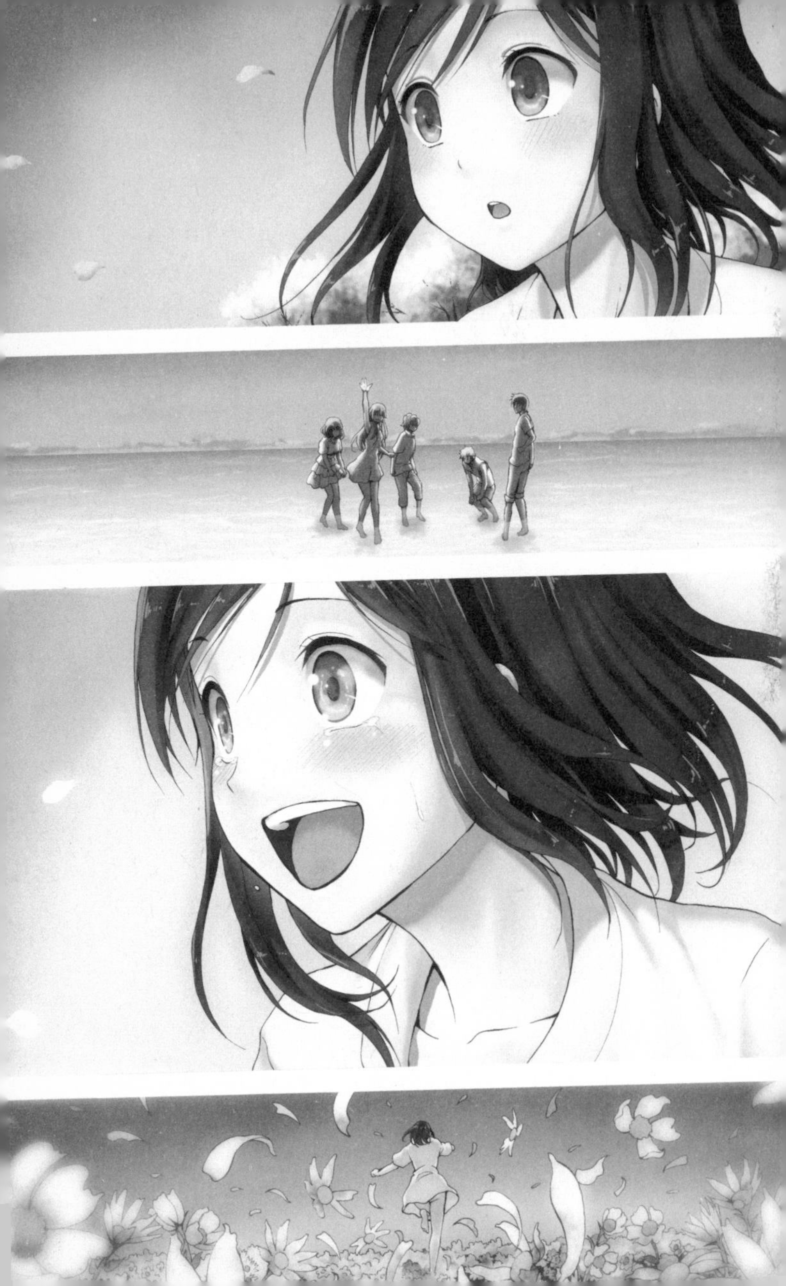

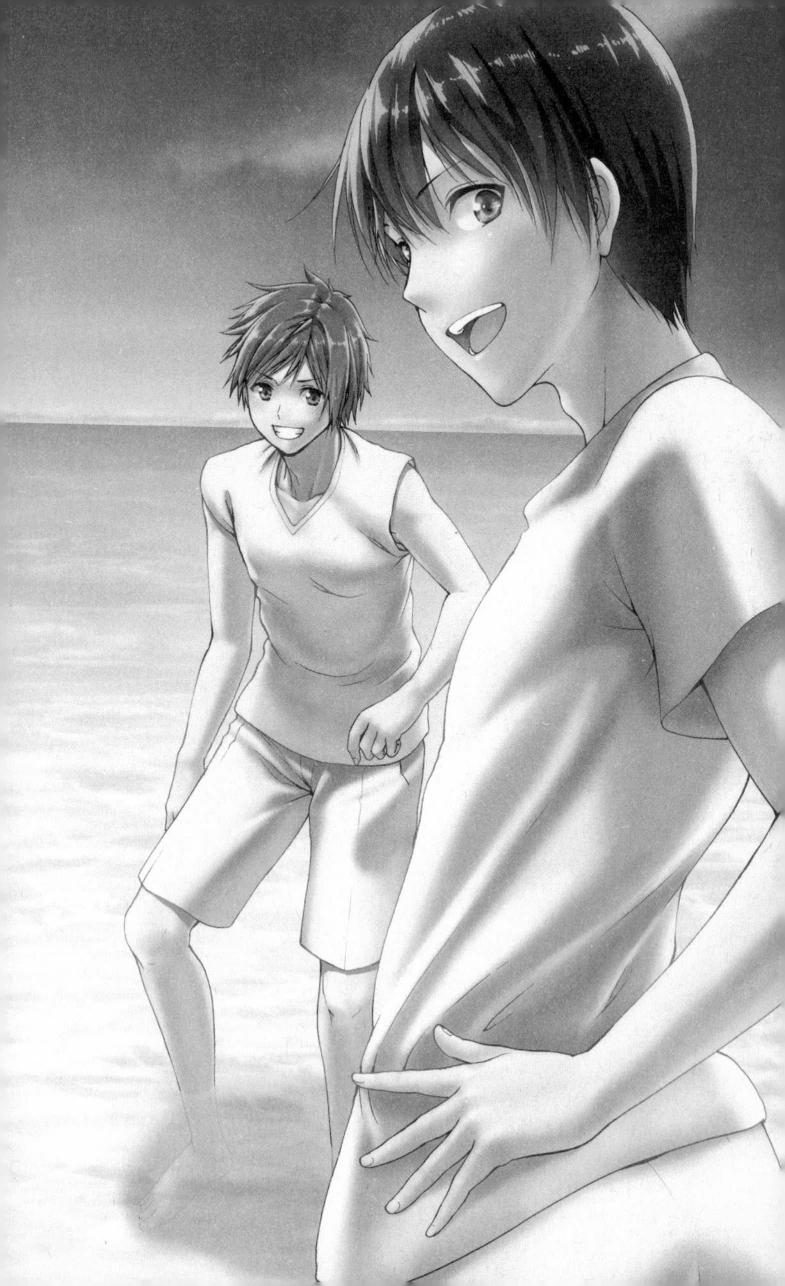

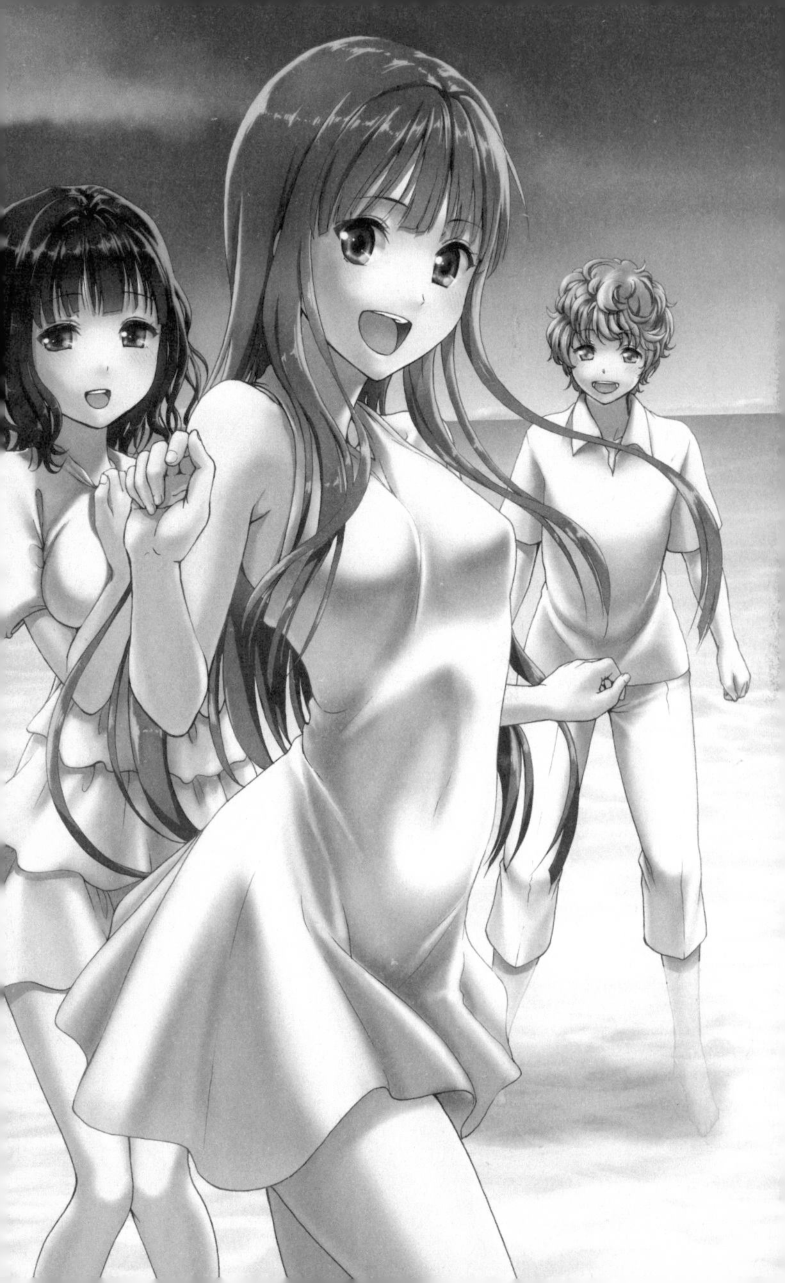

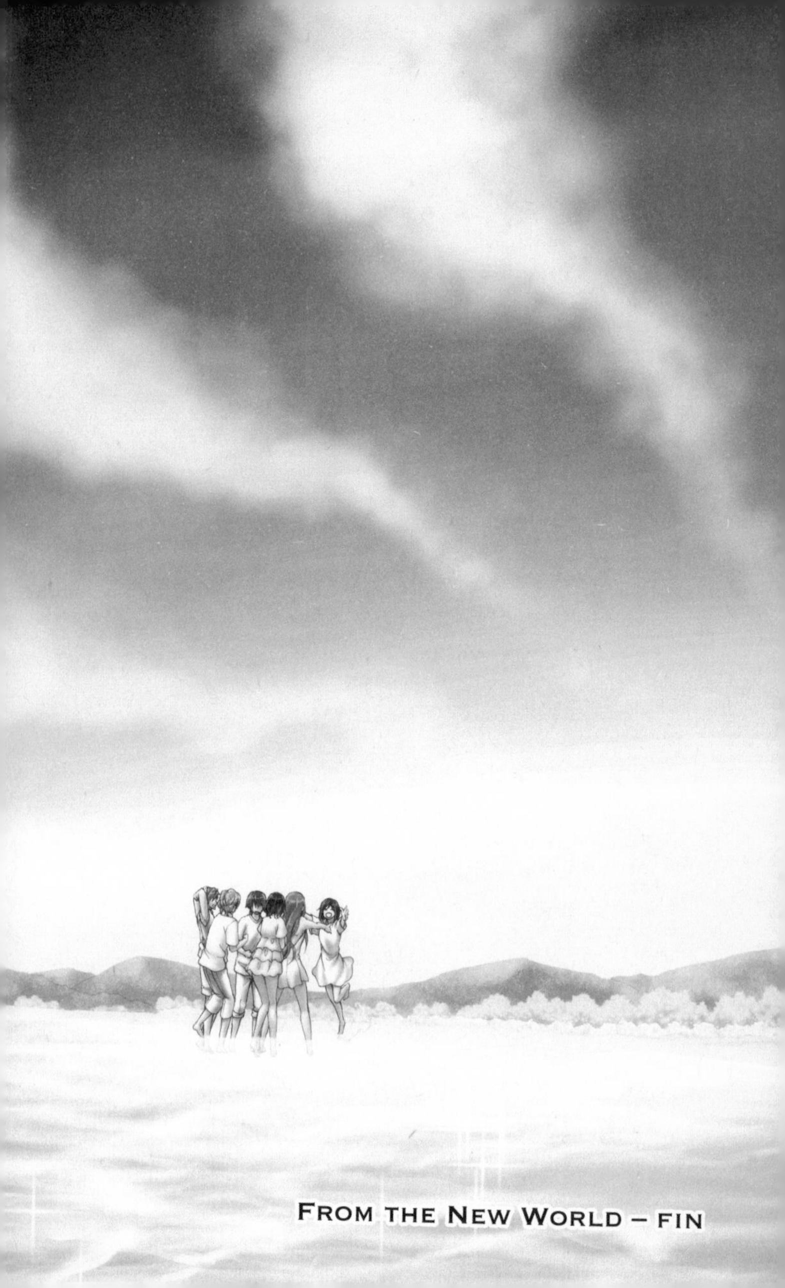
FROM THE NEW WORLD – FIN

Regarding the *From the New World* Manga

Mr. Oikawa, thank you for your hard work. Adapting a novel into manga format is harder than readers tend to imagine. The written word and pictures impact the reader in different ways, and you can't pass over certain things that can be omitted in a novel.

On top of that, because the anime was released beforehand, you had to make sure not to hew too close or to deviate too far, and that must have been quite a hurdle.

I believe, however, that this work magnificently accomplishes the complicated task. You've created a world of your own while remaining faithful to the themes and storyline of the original.

Your Saki exudes a cheerful brightness seen in neither the original nor the anime. The character into whom I invested the most emotion, Squealer, and his desperate struggle despite the deep darkness within him, are sure to forever remain in the hearts of readers.

I suspect that, while working on this manga, you glimpsed a misshapen world a millenium hence, as I did, and as I wish for the reader to do.

This tale has reached its conclusion, but I hope to see you again, Mr. Oikawa.

Readers, please look out for his next work!

Sincerely,
Yusuke Kishi

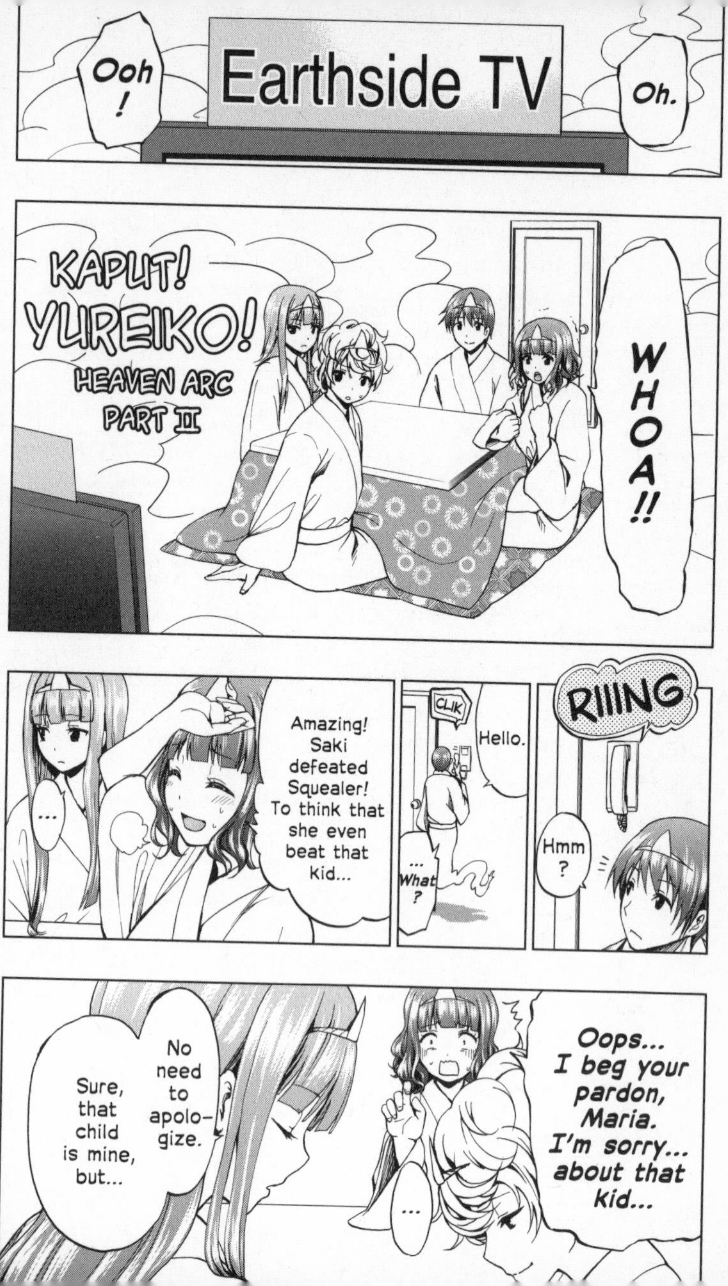
Oh.
Earthside TV
Ooh!
WHOA!!
KAPUT! YUREIKO!
HEAVEN ARC PART II
RIIING
Hmm?
CLIK
Hello.
...What?
Amazing! Saki defeated Squealer! To think that she even beat that kid...
...
Oops... I beg your pardon, Maria. I'm sorry... about that kid...
...
No need to apologize.
Sure, that child is mine, but...

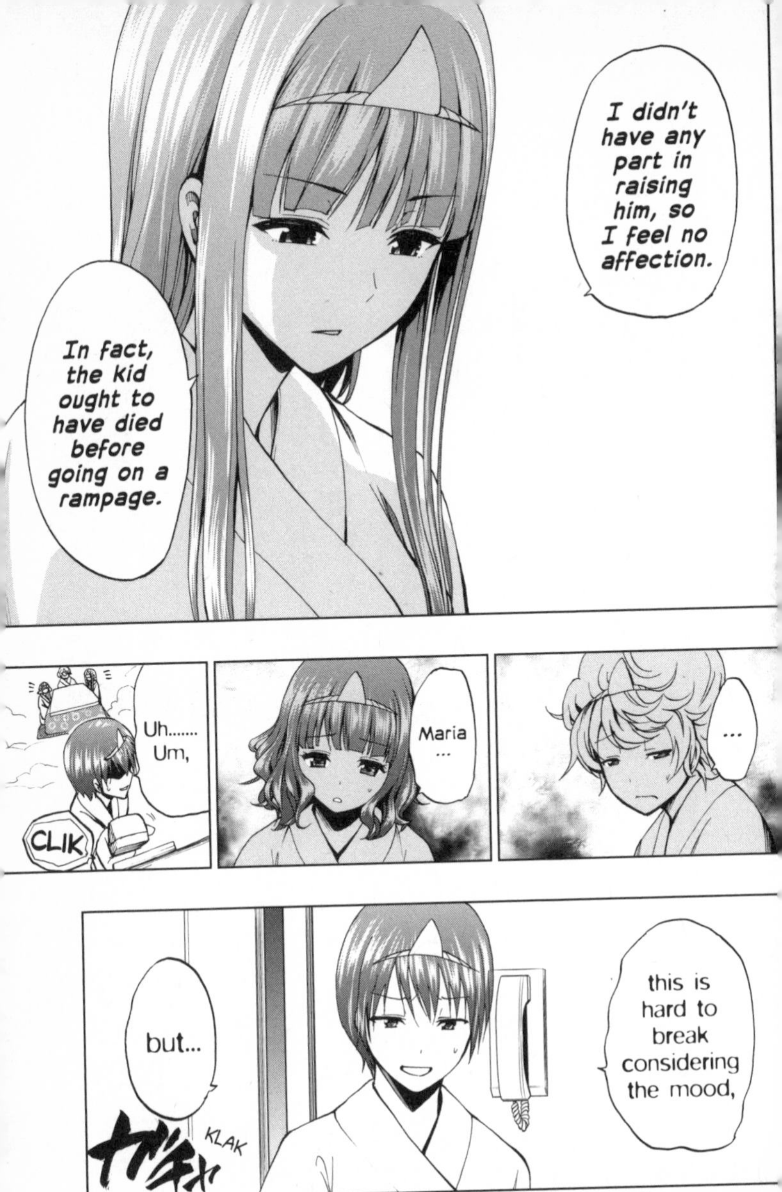
I didn't have any part in raising him, so I feel no affection.
In fact, the kid ought to have died before going on a rampage.
...
Maria ...
Uh....... Um,
CLIK
this is hard to break considering the mood,
but...
KLAK

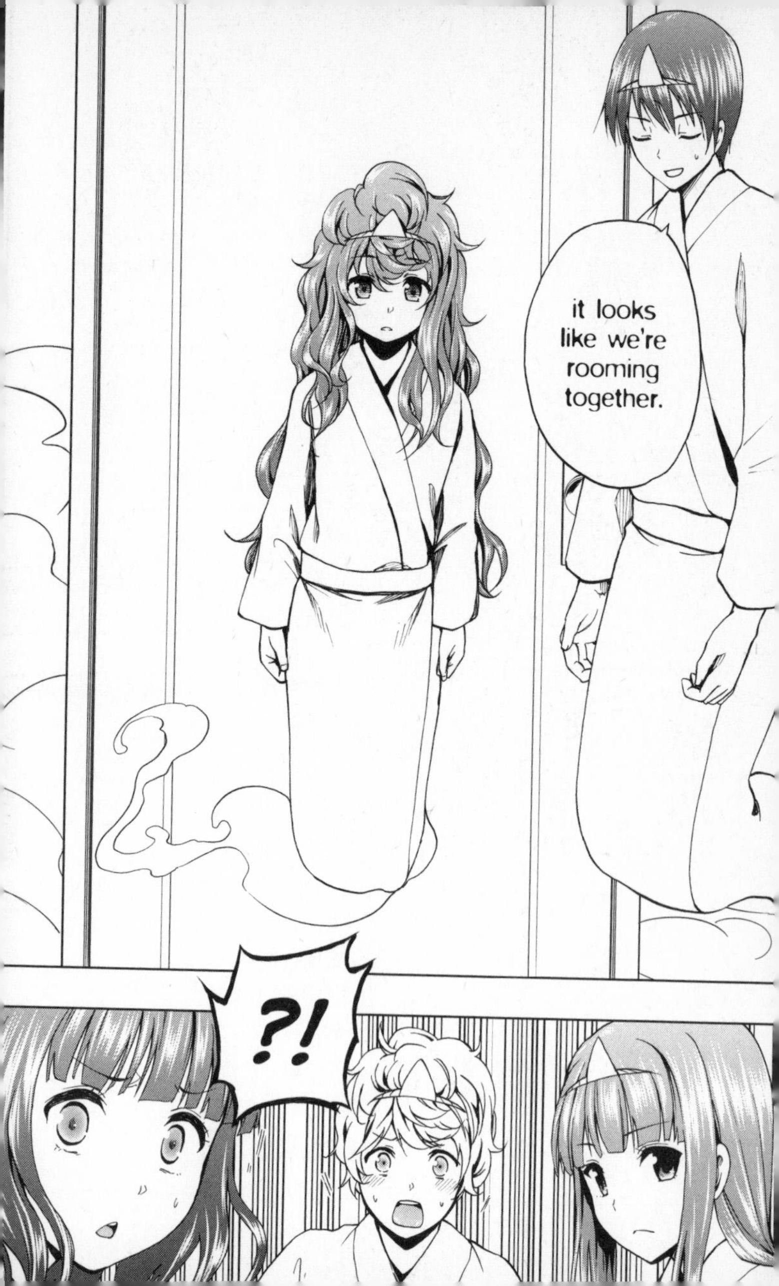
it looks like we're rooming together.
?!

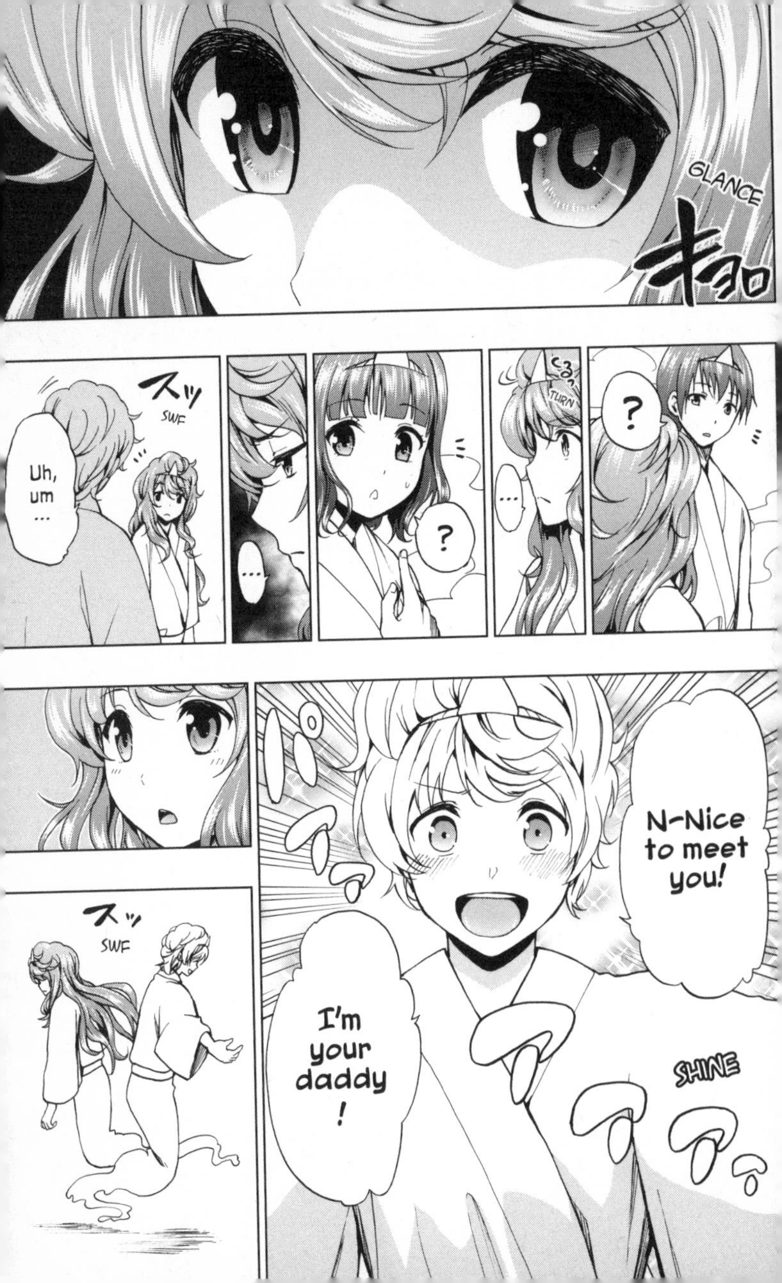
GLANCE
キョロ
?
くるっ
TURN
...
?
...
スッ
SWF
Uh, um ...
N-Nice to meet you!
I'm your daddy!
SHINE
スッ
SWF

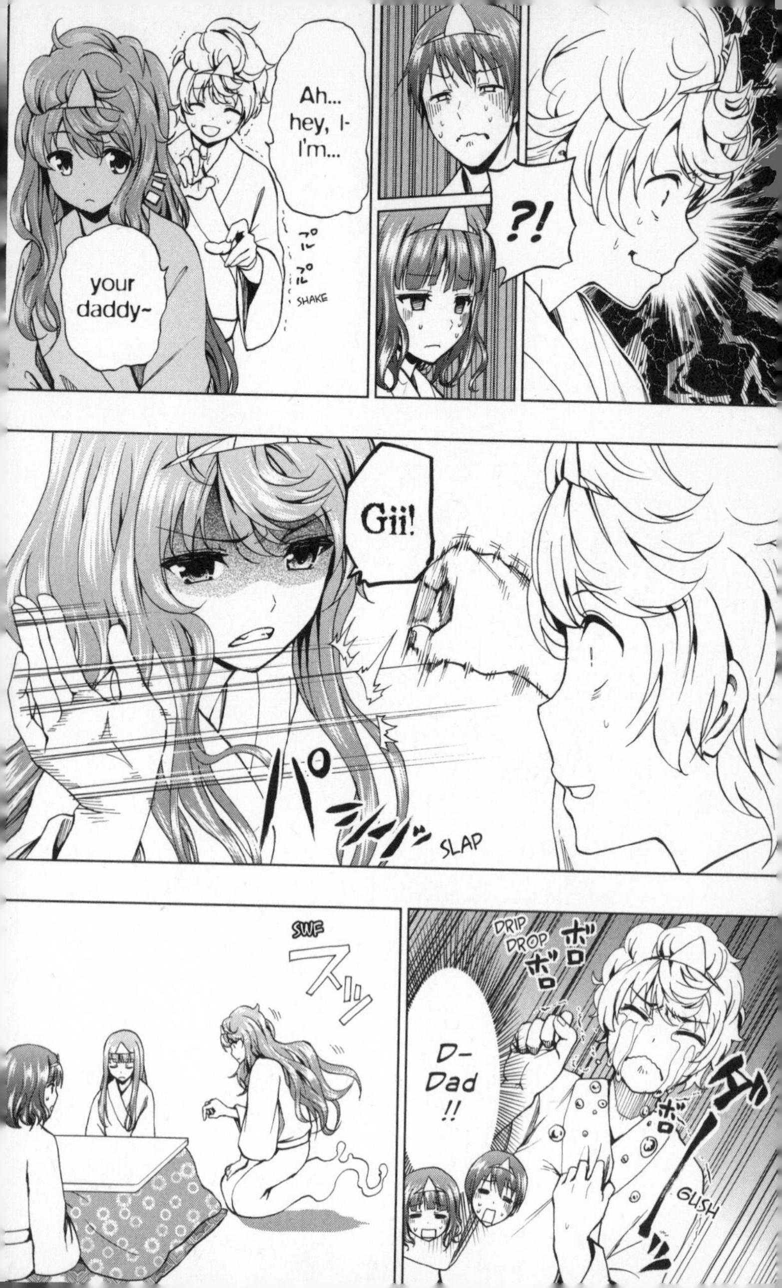
?!
Ah... hey, I- I'm...
プルプル
SHAKE
your daddy~
Gii!
パッ
SLAP
ボロボロ
DRIP DROP
D- Dad !!
ボ
GUSH
スッ
SWF

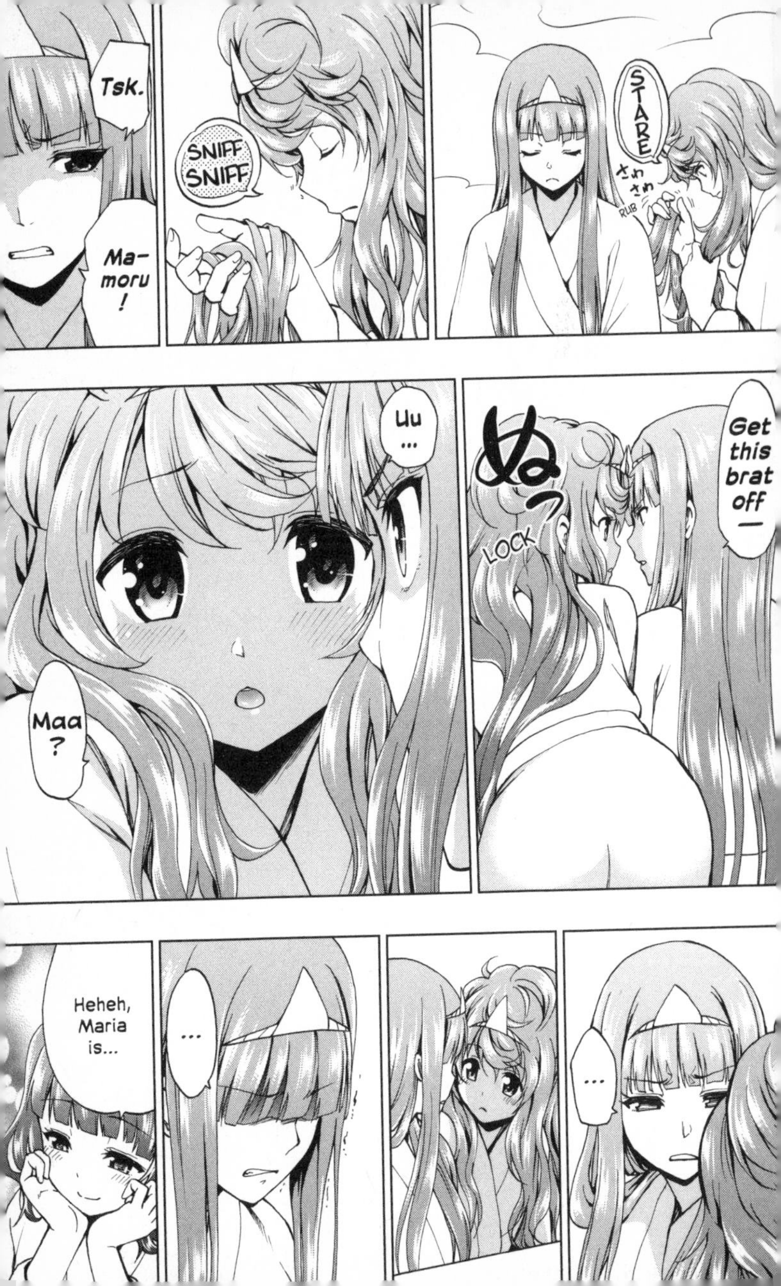
STARE
さわ さわ
RUB
SNIFF SNIFF
Tsk.
Ma-moru!
Get this brat off—
ぬっ
LOCK
Uu...
Maa?
...
...
Heheh, Maria is...

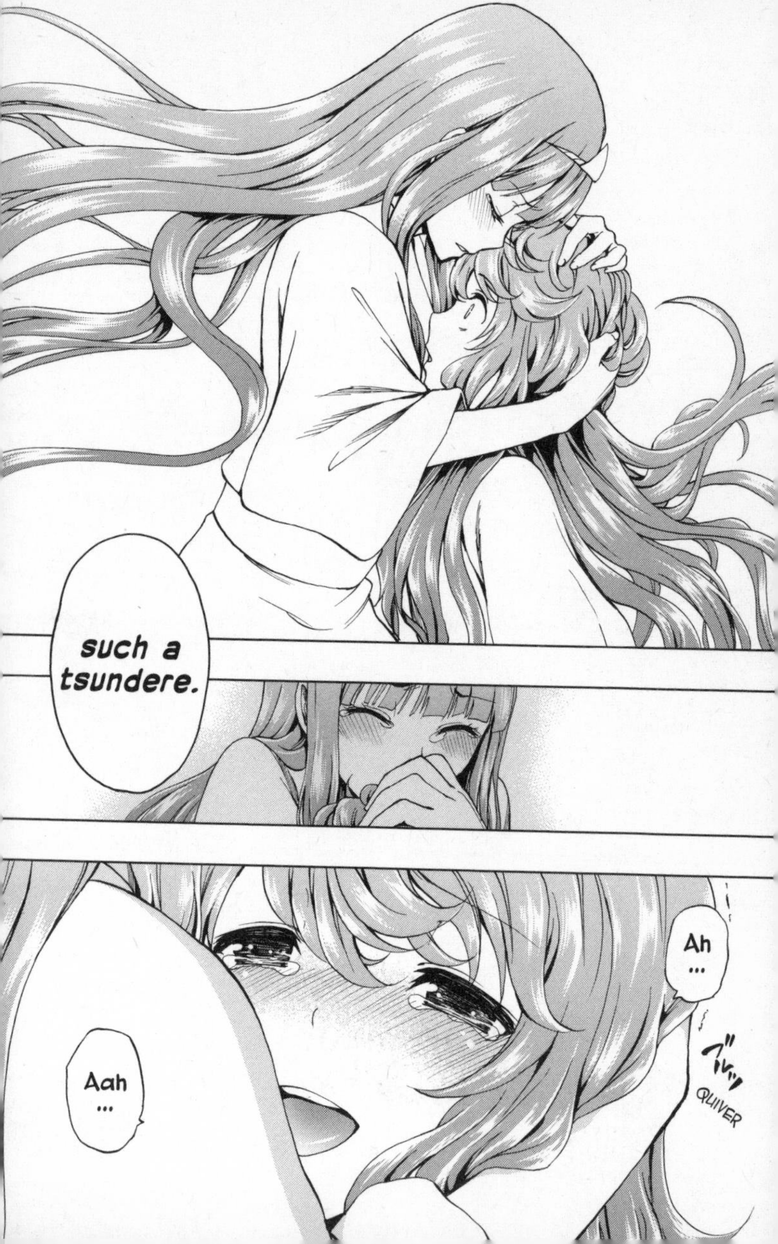
such a tsundere.
Ah ...
QUIVER
Aah ...

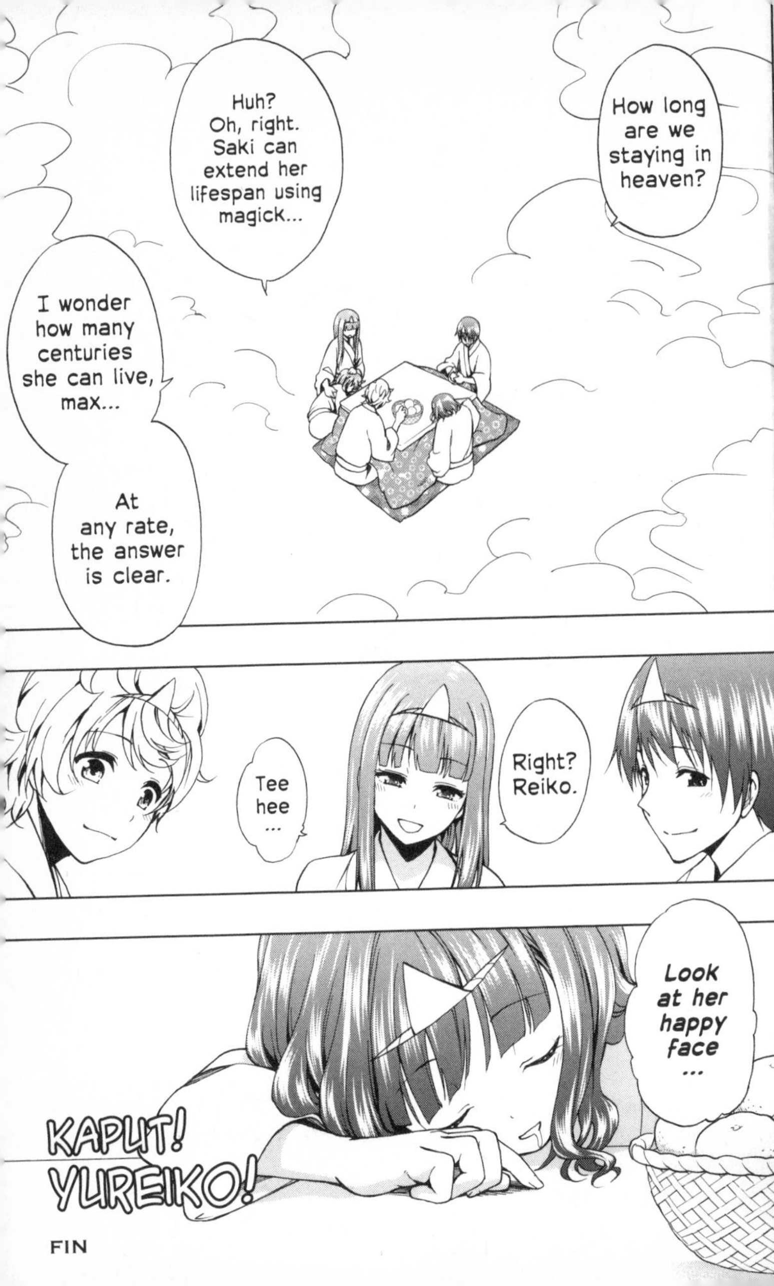
How long are we staying in heaven?
Huh? Oh, right. Saki can extend her lifespan using magick...
I wonder how many centuries she can live, max...
At any rate, the answer is clear.
Right? Reiko.
Tee hee ...
Look at her happy face ...
KAPUT! YUREIKO!
FIN

7th Floor
New York, NY 10016
www.vertical-inc.com